D0927868

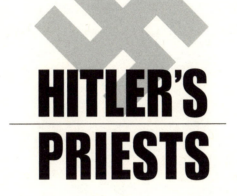

HITLER'S
PRIESTS

HITLER'S PRIESTS

175286310

3375 67765

282.43
S754h

CATHOLIC CLERGY AND NATIONAL SOCIALISM

KEVIN P. SPICER

Published in Association with the United States Holocaust Memorial Museum

NORTHERN ILLINOIS UNIVERSITY PRESS

East Baton Rouge Parish Library
Baton Rouge, Louisiana

© 2008 by Northern Illinois University Press
Published by the Northern Illinois University Press,
DeKalb, Illinois 60115
in Association with the United States Holocaust Memorial Museum
Manufactured in the United States using
postconsumer-recycled, acid-free paper.
All Rights Reserved
Design by Julia Fauci

The assertions, arguments, and conclusions contained herein are
those of the author or other contributors. They do not necessarily
reflect the opinions of the United States Holocaust Memorial Museum.

Endsheet photograph: 1934 Field Mass during Hitler Youth Gathering.
Courtesy of Allgäuer Anzeigeblatt.
Title page photograph: Father Roth greeting Adolf Hitler.
Courtesy of Bundesarchiv.

Library of Congress Cataloging-in-Publication Data
Spicer, Kevin P., 1965–
Hitler's priests : Catholic clergy and national socialism /
Kevin P. Spicer.
p.   cm.
"Published in Association with the
United States Holocaust Memorial Museum."
Includes bibliographical references and index.
ISBN 978-0-87580-384-5 (clothbound : alk. paper)
1. Catholic Church—Germany—Clergy—History—20th century.
2. Catholic Church—Germany—History—1933–1945. 3. Germany—
Church history—1933–1945. 4. Church and State—Germany—
History—20th century. 5. National socialism and religion.
6. Antisemitism—Germany—20th century. I. Title.
BX1536.S65 2008
282′.4309043—dc22
2007041504

DEDICATION

To the men and women who taught me history, especially

Mr. Frank Broschart

Dr. Anne T. Carrigg

Dr. Thomas J. Clarke

Dr. Donald J. Dietrich

Mrs. Clarisse Dixon

Dr. John L. Heineman

Rev. Dr. Brian Hogan, C.S.B.

Dr. James J. Kenneally

the late Mrs. Adelaide Keough

Mr. Richard Mills

the late Rev. Dr. Francis Murphy

the late Rev. Augustine J. Peverada, C.S.C.

Dr. Virginia Reinburg

Professor Judith Sughrue

Contents

Preface

In 1996, as I was sitting in the reader's room of the German Federal Archive in Berlin-Lichterfelde, I came across several letters about Father Karl König of the archdiocese of Paderborn. As I read the letters, the language used by the German state officials to describe König surprised me. They described him as a priest who was highly supportive of National Socialism and extremely open to working for greater cooperation between church and state. Reading such letters jogged my memory to recall a brief mention of similar priests in the pioneering works of John Conway, *The Nazi Persecution of the Churches,* and Guenter Lewy's *The Catholic Church and Nazi Germany.* Lewy had even mentioned König once in his book. Still, I found it difficult to comprehend how a person ordained to serve others and preach Christ's commandment of love could so wholeheartedly embrace the hate-filled ideology of National Socialism. I also realized that the antisemitism present within my Church created a convenient bridge for these priests to embrace many aspects of National Socialism's racial ideology. Even with such initial doubts, my historian's training and curiosity encouraged me to set aside any theological reservations that I held and pursue my findings. This led me to a satellite archive of the German Federal Archives in Berlin-Dahlwitz. Following the leads provided by Federal Archives specialists Maike Maerten and Heinz Fehlauer, I found more letters that contained the names of several other priests who were sympathetic to Nazism. It is then that I realized that I was on to something. At the time I was researching a book on the reactions of Berlin diocesan priests to the Third Reich, so I brought all this information to the Berlin diocesan archivist, Dr. Gotthard Klein, who is also a specialist in modern German history. Dr. Klein confirmed that indeed there was a small, but outspoken, group within the ranks of the German clergy who openly supported Hitler and, at times, promoted National Socialist ideology. He also informed me that no one had written a history exclusively about these priests. That was enough information for me to know exactly what would be the topic of my next book. In the meantime I brought together my research and composed a chapter about these priests in my work on the Berlin clergy.

Over the next eleven years, during spring and summer breaks, I continued my quest to learn more about the lives and choices of the priests who publicly supported the NSDAP. Such a quest has taken me to archives and institutes throughout Germany. As you might imagine, I could not simply approach a diocese or archive and ask, "Who were the priests who openly supported National Socialism through their preaching, writing, and ministry?" Such a question, even to those with no religious convictions, might appear impertinent and perhaps sensationally journalistic in nature. By contrast, I learned that once I had identified a priest who fit into this category, archivists, both church and state, were quite willing to share their records with me. After a final summer of research in 2005, I decided that I had gathered enough information and evidence to begin writing the present work during my sabbatical year. I am confident there are many more clergymen's names to uncover, but I also believe that I present enough evidence in this book to allow the reader to gain a deeper understanding of the motivations behind the life choices of these priests.

As any historian knows, grants from academic-minded institutions, societies, and foundations primarily make research possible. Therefore, for their generous support of my research and writing, I would like to wholeheartedly thank the American Philosophical Society for two Franklin Research Grants, the National Endowment for the Humanities for a summer stipend, and Theodore Z. Weiss and the Holocaust Educational Foundation for a Research Fellowship in Holocaust Studies. In addition, I must thank the administration of Stonehill College, especially Rev. Mark Cregan, C.S.C., J.D., president; Dr. Katie Conboy, vice-president for academic affairs; Dr. Karen Talentino, dean of faculty; and Bonnie Troupe, director of academic development, for offering me faculty professional development grants and a full-year sabbatical to write this book. Likewise, a word of thanks is due to all my department colleagues who supported me during this project, especially Dr. Edward McCarron and Dr. Shane Maddock.

I had the privilege of spending my sabbatical year in Washington, D.C. as a fellow of the Center for Advanced Holocaust Studies of the United States Holocaust Memorial Museum. I am grateful to the center not only for its financial support, but also for its incredibly gifted members, who regularly shared their expertise and provided essential feedback for my work. In particular, I would like to thank Paul A. Shapiro, director of the Center for Advanced Holocaust Studies; Robert Ehrenreich, director of university programs; Lisa Yavnai, director of the visiting scholars division; Benton Arnovitz, director of academic publications; Suzanne Brown-Fleming, senior program officer for the center's university programs; Jürgen Matthäus, Martin Dean, Victoria Barnett, Ann Millan, Aleisa Fishman, Michael Gelb, Geoffrey Megargee, Severin Hochberg, Patricia Heberer, Dieter Kuntz, Gwendolyn Bowen-Sherman, and finally Lisa Zaid. I would also like to express my appreciation to all of the scholars who were fellows with me at the center and who provided critical feedback on this project, especially Richard Breitman, Zvi Gitelman, Judith Gerson, Daniel Magilow, Steven Sage, Christian Goeschel, Krista Hegburg, and Katharina von Kellenbach.

Since this book deals closely with the lives of individual priests, I could have never written this work without the assistance of the archivists of the German diocesan church archives. All of them greeted me with warm hospitality and collegiality and generously answered my follow-up written inquiries. First and foremost I would like to thank Dr. Gotthard Klein, director of the Berlin diocesan archive, who was always there to answer my numerous inquiries and direct me to pertinent sources. I also wish to express my gratitude to Dr. Erwin Naimer, director, and his predecessor, the late Dr. Stefan Miedaner, Augsburg diocesan archive; Professor Dr. Reimund Haas, senior archivist, and Wolfgang Schmitz, associate archivist, Cologne archdiocesan archive; Dr. Bruno Lengenfelder, director, his predecessor, Brun Appel, and his former associate archivist, Dr. Franz Heiler, Eichstätt diocesan archive; Dr. Christoph Schmider, director, Freiburg archdiocesan archive; Dr. Thomas Scharf-Wrede, director, and Gabriele Vogt, associate archivist, Hildesheim diocesan archive; Dr. Peter Pfister, director, and his predecessor, Monsignor Dr. Sigmund Benker; Susanne Kornacker and Christian Schlafner, associate archivists, Munich and Freising archdiocesan archive; Dr. Arnold Otto, director, and his predecessor, Gerhard Sander, Paderborn archdiocesan archive; Monsignor Dr. Paul Mai, director, Regensburg diocesan archive; Dr. Stephan Janker, director, and Thomas Oschmann, associate archivist, Rottenburg-Stuttgart diocesan archive; Dr. Martin Persch, director, Trier diocesan archive; and Dr. Norbert Kandler, director, and his predecessor, Erik Soder von Güldenstubbe, Würzburg diocesan archive.

During the course of my research, I also utilized the archives of several religious communities. The archivists not only provided me access to their archival records, but their religious communities also provided me with warm hospitality and a place to stay during my research. Therefore, I would like to especially thank Emeritus Abbot Stephan Schröer, O.S.B., Abbot Dr. Dominicus Meier, O.S.B., and the Benedictine religious of Meschede's Königsmünster abbey; Emeritus Abbess Luitgardis Hecker, O.S.B., archivist, and the Benedictine sisters of Grefrath's Mariendonk abbey; Abbot Emmeran Kränkl, O.S.B., Father Otmar Wieland, O.S.B., Father Augustin Renner, O.S.B., archivist, and the Benedictine religious of Augsburg's St. Stephen Abbey; Abbot Christian Schütz, O.S.B., Father Matthäus Kroiss, O.S.B., archivist, and the Benedictine religious of Schweiklberg abbey. In addition, I must thank my friend and colleague, Father Elias H. Füllenbach, O.P., who provided me access to documents from his religious order's archive and who hunted down several elusive books for me.

In order to complete my list of brown priests (appendix 2), I had to contact via e-mail, fax, and written correspondence additional diocesan and religious order archives in Germany, Austria, and Poland. Again the archivists were generous with their time as they answered my numerous inquiries regarding essential biographical information of these priests. Thus I would like to extend a special word of thanks to Dr. Josef Urban, director, and Birgit Schäder, Bamberg archdiocesan archive; Dr. Birgit Mitzscherlich, director, Dresden-Meissen diocesan archive; Dr. Edgar Kutzner, director, Fulda diocesan archive; Martina Wagner, director, Limburg diocesan archive; Dr. Hermann-Josef Braun, director, Mainz diocesan archive; Dr. Herbert W. Wurster, director, Passau diocesan archive; Dr. Hans Ammerich, director, and Klaus Karg, associate archivist, Speyer diocesan archive; Dr. Norbert Müller, director, Dr. Norbert Allmer, associate archivist, and Stefanie Appenzeller, Graz-Seckau diocesan archive; Dr. Annemarie Fenzl, archivist, and Dr. Johann Weißensteiner, associate archivist, Vienna archdiocesan archive; Professor Dr. Marian Borzyszkowski, director, Warmińskiej archdiocese archive; Father Engelbert Otte, O.F.M. Conv., provincial, German Franciscan Friars Minor Conventual Province St. Elisabeth; Father Rafael Rieger, O.F.M., archivist, and Dr. Christiane Schwarz, associate archivist, Bavarian Franciscan archive; Father Emmanuel Dürr, O.F.M., archivist, Cologne Franciscan province; Brother Jakobus Kaffanke, O.S.B., archivist, St. Martin's Beuron Abbey; Dr. Clemens Brodkorb, archivist, German province of Jesuits archive; Father Thomas Neulinger, S.J., archivist, and Dr. Martina Lehner, associate archivist, Austrian province of Jesuits archive; and Father Leo Weber, S.D.B., archivist, Benediktbeuern monastery. In addition to these individuals, I would like to thank Anna Łysiak Majdanik and Alicja Szarska for researching biographical information on Breslau priests from the Wrocław archdiocesan archive.

In order to gain a more complete portrait of the priests in this book, I also consulted numerous state and private archives. I would like to thank the archivists and staff at these archives for their help and suggestions throughout my research. I must offer a special word of gratitude to

Professor Dr. Wolfgang Thönissen, director, and Father Dr. Burkhard Neumann, Johann-Adam-Möhler Institute for Ecumenism, Paderborn, who allowed me to access the papers of Father Richard Kleine. Likewise, I would like to thank Reinhold Lenski, Stadtarchiv Böbingen, and Dr. Franz-Rasso Böck, Stadtarchiv Kempten, who granted me access to the papers of Father Dr. Philipp Haeuser. In addition, in Paderborn, Andrea Pollman and in Kempten, Anita Mayr, helped facilitate my research and are well deserving of my gratitude. Irene Bormann, the vice-principal of Eichsfeld Gymnasium, Duderstadt, not only shared with me her school's files on Father Richard Kleine, but along with her husband, Günter, offered me kind hospitality and gave me a wonderful tour of the Eichsfeld region. I am exceedingly grateful to the Bormann family. Also helpful, especially in my initial research, were Jana Blumberg, Heinz Fehlauer, Simone Langner, and Maike Maerten, Bundesarchiv Berlin-Lichterfelde. In addition to these individuals, I would like to thank Dr. Gregor Pickro and Beate Schleicher, Bundesarchiv, Koblenz; Dr. Susanne Wittern, Brandenburgisches Landeshauptarchiv; Gisela Klauß and Alexander Fiebig, Geheimes Staatsarchiv Preussischer Kulturbesitz; Dr. Maximilian Gschaid, Dr. Joachim Lauchs, Dr. Otto-Karl Tröger, and Renate Herget, Bayerisches Hauptstaatsarchiv; Susanne Knoblich and Martin Luchterhandt, Landesarchiv Berlin; Dr. Reinhold Weber, Dr. Christoph Bachman, and Andrea Schiermeier, Staatsarchiv Munich; Christoph Brunken, Niedersächsisches Hauptstaatsarchiv, Hannover; Dr. Silke Wagener-Fimpel, Niedersächsisches Staatsarchiv, Bückeburg; Ursula Lochner, Ludwig Maximilian Universitätsarchiv; Robin E. Cooksen and David C. Lake, United States National Archives, College Park; and David A. Keough, United States Army Military History Institute, Carlisle.

Similar to my research in church archives, it was necessary for me to consult additional archives to answer specific historical questions. I would like to thank the following individuals who took the time necessary to answer my letters of inquiry: Rev. Jesus Torres, C.M.F., undersecretary, Congregation for Institutes of Consecrated Life and Societies of Apostolic Life, Vatican City; Henry Böhm, Bundesarchiv Militärarchiv, Freiburg im Breisgau; F. Eichelmann, federal representative for national security service documents of the former DDR, Berlin; Gunther Friedrich, Staatsarchiv Nürnberg; Dr. Klaus A. Lankheit, Institut für Zeitgeschichte, Munich; Dr. Ursula Basikow, Bibliothek für bildungsgeschichtliche Forschung, Berlin; Franz Schreiber and Marianne Finkl, Stadtarchiv Augsburg; Rainer Rollenmiller, Stadtarchiv Bad Honnef; Dr. Hans-Heinrich Ebeling, Stadtarchiv Duderstadt; and Martina Trettenbach, Stadtarchiv Regensburg.

While I was in Germany, several colleagues discussed my project with me and made helpful suggestions for further research. For sharing their own research and expertise, I would like to thank the late Father Roman Bleistein, S.J., Dr. Ludwig Brandl, Professor Dr. Georg Denzler, Thomas Forstner, Dr. Antonia Leugers, Dr. Brigitte Poschmann, and Professor Father Ulrich Wagener. In addition, I am grateful to Dr. Josef Lettl for personally sending me a copy of his fine study on Johann Pircher's *Arbeitsgemeinschaft.* I would also like to thank Dr. Karl-Joseph Hummel and Dr. Christoph Kösters, Kommission für Zeitgeschichte, Bonn, and Gregor Klapczynski.

Furthermore, I wish to thank many colleagues for providing support and offering critical insights into my research and writing. In particular, I would like to thank Gotthard Klein and Martin Menke and the anonymous readers for Northern Illinois University Press for their critical reading of the entire work. I am also grateful to Robert Anthony Krieg, Rick Gribble, C.S.C., and Thomas Looney, C.S.C., who shared their expertise in theology, and John Santone, J.C.L., who clarified several complicated questions related to canon law. In addition, I would like to thank Doris L. Bergen, Thomas Blantz, C.S.C., Thomas Campbell, C.S.C., Donald J. Dietrich, the late Robert A. Graham, S.J., Beth Griech-Polelle, Gershon Greenberg, Derek Hastings, Peter Hayes, Susannah Heschel, David I. Kertzer, Jacques Kornberg, Shari Lowin, Richard McGaha, John T. Pawlikowski, O.S.M., Michael Phayer, John Roth, Theresa Sanders, Lucia Scherzberg, Erica Tucker, and Susan Zuccotti.

My work was not only strengthened by interaction with scholars in my field, but also through the technical assistance of several individuals. While I was in the D.C. area, Christopher Cooksey tirelessly gave of his own time to assist me as I went through reels and reels of microfilm of Nazi Party records at the U.S. National Archives. Cathy Graupner shared with me her family's photos and documents of her great-uncle, Josef Roth. At the U.S. Holocaust Memorial Museum, Judith Cohen, Maren Read, and Nancy Hartman, archivists in the museum's photo archive, helped to prepare digital images of many of the photos found in this book. Michlean Amir, an archivist in the museum's document archives, aided me in my search to find background information on several photos that I considered to include in this work. Mark Ziomek, the museum's library director, and Vincent Slatt and Steven Kanaley, librarians, provided untold help with questions relating to interlibrary loans and collections. At Stonehill, Glen Everett, director of the Learning Technology Center, and his able staff, also assisted me to prepare digital images of photos. Edward Hynes, director, Betsy Dean, collection development librarian, Heather Perry, reference librarian, Regina Egan and Nora Bellmore, interlibrary-loan specialists, all went out of their way to track down the many obscure titles that I requested. To all of the individuals mentioned above I offer a sincere word of thanks.

During my research visits to Germany, many people provided me with hospitality and lodging. To all I am eternally grateful. In particular, I would like to thank Eduard and Waltraud Burchat, Emeritus Abbot Dr. Odilo Lechner, O.S.B., Abbot Johannes Eckert, O.S.B., Father Valentin Ziegler, O.S.B., and the Benedictine community of St. Bonifaz, Munich; also *Pfarrer* Peter Wehr, *Pfarrer* Bernhard Motter, and *Pfarrer* Michael Höhle, Berlin. While on sabbatical in Washington, D.C., I lived and served in the parish of St. Ann. For their friendship and support I would especially like to thank Rev. Monsignor Godfrey T. Mosley and Rev. William M. Brailsford. In Waltham, Massachusetts, Rev. William T. Leonard and Ann Witham of St. Jude's parish and the Fernald Chapel have continually been sources of encouragement to whom I am always grateful. In Easton, Massachusetts, and in Notre Dame, Indiana, I would like to thank the support of my religious community, the Congregation of Holy Cross, whose daily encouragement to me is a blessing.

I would also like to express my gratefulness to my wonderful parents, John and Gloria Spicer, for their unending love and support. Last, but never least, I especially need to thank my editors, Melody Herr of Northern Illinois University Press, James William Chichetto, C.S.C., of Stonehill College, and Ilse Andrews. I found Jim and Ilse to be extremely gifted editors, whose editorial suggestions made this a better book in every way.

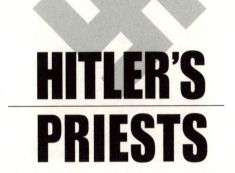

HITLER'S
PRIESTS

Introduction

On December 14, 1930, members of the National Socialist German Workers' Party (NSDAP) from Augsburg and the surrounding areas gathered in the city's historic center for a Christmas celebration. It was an especially festive occasion because the Nazi Party, in the March 1930 national election, had significantly increased its representation in the Reichstag.[1] Those present tasted ultimate victory and believed that their leader, Adolf Hitler, would soon hold a top position in the German government. In turn, the crowd wanted to hear from a dynamic speaker who could both affirm their aspiration for political power and renew their faith in the Nazi movement. When a district party representative introduced the main speaker, the crowd broke into loud cheers and applause. A thin, stern-looking man of medium height with thinning hair took the stage. Donned in a long black cassock, he set down his notes on the podium and announced, "Today the National Socialists of Augsburg celebrate Christmas. That is a fact. Another fact is: a Catholic priest delivers the address at this Christmas celebration upon the special wish of the National Socialists. Both facts are extremely sad—sad for the self-righteous Pharisees."[2] So began the campaign of Father Dr. Philipp Haeuser, a priest of the diocese of Augsburg, a campaign specifically fine-tuned for his Führer, Adolf Hitler, whom Haeuser would support until his dying breath. Not a stranger to right-wing politics, Haeuser had been speaking on behalf of what he called the German movement—broadly and loosely encompassing most right-wing and conservative-nationalistic movements and political parties—since the end of the First World War. However, following his 1930 Christmas address and its subsequent publication by Franz Eher, the NSDAP publishing house, Haeuser would be forever linked to the Nazi Party.

Haeuser was one of the priests U.S. diplomat Robert Daniel Murphy had in mind when in May 1945, following Germany's defeat, he asked Cardinal Michael Faulhaber, archbishop of Munich and Freising, about the "disturbing reports that during the war some of the Catholic clergy in Bavaria fell under Nazi influence." Faulhaber responded frankly that this was "unfortunately true" and admitted that "five priests in his archdiocese did align themselves with the party." The Cardinal then reassured Murphy that he had "relieved" these priests of their "respective offices including teaching in Catholic schools where . . . they had exercised harmful influence." Faulhaber continued, "Three of these men are now dead . . . and the other two have disappeared."[3]

Although Murphy approached Faulhaber with great respect, the disturbing questions he raised still troubled the Cardinal. They forced him to face the difficult choices that priests had to make under National Socialism. Faulhaber and his fellow bishops, however, were not eager to address their institution's failings.[4] Nor were they energetically supportive of the Allies' prosecution of war criminals and denazification efforts, especially regarding the culpability of German citizens during the Nazi years of power.[5] Instead, they wished to emphasize the persecution that the Church had to endure at the hands of both the SS (*Schutzstaffel,* the elite corps of the Nazi Party) and the Gestapo (*Geheim Staatspolizei,* secret state police) and attach blame primarily to these organizations of terror. They also rejected any notion of collective guilt for their fellow citizens. In 1946 Father Johannes Neuhäusler, who a year later joined the ranks of the German episcopacy, made the bishops' stance even more evident when he published a volume that detailed the Nazi oppression of the Church and stressed the resistance of the hierarchy against this onslaught.[6] Most interested parties, including a number of historians, accepted this interpretation. This pattern of defense persisted until the early 1960s, when a new generation of scholars produced studies critical of the Catholic Church's relationship to the National Socialist state.[7] Since then, historians have been involved in an ongoing debate about the Church's role under National Socialism.

As revealed in my previous work, *Resisting the Third Reich: The Catholic Clergy in Hitler's Berlin,* there were many levels of acceptance and rejection of the Nazi state among the German Catholic clergy. Even some clerics who repeatedly and forcefully challenged National Socialism and its antisemitic ideology (and paid with their lives for doing so) had publicly embraced a form of racism sometime during their ministries.[8] Priests, like most Germans, had to resist the lure of National Socialism. Yet, the relationship between church and state in Germany placed priests in a precarious position. In Germany, priests were not only religious figures subject to God first, their diocesan bishop second, and finally to the norms of the Catholic Church's canon law, but they were also pseudocivil servants subject to state regulations.[9] Consequently, when the state mandated in July 1933 that civil servants had to offer the "Heil Hitler" salute, Catholic priests had to comply.[10]

Some Catholic priests did offer the Hitler salute. Those who chose to adopt it often did so specifically when they entered a classroom to give religious instruction in a state school. Although their action provided a poor example for German Catholic youth, most of those who used this greeting did not equate it with full acceptance of National Socialism. Some used it simply to avoid problems with the state. Others used it to join in national solidarity with fellow Germans. Few used it to display a personal commitment to National Socialism. However, there existed a group of 138 priests who regularly used the salute, often to the dismay of their parishioners and fellow clergymen. At least one-third of these priests even enrolled in the Nazi Party. The rest did not join the party, but still chose to identify themselves closely with it and publicly promoted its cause. Clearly, all these clergymen were Hitler's priests, embracing not only the leader but also the *Weltanschauung* (worldview, ideology) of the Nazi movement. There were also a small number of priests who left the priesthood altogether and withdrew from the Catholic Church in order to join the ranks of the SS.[11]

Men who stayed in the priesthood and promoted National Socialism were often derogatorily called "brown priests"—brown being the official color of the Nazi movement.[12] Their acceptance of and devotion to National Socialism, however, ought not to be attributed to one specific event or ideology. Instead, these clergymen, in a fashion similar to the pattern of most National Socialists, aligned themselves to the Nazi Party for different reasons.[13] For some, the events that followed the First World War and the subsequent foundation of the Weimar Republic triggered a moral decline that they believed only National Socialism could arrest.[14] This was particularly true of former soldiers, medics, or chaplains. Others saw membership in the NSDAP as a means to advance their careers in both state and Church or to escape a conflict with their Church superiors. The latter often revolved around issues concerning vocational crisis, celibacy, or alcoholism.[15] Ironically, Hanns Kerrl, the Reich minister for church affairs, cautioned that priests should not "use the party as a screen" to shield themselves from problems with their diocesan superiors.[16] Still others embraced Nazism primarily because of its antisemitism, linked to a belief that Jews were the cause of Germany's misfortune.[17]

Regardless of a particular priest's motives for supporting National Socialism, many Catholics supported Hitler, especially in his initial years of power.[18] Hitler tapped into the mythical longing of many Germans for a national savior. His gift of oratory was also enticing and played into this yearning. Similarly, the words he spoke—especially when he attacked Communism, immorality, and unemployment—resonated in the German Catholic milieu. In the 1920s and 1930s, for example, on any given Sunday it was common to find Catholics throughout Germany sitting in their pews and listening to their priests warn them about the evils of immorality and Communism.

Catholic clergy and most Catholic laity also had much in common with National Socialist antisemitism. Though the Church hierarchy officially rejected the party's extreme racial ideology, it continued to hold negative perceptions of Jews by blaming them for Christ's crucifixion.[19] According to Catholic rhetoric and popular thought, Jews were outsiders and, unless they chose baptism, had little chance of salvation.[20]

Nonetheless, priests and bishops had reason to be suspicious of National Socialism. In fact, in March 1931 the bishops of Germany forbade Catholics to join the Nazi Party. In some dioceses the directives even ordered priests not to provide the sacraments to NSDAP members.[21] Church leaders were primarily concerned that National Socialists would not respect the rights of the Church to operate freely. The bishops also feared National Socialists would call for the creation of a schismatic German national church, the "purification" of the Old Testament, and particularly the sanctification of race, which would discount the efficacy of baptism for Jews who converted to Catholicism.[22] Until March 1933 Hitler compounded these fears further by refusing to clarify the stance of his party toward the Christian churches in general. Instead, he let Point 24 of the Nazi Party program, which stated that National Socialism accepted a "positive Christianity," remain ambiguous. As a result, individual district and local NSDAP leaders assumed the freedom and latitude to issue a wide variety of opinions, both for and against the churches.[23]

Despite the ambiguous and, at times, hostile attitude of the party toward the churches, some Catholics were drawn to it. This number increased slightly after 1930 when the NSDAP became a force in the German Reichstag.[24] The National Socialist emphasis on nationalism also became a prime factor in persuading many Catholics to rethink their position toward the Nazi Party. On January 30, 1933, this situation changed dramatically when Hitler became chancellor of Germany. As National Socialists gradually took over national and local political positions, Catholics feared even more that they would be left out of the political process and labeled traitors by the new government. No practicing German Catholic desired a resurgent *Kulturkampf,* which under Otto von Bismarck's chancellorship in imperial Germany had attempted to suppress the Catholic Church for the broader purposes of the state.[25] This worry repeatedly surfaced in Catholic publications in the years immediately before and after Hitler's rise to power.[26]

On March 23, 1933, in a speech to Reichstag deputies, Hitler took the initiative to calm these fears. In an effort to gain the support for his government, and especially for an enabling act that would place legislative power solely in his cabinet and ultimately in his hands, Hitler promised Catholic and Lutheran Churches that Christianity would serve as the underlying foundation of the German nation. For the most part, the Catholic hierarchy trusted Hitler's promise. A few days later the German bishops lifted their ban on NSDAP membership and publicly recognized Hitler's promise to the churches. However, the bishops chose not to remove their "condemnation of definite religious-moral errors" regarding the *Weltanschauung* of National Socialism.[27] The bishops specifically aimed this rather abstruse complaint at the racial teaching of National Socialism that rejected the efficacy of baptism and sanctified grace. Not surprisingly, several months later, on July 20, the German government under Adolf Hitler signed a concordat with the Vatican state, which promised official government protection and recognition of the Catholic Church and its institutions in Germany, something no other German Reich had dared to grant.[28]

Because of Hitler's concessions, Catholics had ample reason to offer their support to the new German state, at least initially. Catholics could now find reason to differentiate between Hitler, whom they supported, and the Nazi Party, whose *Weltanschauung* they did not fully embrace. It must also be remembered that until the mid-1930s the German state and the Nazi Party were two separate entities.[29] Attacks against Catholic teachings by party members such as the ideologist Alfred Rosenberg only heightened this distinction.[30] Hitler, however, remained above criticism; many Catholics even preferred to believe he disapproved of the writings of Rosenberg and other party members.[31] As a result, a large majority of Germans came to view Hitler as Germany's savior.

Answering the call to assist Hitler, brown priests viewed themselves as chaplains or even missionaries to the right-wing movements of Germany. Normally this meant that the brown priests were not supporters of the Catholic-based Center Party *(Zentrum)* nor of its Bavarian counterpart, the Bavarian People's Party (BVP), but instead were advocates of the far right-wing parties that had been active since the foundation of the Weimar Republic. In fact, many such priests viewed the Center Party and its representatives as traitors to Germany. In their minds the Catholic Church had aligned itself with the wrong political party. To counter this, they sometimes joined the Catholic faction of the German National People's Party (DNVP) or became involved with other smaller right-wing parties or movements. All eventually made their way to the NSDAP: some as members, some as informants, and some as "outside" supporters ever ready to fight for the cause of National Socialism. Catholicism and National Socialism, they thought, were fully compatible. If elements in the party attacked their religious tradition, brown priests were more than willing to attribute this behavior to extremists who were not yet in line with Hitler.[32]

The brown priests, however, always believed that they were almost mystically in line with Hitler and reflected the essence of National Socialism. They also felt that they represented a genuine response of their religious tradition to National Socialism. Most viewed themselves as honorable and devout Catholics who rarely doubted their call to the priesthood. In addition, the majority of the brown priests relished their roles as pastors and teachers and genuinely enjoyed dispensing the sacraments and involving themselves in intellectual parleys about their faith. In fact, more than one-third of them had doctorates in theology or philosophy. Even those who did not hold advanced degrees had received excellent instruction as seminary students either in state and diocesan theological-philosophical colleges or in universities with theology faculties. Yet, despite this education these brown priests did not see the intrinsic evil in National Socialism. Rather, they often created their own national and Germanic vision, a mixture of German Catholicism and National Socialism that neither their Church nor the Nazi Party could fully embrace. For Church leaders, in particular, these priests became renegades who ignored episcopal directives by politicizing their preaching and teaching. And ironically, for state officials and Nazi Party leaders, these same priests were still too Catholic and therefore not fully trustworthy. Indeed, most leading Nazis rejected a Catholicized version of National Socialism, no matter how Germanic.[33]

On the whole, those priests who became brown and who worked for the cause of the NSDAP did so as individuals. Despite a few attempts to bring them together, they were not organized in any way like their counterparts, the German Christians *(Deutsche Christen)*, an overwhelmingly Protestant fellowship, whose members sought "a synthesis of Nazi ideology and Protestant tradition and agitated for a people's church based on blood."[34] Nevertheless, there existed an unfounded, yet intricate, network of communication among brown priests. Many of them knew each other and the nature of the work they conducted on behalf of National Socialism. Many of them also regularly corresponded. When any one of them experienced conflict with his local bishop or religious superior, he might confer in person with a fellow brown priest. In addition, in certain circumstances they appear to have worked together to promote state and party goals in their individual dioceses and churches.

By studying the lives of these brown priests, and especially their writings, we learn how they could justify their support of the National Socialist *Weltanschauung*. Their sermons, speeches, and writings align traditional Catholic religious antisemitism with National Socialist racial antisemitism.[35] This discovery confirms David Kertzer's thesis in *The Popes against the Jews* that the Catholic Church implicitly sustained and carelessly bred a religious, social, and economic antisemitism that ultimately provided a seductive option upon which National Socialism was able to build its broader racial and annihilative antisemitism.[36] Even today the Catholic hierarchy seems incapable of disengaging itself completely from this historical posture. In 1998, when the Vatican's Commission for Religious Relations with the Jews produced *We Remember,* an official statement on the Shoah, it attributed Nazi racial antisemitism solely to neopagan philosophy, as if the Church's own theology at that time did not generate an equal, though variant, form of antisemitism. In like manner, in 2005 Benedict XVI reiterated this same impaired understanding of the Shoah during his visit to the synagogue of Cologne.[37]

In this work I offer a corrective to these reductive theological interpretations and move beyond Kertzer's argument to demonstrate how, on a local and parochial level, the hierarchy was not as greatly troubled by the antisemitism of subordinates as by the brown priests' refusal to eschew politics and obey episcopal directives. The German bishops' primary concern was always the protection of the Catholic Church and its sacramental mission.

This study of brown priests also reveals how all levels of oversight and leadership in the Catholic Church failed to oppose the persecution of Jews and National Socialism's social and territorial goals. Much of the current literature on this subject emphasizes the role of the papacy and the bishops, ignoring the complicity of clergy at the local and regional levels. I raise the issue of complicity not only among the clergy of the highest levels of Church leadership, but also among the diocesan and religious-order priests of parochial rank and station.

I first ask the question: "What induced a Catholic priest to become a brown priest?" In the context of this question, I examine a brown priest's ideological identity, attempting to fathom the theological and social processes that inspired some of his most antisemitic actions and thoughts. Through the use of various examples and case studies from a number of dioceses throughout Germany, I present my understanding of the term "brown priest." I likewise discuss the layers of complicity among the Catholic clergy with the National Socialist state, then examine the theological "brownness" of the German Catholic Church in general.

Next I explore the lives of Hitler's first clerical supporters. I do this through the individual stories of the "Old Fighters" *(Alte Kämpfer)*—hard-core Nazis who had agitated with Hitler as the party maneuvered to gain political power from 1919 through January 1933. I profile brown priests such as Bernhard Stempfle, editor of *Mein Kampf;* Albanus (Alban) Jakob Schachleiter, Benedictine abbot of Emmaus; Dr. Josef Roth, First World War infantryman; and Dr. Lorenz Pieper, grassroots agitator for Hitler, all of whom were key figures in the propaganda machine that drew Catholics toward National Socialism. I point out that there was not simply one single motive for supporting the Nazi Party. Rather, each priest had a variety of individual reasons such as nationalism, antiliberalism, anti-Bolshevism, opportunism, and antisemitism.

Since antisemitism was so central to the National Socialist Party and state, I also examine the life of Dr. Philipp Haeuser, patristic and biblical scholar as well as pastor of Straßberg. Haeuser publicized his antisemitic prejudices more than any other of the brown priests. In his process of denigrating Jews, Haeuser simultaneously deified Hitler. Though his bishop detested Haeuser's renegade nature and attempted to control him, Haeuser's friend, the auxiliary bishop of Augsburg, sympathized with his work and continued to offer him protection. The story of Haeuser under National Socialism starkly reveals the depth and complex nature of antisemitism in Catholicism.

Antisemitism, however, was not the only factor that impelled a priest to support National Socialism. Even more alluring was the temptation of nationalism, as exemplified by Father Anton Heuberger. Pastor of a small parish in the diocese of Eichstätt, almost overnight Heuberger became a media darling for the National Socialist propaganda machine by publicly asking the question, "Can a Catholic priest be a National Socialist?" He soon learned that such a question was anathema in a small, conservative Catholic diocese. His bishop's unwillingness to remove him immediately from office reveals the Catholic hierarchy's lack of understanding of the inherent dangers within National Socialism.

A large number of the brown priests used their academic gifts for immoral social and ethical ends to promote National Socialism's compatibility with Catholicism. In particular, they worked alongside fellow National Socialists to strengthen the exclusionary vision of an Aryan *Volksgemeinschaft* (racial national community). One such individual was the Duderstadt teacher of religion, Father Richard Kleine. Though a rather unimportant priest in the grand scheme of things, Kleine's promotion of National Socialism went far beyond influencing his Duderstadt gymnasium students. That is, six years into the Third Reich, he was able to bring together a circle of National-Socialist-minded priests that included within its ranks such prominent theologians as Karl Adam and Joseph Mayer, both of whom worked for reconciliation between the Catholic Church and the NSDAP. Kleine similarly encouraged his colleagues to work alongside like-minded Protestants in order to promote National Socialism's antisemitic and exclusionary *Weltanschauung*.

Finally I focus on the postwar experiences of brown priests and show how they fared during denazification. While their respective bishops generally disciplined them, almost all of the brown priests eventually made their way back into full-time ministry.

Although this study deals with a small segment of the German Catholic clergy, I hope to provide an avenue through which we can examine the overall response of the Catholic Church and its priests to National Socialism. Many members of the German Catholic clergy succumbed to the attraction of National Socialism at the expense of their perceived Catholic faith, separating their loyalty to the Church as priests of Christ from their allegiance to the state as advocates of a precarious nationalism. The brown priests, however, never saw the theological discrepancy between faith and hate, partly owing to their own deep-seated antisemitic feelings that were an antecedent to their public commitment to National Socialism. Sadly, these feelings, though never going as far as antisemitic actions, nonetheless compromised their faith when Nazism convinced them that hatred of Jews and love of neighbor were not mutually exclusive choices in prewar Germany. It is even sadder that the Catholic pre-Vatican II tradition inadvertently supplied these racist feelings with a theological lie (i.e., Jews killed Christ and for that reason were theological contaminants), which enabled these clergymen to bring antisemitism into harmony with their priesthood. Indeed, the Christian antisemitism that often lay dormant within them as priests ultimately served as a poisonous seed feeding the racial, annihilative National Socialist *Weltanschauung*. This book examines the lives of these men as "brown priests" and shows how their personal choices or the historical circumstances surrounding their choices ultimately affected their commitment to both God and Hitler.

1—Adapting Catholic Teaching to Nazi Ideology

At the end of the Second World War, a report from the American Third Army stated, "The question who is a Nazi is often a dark riddle. . . . The question what is a Nazi is also not easy to answer." Despite these challenges, the Allied Powers (France, Great Britain, the Soviet Union, and the United States) individually created a complex denazification system with tribunals to determine who had been an ardent supporter of National Socialism. In its occupied zones (Hesse, northern half of Baden-Württemberg, Bavaria, and southern part of Greater Berlin), the United States developed a detailed *Fragebogen* (questionnaire) that asked German citizens to state if they had ever been a member of the NSDAP or of any of its related organizations. In turn, the Americans had access to the party's membership card catalogue in order to verify the respondents' answers.[1] Even with these resources, the occupying powers faced a mammoth task that often relied on the willingness of individuals to incriminate themselves or others.

Many members of the German clergy shared their bishops' negative appraisal of denazification. In particular, Father Hermann Schmidt of the Fulda diocese considered denazification so full of biases that he lodged a formal complaint with the American army. Schmidt's objection concerned the mandatory removal of anyone from his or her place of employment, especially if the person had joined the NSDAP prior to May 1, 1937—the date when all state employees (excluding priests) had either to join the party or relinquish their positions. Schmidt held that many individuals who had joined the party were initially misled by its promises. This fact, he said, was "understandable and forgivable." According to him, "only a few of them were politically so well trained that they could foresee the true backgrounds of the diabolically refined camouflage of the [Nazi] system." However, once the NSDAP leadership revealed its true intentions, he believed many of the members changed their outlook and became "embittered opponents of the party." This unsubstantiated claim has little basis in truth. Nevertheless, Schmidt explained his position further by arguing that the NSDAP had legitimately assumed power. "Foreign governments recognized it without reservation . . . and allowed their flags to fly next to the swastika during the Olympics." Germans only acted in the same fashion. Additional factors also encouraged many Germans to turn toward National Socialism. In particular, the "hopeless economic situation" at the end of the Weimar Republic drove many Germans into Hitler's arms. "Millions were unemployed. Dreaded Communism with its history of organized bloodshed in Russia threatened to bring about a violent coup that would wipe out the intelligentsia and the middle class. Since the party system of the Weimar Republic, because of its hopeless fragmentation, no longer offered any protection against Bolshevism, many saw in the powerful NSDAP the one hope of rescue from the chaos." In Schmidt's opinion, Hitler and his party accepted this challenge and worked tirelessly to come up with a kind of German New Deal to restore order and German honor. With these successes in mind, Schmidt listed what he believed to be the Hitler regime's achievements that had won over Catholics as well as millions of other Germans. For him, these included: "The swift reduction in unemployment, the many social and hygienic measures for the *Volk,* the initial fight against immorality in literature and in the streets, the conquest of the former conflict within the *Volk,* the signing of the Reich-Vatican Concordat, and the silencing of all religious polemics, the initial claimed desire for peace, the banished threat of Bolshevism!" These swift "actions," Schmidt argued, created "a wave of trust" in Hitler and the new government "by the *Volk.*" Schmidt admitted that even Catholic clergy found themselves caught in this rush of support for National Socialism. According to him, "many priests and some bishops were themselves at first swayed from their former stance of opposition, and indeed not at all out of opportunism. It seemed as though National Socialism had been misjudged. . . . Thus, the other former objections—that the NSDAP was the party of the brutal fighters in streets and halls of war agitators, and of enemies of religion seemed to be invalid."[2]

In his analysis Schmidt revealed many of the determinant factors that drew Germans, Catholics and Protestants alike, to National Socialism. Similarly, he correctly observed that many Catholics who supported the NSDAP initially, gradually changed their stance over time, particularly when the policing agents of the state and party began to encroach on Church freedoms. This is much less true, of course, of those Catholics who became registered members of the NSDAP. Nevertheless, problems arise from Schmidt's reasoning primarily because he offered his views devoid of any consideration of antisemitism and its lethal effect on his fellow German-Jewish citizens under National Socialism. Similarly, Schmidt's tone and phraseology, which suggest his frustration with denazification, also reveal his desire to limit its scope. In turn, it is possible to assume that Schmidt supported the arrest and prosecution of only the most ardent Nazis. The rest he was ready to forgive because, in his own mind, they had only joined the majority of Germans who also initially shared a similar trust in Hitler and the NSDAP.

Indeed, after the bishops lifted their prohibitions against National Socialism, many of the Catholic clergy like Schmidt joined their fellow citizens and welcomed the first efforts of the new German government. This is not to say that priests were not involved with the party prior to March 1933. Certain members of the clergy, for example, agitated openly on behalf of the NSDAP throughout the 1920s. In addition, there were priests who welcomed Hitler and joined their more right-wing-oriented parishioners in a united effort to place pressure on the German hierarchy to rescind its prohibition barring Catholics from joining the Nazi Party. The task now is to distinguish between those priests who were outwardly nationalistic (associating the party with their aspirations for national recovery) and those who were ardent supporters of the NSDAP and its *Weltanschauung*. As I will show, the line between these two categories vacillates, especially in the years immediately following Hitler's appointment as Reich chancellor, making it difficult for some priests to sustain a sufficiently consistent identity as nonpartisan priests.

After March 1933 Catholics often received mixed messages from their bishops and priests concerning their participation in the state. Prominent Catholic priests and scholars, including the Münster systematic theologian Michael Schmaus and the Braunsberg church historian Joseph Lortz, produced a series of persuasive studies entitled, "Reich and Church," which promoted reconciliation between National Socialism and Catholicism.[3] Similarly, the Tübingen systematic theologian Karl Adam wrote "German Ethnicity and Catholic Christianity," in which he appropriated the vocabulary of Nazism such as *Blut* (blood), *Boden* (soil), and *Volkstum* (ethnicity) to discuss the question of race and, more specifically, address the relationship of National Socialism to German nationalism and Christianity.[4] Wilhelm Berning, bishop of Osnabrück, concretized these theological "clarifications" further when Hermann Göring, minister president of Prussia, appointed him *Staatsrat* (councilor of state)—a title he used repeatedly in his correspondence.[5] Although this position had become relatively ceremonial in the Third Reich, Berning helped legitimize the new government by accepting a position in it. Moreover, in April 1934, Berning published *Catholic Church and German Ethnicity,* in which he attempted to critically reinterpret National Socialism's *Weltanschauung* through a Christian prism. Despite his best efforts, his words, at times, betrayed his sympathy for the Hitler movement. Likewise, in his conclusion, he lessened the impact of his earlier criticism by praising the German government for its effort to address societal concerns and by expressing a desire for more cooperation between the government and the Church.[6] By contrast, seven months later, in a Hannover lecture, Berning spoke more critically about National Socialism, especially its racial teaching.[7] Despite the bishop's change in tone, SD (Sicherheitsdienst, security service) leader Reinhard Heydrich still presented the possibility of Berning becoming the next bishop of Berlin on account of "his alleged sympathies for National Socialism." Ever skeptical of clerical motivations, Heydrich also added that the bishop's ambitiousness would drive him to seek "the Cardinal's hat" and "in this way then work for Rome against Germany, like every other bishop."[8]

By repealing their prohibitions against the NSDAP, the German bishops placed themselves in an awkward situation, rendering their about-face open to quirky interpretations. Was their change brought about for diplomatic or nationalistic reasons, or both? Were they attempting to cover themselves in one place of negotiation, only to open themselves up in another place? Or were they pragmatically responding to the reality of a new government and simply trying to make the best out of a challenging situation? Since the Church had not gone underground during the Third Reich, it had to operate in the public arena. Its civic posture therefore had to be reckoned with and accounted for. In addition, the July 1933 Concordat had solidified the public existence of the Catholic Church in Germany in such a way that, as an institution, it had to take on the dual role of being both advocate and vigilant onlooker of the new government. The Church's twofold role would play itself out over the coming years. From the state propagandists' perspective, the repeal of the prohibition simply revealed the Church's outright acceptance of the government and its policies for the sake of the public good. Thus, when a new Catholic bishop followed the tenets of the Concordat and took his oath to the state, such an oath not only strengthened and confirmed the Weimar Constitution's Article 137, which called for such a pledge, but also reaffirmed the idea of a close church-state relationship in the minds of Catholics.[9] In addition, the 1934 *German Leadership Lexicon,* which contained pictures and brief biographies of all public leaders in the Reich, only confirmed this church-state connection by including entries on each of the bishops, which they either personally wrote or approved. In his entry, Bishop Berning made sure to include his *Staatsrat* title.[10]

Naturally not all the bishops were as enthusiastic toward the state. One such prelate at the time was Konrad von Preysing, bishop of Eichstätt, who, on May 31, 1933, warned his fellow bishops not to adopt the regime's language such as "new order" or "new state" in reference to the government. According to Preysing, any acceptance of the Nazi *Weltanschauung,* which he believed was inconsistent with the Catholic faith and moral life, would only assist state Nazi leaders in their attempt to identify the NSDAP with the state.[11] Unfortunately, few of the bishops shared Preysing's views fully. Instead, a wide range of individual responses followed. The rejoinders of most bishops fell in the middle and followed the pattern of Johannes Baptista Sproll, bishop of Rottenburg, who, in a January 1934 speech before a gathering of his clergy, specifically spelled out the actions of the state that Catholics should be ready to support. Sproll declared emphatically, "We take a positive view of the new state. We are gladly ready to recognize what the new state strives for and has achieved in various areas." He then went on to give thanks to the state "for the defeat of Bolshevism, . . . the rejection of many liberal ideas, the aspiration to a true *Volksgemeinschaft,* the articulation of a leadership principle, . . . the struggle for just treatment of Germany by other nations, . . . the strengthening of the moral force of the *Volk,* the battle against filth and rubbish, the ousting of prostitution from the streets, the protection of family values, and the purposeful population policy. In all these points we happily support the efforts of the government. We will also gladly work together in the struggle for the elevation of the status of farmers, against unemployment, and against hunger and cold." Despite this positive outlook, Sproll still concluded his talk with this caveat, "However, we must take a position against laws that go against our conscience as it is said in Scripture: 'One must obey God more than man.'"[12]

Probably the bishop most open to the state was Conrad Gröber of Freiburg, who, during the early years of the Third Reich, was often referred to as the "brown bishop." Gröber had such high hopes for cooperation among the state, party, and Church officials that he became a "supporting member of the SS," an infamous fact that a lawyer defending the SS in the Nuremberg trials forced him to confess.[13] Gröber also gave his blessings to the Working Group of Catholic Germans (Arbeitsgemeinschaft Katholischer Deutscher, AKD), a laity-run organization founded in the fall of 1933 by Franz von Papen, Reich vice-chancellor, and approved by the NSDAP to promote cooperation among the party, state, and Church.[14] The group's leadership had turned to Gröber for support after Cardinal Adolf Bertram, archbishop of Breslau and senior prelate among the German bishops, had turned down its request for the German Catholic hierarchy's official recognition. Bertram specifically objected to the group's bid to assist the Church in church-state conflicts and its desire "to strengthen the German national consciousness" among Catholics. In the former proposal Bertram feared a possible conflict with the authority of the hierarchy, while in the latter he feared it sounded more as if "only the Catholics" were "lacking love for Germanness, nation, fatherland, and loyalty."[15]

In 1933 Gröber made it clear that he supported close church-state relations. In April he became the first German bishop to stand publicly behind the government. The *Kölnische Volkszeitung* reported that, during a speech, Gröber "did not allow the least doubt that Catholics should not reject the new state, but have a positive outlook toward it and must single-mindedly work with it, but with dignity and with seriousness and without provocation and useless martyrdom."[16] On June 28, 1933, on the eve of the signing of the Reich-Vatican Concordat, Gröber strengthened his stance by exhorting his priests "to avoid anything in sermons, Christian teaching and religious instruction, as well as in association activity and private discussions, which could be interpreted as criticism of the leading personalities in the state and community or of the state-political views that they advocate."[17] By making such statements the archbishop muted any impetus among his clergy to resist the government. Gröber, however, was not alone, because many of his fellow bishops issued similar statements, primarily to prevent any last-minute problems before the Concordat was signed.[18] Nevertheless, Gröber's public support of the state always went a step further. For example, in October 1933, in a speech delivered in Karlsruhe, Gröber not only thanked the government representatives who were present, but also announced that he stood "completely behind the new government and the new Reich." He continued, "Why should I not do this? We know what the new government strives after. It has concluded a treaty with the Holy See, which exists not merely on paper but is intended to be a vital life of German Catholics. One of the first statements of the Führer was Christian. He has raised his hand against all those who came charging against the cross. We know that the *Volk*'s well-being and the *Volk*'s greatness are only achievable from the roots that are the same as the roots of the cross."[19] Though Gröber made it clear at the time of his speech that he supported the Hitler government only because of its overtures to Christianity, he still at the same time left little room for Catholics laboring to oppose it.

By 1935 Gröber revealed a gradual shift away from the regime, especially after various ministries of the state had encroached on Church-related areas and arrested clergymen for statements or actions perceived as hostile to state interests.[20] Yet, as late as 1937 Gröber still showed his public allegiance to the state when he unequivocally permitted his diocesan priests who taught religion in state schools to offer the newly required oath of allegiance to Hitler. Gröber gave this permission despite resistance to this measure in other German dioceses and among his own clergymen.[21] In addition, in the same year, the SS ironically asked Gröber along with other diocesan officials to withdraw their memberships from its supporting organization. Though most officials complied, Gröber refused to voluntarily withdraw his name and thereby forced the SS to expel him.[22]

During the early 1930s not only did some of the German bishops strongly encourage Catholics to support the Hitler government, but leading members of the clergy also took up this call. In particular, Father Marianus Vetter, a Dominican and the preacher at St. Hedwig, the cathedral of the Berlin diocese, walked a precarious line between nationalism and promotion of National Socialism. At first, it appeared as if Vetter had co-opted the language of National Socialism in his sermons to help Catholics to focus more on their faith and less on the purely ideological rhetoric of the party and state. Such an effort took place on June 25, 1933, when he preached before a crowd of over forty-five thousand Catholics at the thirty-first *Katholikentag* (National Catholic Convention) held at the Berlin-Grunewald stadium. Greeted by a large choir from forty-one parishes, Vetter preached about preparation for the kingdom of God. In his sermon Vetter addressed Pope Pius XI as the "Führer of Christianity" and added that the divine Führer was "one who clearly" grasped the "new world view in himself" and delivered it to humanity with "prophetic strength." This person, according to Vetter, was Christ, "who must again become King in all areas of life." If this were to be accomplished, the "people of the earth shall again become a true, holy Reich, a kingdom of Christ." In order to bring this about, Vetter exhorted his audience to participate in the work of the Church and follow Christ, who called them to build "a holy Reich in your own person, in your own family and in your own *Volk*." Thus Catholics could participate in the Christian task of the German people by building the *Volksgemeinschaft* "in the spirit of Christ." Vetter stated that this was not to be done alone but in "spiritual unity with our Protestant members of the *Volk*." Together the two could proclaim, "Germany awake—onward toward Christ!"[23]

By September 1933 Vetter's support for the state had intensified. In a sermon commemorating the ratification of the Reich-Vatican Concordat, Vetter exposed an increasing trust in the Hitler government. This particular occasion had great significance for Nazi propaganda because Bishop Cesare Orsenigo, the Vatican nuncio to Germany, presided at the mass. Numerous Catholics, many of whom were members of the National Socialist Party, were also in attendance and after the Eucharist sang the German national hymn and the Horst-Wessel song. In his sermon, Vetter stated that the Concordat should be viewed as a treaty that guaranteed the continuation of the mission of the Catholic Church in Germany and not as a compromise with the state. Hitler as "a man with a highly developed sense of responsibility toward God, sincerely concerned with the welfare of the German people in keeping with God the Creator's will," would ensure the government's protection of the Church. At the same time the Concordat would guarantee "full choice of religious affiliation and the public exercise of the Catholic religion." In turn, the Church would "include the state and *Volkstum* in its activity, in its prayers, and in its blessings" and all "spiritual leaders and pastors of every German diocese" would take "an oath of loyalty to the fatherland and its constitutional government."

Up to this point in his sermon Vetter essentially explained the motivation behind the Concordat and its basic tenets by portraying the Church as an equal partner in a treaty that benefited both sides. By contrast, in the middle of his sermon Vetter offered a broader interpretation of the Concordat's aim: to integrate "the Catholic portion of the population into the *Volksgemeinschaft* of the new state." Such language struck a resonant chord in the hearts of many of his listeners, challenging them to put aside any lingering fears of a *Kulturkampf*. The Concordat, he told them, guaranteed Catholics full membership in the German *Volksgemeinschaft*. For this reason, he encouraged them to "personally adopt the oath of loyalty toward our country and government sworn by our bishops" by seeing it as a "responsibility toward God and an expression" of their "love to be not just Catholic Christians, but Catholic Germans as well."

Vetter then concluded his sermon by proclaiming Christ as "savior of the world," who had "awakened our German *Volk* to a new life" and "will incorporate us into his Reich." Christ was the one who also secretly called out to the German *Volk:* "I say to you, Germany arise."[24]

Even before the thanksgiving service took place, the NSDAP regional office of Greater Berlin reported to Hitler's Reich chancellery that "a National Socialist Catholic priest will give the sermon."[25] Vetter's homiletic enthusiasm for the new government and his clever textual juxtaposition of National Socialist jargon with Christian imagery might have made it difficult for the listener to understand the priest's motivation. By emphasizing such Christian phrases as "arising to new life" and the "kingdom of God" in his sermon, Vetter sent mixed messages to his congregation, especially since the Nazis had used similar phrases in their speeches and writings to refer to the promises of the Third Reich. Similarly, in his preaching Vetter did not encourage Catholics to set themselves apart from the "reawakening" of the German state, nor did he specifically invite them to align themselves with Nazism. Rather, he offered them an invitation to test their patriotism on the basis of their Catholic faith while he simultaneously encouraged them to remain open to the German government. Interestingly enough, in 1937, after he left Berlin to become superior of the Dominican community in Cologne, Vetter himself admitted in a sermon that his previous desire for harmony in church-state relations encouraged him to make such generous overtures and concessions to the state. According to Vetter, his work for "peace" went so far that at times he "was suspected of being a secret member of the party."[26]

Though Marianus Vetter was neither a brown priest nor a secret member of the party, his words, at least in 1933, served as an entreaty to Catholics to accommodate themselves to National Socialism and the German state. In this regard, Vetter's life reveals the challenging choices that priests had to make under National Socialism. Vetter had the difficult task of balancing his love of the Church with his nationalism. His efforts to balance these two attachments under the Third Reich were further complicated by the growing entanglement of German nationalism with the NSDAP. Though the Church had traditionally condemned radical nationalism, many Germans, including Catholic clergymen, were still unable to or did not wish to separate nationalism from the NSDAP. It seemed each grew as a component of the other, making it difficult to discriminate between the two entities. For that reason, many priests neglected or refused to reflect carefully on the consequences of their pastoral actions in relation to the state and party. Like many Germans, they felt (or outwardly acted as if they believed) that nationalism and the NSDAP went hand in hand and encompassed similar economic and social goals for the common good that involved the cooperation of all responsible citizens. As late as 1940, Father Heinrich Molitor, a pastor in the city of Mainz, offered a clear portrait of this mode of conduct. In addition to his parish duties, Molitor also had the responsibility of serving as a chaplain to the soldiers stationed within his local area. In November he agreed to preside at the burial of SS Corporal Rheingan in the cemetery chapel. Accompanied by an unnamed priest, Molitor arrived at the cemetery in the automobile of his ordinary, Albert Stohr, the bishop of Mainz, which the bishop had personally lent to him for this occasion. Following the funeral, Molitor, dressed in his chaplain military uniform accompanied the body and a contingent of uniformed SS men in a procession to the place of burial. There Molitor delivered a twenty-five-minute sermon about "loyalty and love of fatherland," in which he "cleverly weaved in some Church faith teaching." The newspaper reporter who covered the event commented that Molitor's speech "made a great impression."[27] This display did not please the SD. Not wishing to give the impression that the SS and Catholic Church were closely linked, it recommended that SS men not be allowed to appear in formation at future funerals of their comrades.[28]

Despite his actions, Molitor was not a brown priest. That is, while his words and actions might today convey the aspirations of an overly nationalistic individual, he was at the time merely carrying out his priestly sacramental duties, albeit wearing a military uniform and blessing the body of a deceased Catholic member of the SS. The case of Father Bruno Bayer of the Augsburg diocese reveals a similar pattern. After the war the local denazification tribunal called Bayer in to explain his actions during the Third Reich. In particular, the tribunal concerned itself with a March 1936 report in Bayer's local newspaper, *Aichacher Zeitung,* that covered a rally in Oberwittelsbach on the eve of the March 29, 1936, Reichstag election during which Bayer had publicly praised the "merits" of Hitler and made a "stirring appeal" to those present "not to become traitors to the people's chancellor Adolf Hitler." Following the March 7 reoccupation of the Rhineland by German troops and the dissolution of the Reichstag, the March 29 "election" was primarily a referendum that asked German voters whether or not they supported the policies of Adolf Hitler. The yes vote both ratified the decision to reoccupy the Rhineland and justified the decree to dissolve the Reichstag in favor of a new membership. Since the reoccupation overturned a major clause of the despised Versailles Treaty, it is no wonder that 98.9 percent of the German population voted in favor of their Führer.[29]

When a tribunal member asked Father Bayer if he had supported Adolf Hitler's policies by making the above statements, the priest did not deny it. Still, Bayer did assert that the reporter exaggerated a bit in his details about his level of enthusiasm.[30] In essence, Bayer's tone was only slightly stronger than that of the German bishops. Generally, the bishops supported the referendum by using patriotic language without specifically praising Hitler, his government, or party. At the same time the bishops were forthright in making known to Catholics that their stance in no way endorsed any "measures and statements," presumably by the state, that were hostile to the Church and its pastoral mission.[31] Following laudatory nationalistic language, such a fine distinction may have been easily lost on ordinary Catholics.

Like Bayer, Father Friedrich Pfanzelt, pastor of Dachau, was also called before a denazification tribunal to explain his actions in the early years of the Third Reich. Allegedly in November 1934, Pfanzelt gave a speech before the Dachau SA (Sturmabteilung, storm troop) members of his parish entitled "Act Manly and Be Strong," in which he encouraged them to use their entire strength to help Hitler rebuild the Reich. Following his strongly worded, nationalistic speech that touched upon weighty topics, such as the Versailles Treaty, revolution, inflation, and unemployment, Pfanzelt celebrated mass for the SA men, 90 percent of whom were Catholic.[32] After the war a witness testified that Pfanzelt also blessed the SA flags that were present.[33] Furthermore, only a month prior to this event, the NSDAP *Kreisleiter* (district leader) had written a letter to the Bavarian government on Pfanzelt's behalf in which he attested that the priest had in no way proved himself to be an opponent of the party but had made it clear that he did not agree with the "machinations" of the Catholic-based Bavarian People's Party.[34] The *Kreisleiter* also supported Pfanzelt after Johann Schober, an SS man, had denounced him for encouraging him to turn against the party and for making derogatory statements about the state during the sacrament of penance and in a subsequent discussion.[35] As Pfanzelt's lawyer argued during the denazification proceeding, the priest was under tremendous pressure to carry out his ministry in Dachau, the home of the first official concentration camp, where a significant number of SS men were stationed. On several occasions during the Third Reich, SS men, who routinely distrusted churches, even attempted to entrap the priest. They were particularly troubled by his ministry to concentration camp prisoners.[36]

Despite Pfanzelt's pastoral zeal, especially in his outreach to prisoners, he did have a personal history of supporting a conservative, right-wing agenda. In January 1932, for example, officials of the Munich archdiocesan chancery felt compelled to write to Pfanzelt and ask him to clarify the remarks he had made in Pellheim during a rally for the protection of the Bavarian homeland.[37] Pfanzelt gladly responded to their request by proudly informing his diocesan superiors that he had indeed spoken in Pellheim and had also planned to speak to two additional communities about the importance of protecting "our dear homeland from Bolshevism and ungodliness." He explained that it was a "demand of the heart" for him to speak out against these "great dangers."[38] Evidently, the chancery did not find anything objectionable in Pfanzelt's explanation and allowed him to fulfill his future speaking engagements. The denazification tribunal also found that Pfanzelt's actions during the Third Reich did not justify punishment and exonerated him. The tribunal dwelled neither on Pfanzelt's pre-1933 foray into conservatism and nationalism nor on his 1934 interactions with the SA, but instead focused on his pastoral work and on his persecution at the hands of the SS and Gestapo.[39] Although the denazification tribunal cleared Pfanzelt of any wrongdoing in the Third Reich, his actions during this period offer a clear example of how some priests flirted with National Socialism without embracing it fully. In a sense, he allowed his cassock to get dirty, but washed it before the "brown" stain set in permanently.

National Socialism was alluring not only to Pfanzelt and Bayer, but to many members of the German Catholic clergy. Though the state and party often had a tenuous relationship with the Church and its priests, clergymen could not evade the state's and party's promotion of nationalism and unity among the German *Volk*. These factors in particular encouraged priests to avoid actions that might appear antinationalistic, or even anti-German. In addition, priests often attempted to forge a positive working relationship with local state and party officials in an effort to protect their parishes and associated organizations. However, this is not to say that, behind each overture that priests made to the party or state, there were not also a variety of motivations, including sympathy for one or more aspects of the National Socialist *Weltanschauung*.

The priests of the archdiocese of Freiburg in the southwestern state of Baden exemplify this diverse response of the Catholic clergy to the German state and the National Socialist Party. Their actions during the Third Reich also further reveal the complexity of attributing the "brown" label to a priest's identity. In 1937, for example, the archdiocese of Freiburg had 1,546 ordained priests, of whom approximately 488 served in the Catholic parishes and institutions of the state of Baden.[40] A report by the Nazi Party categorized 60 of these priests, or 8.1 percent, to be politically reliable and sympathetic to the aims of the state and party.[41] The party would have received information on these clergymen primarily through the Gestapo and SD, who in turn collected information from informers and from personal encounters with these priests. Among the sixty priests alluded to, the party judged Father Paul Bleichroth's attitude toward it as "formerly unknown," but "today good and reliable." It also judged Father Konrad Marbe to be "uninterested in politics before our seizing of power," but now "favorable," especially because he "propagandize[d] strongly" for the NSDAP "in existing Church organizations." When it focused on Father Hermann Kast, the party was more reserved. Though he had "not come out politically," it still viewed him as promising because he had executed "his office as [an] educator according to [the] principles of [the] National Socialist state." Father Karl Behringer, on the other hand, caused the party greater concern since he "publicly" affirmed the "party (flag-waving, processions, and press)," but his "inward attitude towards [the] party [remained] doubtful." Even worse, it worried that he held "great influence" over the "population and also on fellow party members." In many other cases the party described a priest simply as having a "good" or "friendly" attitude toward it without offering any further comments. Still, these descriptions offer contemporary historians a means by which to distinguish between those priests who were opponents of the party and those who were sympathizers. For example, the party described Father Artur Oswald as "reticent and malicious" and Father Fabian Dietrich as a "party opponent [who] was reported to [the] Gestapo several times." Father Joseph Fritz, another parish priest, received even stronger criticism when the party described him as a former "open, hateful agitator" who today carried out his work "only in secrecy."

The tangible actions of the sixty priests deemed favorable to the state and party reveal a contrasting spirit of activity and enterprise. Twelve of them, for example, eventually ran afoul of the Gestapo at some point during their ministry.[42] Nevertheless, none of them directly opposed the state or party for political reasons, but instead came into conflict because of their pastoral ministry. Of these twelve, three had problems with the local NSDAP leadership in either 1933 or 1934, primarily regarding statements they had made publicly, which a NSDAP member perceived as hostile to the state.[43] In 1937 the Gestapo questioned an additional four priests for either reading or distributing copies of the papal encyclical "Mit brennender Sorge" (with burning concern), which was critical of the German government and the NSDAP for their treatment of the Catholic Church and its organizations.[44] The other five priests ended up in conflict with the state either over comments critical of the state's treatment of the Church or over pastoral work with youth that conflicted with the efforts of the Hitler Youth (HJ). In 1941 the latter even led to the arrest of Father Albert Riesterer, who spent more than three years in the Dachau concentration camp for ignoring a Gestapo prohibition that blocked him from returning to his former parish.[45]

To make the matter even more complex, only five of the priests—Fathers Theodor Böser, Carl Robert Lehrmann, Karl Theodor Leuchtweis, Johann Gottfried Riegelsberger, and Rudolf Sigi—left behind any evidence that would reveal sympathy for National Socialism. After the Second World War, Böser and Leuchtweis, for example, admitted in the military government's *Fragebogen* that they were members of the National Socialist Welfare organization, or NSV, which, by promoting the health and well-being of the German *Volk,* directly supported and advocated the NSDAP racial principle. According to the party's report, Lehrmann was also a member of this organization. In the case of Riegelsberger, in early 1937 the pastor of Ottenheim, where he served, evaluated Riegelsberger's relationship with state authorities as "very good!" and added that "for today, he is the right man."[46] In addition, the acting mayor of Ottenheim and National Socialist supporter, Heinrich Benz, had years later protested to Archbishop Gröber for transferring Riegelsberger, among other priests, to a different parish. According to Benz, the parish would never get "a man of quality such as Father Riegelsberger." He even attributed the 30 percent increase in mass attendance to the priest's presence.[47] Still, neither of these statements definitely reveals that Riegelsberger had National Socialist sympathies. The situation of Father Rudolf Sigi, parochial vicar in Engen, is much clearer. In April 1936 his pastor, Father Emil Dreher, informed Archbishop Gröber that Sigi had preached a sermon with "figures of speech favorable to National Socialism."[48] In the same month the Freiburg chancery received several letters from National Socialists who requested the transfer of the "politically untrustworthy" Fathers Dreher and Wilhelm Hauswirth. The latter was also a parochial vicar in Engen and Sigi's peer. According to the NSDAP local leader, the transfer of Father Hauswirth would allow "peace" to exist in the parish.[49] This situation intensified to such an extent that Emmi Krucker, the local leader of NSV, circulated among Engen's parishioners a petition of support for Sigi.[50] As the conflict escalated, in July 1936 Father Dreher pleaded to the chancery to have Sigi transferred because Sigi made use of the party to work against him.[51] Evidently the chancery took Dreher's side and transferred Sigi, making him parish administrator in Pfaffenweiler. After this point, Sigi, who now found himself in a position of authority, kept out of conflict, at least with his fellow priests.[52]

Though one can describe only two of the sixty priests as outwardly and ideologically sympathetic to National Socialism, one additional factor helps to explain why they all might have been, to some degree, sympathetic to National Socialism and, at the very least, radically nationalistic: their military service. Out of the sixty priests in the report, thirteen served as soldiers in the First World War before their ordination, including Father Paul Robert Bleichroth, who was a prisoner of the French from September 2, 1918, through March 19, 1920.[53] Most of the thirteen also saw front-line combat and were either wounded or gassed. In addition to the thirteen who served as soldiers, four priests served as chaplains, either in hospitals or in front-line ministry.[54] Three additional priests, Fathers Albert Riesterer, Robert Alfons Schlund, and Erwin Schweizer, also served as military chaplains in the Second World War. Riesterer only served for less than four months before the military released him from service and before the Gestapo arrested him.[55] In contrast, in July 1940 Schweizer boasted to the Freiburg chancery that he was the first priest of his archdiocese to serve as a military chaplain in (what was to become) the Second World War.[56]

Although an examination of the Freiburg archdiocesan priests in Baden does not yield a definitive judgment regarding these priests' pastoral or ideological motives for cooperating with certain party and state organizations, a portion of the clergy inspected portrayed itself, at least in 1937 and 1938, as state and party loyalists. In many respects, this revelation could simply mean that such priests stayed far away from politics, preached solely about religious matters without making even the slightest allegorical reference to contemporary politics, and worked to create an amicable relationship with local state and party officials. At the same time, the NSDAP's "positive" designation of certain clerical loyalists could also be on target, laying bare certain right-wing affinities that had always been present in these priests. Either interpretation is still significant when one considers that by 1937 church-state relations had deteriorated drastically and that the Vatican had to take a dramatic course of action that ultimately resulted in the promulgation of the controversial encyclical "Mit brennender Sorge." This in turn meant that a priest had to rise above the turmoil of church-state relations in order to carry out his pastoral mission. To do this well and on a local level, he first had to exhibit pro-state or pro-party sentiments convincingly. Needless to say, genuine feelings of sympathy for the party and state or overtures based on purely pragmatic considerations could have prompted each of these priests to act favorably toward party and state officials. According to Nazi officials, however, some priests seemed more than others representative of party interests and more genuine in their response to party *Weltanschauung*.

This examination shows how difficult it was (and still is) to label a priest "brown." The majority of the priests discussed here displayed, at best, a public willingness to work with state and party representatives. In addition, some German priests adapted more readily than others to this state of affairs under National Socialism. Still, hardly any of the priests in this study endeavored to serve the Führer by openly preaching Nazi policies or by publicly working for the ideological goals of National Socialism. Instead, most of these priests fell on one side or the other of a flexible line separating "black" (color of clerical attire for Catholic priests) from "brown," a line made visible and fluid through circumstance, conviction, and need. On this changeable, precarious line, priests tactfully negotiated, on the one hand, the ideological demands of party and state and, on the other, the eternal claims and challenges of the Church.

One of the sixty priests that the party designated as politically reliable complicates this discussion. The party described the attitude of this priest, Father Wilhelm Maria Senn, pastor of Flehingen, and then Sickingen, as "good"—a designation given to many of the sixty priests. However, in comparison to the Catholic priests discussed earlier, Father Senn had a long history of publicly venting his antisemitism and openly identifying himself as a supporter of National Socialism even before Hitler came to power. For example, in 1931 he published *Catholicism and National Socialism: A Speech Concerning German Catholicism* and, in 1932, *Halt! Catholicism and National Socialism: My Second Speech to German Catholicism and to Rome*. Both works offered a positive portrayal of National Socialism and encouraged Catholics to embrace the Hitler movement. Senn also used these works to propagate what he found most attractive in National Socialism—its antisemitism. To this end, in *Catholicism and National Socialism,* Senn asked, "Is our Catholicism Judaized?" He answered this question with a resounding, "Yes! We are Judaized—to a highly frightening degree Judaized" and then proceeded to portray a world in which Jews controlled everything—from politics to the press and culture. According to him, Catholicism was Judaized because it refused "to protect Christianity and *Volkstum*" by caving in to Jews, who derided every challenge as "antisemitism."[57]

Even though by 1937–1938—the years when the party composed its report on the Baden Catholic clergy—Senn had cut back his public activity for National Socialism, partially because of his recurring health issues, the party's use of the label "good" to describe his relationship with National Socialism might strongly suggest that the lives and choices of his fellow priests who received the same designation need to be reevaluated. Perhaps the evidence of their activities during the Third Reich does not accurately portray the full extent of their acceptance of National Socialism. On the other hand, it must always be remembered that the policing mechanisms of the party and state did not always correctly evaluate an individual's political outlook or motivation. The Gestapo or SD regularly labeled individual priests as opponents to the state, even though these individuals rejected such an antinationalist categorization. Quite often such priest "opponents" challenged the state out of pastoral concerns, especially when the state encroached upon Church life and their pastoral sensibilities. Likewise, the Gestapo or SD could also have labeled some priests as supporters of the state, even though these individuals never outwardly spoke on behalf of the Nazi Party or state.

Who then were the brown priests? They were those clergymen who had become members of the NSDAP, especially those individuals who signed up before Hitler came to power. Alongside these clergymen were other priests who never joined the party, but who publicly supported Adolf Hitler and the Nazi Party through their ministry, preaching, and writing. Apolitical fellow clergymen and Catholic laity regularly identified such individuals as *braune Pfarrer* (brown priests), who worked closely with National Socialists or who promoted the goals of Hitler's movement. Normally such a clerical identification meant that a brown priest embraced not only the ultranationalism of the NSDAP, but also other aspects of its *Weltanschauung*—even those that conflicted with Church teaching. Of course, there were limits even to what a brown priest might support. Nevertheless, despite differences with the state or party on individual issues, most brown priests refused to separate themselves completely from National Socialism.

Father Wilhelm Senn was not the first clergyman who risked his ministerial career and priesthood to agitate for the cause of Hitler. No, there were several other "Old Fighters," the affectionate label with which National Socialist comrades who were part of the movement before 1933 identified themselves. These joined Hitler in the "trenches" and helped him strengthen the party throughout the 1920s.

2—In the Trenches for Hitler

On April 12, 1933, Gustav Staebe, editor of the southern German edition of the *Völkischer Beobachter,* the National Socialist newspaper, ran a brief notice requesting all Catholic priests who stood by "Adolf Hitler and his ideas" to submit their names and addresses to his newspaper. Staebe assured the priests of confidentiality.[1] This appeal came only two weeks after the German bishops had allowed Catholics to join the NSDAP. Many priests took advantage of the reversal of the bishops' prohibition and publicly professed their support for the Hitler movement. Father Franz Sandkuhl of the archdiocese of Munich and Freising wasted no time in sending Staebe his reply. Sandkuhl proudly boasted that he stood by Adolf Hitler with his "whole heart" and commended the NSDAP for doing "more for the Church than the Center and the Bavarian People's Party had done in years." He confided that he had kept his National Socialist convictions secret only so that his Church superiors would not block his appointment as a religion teacher at a state academy. Now that his bishop had reversed his stance, he would apply for membership in the NSDAP.[2] In a matter of days Sandkuhl joined the party and became member No. 3,213,295.[3]

Staebe was pleasantly surprised by the number of responses he received from Catholic priests.[4] Though many of those were priests who had just made their support for Hitler public for the first time, a few were longtime adherents. Among the latter was Father Christian Josef Huber of the Augsburg diocese who reported, "I have been since the beginning a supporter of the movement and became a member of the party in 1922 or 1923 and during this time also actively agitated for it."[5]

As party official Martin Bormann commented, "On the whole only a minuscule number of priests joined the NSDAP before 1933."[6] One of the most significant reasons for this was the close bond between the German Catholic Church and the Center Party and its more conservative Bavarian counterpart, the Bavarian People's Party. Responding to a form of anti-Catholicism in the German states in the second half of the nineteenth century and on the heels of a united Germany with its anti-Catholic *Kulturkampf* policies, the Center Party had earned its right to represent Catholic interests in the German political process.[7] Though not every German Catholic was a member of the Center Party or had even voted for it, most Catholics and bishops expected their priests to promote its interests. If a priest dared to separate himself from the Center Party, a plethora of right-wing, nationalist parties awaited him.[8] Furthermore, in the early 1920s many of the priests who would eventually declare allegiance to National Socialism still actively participated in the parties and organizations that sought the restoration of the prewar monarchy. The few priests who did seek out the NSDAP found its raw antisemitism and ultranationalism particularly appealing.

In order to understand why a priest chose to support or agitate publicly for the NSDAP prior to 1933, one must first look at the history of the party and study the issue of membership and identity chronologically and contextually. Founded by Anton Drexler in 1919, and originally called the German Workers' Party, the NSDAP operated in the Bavarian *Hauptstadt* (capital) of Munich at the "brown house," where the party's central office was located and where, in 1920, it published its first political program.[9] Originally it attracted a number of priests, primarily from the overwhelmingly Catholic Bavaria. The party gradually began to branch out as enthusiasts and supporters founded local groups throughout Bavaria and in other German states.[10] Whereas the party grew significantly in the latter part of 1922 and into 1923, it actually had no more than fifty thousand members prior to the 1923 putsch when Hitler and his followers attempted a coup d'état in Munich.[11] Nevertheless the party was able to attract the attention of a few, select Catholic clergymen, who traveled to Munich to agitate for Hitler. Similar to that of the party, the rhetoric of these Hitler-supporting clergymen was ultranationalistic and antisemitic.

The 1923 putsch brought an unexpected halt to the spread of National Socialism and a decrease in its ranks. Hitler's subsequent arrest and imprisonment and the Bavarian state government's prohibition of the NSDAP led to the movement's fragmentation. Alfred Rosenberg, Hitler's self-appointed replacement, fought with both Erich Ludendorff, the former World War I general, and Albrecht Graefe, a right-wing, völkisch (racial-nationalist) leader, for control of the former NSDAP and the *Völkisch* movement.[12] The *Völkisch* movement encompassed a variety of right-wing groups that were extremely nationalistic and antisemitic and, more often than not, rife with religious underpinnings.[13] After the Bavarian Supreme Court ordered Hitler's parole on December 19, 1924, and Bavarian Prime Minister Heinrich Held rescinded the state's ban on the NSDAP on February 16, 1925, the Nazi movement did not rebound immediately.[14] Many former members or supporters could not overlook the militant action of the putsch and the chaos that ensued from it. As Father Christian Huber attested, "As a result of the confusion after the putsch in 1923, I became estranged for some time without relinquishing the *Weltanschauung*." Even prior to the putsch Huber began to turn away from National Socialism because of the anti-Catholicism of some of its leaders and speakers. He would not start agitating for it again until 1928.[15] During this postputsch period other National Socialist supporters among the clergy turned to rival *völkisch* groups as a means of channeling their antidemocratic and nationalistic yearnings.

The surprising results of the 1930 Reichstag election altered the situation in favor of the NSDAP. The German voters gave the NSDAP a 15.7 percent increase over its previous election return, which expanded the party's Reichstag representation from 12 to 107 seats.[16] With the weakening of the Weimar democracy, the threat of Communism, and the economic problems of the world depression, the Nazi Party and its rhetoric had become more attractive to many Germans. It now became clear to many Germans that among the various fatherland (nationalist) and *völkisch* associations and parties the Nazis would prevail as the leading political representative of an ultranationalistic and antisemitic ideology.

Up to this point, the German bishops had largely ignored the NSDAP and the *Völkisch* movement. In 1921, for example, the German bishops had issued pastoral instructions for their priests in regard to those associations they deemed harmful to Catholics. Although these directives specifically mentioned only Socialists and Freemasons, they forbade membership in any party or organization whose outlook was detrimental to Christianity and the Catholic Church. The instructions also enabled a priest, if pastorally warranted, to withhold the sacraments and Church burial from anyone whose participation in such a pernicious party might cause public scandal.[17] A bishop could also have referred to these directives if he wished to limit a Catholic's involvement in the Hitler party. Until 1930 the bishops did not deem this action necessary. At best, they individually issued general, tentative statements critical of right-wing, militant, fatherland associations without ever fully prohibiting outright Catholic membership.[18]

In 1930 the state of affairs changed, since the NSDAP had made such notable progress. Now the situation forced the bishops to act, primarily because Hitler continually declined to clarify his party's view on churches and refused to prevent individual Nazis from speaking critically against the Church. Thus, if the 1930 elections encouraged a Catholic priest to support the NSDAP publicly, the bishops' 1931 prohibitions against it forced him to keep his sympathies secret. Only a few priests publicly declared their support of the NSDAP and agitated for its interests. These priests boldly challenged their bishops' prohibitions against the NSDAP and proudly bore their "persecution badge" at the hands of their Church superiors as a form of "martyrdom" for the cause of Hitler.

The majority of Catholic clergymen who considered themselves Old Fighters had discovered National Socialism long before the failed putsch. They had attached themselves to the party from its infancy when the party needed support from anyone who held an influential position in German society. In addition, these priests became involved in National Socialism during a time when its party leaders did not always hold fast to Point 24 of the 1920 party platform, which championed a "positive Christianity" that was not bound "to any particular denomination."[19] Although Hitler did not originally emphasize a clear separation of party politics from religious-denominational issues, he aimed from the beginning to create a national party that would unite all Germans across religious and social spectrums. This would be a particularly challenging task for any party, but especially for the NSDAP, since it had located its headquarters in ultra-Catholic Munich. Only later did Hitler make a clear separation between politics and religion a central concern. Hitler felt compelled to take a strong stance against mixing religion and politics, especially after recognizing how divisive religion was in other *völkisch* parties and associations and, in particular, in the remnants of the NSDAP while he was in prison.[20] Of course, Hitler and other party leaders were not shy about invoking religious imagery and language for propaganda purposes.

Despite Hitler's efforts to separate his party politics from religion, in May 1923 the Nazi Party was so favorable to religion that its party newspaper, the *Völkischer Beobachter*, began publishing weekly schedules for Catholic masses and Protestant worship services, accompanied by a prayer for Hitler. The prayer ran: "O God, preserve our Führer, lead him on the right path and bless his work."[21] Around the same time other newspapers reported that Catholic priests had been openly agitating for the National Socialists. On July 11, 1923, *Vorwärts*, the official organ of the Social Democrats, ran an article on its front page with the headline "Bavarian Priests as Supporters of the Swastika. Rebellion against the Pope?" The reporter wrote, "It is no secret that a large part of the Bavarian clergy completely devotes itself to supporting the swastika. . . . In Bavaria there is today no nationalist event at which some Catholic priest does not give his 'blessing.'" The reporter also lamented that priests had acted as "Catholic National Socialist Storm Troop preachers" and called on the bishops to "put an end to this nonsense and put the priests in question in their place to fulfill their Catholic duties."[22] In October 1923 Heinrich Held, then head of the Bavarian People's Party in the Bavarian state parliament, addressed similar concerns in a letter to Cardinal Michael Faulhaber, the archbishop of Munich and Freising. Held wrote, "Even priests have become enmeshed in National Socialist ideas and allow themselves to be shamefully misused as agitators. . . . Under the guise of field masses, the Catholics, particularly the Catholic youth, are misled about the true intentions of the leaders of the movement."[23]

Finally, in August 1923, the diocese of Regensburg stepped in to prevent a member of its clergy from blessing a NSDAP flag. The chancery official argued that the diocese had to refuse this request not only because it was a political symbol, but also because the NSDAP was "undoubtedly anti-Christian in nature."[24] Still, at this time the German bishops and chancery officials did not consider the party significant enough to warrant determined action. Rather, each diocese dealt individually with any problems arising from clerical involvement in the NSDAP or in other right-wing movements.

In many regions of Germany, and even in Austria, there was clearly some initial form of cooperation between members of the local clergy and the Nazi Party. As far away as the diocese of Graz-Seckau, Father Ottokar Kernstock, a member of the Austrian Congregation of the Canons Regular of St. Augustine, composed the poem "The Swastika," which the newly founded Fürstenfeld NSDAP local group requested on the occasion of a flag-blessing ceremony.

The swastika in the white field
On a background of fire-red
Proclaims freely and plainly to the world
The joyful tidings ahead:
That those who gather about this symbol
Are German, not just by saying so,
But by intent, kinship, and soul.

The swastika in the white field
Was culled as the nation's symbol
On a background of fire-red
In hard times and fateful
When, in deep pain and distraught,
The fatherland for help cried out,
Dear fatherland in the death-throes of shock!

The swastika in the white field
On a background of fire-red
Inspires us with courage bold.
No heart beats faint-hearted
Nor will be disloyal;
God's in league with us.
We fear neither death nor the devil.[25]

Kernstock, who was well into his seventies when he composed this poem, passed away in 1928. Though an ardent nationalist and an anti-Communist—both traits he shared with National Socialists—he publicly distanced himself from the Hitler movement in protest of the manner in which the National Socialists had misappropriated and published his poem without his permission.[26] Still, the "Swastika" poem continued to serve the interests of party propaganda for years.

Among the more prominent clerics who supported National Socialism were Alban Schachleiter, O.S.B., former abbot of the Emmaus monastery in Prague; Dr. Bernhard Stempfle, O.S.H., Hieronymite religious and priest; Stempfle's protégé, Christian Josef Huber, priest of the archdiocese of Munich and Freising, who in 1922 was incardinated into the diocese of Augsburg; Magnus Gött and Johannes Baptist Müller, both priests of the diocese of Augsburg; Josef Roth, priest of the archdiocese of Munich and Freising; and Dr. Lorenz Pieper, priest of the archdiocese of Paderborn.

The NSDAP did not have to seek out these clergymen. The seven were already suffused with the *Weltanschauung* of Nazism. These priests were also staunch ultra-nationalists and, with the exception of Schachleiter (who rarely publicly displayed his ingrained dislike of Jews), rabid anti-semites. All believed that the Versailles Treaty was unjust and was signed by an illegitimate, Socialist Weimar government under the control and corrupting influence of leftist Jews. All were steadfast in their determination to reform the German state and replace it with an authoritarian nondemocratic regime. Finally, each priest had firmly convinced himself that it was his divine task to assist in this Nazi undertaking for the salvation of the German *Volk*.

First Impressions

If someone could have appointed a leader from among the brown priests, he or she would have bestowed the "privilege" upon Abbot Alban Schachleiter.[27] He clearly earned this position for a variety of reasons: the prominence of his ecclesiastical office, his age and years of exceptional service to the Church, and his resolute approval of National Socialism—a factor that Hitler acknowledged in giving his personal attention to Schachleiter until the abbot's death in 1937. Schachleiter met Hitler in 1922 at a luncheon given by Erna Hanfstaengl, the sister of Ernst "Putzi" Hanfstaengl, a friend of Hitler's, Harvard graduate, and early NSDAP supporter.[28] After an earlier meeting with the abbot, Hanfstaengl made an overture to Schachleiter to meet Hitler.[29] According to Hanfstaengl, "Hitler and Schachleiter were very soon engrossed in a stirring exchange of ideas."[30] Hanfstaengl was especially happy about the lively exchange of ideas because the rhetoric of some party speakers, which had alienated many Bavarian Catholics, had worried him for some time. As he pointed out, Schachleiter had a "certain amount of sympathy for Hitler's general political line," but "deplored the party's anticlericalism."[31] Though Schachleiter would always maintain his allegiance to Hitler, he would also repeatedly attempt to inform him of any party action that he thought was detrimental to the Church's pastoral mission.

By the time Hitler met Schachleiter, the abbot had been in Germany for several years. Though born in Mainz in 1861 and raised in Germany, Schachleiter had left his native country in 1881 to enter the Benedictine monastery of Emmaus in Prague, which at the time was located in the Austro-Hungarian Empire.[32] There, as a young monk and priest, Schachleiter worked tirelessly to defend Catholicism against the *Los-von-Rom* (Break

Away from Rome) movement, which encouraged Austrian Catholics to leave the Catholic Church and become Protestants in order to prepare Austria for a future union with the German Reich.[33] To help in this defense, Schachleiter founded a local chapter of the Bonifatius Association, whose mission was to promote the Catholic faith through religious literature and homeland missionary work. Through this association Schachleiter emphasized German nationalism, albeit Catholic in nature, to suggest that Catholicism and one's German identity or nationalism were not two mutually exclusive alternatives. In June 1906 Pope Pius X publicly acknowledged Schachleiter's heroic defense of the faith. Schachleiter's monastic brothers also recognized his leadership qualities and, on July 2, 1908, elected him abbot.[34]

Since Emmaus was part of the Beuron Benedictine congregation, it had clear ties with Germany. As nationalism became an increasingly prominent issue in the Austro-Hungarian Empire, the monastery became "not only a spiritual, but also a political center." In particular, Schachleiter increasingly preached a radical German nationalism and aligned himself politically with the Austrian Catholic monarchy.[35] After the monarchy fell, Schachleiter and his monks were *persona non grata* in the emerging Czechoslovakian state. Upon hearing rumors that the monks had a secret radio transmission center in the monastery's basement and had money tucked away in their closets, local Czech nationalist groups routinely searched Emmaus and took what they desired. All the while the local Czech press kept fueling these rumors. Schachleiter soon realized that his pro-German stance had made it impossible for him to stay in Prague. Therefore, on December 8, 1918, he fled the city. However, before he reached an area that was primarily Austrian-German, a group of Czech soldiers arrested him. After a brief, though horrifying, confinement in Benesov, where a crowd of Czech nationals surrounded his detention cell and demanded his execution, Schachleiter was released and escorted safely out of the area. He then traveled to Linz and stayed briefly with Johannes Evangelist Maria Gföllner, the bishop of Linz.[36] While he was in Linz, the canons regular of St. Augustine—the same religious community to which Father Ottokar Kernstock belonged—welcomed Schachleiter into their St. Florian monastery. He was a guest there from December 1918 until October 1919, when he ventured to Munich.[37]

In a short period of time Schachleiter's life had changed drastically. One day he was the leader of more than one hundred religious priests and brothers and a spiritual guide and political advocate of German nationalism and culture in Prague, then, within a day, he became a beleaguered refugee on the run without any place to call his own. Further-more, after his departure from St. Florian and his subsequent arrival in Munich on June 15, 1920, Schachleiter, at a distance, resigned his office as abbot of Emmaus.[38] However, the Vatican did not forget this untiring crusader of Catholicism. On March 21, 1921, during a private audience, Pope Benedict XV named Schachleiter titular abbot of Sponheim, a for-mer Benedictine abbey in the Rhineland-Palatinate.[39] Though this title offered Schachleiter little authority and no real ecclesiastical power, it did bestow an honor upon him and strengthened his resolve to press forward. By this time his intense devotion to Germany had developed into an extreme form of nationalism. Instead of preaching love of neighbor and peace among nations, the most basic Christian message, Schachleiter began to accept speaking and preaching engagements from right-wing groups extolling him to champion Germany's virtues and to exhort German citizens to cross a battle line, so to speak, to fight any-one who stood in the way of Germany's rise to greatness. Schachleiter, however, was not leading this charge. He was merely serving as a precur-sor, a kind of neo-John the Baptist, to the one who would eventually rise to power, his newfound savior, Adolf Hitler.

In contrast to Schachleiter, whose attraction to Hitler derived from his German nationalism and anti-Catholic experiences, especially his re-cent expulsion from Prague and his loss of an ecclesiastical position, Fa-ther Bernhard R. Stempfle, O.S.H., saw in Hitler a fellow traveler who shared his detestation of Jews. Konrad Heiden was right on the mark when, in his biography of Hitler, he described Stempfle "as an antise-mitic journalist, a political conspirator—all in all, an armed bohemian in priest's robes."[40] Hitler clearly saw in the priest something that he es-pecially liked since sometime in the early 1920s he allowed Stempfle to become a member of his trusted inner circle.[41] Though some of Hitler's followers, especially Alfred Rosenberg, were jealous of Stempfle and at-tempted to portray him publicly as an opponent of the NSDAP leader, Hitler ignored them.[42]

Prior to meeting Hitler, Stempfle was Pater Bernardo, a priest and reli-gious of the Poor Hermits of St. Hieronymus of the Congregation of St. Peter of Pisa.[43] After his ordination in November 1904, his religious su-periors assigned Stempfle to the order's monastery, Sant'Onofrio, in Rome.[44] By this time, his religious community was experiencing a lack of vocations and a dwindling number of members.[45] Perhaps troubled by this development and the postwar situation, Stempfle left his monastery in 1918 and returned to his family's home in Munich.[46] An apostolic visitor to Sant'Onofrio thereafter reported that Stempfle was a "hopeless subject," who "after the end of the war remained with his family without any permission. . . . There he did not exercise his priesthood and seemed to have been reduced to the lay state."[47]

In spite of this conclusion by an official of the Holy See, the German press regularly identified Stempfle as a priest.[48] Stempfle, however, did not publicly refer to himself as "pater," but rather as "professor."[49] Some newspapers even addressed him as "Herr Doktor," though it is unclear if he ever earned an advanced degree beyond that required for ordination.[50] Still, the apostolic visitor was probably correct in his judgment that Stempfle no longer exercised his priesthood.[51]

If so, Stempfle still retained a sense of concern for his Church and tradition.[52] In January 1919, for example, he spoke at a gathering of the Bavarian People's Party in Mühldorf and articulated the political goals of the newly founded "break-off" sister of the Center Party. During this speech he also defended Catholic priests against attacks by the Social Democrats.[53] Shortly thereafter, he joined the Bavarian People's Party in its campaign against Johannes Hoffmann, the new Bavarian education minister and Social Democratic Party member, whose proposed school reforms threatened the future of religious education in public schools and called for the removal of clerical supervision in school districts.[54]

Stempfle also aligned himself closely with the Bavarian monarchy, and he often was the featured speaker at events sponsored by associations that supported monarchical restoration.[55] Though his support of both Catholicism and of the monarchy might be seen as positive attributes of a good Bavarian, one could hardly describe Stempfle in this manner. Instead, his interests in Catholicism and the Bavarian monarchy betrayed an ever deeper and more pervasive than normal Bavarian parochialism and nationalism, gradually shifting to the extreme right of the political spectrum. Thus Stempfle supported the Bavarian People's Party, the Church, and the monarchy because they stood as bulwarks against everything he opposed in postwar German society, especially socialism, communism, and democracy. And, similar to his future National Socialist comrades, Stempfle was convinced that Jews were behind everything that tore apart the fabric of German society.

Stempfle was not content with simply offering occasional talks and lectures on subjects that he found to be plaguing Germany. In 1919 he used his solid writing skills to join the staff of the *Miesbacher Anzeiger,* a provincial, antisemitic newspaper "so closely akin to the *Völkischer Beobachter* of the Nazis that both were always named in one breath by their common political opponents."[56] By 1922 he had become the paper's editor.[57] While Stempfle hid his vile attacks behind a series of aliases, such as "Redivivus" and "Spectator Germaniae," he published enough material under his real name to earn an infamous reputation. A rival newspaper editor described the deceptive method of Stempfle's journalistic style in the following manner: "The single weapon that Herr Stempfle knows how to use with virtuosity, however, is bluff and still more bluff. . . . The entire political outlook of this paper [*Miesbacher Anzeiger*], if one wants to call it that, is focused on stirring up hatred between people as well as poisoning the political atmosphere in the city and the countryside with clandestine rumors and confessional secrets."[58]

In article upon article in the pages of the *Miesbacher Anzeiger*, Stempfle assailed anyone who represented a pro-Weimar position, particularly Germany's Jews. Preposterously, he accused them of unlawful acts such as harboring criminals, promoting inflation, and practicing price control.[59] Likewise, he did everything possible, both in his newspaper and in other newspapers such as the *Völkischer Beobachter*, to rile the German population against its fellow Jewish citizens.[60] Thus, by the time he met Hitler in the early 1920s, Stempfle was already well groomed and ready to join the NSDAP leader's inner circle.

Just as Stempfle began his journalism career with the *Miesbacher Anzeiger* in 1919, Cardinal Faulhaber assigned Father Christian Josef Huber as a parochial vicar to the Assumption of Mary parish in Miesbach. This was one of several one-or-two-year assignments that Huber, like any newly ordained priest, had to endure before his bishop gave him a more permanent ministerial position. It is surprising that his superiors had agreed to ordain him at all, since in 1912, three years before his June 1915 ordination, Huber temporarily left the seminary. Huber explained to his parents that it was "impossible" for him "without vile hypocrisy to swear the antimodernist oath."[61]

On September 1, 1910, Pope Pius X had mandated that all priests, religious superiors, and seminary professors had to take the antimodernist oath.[62] Primarily, it prescribed acceptance of Neo-Scholastic theology and a rejection of modern philosophical categories and methods of historical-critical analysis. Yet, just over a year later, Huber had put aside his doubts and reentered the seminary.[63]

Soon after his ordination in June 1915 Huber volunteered as an unpaid medical orderly for the army. His own war experience, coupled with Germany's surrender, affected him significantly, and his curiosity about new ideologies, which almost caused him to leave the seminary, increased. Upon his return home Huber immersed himself in *völkisch* thought. Therefore, by the time he reached Miesbach, he did not need the encouragement of Father Bernhard Stempfle or his *Anzeiger*. On Sunday, October

5, 1919, before a large crowd, Father Huber was finally able to articulate his *völkisch* beliefs by giving a speech entitled "The Wandering Secret." In dramatic form, with great emphasis on diction and pitch, Huber gradually and seductively roused his audience from silence as he disclosed to them the secret: "The Lord of the World, Judas Iscariot," the apostle who turned his back on Christ and betrayed him. According to Huber, such a creature embodied the fullness of Jewish decay and debauchery. Jews were money-grubbers, power-hungry, shamelessly brazen, sneaky, untrustworthy, manipulative, and bolshevistic. In no way should his audience take his warnings lightly, because the day was not that far off when "the wealth of the world will belong to Jews." Stempfle eagerly gave Huber's talk front-page coverage in two consecutive issues of the *Anzeiger*. And as if he were following the preferential racial guidelines of National Socialism, Stempfle twice mentioned the blondness of Huber's hair.[64]

Huber's increased involvement in the *Völkisch* movement did not strengthen his priestly vocation. Rather, it increasingly unsettled him. In February 1920 he moved to Munich and became vice-president of the Catholic Central Journeymen's Association. A year later he also accepted a parochial vicar position at Munich's Bürgersaal Church. Still spiritually unsettled, in September 1921 Huber sought admission to the Munich Benedictine community of St. Bonifaz.[65] Interestingly enough, at this time St. Bonifaz was also the home of Abbot Alban Schachleiter, though it remains unclear if they ever met. What does remain clear is that during his time in Munich Huber had significant contact with the NSDAP, which increased his interest in Germany's extreme-right-wing movements and ideologies.

It appears that Huber did not want to become a Benedictine religious but instead sought incardination into the diocese of Augsburg.[66] Through the support of a local Catholic nobleman, Huber received an appointment as parochial vicar of the Holy Trinity parish in Kronburg.[67] Huber was quite popular among the inhabitants of this small, but historic, Bavarian town.[68] In 1922 Huber befriended Father Magnus Gött, pastor of Mary of the Snow parish in the neighboring town of Lehenbühl near Legau. Soon the two priests shared a great friendship, and over time Huber became Gött's mentor and guide into the National Socialist movement.

Huber was lucky to strike up this friendship, since Gött was not the most cordial of individuals. In the past, when Gött was parochial vicar of the St. George parish in Augsburg, he had had a public falling-out with his pastor. Gött was so vindictive in his criticism of the pastor that he brought the conflict into the local press. At the same time he publicly accused his bishop, Maximilian von Lingg, of "ruling like a pasha." Lingg did not like this treatment in the least and disciplined the impudent priest by transferring him to the remote village of Altusried. Thus Lingg, while he was bishop, made sure that Gött would not be able to return to serve in a larger or more significant parish but minister only in rural communities. In 1912 this pattern finally brought Gött to Lehenbühl, where he would remain for over twenty years.[69]

Gött made the most of his situation in rural Lehenbühl, not only doing pastoral work but also writing a weekly political column entitled "How It Is and Stands in the World" for the *Legauer Anzeiger*. Instead of promulgating right-wing rhetoric only, in 1917 he surprisingly advocated peace without annexation, expressed great sympathy for the working class and Social Democracy, and even criticized Kaiser Wilhelm II. Though Gött did not hold the same array of opinions as many within the *völkisch* camp, he shared one ideological trait with the majority of them: antisemitism. Over time his antisemitism tainted his entire worldview. He began to attribute the decay of the Weimar "party state" to Jews and blamed all of Germany's misfortunes on them. Gött was so negative in his portrayal of Jews that a military official, fearful of the effects that the priest's hateful rhetoric might have on his listeners and readers, summoned Gött to Munich and ordered him to tone down his antisemitic remarks.[70]

Gött may have temporarily softened his rhetoric, but soon he and Huber began running joint evening "discussions" in their parishes as a means of fostering and spreading National Socialism among their parishioners. Gött drenched himself in National Socialism to such an extent that he even began to fantasize about founding a religious community whose members' sole mission would be to travel throughout Germany as itinerant preachers, exhorting the citizenry to live according to a "new social, patriotic, and Christian foundation."[71]

Huber was also a devoted disciple of National Socialism and the *Völkisch* movement; but, in contrast to Gött, he paid particular attention to its leaders and speakers' comments on religion. In particular, Huber became quite concerned about the growing anti-Catholic rhetoric of some NSDAP and *völkisch* speakers, especially Erich von Ludendorff.[72] This gradually caused Huber to question his relationship with National Socialism and the *Völkisch* movement. The violence of the 1923 putsch and the chaos that ensued with Hitler's arrest and eventual imprisonment also dismayed Huber and led him to separate himself from the NSDAP temporarily.[73] Though the party's questionable relationship with

Catholicism also concerned Gött, he was not ready to desert the *Völkisch* movement. Rather, he lashed out at his "friend," publicly attacking Huber in his newspaper column as a "deserter who had abandoned the *Völkisch* movement in its time of misery."[74] Huber's "desertion," however, would not last long. The allure of National Socialism was too strong for him, which eventually led him to rejoin its ranks.

During the course of the 1920s Fathers Josef Roth and Lorenz Pieper developed a close bond of friendship in their zeal for and support of National Socialism. Roth and Pieper also shared an intense hatred of Jews, which led them, at least initially, to embrace the racial antisemitism of National Socialism.

Born in 1897 in Ottobeuren, Roth voluntarily fought in the 19th Bavarian Reserve Infantry during the last two years of World War I. Though this experience hardened him considerably, he still decided to pursue a vocation to the priesthood, which his family had instilled in him since childhood. On December 1918 Josef entered the seminary and began his study of theology in preparation for ordination as a priest of the Munich and Freising archdiocese.[75] Despite his theological studies in Passau and Munich, Roth maintained contact with his former fellow soldiers and from April until August 1919 became a member of the *Freikorps* Oberland. He was also active in the *Wachregiment* Munich.[76] Both paramilitary groups consisted primarily of former soldiers who banded together in postwar Germany to protect the homeland from internal and external "enemies."[77] This military duty included the quelling of the Communist uprising in Munich in early May 1919. Roth also became involved with the German *Völkischer Schutz- und Trutzbund* (People's Protection and Defense League), an extremely nationalistic, antisemitic, and militaristic league that often turned to violence and bloodshed to achieve its purposes. In 1919, as a result of his involvement, Roth helped to found a branch of this organization at the University of Munich.[78] Roth's seminary superiors were either ignorant of his right-wing involvement or simply overlooked it when they recommended him for ordination. On June 29, 1922, Cardinal Michael von Faulhaber ordained Roth to the priesthood and assigned him as parochial vicar of Indersdorf.[79]

Almost immediately Roth publicly identified himself and sympathized with the *Völkisch* movement. In June 1923 he published three consecutive articles in the *Völkischer Beobachter*, entitled "Catholics and the Jews." He later enlarged his articles into the tract *Catholicism and the Jewish Question*, which Franz Eher, the official publishing house of the NSDAP, published in August.[80] Preceding Hitler's *Mein Kampf* by only a few years, Roth's work dealt with the Jewish question in almost equally harsh terms. Roth argued that Catholics had to move beyond their "catacomb antisemitism" and embrace the full teaching of their religion, which revealed an inherent opposition between the Christian religion and Judaism. According to Roth, and in contrast to many theologians, it was not anti-Christian to profess a racial antisemitism, but rather a religious "duty." Jews, he stated, transmitted immorality through their Jewish blood, which Catholics must resist. Consequently, for Roth, the Christian command to love one's neighbor excluded Jews, because from the beginning every Jew was "already a latent danger for the Christian religion and morality," and for that reason "the Jewish race on account of its demoralizing influence inherent in its nature" had to be "eliminated from the public life and religion" of the German *Volk*. Roth assured his readers that this was the only true way to show genuine "love of neighbor toward Jews." If any Catholic had qualms about this practice, Roth assured them that the struggle to defend their homeland against Jewish national influence was "not a violation of the Christian love of neighbor" but a patriotic duty. Otherwise, he argued, Christ would also have to be "considered as un-Christian when he drove the traders and moneylenders from the temple." Furthermore, it was a "distortion of the command of Christian love of neighbor to demand that one should let go all unworthiness unhindered." Then he assured his readers that antisemitism today was "an act of self-defense. All Christian moral conditions for just self-defense" were present in their "stance against Jewry."[81]

Roth also insisted that "something must be done by Christianity and individual Catholic Christians to save, preserve, and protect its sacred goods by the elimination of Jews from public life." This, however, could not be accomplished by merely having the swastika as a "house ornament," nor through "new German names of the month" or "tasteless antisemitic treatises and slogans." For Germans to attempt merely to limit the "influence and activity of Jews," generally or by simply conducting "boycotts" against their businesses, would be "of little use." Rather, he insisted, Germans had to strike hard and elevate the Germanic *Volk* to eliminate "the worst influences." Germans could only accomplish this by duplicating the methods of the Inquisition and by totally eliminating the Jews' "rights as citizens." This would include expelling them "from all state offices," denying them "licenses for any trade and commerce," and prohibiting them from "any literary and propaganda activity."[82] Roth's proposed exclusionary measures against Jews were later echoed in the legislation that Hitler's government enacted during the course of the Third Reich.

In *Catholicism and the Jewish Question* Roth also showed that in his antisemitism and nationalism he was not alone among the German clergy. He twice quoted from the work *Jew and Christian,* by Father Dr. Philipp Haeuser.[83] Unlike Haeuser, however, Roth neglected to submit his tract to Cardinal Michael von Faulhaber as required by canon law. When Faulhaber learned of Roth's infraction he became incensed. Most probably the boldness of Roth's move, especially as a young, newly ordained member of Faulhaber's diocesan clergy, angered the cardinal archbishop most. In no time, Faulhaber called Roth into his office and verbally reprimanded him. It is unclear how Faulhaber viewed Roth's reasoning because he never recorded his thoughts about its diabolical contents. Despite the seriousness of the situation, Roth initially remained quite obstinate in his unwillingness to acknowledge fully Faulhaber's authority.[84] However, reflecting on the implications of his actions in relation to his future priestly career, Roth soon sent off a letter to Faulhaber in which he pledged his fidelity, disclaimed any wrongdoing, and promised obedience to him in the future. Roth would continue to follow this same pattern of defense in future encounters with his diocesan superiors.[85]

Immediately following the war, Father Lorenz Pieper also attached himself to various right-wing groups. Born in Eversberg, Pieper received a classical education at the Paderborn Gymnasium. Ordained in March 1899 for the Paderborn diocese, and after a few years of teaching on the secondary-school level, Pieper undertook doctoral studies in economics in Berlin and then at the University of Munich. In 1903 he published his dissertation "The Situation of the Miner in the Ruhr District," in which he revealed his social and pastoral concern for the working class. Still, even in this prewar period, a conservative right-wing slant marked his political views, especially in articles like "More Willingness for Sacrifice in Political Life!"[86] From 1903 to 1917 Pieper worked as a staff member in the Mönchengladbach central office of the Volksverein for Catholic Germany. Since 1890 the Volksverein had promoted Catholic values in the socioeconomic realm through education.[87] Through this association Pieper traveled throughout Germany, recruiting and lecturing while simultaneously receiving first-hand experience of the Catholic political world. While working with the Volksverein, Pieper became particularly interested in motion pictures, published articles on their implications for society, and in 1916 even served a year in Brussels, Belgium, as a film consultant during the German occupation.[88]

Since his ordination Pieper had held a series of varied ministries that took him far from his home diocese and into contact with important individuals. Hence, when his bishop assigned him in April 1917 to parish ministry in Geseke and subsequently, in August 1917, to Hüsten, Pieper's life changed drastically.[89] Coupled with these reassignments, Pieper, like his fellow Germans, had to contend with the consequences of Germany's losing the war and its immediate aftereffects on his homeland. Pieper's first reaction was to withdraw his membership in the Center Party sometime before 1918.[90] In November of the same year Pieper likewise described democracy as a "farce."[91] Clearly, Pieper had no tolerance for a German republic in which the masses elected representatives from multiple political parties. In this climate, he soon began his search for a new party that would represent his increasingly nationalistic and antisemitic interests.

By November 1919 Pieper solidified his turn to the right when he attempted to establish local branches of the German *Völkischer Schutz- und Trutzbund*.[92] Two years later Pieper turned his attention to expanding and strengthening the Hüsten area *Jungdeutscher Orden,* or Jungdo (Young German Order), a right-wing fatherland association that had much in common with other *völkisch* groups.[93] Pieper fervently worked to instill a Catholic "spirit" into this association. In July 1921 he reported with great pleasure that the Jungdo "has experienced a wonderfully quick dissemination" in the areas directly north of him. Just under a year later Pieper recorded that he took part in a "gigantic rally of the Jungdo in Elberfeld" in which twelve thousand men took part. In order to follow the developments of the various right-wing groups, Pieper also subscribed to Stempfle's *Miesbacher Anzeiger,* which he judged "excellent," especially because "the editor really has wit and style."[94]

Pieper also followed the development of the NSDAP. In February 1922 he first mentioned the efforts of the Hitler movement in his diary. He swore that if he were in Munich, he would do everything he could to help it.[95] By July 1922 he excitedly noted that a local group of the NSDAP had only recently been founded in nearby Hagen and that he had agreed to "prepare an introductory gathering of the National Socialists" in Hüsten.[96] Pieper was especially attracted because he found many similarities between the German *Völkischer Schutz- und Trutzbund* and the NSDAP. This became even more important to him when right-wingers assassinated German Foreign Minister Walter Rathenau on June 24, 1922, and individual German states began to ban the *Schutz- und Trutzbund*.[97] Pieper assured himself that "a way will be found for it [the *Bund*] to come to life again in a different form. It would be best," he thought, "if it slipped in under the guise of the National Socialist Party."[98]

In October 1922 Pieper had the opportunity to hear Hitler speak. He testified, "I have until now actually never heard so fascinating a speaker as Hitler."[99] Later that same month Pieper noted that the "progress of the Hitler party" was for him "a joy of the heart."[100] Pieper had been convinced by him that Hitler was the "born *Volksführer,* who could captivate the masses."[101] By the end of November Pieper felt confident to state, "The future belongs to the Hitler party *alone,* and I am convinced that it will soon be attacked in Bavaria. However, in less than *one year* Bavaria will be ripe for a Hitler victory."[102] At this point, Pieper decided that he did not wish to be left behind as the National Socialists made their way to power. Therefore he decided to go to Munich, and, with "fire and flame" and "every last bit of strength," agitate for National Socialism.[103] As soon as he was finished with his priestly Easter duties in Hüsten, Pieper boarded the first train bound for the Bavarian capital.

1923—The Year of Decision

The year 1923 was a momentous one for the *Völkisch* movement, especially for the NSDAP. Throughout the year a feeling of impending victory resounded throughout the ranks of Hitler's followers. Ultimately, of course, this would lead to the failed Beer Hall Putsch in November 1923, but no one anticipated this loss as the new year began. Certainly not Father Bernhard Stempfle. Rather, he started 1923 by speaking in Miesbach to the Schliersee local NSDAP group and the Oberland *Freikorps,* of which Father Josef Roth was a member. Stempfle recounted the "glorious" past of German history such as the 1870–71 defeat of France and compared it to the bleak situation in which Germany now found itself, both economically and politically. He assured his listeners that they would become "the salvation of the German fatherland."[104]

While Stempfle was making the rounds in Bavaria's countryside, working the small towns, Abbot Schachleiter had already located himself at the epicenter of the *Völkisch* movement, Munich.[105] Schachleiter became the first brown priest to make a splashing debut in the right-wing capital by accepting an invitation to preside at a memorial mass for Albert Leo Schlageter. Schlageter was a devoutly Catholic World War I soldier and *Freikorps* member whom the French had arrested for terrorist activities during the French Ruhr occupation. From 1923 to 1924 French and Belgian troops had occupied the Ruhr region, Germany's main area of heavy industry, in response to the German government's failure to meet the war reparation payments that the Treaty of Versailles stipulated.[106] Tried and convicted by a French military court, Schlageter was sentenced to death, which twelve army sharpshooters swiftly carried out on May 26, 1923. Subsequently Schlageter became a martyr for the right-wing cause.[107]

Since early 1921 Schachleiter had been speaking to right-wing groups throughout Bavaria. By September 1922 archdiocesan officials had already received a complaint about his activism and felt compelled to confront him. The chancery demanded that he "refrain from further talks" with "political contents" because they were "inopportune in our unstable and difficult time."[108] Though Schachleiter obediently received the politely worded archdiocesan request, in typical fashion he ignored its contents.

But the events of June 10, 1923, were impossible for the Munich archdiocese to ignore. While family and friends buried Schlageter in his hometown of Schönau, Baden, in the archdiocese of Freiburg, following a large and celebratory procession by train from Düsseldorf, the Catholics of Munich would honor him with a requiem mass in the basilica of St. Bonifaz Benedictine Abbey. The crowd filled the basilica to capacity. Representatives from the various fatherland and *völkisch* groups, including the NSDAP—all bearing flags—marched in, approached the sanctuary and altar, and stood at attention on both sides. Schachleiter greeted each flag-carrying representative by blessing the flag with holy water.[109] After the proclamation of the gospel, Schachleiter delivered "a burning sermon of love of fatherland."[110] One of the nationalistic-minded congregants, a member of the SA, described its emotional impact as having moved him "into an almost holy enthusiasm."[111] The abbot proclaimed Schlageter "a martyr for German concerns" who "fell in the service of the fatherland and comes before the judgment seat of God as a victim of the most loyal fulfillment of duty." After rousing his listeners, he concluded by assuring them that "salvation for Germany could take place only in the spirit of deep patriotism and sacrificial willingness and firm unswerving belief in God."[112] A few weeks after Schachleiter extolled the deeds of Schlageter, the Capuchin friars of the Bavarian city of Kempten held their own requiem mass, which included a fiery, nationalistic sermon and a politically oriented speech by a National Socialist for the fallen *Volk* hero.[113]

As the various commemorations for Schlageter were under way, Father Lorenz Pieper arrived in Munich with his NSDAP membership card No. 9,740 in hand.[114] With no place to live, Pieper blithely claimed that he would reside with Hitler.[115] The Nazis soon made use of Pieper's preaching skills. Before long, Pieper found himself thrust into a lecture tour for the Nazi Party, traveling throughout Bavaria and into Württemburg, posing the question: Can a Catholic be a National Socialist? Yes, Pieper answered, there was no contradiction between National Socialism and Catholicism. The Hitler movement stood on the "basis of positive Christianity" and continually fought for "Christian education and the denominational school."[116]

In his speeches Pieper also promoted National Socialist racial theory. He proclaimed, "God Himself has created the different peoples according to blood, nature, and race and therefore desires the difference of blood, of peoples, and of race. He also desires that that which he created remains pure. Therefore, one must oppose everything that harms the purity of race. Therefore, the racial standpoint of National Socialism corresponds with Christianity absolutely." For Pieper this practically meant the complete separation of Christians from Jews. To illustrate his belief, Pieper stated, "In the spirit of Christ, we must therefore oppose Jewry. . . . We have the right and duty to protect ourselves against it." Then, quoting Father Josef Roth's articles against Jews almost verbatim, Pieper argued, "Each Jew is from the beginning a hidden danger for the Christian religion and, therefore, the Jew must be eliminated from the public life of the Christian peoples." Pieper concluded, "A committed Christian and Catholic must be an antisemite."[117]

Pieper's lectures demonstrate the influence of Roth's antisemitic thought upon Catholics, especially those who were already sympathetic to a *völkisch Weltanschauung.* Not surprisingly, on the weekend of September 1–2, 1923, a contingent of the *völkisch,* paramilitary, and fatherland groups chose Father Roth, along with Father Anton Braun, a religion teacher, to preside at a prayer service in Nuremberg on *Deutscher Tag* (German Day), a celebration of the German victory against France in the 1870 battle of Sedan. More than one hundred thousand people were in attendance, including Hitler, General Erich Ludendorff, Prince Louis Ferdinand of Bavaria, and Pastor Helmuth Johnson, a Protestant minister and the Bavarian Jungdo leader.[118]

A nondenominational prayer service was the first order of the day. The massive crowd filled Nuremberg's *Deutschherrnwiese,* a sports field and park, to overflowing capacity. Roth had never experienced so large a congregation. Confident in his mission, the young priest approached the makeshift pulpit, looked out upon the masses, and addressed the crowd with "blazing words."[119] Rather than speaking about love and forgiveness, Roth preached about revenge and destruction. Germany had to free itself from the bondage of the Versailles Treaty, deal promptly with its enemies, and remain loyal to a heroic, militant Christ. If Germany truly dealt with these issues, Roth promised, "a new *Volk*" would arise and the "power of Jewish money and foreign henchmen" would come to an end. However, this would happen only if Germans chose a "path to salvation" through militancy—with weapons if necessary. The German *Volk* had to remain strong by protecting its "ethnicity" and refusing to cave in to the false teaching of love of neighbor. Germans needed to follow Christ, "the heroic strongman who was thrown at the feet of his opponents, scourged, and asked no one to mourn for him on the way of the cross to Jerusalem." Jesus came into the world "not to bring peace, but the sword, to throw fire into the world with the intention to burn it." Roth then concluded his harangue by praying, "Hear us, you mighty God, heavenly Führer of battle! Lead us, even if our lot is to sink into the grave. Praised be your name. Thy kingdom, power, and glory be yours for ever and ever!"[120]

The crowd answered Roth's "stirring" call to battle with a unanimous "Amen!" in a chorus of shouts and cheers. Then it marched in an "immense procession" through the streets of Nuremberg. For two hours Prince Ludwig Ferdinand inspected these "troops" as they passed by him through the city's market square.[121]

Two months later, in the evening of November 8 and into the early morning hours of the ninth, Hitler led his fellow party members in an attempted putsch. Before it was over, fourteen of Hitler's followers along with four state policemen lay dead. Hitler fled from the scene to Putzi Hanfstaengl's home in Uffing, forty-three miles south of Munich, only to be arrested on the evening of November 11. A major trial ensued, enabling Hitler to plead his case before sympathetic judges. Though convicted of high treason on April 1, 1924, Hitler received only a five-year prison sentence along with a relatively small monetary fine. Hitler's resignation from the NSDAP in July 1924, together with his imprisonment in the Landsberg fortress and a state ban on the NSDAP, left the future of the party in question.[122]

Rebuilding the Party

The Hitler putsch caught most of the brown priests by surprise and caused many of them to question the future of the NSDAP. In his journal Father Lorenz Pieper captured their collective feelings when he wrote, "Poor Hitler! . . . And the Jews have this lame triumph! Hitler in jail? I cannot grasp it. . . . How can a 'German,' a 'soldier' dare to put his hand on this fiery fanatical German, on this man who shed his blood for Germany in the war?"[123] Pieper recorded these words at his parish rectory in Wehrden, where his bishop had assigned him upon the priest's return from Munich in October 1923. He had returned to his diocese out of fear of canonical suspension and of losing his monthly income. Hitler had also encouraged Pieper to return to full-time ministry in order to avoid ecclesiastical suspension.[124]

Paderborn diocesan officials had been fully aware of Pieper's right-wing sympathies ever since he had deserted his parish earlier that spring to agitate for Hitler. They also knew about his continued support of the Jungdo. However, they had not yet firmly reprimanded him. Father Josef Arnold Rosenberg, his vicar general, only ordered him to return to the diocese and resume his parish ministry. If diocesan officials wished, they could have used the German bishops' 1921 directives concerning associations they deemed harmful to Catholics as the basis for reprimanding a Catholic whose membership in such a group caused scandal for the Church.[125] After March 5, 1924, they could also have turned to Cardinal Bertram's statement on "new organizations" in which he specifically mentioned the Jungdo and Stahlhelm (League of Frontline Soldiers) and then used "etcetera" to include a multitude of other groups. Bertram did not specifically mention the NSDAP, though he did acknowledge the need for Catholics to exhibit a healthy nationalism and love of fatherland while warning them against a "fanatical emphasis on a one-sided nationalism." Overall Bertram did not take further steps to ban Catholic membership in such organizations but left the question open for further study.[126]

Though Bertram's statement did not exclude membership in the "new organizations," it offered enough impetus to Kaspar Klein, the bishop of Paderborn, to ask Pieper "to refrain from public appearances for the Jungdo." At the same time Klein did not restrict Catholic membership in this organization. Pieper stubbornly fought his bishop and remained in the Jungdo by interpreting Kaspar's order strictly as a request to refrain from supporting it in public appearances.[127] By the fall of 1924 Pieper was still working arduously to promote Catholicism within the Jungdo.

In order to solidify this effort, on October 18, 1924, Pieper joined a group of like-minded individuals at the Hotel Löffelmann in Paderborn to discuss the establishment of a Nonpartisan Association of National-Minded Catholics, which would promote "national spirit, the realization of greater-German thought, the reconciliation of denominations and classes, and the collaboration with Protestant Germans for the reconstruction of Germany." Pieper supported this agenda but took exception to their "attack against political Catholicism," which he found too divisive for religious and national concerns. After subsequent discussions, in November 1924 the group that met at the Löffelmann Hotel officially founded an overarching, right-wing Association of German Catholics (RdK). This effort was destined to fail, since not all right-wing associations agreed to participate, and soon after its establishment the RdK appeared to be an "appendage of the Jungdo," never fully developing into a separate organization. At most, pro-NSDAP Catholic groups such as the League of Catholic Germans' "Cross and Eagle" and the Working Group of Catholic Germans, founded much later, inherited the work begun by the RdK.[128]

Undaunted by the failure of the RdK, on August 12, 1925, Pieper renewed his NSDAP membership, as No. 15,406, after the party's refounding in late February.[129] Two weeks later the German bishops issued a statement warning Catholics against membership in fatherland associations and specifically stating that the Church would "not tolerate" priests who were active in them.[130] Pieper did not vanish from the *völkisch* scene but merely limited his public appearances.

Despite this new restriction, Pieper maintained his allegiance to Hitler and on occasion traveled to listen to him or other NSDAP speakers in nearby towns.[131] His local agitation for Hitler also benefited the Nazi Party to the extent that in state and national elections it increasingly gained more votes from the population in and near his parish boundaries.[132] Pieper was not the only priest to rally support for the NSDAP during elections. Even during the party's 1924 ban, Father Magnus Gött, through his column in the *Legauer Anzeiger,* persuaded Catholics in his own and neighboring parishes to vote for *völkisch* candidates. His neighbor, Father Johann Wiedemann, attested that in Legau the *völkisch* parties "received only twenty-three votes less than the BVP" and attributed this "directly to Gött's agitation." Of course, Gött's ranting in the *Legauer Anzeiger* did not go unnoticed. By the spring of 1924 Augsburg diocesan officials threatened him with suspension if he continued to advocate for the *völkisch* cause.[133]

"Professor" Bernhard Stempfle meanwhile continued his role as a close confidant of Hitler and trusted member of his inner circle. In particular, Hitler utilized Stempfle's writing and editing skills, perfected in his years as editor of the *Miesbacher Anzeiger,* to edit his two-volume political testament, *Mein Kampf.* According to one Hitler biographer, Stempfle "had read the proofs and struck out passages that were politically objectionable."[134]

Stempfle would soon have plenty of time to dedicate to Hitler and the NSDAP. In January 1926, a change in ownership of the *Miesbacher Anzeiger* resulted in Stempfle's ouster.[135] Soon after, he became an assistant to

Friedrich Josef Maria Rehse, whose Archive for Contemporary History and Journalism would eventually serve as the foundation of the NSDAP's archive.[136] Stempfle also involved himself in the efforts of the Catholic Association for National Politics—a reactionary, right-wing, pro-Nazi group of Catholic professionals.[137]

Hitler's release from prison and the refounding of the NSDAP led other priests, such as Father Johannes Müller, to support its cause.[138] Müller not only encouraged his parishioners to support National Socialism, but his acceptance of the *Weltanschauung* based on the National Socialist view of *Volksgemeinschaft* encouraged him to adopt Protestant liturgical practices and integrate them into Catholic sacramental life. This included the introduction of a common, collective confession of sin and the granting of general absolution in place of an individual's reception of the sacrament of reconciliation.[139] Such an adaptation embraced the National Socialist notion of perfection and reflected the spirit of the German Aryan race, whose members dared not display any weakness, especially by individually admitting sin to a priest in the sacrament of penance.[140] At the same time such a practice mirrored the dismantling of barriers among Christian denominations in an effort to reflect the unity of all Germans in their religious practice.

Naturally Müller's diocesan superiors soon confronted him. After failing to resolve the issue through correspondence, Bishop Maximilian von Lingg sent Father Max Weishaupt, a chancery official, to confront Müller personally. Müller learned of Weishaupt's visit moments before his arrival and "barricaded the rectory door with furniture and would not allow him inside." Müller's behavior was quite unusual and caused chancery officials to question his sanity.[141] In the end, Lingg demanded Müller's resignation as pastor of Röfingen. On June 11, 1929, under great duress, Müller complied but refused to acknowledge the legitimacy of the resignation and unsuccessfully bombarded his diocesan superiors with letters of protest and litigation into the early 1940s.[142]

Abbot Alban Schachleiter's right-wing endeavors also caused him problems, first with the local Benedictine community and then with Munich diocesan officials. Not long after the extremely nationalistic liturgy for Schlageter, Abbot Bonifaz Wöhrmüller, O.S.B., informed Schachleiter that he could no longer reside at St. Bonifaz because the Benedictine community there did not in any way want to become a spiritual center for Catholics in the *Völkisch* movement. Schachleiter moved to the Benedictine abbey of Schäftlarn, immediately southwest of Munich, until the abbot there grew tired of his right-wing politics. After that, he moved to the Munich House of Studies of the Beuron Benedictines.[143] Then, in March 1926, Schachleiter attempted to bridge the gap among various Christian denominations during a sermon delivered in the Court Church of All Saints. In that sermon, he exhorted Catholics to forgo their approach to Good Friday as a "deadly serious day of mourning," in which they dwelled on Christ's suffering and death, and instead adopt the view of Protestants who celebrated the day as the "greatest religious holiday" of all when Christ through his death offered salvation to the world.[144] Immediately the Munich secular and Protestant presses exaggerated Schachleiter's comments, setting the abbot in opposition to Cardinal Faulhaber over the true meaning of Good Friday. In turn, some newspapers portrayed Schachleiter as a promoter of harmony between Catholics and Protestants.[145] The National Socialist *Völkischer Beobachter* also came to Schachleiter's defense and even accused Faulhaber of prohibiting Schachleiter from preaching.[146]

In the spring of 1927 Father Josef Roth invited Schachleiter to preach a sermon in St. Ursula in Munich, where Roth served as parochial vicar. Schachleiter used the opportunity to espouse his nationalistic views. On June 11, Cardinal Faulhaber gently reprimanded him for this and let the abbot know that in the future he would continue to monitor Schachleiter closely. However, Faulhaber was not privy to the sermon's contents and therefore did not have the means to critique the material specifically. Instead, Faulhaber simply informed Schachleiter that he hoped the sermon was "a real service to the kingdom of God and to the soul, since the Catholic priest does not receive his mission to please nationalist circles or even those of other denominations."[147] Four days later Schachleiter replied to Faulhaber with a letter that firmly denied any wrongdoing. Invoking God as his witness, Schachleiter disavowed uttering "even a word" with the intention "to please nationalist groups or even those of other denominations." Then he lied outright to Faulhaber by stating that he had "only mentioned nationalist concerns two times in sermons, once in the homily for the Schlageter memorial mass in St. Bonifaz (June 1923) and once in a sermon in St. Peter (May 1921)" in order to "defend the mother of God against the accusation that she deserted" Bavaria in the "war and in the revolution. Both were misunderstood," and since then he had "never again used the pulpit" for this purpose.[148]

Even after this exchange with the Cardinal, Schachleiter never removed himself fully from right-wing politics. Even when he turned down a speaking engagement or a request to preside at a liturgy, rumors went around that placed him in controversy. Thus in 1929 Schachleiter thought it best to turn down a request to preside at an outdoor mass to begin the Stahlhelm Day rally in Munich, but the rally organizers still printed the abbot's name on the official program. Not only did Cardinal Faulhaber believe that Schachleiter had ignored his request to avoid mixing nationalistic and political concerns with liturgy, but the abbot's apparent participation became the topic of discussion at the September 10 meeting of the Bavarian bishops.[149] Following this discussion, Faulhaber reprimanded Schachleiter with a strongly worded letter.[150]

Such encounters found Faulhaber seeking counsel from his fellow bishops, from Benedictine leaders, and ultimately from the Vatican about how he should deal with Schachleiter.[151] Soon after the Bavarian bishops' meeting, Faulhaber wrote to Dr. Raphael Walzer, O.S.B., the archabbot of the Beuron archabbey and Schachleiter's immediate Benedictine superior, and then ultimately to the Vatican's Congregation for Religious. Faulhaber informed Walzer that Schachleiter had taken up residence as a chaplain in the retirement home Leo House in Bad Aibling, thirty-eight miles south of Munich.[152] Through the assistance of the Vatican's Congregation for Religious and the Munich nuncio, Monsignor Alberto Vassallo di Torregrossa, Faulhaber had also arranged to have the Leo House domicile available for Schachleiter.[153] At that time Faulhaber was happy to report that Schachleiter refrained "from any public appearances" and spent time "in Munich only for urgent matters such as visiting a doctor."[154]

By 1931, however, Faulhaber's concern over the National Socialist Party was changing radically. Thus, on February 10, Faulhaber banned Catholic membership in the National Socialist Party. After taking such a stance, Faulhaber could no longer tolerate Schachleiter's political activism. But no matter how far he removed Schachleiter from Munich's political spotlight, the National Socialist Party always found a way to bring him back to the fore of national attention.[155] The *Völkischer Beobachter* could not resist running articles about and pictures of the grandfatherly churchman in his rustic but imposing Benedictine habit, smiling while offering the Hitler salute. Indeed, it was ever so easy for a newspaper editor to manipulate the truth and portray the "loyal, national, patriotic" abbot as a persecuted victim of the tyrant Faulhaber and an unpatriotic Catholic Church.[156]

Of course, the newspaper coverage that Schachleiter received from the Nazi press infuriated Faulhaber. Faulhaber told Nuncio Vassallo confidentially that he could not understand how a high churchman could permit himself to be portrayed in the *Völkischer Beobachter*—the same newspaper that "incessantly blasphemed the Holy Father and the Church"—as the "only German patriot" among the Catholic clergy.

Faulhaber also feared the effect on German Catholics of Schachleiter's positive stance toward National Socialism. He worried that Catholics might feel free to go against their bishop's restrictive pastoral instructions regarding membership in the Hitler party.[157]

Though Schachleiter left Munich, he created an even more complex problem for Faulhaber in Bad Aibling. Shortly after the abbot's arrival there, Protestants and committed National Socialists Wilhelm and Gildis Engelhard befriended him and invited the abbot to reside in their home in the neighboring Bad Feilnbach. Feeling persecuted and unwanted by his own Church, Schachleiter happily took up residence in their home, which he named Haus Gott-Dank (House Thanks be to God). He treasured in particular the attention that Frau Engelhard lavished upon him and the time she spent preparing special meals for him that took into account his troublesome diabetes. The Engelhards, however, did not act out of pure Christian concern. Rather, both of them saw the unique opportunities that could result from caring for a "friend" of Adolf Hitler.[158] No matter how genuine the Engelhards' intentions were, Schachleiter's acceptance of their offer was scandalous to Catholics. Not only was he, as a vowed religious, living outside his assigned Catholic religious institution, but he was also residing in the house of a Protestant couple. Moreover, and probably the worst in the eyes of Church officials, Dr. Engelhard had a medical practice far outside Bad Feilnbach and was away from home during the regular work week.[159] This left Abbot Schachleiter home alone with Frau Engelhard! Rumors sprang up, and before long Gildis Engelhard had received the unofficial title "Frau Abbot."[160] Despite such rumors, there is absolutely no evidence that Schachleiter broke his vow of celibacy.

By early 1931 Schachleiter had caused so many problems in the surrounding communities that Father Ludwig Zach, the pastor of neighboring Au, with which the parish in Bad Feilnbach had a filial relationship, wrote directly to Cardinal Faulhaber. Zach reported that Schachleiter's pro-National Socialist stance had "confused" local Catholics, especially in Bad Feilnbach, a town already significantly under Nazi influence. This caused among Catholics a great deal of "mistrust against the non-National Socialist priests."[161] Faulhaber appreciated receiving this report and thanked his loyal priest. He assured him that the trouble would soon end, after Catholics read and accepted the Bavarian bishops' prohibitions against the NSDAP.[162] In April 1932 Zach again wrote to Faulhaber to report that in the neighboring town of Litzldorf a NSDAP speaker had declared, "We have one hundred priests in our ranks, one of whom is a man we all know well, the abbot of Feilnbach. He belongs to our movement." Though Zach was pleased to report that the "church-minded people of Feilnbach have no wish other than that Herr Abbot disappear immediately from Feilnbach," he expressed his concern that support for the NSDAP was growing rapidly among the local population.[163]

That same spring Schachleiter rallied for Adolf Hitler's election campaign for Reich president. The abbot even produced an election leaflet that not only exhorted "Christian *Volk*" to vote for Hitler, but also attacked the Catholic Center Party.[164] Now the Munich chancery took swift action. Diocesan officials ordered Schachleiter to leave Bad Feilnbach altogether and return to Leo House, where they believed they could control him better.[165] When Schachleiter informed archdiocesan officials that he could not obey their directive, Dr. Engelhard defended "his" abbot by producing a public "report" on the situation.[166] At the same time, in an effort to declare his independence from Faulhaber's authority, Schachleiter freely distributed copies of Pope Benedict XV's apostolic breve that named him Abbot of Sponheim.[167] Soon the situation in Bad Feilnbach became a scandal for the Munich archdiocese. On June 24 Faulhaber informed Schachleiter that the latter would lose his faculties in the archdiocese if he did not move before July 10, 1932. Faulhaber specifically blamed the situation on Engelhard's letter and the spread of the apostolic breve. However, he did not mention anything about Schachleiter's failure to obey Faulhaber's prohibitions against National Socialism.[168]

In response Schachleiter considered issuing a public appeal and sent a draft to Father Josef Roth, who attempted to dissuade Schachleiter from publishing it. In particular, Roth warned the abbot about placing himself directly in the middle of the already existing tensions between the Church and the NSDAP. Roth also cautioned him about his use of language, which he believed might fuel the fire for those in the Nazi Party who were enemies of the Church.[169] Apparently, Schachleiter listened to his young friend and decided not to pursue this tactic. Later he would even claim that he had never received the cardinal's letter that threatened suspension of his ecclesiastical faculties.[170] Evidently Faulhaber believed that Schachleiter, as a high-ranking churchman, would respect his authority in the area of ecclesiastical privilege. We have no evidence that, after the incident, Faulhaber regularly checked to see if Schachleiter had obeyed the prohibition.

In the meantime Schachleiter turned his attention to overturning the German bishops' prohibitions against the NSDAP and integrating Catholics into the Hitler movement. To this end, on October 6, 1932,

Schachleiter wrote to Hitler and cautioned him that "if the Catholics do not join the NSDAP, the danger exists that National Socialism will become a purely Protestant movement. . . . Is this not the time to say a few words to reassure Catholics?" He pointed to Father Wilhelm Senn's two works on Catholicism and National Socialism as examples of how Catholicism and National Socialism could be compatible. He also offered regularly to write newspaper articles that would promote harmony and understanding between Catholicism and Protestantism. Last, Schachleiter assured Hitler that he prayed daily for electoral victory of his Führer and party.[171] Little was he aware how soon these prayers would be answered!

While Schachleiter occupied himself with promoting the NSDAP in southern Bavaria, Father Josef Roth did his best to agitate for the party in Munich.[172] As parochial vicar at the St. Ursula parish, located in the heart of the Bavarian capital, Roth had the ability to reach a wide range of Catholics. In addition, Roth attempted to communicate the *Weltanschauung* of the NSDAP to more intellectual-minded Catholics through tracts and articles in newspapers and journals and to propagate *völkisch* concerns by working with the Jungdo, the Stahlhelm, and other right-wing groups.[173]

Like many of the brown priests, Roth viewed himself as a "prophet" within the *Völkisch* movement, called to "awaken and enlist" Germans, specifically German Catholics, to its cause and to their ultimate destiny. In 1925, in a lecture entitled "God and Fatherland," Roth argued that the essence of being German and having a national will existed "in Germans in a mysterious way." This will could bear fruit only if Germans aimed for unity in their German ethnicity. By insisting on maintaining their own organizations, especially in the political realm, Catholics drove "the best fatherland organizations into Protestant hands, many even into anti-Church ones." Still, fatherland organizations could exist alongside Catholic associations, since they served different purposes. While they had different goals, they shared a Christian basis in which the "love of God together with the love of brother of the religion of Christ" served as the "first community-building strength of the German *Volksgemeinschaft.*" The second community-building strength developed from the "old German army and from the war: it is the spirit of brotherhood that we experienced as something profound and life-fulfilling in the war and that we brought back to our *Volk* and specifically to our youth as a sacred conquest from the front and that no one who did not serve at the front could understand and imitate." Together, the "Christian German spirit of the front-line soldier" and "the brotherly love of

Christ" offered the national movement its inclusive basis and significance. Catholics could not remain deaf to the national awakening movement, for otherwise a *Kulturkampf* might again result.[174]

The publication of the tract ensured that Roth's talk would be widely distributed. Soon thereafter Roth found himself in a difficult position with his ecclesiastical superiors, who objected to the address's contents and especially to Roth's failure to obtain permission to publish it. In response, Roth justified himself in a public letter, which was published in *Warmia,* an East Prussian newspaper associated with the nationalist and conservative German National People's Party. In the letter Roth blamed the newspaper's publishers for releasing the tract before he obtained approval from Cardinal Faulhaber. He also stressed that he had no desire to place himself in opposition to the German bishops, but also made it clear that he believed it was fully acceptable for Catholics to belong to a Catholic association and a fatherland association at the same time.[175] By reacting in such a fashion, Roth revealed that, at least in 1925, he was still quite concerned about any repercussions he might receive from his diocesan superiors on account of his actions.

Despite his concessions to diocesan officials, Roth refused to be deterred from spreading the *völkisch* message. His actions portray an individual who felt compelled to pursue such a mission. His public words clearly reveal how deeply his experience of battle and defeat affected his worldview. In his mind he was still a soldier engaged in battle for the soul of the fatherland and therefore challenged anyone and anything that he viewed as harmful to his fatherland. In his article "Catholic Pacifism?" in 1926 Roth viciously attacked both the Pacifist movement within German Catholicism and the democracy of the Weimar Republic.[176] Again, in 1929, Roth published a similarly worded essay, "The Path of the Front-Line Soldiers," in which he detailed the suffering that his generation had to endure in postwar Germany. According to Roth, "crafty politicians of all directions" misused him and his fellow soldiers. Such maltreatment led to the "total disintegration of the community" and tore apart the "manly soul" of his nation and of his comrades. Nevertheless, Roth prophesied that a time would "come when the silent martyrdom of the front-line soldiers will change into their victory for the nation."[177]

In all of these postputsch publications Roth was quite careful to avoid the harsh language he had initially used to describe Jews. It appears he had learned his lesson following Cardinal Faulhaber's reaction to *Catholicism and the Jewish Question.* Though Faulhaber had never specifically discussed the 1923 tract's contents, Roth knew that he had published several works since 1923 without Faulhaber's permission and that these had not raised the ire of his cardinal archbishop or chancery officials. In addition, a September encounter with his vicar general, Father Michael Buchberger, following his 1923 Nuremberg German Day address and on the eve of the putsch, solidified this more cautious approach. According to Roth, Buchberger called him to his Munich office and told him, "You have caused enormous harm to the Church. An influential member of the Jewish community came to me after being informed of your address that you delivered on German Day in Nuremberg. [He did so] in order to raise an objection against your activity. This Jewish individual threatened no longer to give any donations to Catholic charities if I do not take action against you on account of your speech and on account of your work *Catholicism and the Jewish Question*. If we no longer receive any support from the Jews, the Church will suffer too much harm. Therefore, you shall no longer speak in a *völkisch* spirit."[178] As a result of such meetings, Roth quickly learned that, in order not to create greater problems for himself, he had to avoid using explicit racial antisemitism.

Despite what Roth had learned, his antisemitic worldview caused him further problems. On February 8, 1929, the *Antisemitische Zeitung*, published in Cologne, reprinted sections from his 1923 tract on the Jewish question.[179] On March 20 a representative from the Cologne branch of the German League for Human Rights informed Faulhaber about the article and asked if he had given Roth ecclesiastical approval for its publication.[180] Faulhaber had his secretary, Father Rudolf Hindringer, check into the situation to see if Roth had been behind its reprinting.[181] Roth realized the seriousness of the inquiry and immediately replied to Hindringer by explaining that the newspaper had published the article without his permission. Roth noted, "Even if I had the permission [from the cardinal], I would not use it to publish in such an inferior publication."[182] In turn, Father Hindringer more or less used Roth's explanation verbatim to compose his response to the German League for Human Rights. No one, however, from the Munich archdiocese bothered to address the antisemitic nature of the article.[183]

Despite Roth's reserve, his publications after 1929 indirectly reveal that he never strayed far from his 1923 worldview. In 1930 he boldly published his Munich Stahlhelm Day address, in which he warned Catholics not to allow their "spiritual Catholic standard of living to be dominated by writers who come from Jewish or other non-Catholic mentalities." True Christianity, he argued, was "not only a religion of love and submission, but also a religion of authority and justice."[184]

Roth, like many brown priests, feared that his Church had begun to lag behind the "awakening" and rebirth of Germany. In his mind Catholicism had allowed itself to become weakened by a variety of forces, including pacifism, democracy, and German Jewry. In 1932, Roth added feminism to this list of Catholicism's afflictions. In his essay "Feminism in the Present Public Life," Roth decried the feminization of Christianity, which expressed itself physically by the lack of male participation in the liturgical life of the Church and theologically by the "too frequent overemphasis on the social and humanitarian." Roth exhorted Catholics to stand against such feminization "in all decisiveness" because "service to neighbor" was "not the essence of Christianity." Catholics today, he argued, should "no longer desire mercy and alms," but rather want "authority and justice." Then, just as he had anticipated the Nazi racial policy to come, Roth offered a logic for the party's eventual euthanasia policy. "Feminist-sentimental humanism feels sorry for the individual criminal while forgetting state and society; it protects the worthless and decaying as never before, but at the same time it wants to abolish the lawful protection of budding life. In Germany we maintain over four hundred mental and nursing homes, most of them splendidly furnished and provided for, to care for the hundreds of thousands of incurably ill individuals—while hundreds of thousands of talented and healthy national comrades pay rent, suffering privations by living in primitive apartments and slowly going to rack and ruin."[185] Though such a declaration clearly violated Catholic moral principles, no diocesan official specifically challenged Roth.

Roth was soon vindicated. On January 30, 1933, with the encouragement of a series of conservative politicians, President von Hindenburg appointed Hitler chancellor of Germany. Then, just two months later, on March 28, the German bishops lifted their prohibitions against the NSDAP. From this point onward, Catholics could freely declare their membership in the Nazi Party and, with the exception of racial policy that denied the efficacy of the sacrament of baptism, profess its *Weltanschauung*. But the brown priests were soon to find out how difficult it would be in the new German state to be brown and black at the same time.

Abbot Albanus Schachleiter, O.S.B., preaching at a NSDAP rally, flanked by members of the SA and Hitler Youth. (BArch B NS 26/1323)

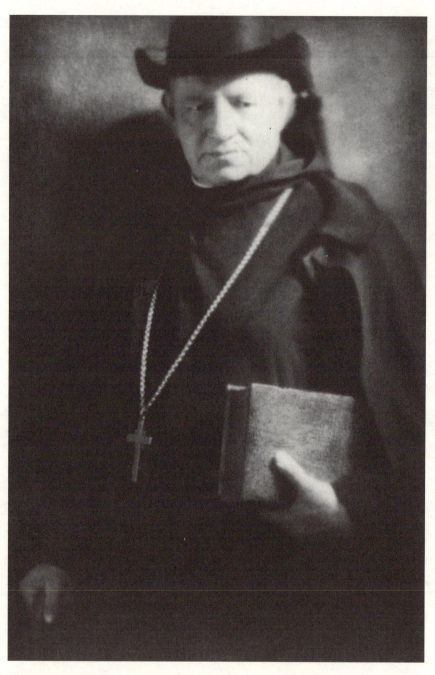

A publicity portrait of Abbot Albanus Schachleiter, O.S.B. Schachleiter always wore his traditional Benedictine habit when propagandizing for the National Socialist movement. (BArch B NS26/1323)

Roth, Schachleiter, Pieper, and Huber enjoy cigars while sharing stories during their Bad Feilnbach gathering. Pieper and Huber display Nazi Party pins on their lapels. (AAK NL Pieper)

Bernhard Stempfle, O.S.H., curator of the Rehse Archive, talking with Adolf Hitler. (LofCong 3983 G)

(right, above) A 1937 wedding photo of former Munich priest Albert Hartl, who had become an SS officer, and League of German Girls (BDM) unit leader Marianne Schürer-Stolle. (BArch B SSOA)

(right, below) Seminarian Albert Hartl's photograph in his student file at the Ludwig Maximilian University in Munich. (ALMU Studenten-Kartei)

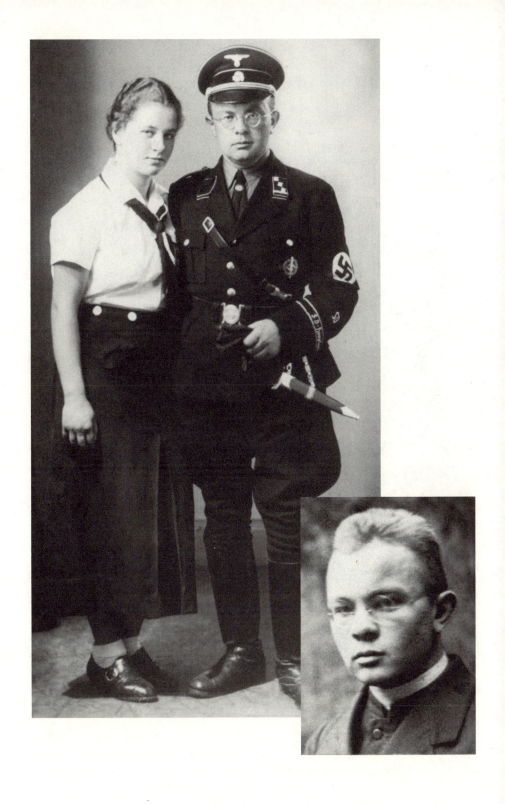

Studienrat Richard Kleine posing for a photograph in his Duderstadt classroom in 1963. (MIO NL Kleine)

In Christus leuchtet uns die Hoffnung
seliger Auferstehung

Dem steten frommen Gedenken wird
empfohlen hochw. Herr

Johann Pircher

Priester der Erzdiözese Wien
Religionslehrer i. R. in Bischofshofen

welcher am 12. August 1953, im 43.
Jahre seines Priestertums, im Alter
von 68 Jahren, nach Empfang der
Gnaden der hl. Sterbesakramente, zum
Herrn und Gott heimgegangen ist.

Selig sind die Toten, die im Herrn sterben,
von nun an, spricht der Geist, sollen sie ruhen
von ihren Mühen, denn ihre Werke folgen
ihnen nach.   Off. 13/12
     Herr, gib ihm die ewige Ruhe!

Druckerei L. Stepan's Wrw., Bischofshofen

(above) Ordination photograph of Josef Roth and his family, June 1922. (Courtesy M. Catherine Graupner)

(left) Portrait of Father Johann Pircher from his 1953 death announcement. During the Third Reich Pircher worked endlessly to promote National Socialism in his native Austria. (DAWien)

(above) Kaplan Roth walks by the
Obelisk on Munich's Karolinen-
platz in November 1934. (AAK NL
Pieper)

(right) In a rare photo, *Kaplan*
Roth, wearing his priestly attire,
enjoys smoking a cigar. (AAK NL
Pieper)

Father Roth greets Adolf Hitler during a NSDAP rally in Nuremberg. The Nazi Party had invited 'Old Fighters' such as Roth, Abbot Schachleiter, and Pfarrer Haeuser to attend as its honored guests. (BArch K NL 898 Roth)

Pfarrer Philipp Haeuser, biblical exegete, political theologian, and champion of the German movement, in his study at the rectory of his Straßberg parish. (StA Bobingen Haeuser Sammlung)

Pfarrer Haeuser presiding at a field mass on Pentecost Sunday 1934 during an Augsburg Hitler Youth gathering. (Courtesy of *Allgäuer Anzeigeblatt*)

Haeuser delivering one of his many political-theological speeches before an eager NSDAP audience. Behind him hangs a portrait of Hitler. (StA Bobingen Haeuser Sammlung)

Dr. Lorenz Pieper in his study, trying to keep up with the high volume of correspondence that he received daily. (AAK NL Pieper)

Pfarrer Anton Heuberger visiting the grave of his deceased brother, Georg, in the military cemetery in Pocarevac near Belgrade. This visit would inspire Heuberger's *Open Letter,* in which he would ask whether it was possible to be a good priest and, at the same time, a good National Socialist. (DAEI)

3—The Old Fighters under Hitler's Rule

Hitler's appointment as chancellor and his solidification of power during the first six months of office drastically changed how brown priests operated in public. Those priests who previously had to conceal their affinity to National Socialism from their ecclesiastical superiors could now profess it openly. Similarly, many of them received support from local NSDAP officials when conflicts arose with their bishops. However, many bishops did not even attempt to restrict or reprimand their brown priests—often out of a desire for harmonious church-state relations, but frequently out of fear of repercussions from state or party officials. For example, in 1936 Bishop Matthias Ehrenfried of Würzburg admitted to a colleague that he "would have long ago suspended Father Huber" if he "lived in normal times." Ehrenfried feared, however, that such a response might be interpreted as "politically motivated." The climate had clearly changed for any supporter of the NSDAP. Nevertheless, Father Huber firmly believed that Bishop Ehrenfried viewed "every priest who profess[ed] a National Socialist *Weltanschauung* as a traitor to the Church."[1] Though not every bishop held such a view, in general the German episcopacy regarded any priest who appeared to work against the interests of the Catholic Church as disloyal and endeavored to silence the voice of any cleric who took the state's side in a conflict.

Even more difficult than having to endure a strained relationship with diocesan superiors was the party's process of sidelining brown priests. While in certain circumstances this happened immediately after Hitler took office, normally this was a gradual process. As local party leadership changed, the more recent recruits often failed to recognize the efforts of the Old Fighters, especially of the priests among this group. Many of these younger Nazis also renounced their ties to organized religion and saw no reason to work with Catholic priests, even if they were party members. Tensions in church-state relations definitely affected this situation for the worse.

Father Magnus Gött experienced this estrangement as early as 1926. In December of that year and into the first months of 1927, Gött addressed this breach of trust in an exchange of letters with Hitler. In particular, the anticlericalism of the NSDAP greatly concerned him. Gött realized that anticlericalism was not something unique to National Socialism alone; he also saw it present in other political movements throughout Europe. Nevertheless, as a priest he felt compelled to address its presence in his favored political party.[2] In February 1927, Hitler replied to Gött by rehearsing his often-stated religious policy, "It is not the task of my movement to gather faithful and dedicated Christians, but to win back all those elements of the nation and of its spiritual and moral culture that it had already lost."[3] Gött did not accept this explanation at face value and on February 10 pushed Hitler further, asking him to be more considerate of religion. Gött also admitted that he had experienced a "strong cooling off" of his "former enthusiasm" for Hitler's work. Nevertheless, he stated that he still subscribed to Hitler's "political program line by line," but could not accept his approach to religion.[4] Just under a month later, Hitler reiterated his earlier rejoinder to Gött. He told Gött that he did acknowledge his complaint that the NSDAP was "too 'meager' in a religious sense," but added that he feared that if the political parties meddled "too much in religious matters," religion would become more and more politicized and would end up in a situation that one day might bring it harm. "Under all circumstances" Hitler considered it "unfortunate" if religion in any form became "mixed up with politics."[5]

Hitler's response did not please Gött. In 1929, the Augsburg priest could finally express his displeasure publicly after his bishop lifted Gött's prohibition against publishing. In the *Legauer Anzeiger* Gött "praised the politics of Brüning" but distanced himself from Hitler. He made it clear that the NSDAP had been "too much defined by academics" for his taste and "represented too strongly the interests of the middle class" while neglecting the working class. For this change of position, in September 1932 the diocese rewarded Gött with a larger parish in Schrattenbach, near Kempten. By 1934 Gött had become fully estranged from the NSDAP and even began to regret privately his public expression of antisemitism.[6]

Professor Bernhard Stempfle, on the other hand, was not as eager as Gött to remove himself from a connection with the NSDAP before Hitler came to power. While Gött publicly distanced himself from the Hitler party, Stempfle published an antisemitic work, *Public Prosecutor! Charge Them for Inciting Class Struggle,* which contained brief excerpts from a wide variety of authors. Under headings such as "The Destroyers of Morality" and "The Jews Are Our Misfortune," Stempfle attempted to attribute all of "society's ills" to Jews. He also concluded his work by quoting from the writings of Fathers Josef Roth and Philipp Haeuser, reminding his readers that "a Christian has to be an antisemite!"[7]

On January 1, 1934, Stempfle finally joined the NSDAP. However, his stay in the party was not very long. On Monday, July 2, 1934, during the Röhm purge, when Hitler, with the help of Himmler and the SS, consolidated his power by having more than a hundred individuals whom he believed to be a threat to the state and party murdered, SS men in civilian clothes took Stempfle into the forest near Harlaching, not far from Munich, struck him "on the back of the neck with some heavy weapon," and shot him three times.[8] Stempfle's murder came in the wake of his abduction the previous day when four SS men dressed in civilian clothes took him away from the room he had rented from the Lutz family in Munich. On the day of his murder four Gestapo agents also confiscated all of Stempfle's possessions.[9] Though Stempfle had made plenty of enemies as a journalist, the exact motivation for the murder remains a mystery. One contemporary author suggested that Stempfle had to be murdered to conceal intimate knowledge he had of an affair between Hitler and his niece, Geli Raubal, who had committed suicide in September 1931 under mysterious circumstances.[10] There is no way to substantiate this theory, however.

Unlike Stempfle, Father Christian Huber did not know Hitler personally. Estranged from the party since the failed putsch, in 1928 Huber began to agitate again for the NSDAP in his Sandizell parish. In 1930 Huber decided not only to work on behalf of the NSDAP, but also to defend it with force if necessary by obtaining a weapons' permit that allowed him to own two rifles and a pistol.[11] Soon things took a quick turn for the worse for Huber. In December 1930 he attempted to leave parish work and apply for a position as a high-school religion teacher. Well aware of Huber's activities and not wishing him to influence Catholic youth, the Augsburg chancery intervened in the process.[12] A month later the Bavarian State Ministry of Education informed Huber that according to state law he was too old to begin a full-time teaching career and denied his request.[13] Less than a week later Huber was in possession of a doctor's note that diagnosed him as suffering from "nervous exhaustion" and prescribed a thirty days' rest, specifically in Munich.[14] It seems possible that during this time Huber was making a strenuous attempt to agitate for National Socialism before a wider audience, i.e., as a teacher in a gymnasium or as a National Socialist speaker in Munich. The Augsburg chancery ignored his regular requests for a brief sabbatical until, in November 1932, it offered him early retirement with pay.[15] Huber immediately packed up his possessions and moved to Munich. By April 1933 he had become a registered member of the NSDAP and the SA.[16] He also worked to instill a National Socialist spirit in the Munich Catholic Journeymen's Association, where he still maintained contacts from his previous chaplain assignment.[17]

In June 1935 Huber again began to become restless due to his nonparochial presence in Munich and wrote the Augsburg chancery to request a parish assignment. He assured his superiors that his health was fully restored.[18] Augsburg chancery officials, however, were not yet prepared to offer Huber full-time parish work. Nevertheless, through the assistance of state officials, Huber received an appointment as a director and chaplain to the Rohesche Home for the Poor and Aged in Kleinwallstadt in the Würzburg diocese.[19] Immediately at the beginning of his new assignment problems began to surface. In April 1936 Bishop Ehrenfried felt compelled to confront Huber about his questionable political behavior and told him, "In public addresses you have repeatedly addressed and described political and national questions while also touching upon religious, moral, and Church matters in a manner that has created offense to Catholics. We have continually overlooked this with patience." This time the bishop told Huber he had gone too far. As a result, on September 1, 1936, Ehrenfried withdrew Huber's ecclesiastical faculties for the Würzburg diocese.[20]

Despite this difficult situation, on August 30 Huber wrote Joseph Kumpfmüller, the bishop of Augsburg, that out of "self-respect" he could not leave his assignment. Instead, he asked him for permission to say mass in the home's private chapel, with his mother as the sole congregant.[21] Huber's stubborn stance made the situation unbearable for both the Augsburg and Würzburg dioceses because ultimately there was not much they could do, since the state had hired Huber. Normally chancery officials could easily work with state officials to remove a priest if necessary. However, as both chancery staffs found out, they did not live in normal times. Even worse, as Huber's difficulties with diocesan superiors increased a new opportunity to exploit would always come his way. In this case, through the machinations of Albert Hartl, a former priest of the Munich archdiocese, SS lieutenant, and member of the SD, Huber was invited to intensify his work as an informant for the SD in Munich. Huber had already been a longtime, though intermittent, informer for the SD.[22] Hartl, though, had no desire for Huber to compromise his standing in the Church and become less useful as an informant.

In September 1936 the Würzburg vicar general, Father Franz Miltenberger, informed Huber that Bishop Kumpfmüller had agreed to allow him to be named a *Kommorant,* a priest who officially resided in a town and collected diocesan pay, but who did not hold a specific pastoral position.[23] Huber was not yet ready to relinquish his position at the Rohesche Home and give up the little control that he had over his life, but he realized that this situation would not easily resolve itself. Huber's brother, Stephan, also a member of the NSDAP, knew of his sibling's plight and wrote on his behalf to Franz Xaver Eberle, auxiliary bishop of Augsburg and vicar general, and asked the bishop to assist his brother in obtaining a pastorate. He made it clear in his letter that the diocese had persecuted his brother "on account of his National Socialist outlook."[24] Sympathetic to the request, Eberle promised to do "what was possible" for his brother.[25] Such assistance even led Huber to contemplate a move to the Regensburg diocese as a *Kommorant* in order to accept a state archival position.[26] But before this move took place, the Augsburg chancery intervened and sent their counterpart in Regensburg a very unflattering letter about Huber.[27] In the end Huber remained stuck in Kleinwallstadt.

By March 1937 Huber had begun experiencing severe financial problems.[28] However, instead of going to his bishop to make amends, Huber intensified his work for the NSDAP. In January 1938 Father Ludwig Spangenberger, the local pastor of Kleinwallstadt, reported to the Würzburg chancery that Huber was "a member of the SA and performs regular SA duty in uniform. Quite some time ago, during a gathering of civil servants here, he recommended the writings of [Alfred] Rosenberg as good reading. More recently, at a party gathering he strongly objected to those who support the Catholic denominational school." He added that Huber was "even more sinister in his indirect influence. All community elements that are hostile to the Church gather around him and derive support from him." Spangenberger also wondered if Huber was behind the two Gestapo interrogations he had been forced to endure and the recent summons he had received to appear in the Obernburg district court.[29]

When the Würzburg chancery officials received Spangenberger's report, they shared it with their colleagues in Augsburg. The report confirmed their resolve to begin canonical proceedings against Huber.[30] However, their main witness, Father Spangenberger, refused to participate. Perhaps out of fear of state retaliation, or perhaps out of pastoral concerns, he stated that he only wanted Huber to return to his home diocese. He added, "I consider it my moral obligation to make it known that this overture for him to return must be made soon, as otherwise it might be too late."[31]

Father Spangenberger was correct in his prediction. On October 9, 1941, Huber left active ministry by withdrawing from the Catholic Church. Several months later, on New Year's Day 1942, Huber married Rosa Albert in a pseudoreligious state ceremony.[32] In the same month Bishop Kumpfmüller responded by initiating canonical proceedings against him.[33] Huber ignored his bishop's request to defend himself in the proceedings. As a consequence, on June 24, 1942, the Augsburg diocese's consistory confirmed Huber's apostasy and upheld the excommunication that he had automatically incurred twice—at the moment he left the Church and when he, as an ordained priest, entered into civil marriage.[34] At this point, Huber cared little how his superiors viewed him. Instead, he obtained a civil service position as an archivist in the Aschaffenburg City Archive and continued his work with the NSDAP. Rosa and Christian Huber also put to use the apartment that Huber had at the Rohesche Home in Kleinwallstadt, making it—to the ultimate dismay of the Franciscan nuns who also lived and served there—their marriage home.[35]

Similar to Huber, Father Lorenz Pieper also ran afoul of his bishop. On January 15, 1933, just two weeks before Hitler took office, Archbishop Kaspar Klein removed Pieper as administrator of Halingen. Klein could easily take this action because Pieper's parish was the filial church of the nearby Mendon parish. Klein, however, did not proceed discreetly. Instead, he issued a press release detailing Pieper's removal in order to serve as a warning to any other priests who wished to defy the stance of the German bishops toward National Socialism. In it he stated, "The diocese was forced to take these measures out of pastoral concerns. The personal files of this priest consist of two full, heavy files of documentation that justify this action. The peculiar characteristics of this priest are reflected in the stubbornness and incorrigible obstinacy that he indulges in a special way and the arrogance that leads him constantly into new conflicts and impertinence toward superiors. He considers it appropriate always to test the extreme boundaries."[36] In defiance of their bishop, citizens of Halingen printed a full-page tribute to their pastor in their local newspaper.[37] Despite further protests from his parishioners, Pieper had no choice but to obey the directive of his bishop. Upon leaving Halingen, he chose to move to his hometown of Eversberg. On Sunday, February 2, more than five hundred of the town's inhabitants came out to greet their local "celebrity." A reporter commented that "the entire thing resembled the arrival of a bishop and was the best example of the popularity of this man who is respected among all members of the *Volk* on account of his genuine character."[38]

The remainder of Pieper's career under National Socialism was uneventful. For a short time in 1934 local authorities appointed him district school advisor in Arnsberg. Pieper moved from there with the help of the state to Marienthal near Münster in August 1934 to accept a chaplaincy job in a state sanitarium. In April 1936 he accepted a similar ministry position in a state sanitarium in Warstein, where he remained until 1942, when he ran into difficulty with the state for opposing its "secret" euthanasia program directed against individuals with mental and physical handicaps.[39] Even for a dedicated brown priest like Pieper the National Socialist state went too far with its eugenics policies.

At times Abbot Schachleiter also felt compelled to question the policies of the state, especially those that directly conflicted with Catholicism. Yet, no matter how much Schachleiter disagreed with a particular policy or ideological point, his fondness for Hitler prevented him from separating himself from the NSDAP. In early February 1933 this stance would create problems even greater for Schachleiter than derived from any ongoing or past conflict.

On January 21, 1933, Johannes Maria Gföllner, bishop of Linz, Austria, published a pastoral letter in which he critically questioned National Socialism's relationship with Christian churches and its anti-Christian *Weltanschauung*, especially as found in the writings of the chief party ideologist, Alfred Rosenberg. Though Schachleiter also disagreed with Rosenberg's work, he did not believe National Socialism was incompatible with Catholicism. Upon reading Gföllner's letter, Schachleiter immediately published in the *Völkischer Beobachter* a retort under the headline "In Reply to the Linz Pastoral Letter, a Word of Reassurance for Faithful Catholics."[40] According to Schachleiter, Hitler had no secret intentions toward the Christian churches, but viewed Catholicism "as a valuable support for the continued existence of our *Volk*." In turn, Hitler's program was "absolutely not a religious program," but a "political, cultural, social, and economic" one that labored for "the political freedom of the German people" and joined the Church in its battle "against Marxism."[41]

Schachleiter resolutely refused to say anything negative about Hitler. For him, Hitler was truly a savior who was destined to restore Germany to unparalleled glory. If there was anything wrong with National Socialism, Schachleiter would attribute it exclusively to its misguided followers such as Alfred Rosenberg, who he believed misinterpreted Hitler's "purest intentions." The German bishops, however, did not accept this distinction. They were generally of one mind and stood behind their 1931 prohibitions against the NSDAP.

Once again Schachleiter's action infuriated Cardinal Faulhaber, who attempted to restrain the abbot. On February 4, 1933, Faulhaber wrote Nuncio Vassallo and asked him to inform Rome that Schachleiter had spoken directly against the German bishops in his *Völkischer Beobachter* article. Faulhaber also told Vassallo that he could "not suspend Schachleiter" because he was not "under his jurisdiction," even though it was within his right to discipline Schachleiter canonically.[42] Nevertheless, Faulhaber did publicly announce the removal of Schachleiter's ecclesiastical faculties.[43] Once Faulhaber made his stance toward Schachleiter public, the abbot released his own statement to the German press, agreeing to the terms of the ecclesiastical prohibition.[44]

Almost overnight the "Schachleiter Linz affair" became national news. It is particularly interesting to read the newspaper coverage of the affair written in the waning days of a free German press. After Hitler came to power, the state gradually curbed the broad freedoms that the press had experienced under the Weimar Republic. This was especially true after the February 27, 1933, burning of the German Reichstag. Hitler's government placed the blame on Communists, though it is still unclear who actually started the fire. A day later President Hindenburg signed the Decree for the Protection of the People and State, which suspended the Weimar constitutional sections that related to freedom of speech and press, and in their place gave state governments a wide range of options to restore "public security and order."[45] This law enabled the Gestapo and local police to shut down any presses that published works or newspapers critical of the new government. At the same time individuals sympathetic to the new state took over the editorial boards of many newspapers. In early February 1933, however, most newspapers still offered unbiased reporting, but, even at this early date, some newspapers had already altered their editorial style. Thus, in Freiburg im Breisgau *Der Alemanne* compared Schachleiter's plight and prohibition to the situation previously experienced by its own local celebrity, brown priest Father Wilhelm Senn.[46] By contrast, the reporting in Berlin's Catholic newspaper *Germania* was quite critical of Schachleiter.[47]

On February 9 Bishop Gföllner offered his own reply to the affair by publishing an "Open Letter to Abbot Albanus Schachleiter, O.S.B." in the *Linzer Volksblatt*. Gföllner portrayed Schachleiter as naïve, especially in his understanding of Hitler's attitude toward Jews and its implications for Catholicism. This did not mean, however, that Gföllner heroically defended Jews or Judaism in any way. Rather, Gföllner defended the Judeo-Christian heritage, such as the validity of the Old Testament as divine revelation from God. By taking such a stance, the Linz bishop defended his Church against any attempt by Nazi ideologists or speakers to portray it as a religion "foreign" or "alien" to Germans. Gföllner noted, "Hitler raises the accusation that the foundation of the Catholic Church is corroded and undermined by the poison of international world Jewry." In the same vein, he noted that Hitler also claimed that "both Christian denominations, including the Catholic Church, sit back and watch indifferently the desecration and destruction of innocent, young, blonde German girls by the Jews."[48]

While Gföllner defended his stance, local members of the Munich clergy also involved themselves in the conflict. In mid-February 1933 Father Jakob Albrecht, pastor of Bad Aibling, who had to contend with Schachleiter regularly, published in his parish's newsletter his own perceptions of the affair.[49] In particular, he stated, "It must certainly be clear to Abbot Schachleiter as a learned theologian that the racial theory and the other cultural-political teachings of National Socialism are erroneous and, therefore, affiliation with them is irreconcilable with the Catholic conscience and with the religious doctrine and moral teaching of the Church."[50] In a separate case, Father Emil Muhler, pastor of St. Andreas in Munich, during an address to the Munich Catholic Women's Association, attempted to undermine the abbot's personal reputation, even among National Socialists. In this undertaking, he tried to portray Schachleiter as a liar and coward for fleeing harassment in Prague and for embellishing his flight with stories of impending imprisonment and possible violent death at the hands of the local Prague inhabitants.[51] Cardinal Faulhaber later admitted that he had provided the information for Muhler's "attack" but resented Muhler's approach and the formulation of his argument.[52] Shortly thereafter Muhler would end up in "protective custody" for spreading negative reports concerning the state.[53]

While Albrecht and Muhler challenged Schachleiter in the public forum, clergymen from the Feilnbach and Bad Aibling area did their best to ensure that the abbot obeyed Faulhaber's prohibition. Father Ludwig Zach, the pastor of Au, reported to the Munich chancery that Schachleiter regularly attended the 6:00 a.m. mass in his parish and sought reception of the Eucharist. Zach also truly worried about the effect this was having on the parishioners and feared they might think, "Communion is for those who are not in mortal sin. If Abbot Schachleiter goes to communion, then his behavior can only be a tiny, venial sin. Why then is so much fuss being made about his situation? There cannot be much wrong with him."[54] To confront this situation the local clergy worked with the Munich chancery to prohibit Schachleiter from receiving communion. On March 18, 1933, this prohibition went into effect.[55]

As the Schachleiter events unfolded, Nazi officials kept Hitler abreast of their development. The previous October Schachleiter had written directly to Hitler to inform him that the Emmaus monastery was no longer sending him a monthly stipend.[56] Schachleiter's tenacious support of National Socialism so impressed Hitler that in March 1933 he rewarded Schachleiter with a monthly subsidy of 200 reichsmark "as long as he need[ed] it."[57] During a March 7 meeting of Reich cabinet ministers, Hitler even suggested that the clerical advisor to the German ambassador at the Vatican be replaced with a man "such as Abbot Schachleiter."[58] On March 20, right before the opening of the Reichstag, Hitler also turned to Schachleiter and asked him to take a night train to Berlin in order to say mass for him.[59] Hitler did this after refusing, because of the bishops' prohibitions against the NSDAP, to take part in the Catholic mass scheduled for this occasion. Schachleiter "sadly" declined the unique request, citing Faulhaber's suspension.[60] This response did not please Hitler, who ended up joining his minister of propaganda, Joseph Goebbels, at Berlin's Luisenstadt Cemetery for a secular ceremony for fallen SA men.[61]

Hitler was not the only National Socialist to stand by Schachleiter. On March 21 the local SA organized a rally in Feilnbach in support of Schachleiter. More than two thousand people attended the demonstration, filling the streets of the town.[62] Schachleiter joyfully gazed upon the crowd and proclaimed, "It delights me to be able to state here: the Führer has repeatedly declared and has included it in his official program that the National Socialist movement has its basis in positive Christianity. That is to say, the new freedom movement shall be something truly Christian, a *Volk* movement that professes our Lord and Savior, that lives this profession in word and deed. Take this to heart, my friends!"[63] Schachleiter ended his remarks with the "Heil Hitler" salute. A few days later, the Feilnbach town council named Hitler, Richard Wagner, and Abbot Alban Schachleiter honorary citizens.[64]

Though he received these accolades from National Socialists, the bishop's prohibitions and the suspension of his ecclesiastical faculties greatly disturbed Schachleiter. While he was a staunch supporter of Hitler and National Socialism, Schachleiter also viewed himself as a devout Catholic and servant of God. Similarly, Schachleiter apparently believed that in his ministry to National Socialists he was saving many souls from leaving the Catholic Church.[65] Consequently, by late March the prohibitions against him started to bother Schachleiter considerably. He even confided to Hitler that in addition to his not being able to say mass and take communion, a priest had refused him absolution in the confessional. Despite this, he promised to remain resolute in his support of Hitler and wrote, "All of this only because I said in my [Linz] article exactly what the bishops themselves now say and *must* concede!"[66] Here Schachleiter referred directly to the March 28 lifting of the German bishops' prohibitions against National Socialism. In Schachleiter's mind the German bishops were all hypocrites for the way they had treated him. On April 6 he pointed this out in a letter to the editor of the *Völkischer Beobachter,* stating that his suspension from active ministry was the result of his support for the NSDAP and not of some earlier controversy over his living situation.[67] A few days later the *Völkischer Beobachter* ran a very sympathetic picture of Schachleiter with its own interpretation of the situation, which the editors tried to encapsulate in one sentence: "Abbot Schachleiter . . . disobeyed the order of the pope to return to a monastery, [disobeying] in order to continue to work in the National Socialist movement, and . . . was as a result suspended from his office."[68]

At this point Pope Pius XI still had not become involved in the affair. If at all, he was aware of it only through his secretary of state, Cardinal Eugenio Pacelli, who had been in communication with Cardinal Faulhaber.[69] Primarily, the Holy See's Congregation for Religious had been the intermediary contact between Faulhaber and the Vatican.[70] Still, Faulhaber continued to do his best by calling upon every possible authority figure to force Schachleiter to return to Leo House or to a Benedictine abbey. This included seeking the assistance of Fidelis von Stotzingen, O.S.B., the abbot primate of the Benedictine order, who unsuccessfully ordered Schachleiter to take up residence in the Neresheim abbey, northwest of Augsburg.[71] In mid-April Faulhaber admitted to Archabbot Walzer of Beuron that he had "become convinced that the abbot primate did everything possible to clear up the tragic affair, but that the Congregation for Religious obstructed the matter out of significant fear of interfering in a political matter or in the concerns of a religious community." At this point Faulhaber realized that the Congregation did not have a complete understanding of the new political situation in Germany and therefore held opinions such as "the German

Volk would never believe an abbot more than the German bishops." To his credit, the Munich cardinal realized that this might not be the case any longer under a National-Socialist-led government.[72] In his reply Walzer concurred with Faulhaber's analysis of the situation and even admitted that Schachleiter had threatened him "in the worst ways." He then confided to Faulhaber that his own situation at present had publicly forced him to be silent on the issue. Walzer concluded that "the state of mind of the poor man [Schachleiter]" was such that nothing would "be achieved either through pastoral or other actions or with an ecclesiastical trial."[73]

By mid-May all of these efforts seemed null and void after Adolf Hitler made a personal visit to Haus Gott-Dank to congratulate Abbot Schachleiter on the occasion of the golden jubilee of his priestly ordination. Though Hitler stayed for only fifteen minutes, it was the most excitement the people of Feilnbach had experienced in their town in years.[74] Afterward Schachleiter felt vindicated regarding his current struggles and reinvigorated enough to push forward on behalf of Hitler. On May 25 he spoke before a crowd of three thousand people in Trudering, a suburb of Munich, during a memorial service for Schlageter. The following day the *Völkischer Beobachter* dedicated one fourth of its front page to a photo of Schachleiter. In the photo Schachleiter is offering the "Heil Hitler" salute and standing in a makeshift pulpit flanked on both sides by SA and SS men and by Hitler Youth bearing flags.[75]

The personal encounter with Hitler and the Schlageter event that followed taught Abbot Schachleiter that if he conformed to Faulhaber's wishes and returned to Leo House, the Munich Church authorities presumably would allow him to continue his efforts for the NSDAP without any interference. At the same time, Schachleiter was truly suffering spiritually as a result of being deprived of receiving the sacraments and presiding at liturgies. Secretly, Father Josef Roth did bring Schachleiter communion on occasion, but his infrequent visits were hardly able to fill Schachleiter's spiritual void.[76] Seidler, an SA *Sonderkommissar* (special commissioner), whom Schachleiter had befriended, even attempted to intervene in his behalf with Cardinal Faulhaber.[77] Faulhaber, of course, was extremely gracious to the SA man, and attempted to explain the situation in words he could understand, "Translate the case into your situation and assume that an SA Führer has disobeyed an order of the highest-ranking Führer in the same way. It is not up to me to say a word. The highest Church authorities have dealt with the case of Schachleiter quite leniently. In other, similar cases in which a monk persists in his disobedience, he is expelled from the order and prohibited from wearing his religious habit." Faulhaber then shared his greatest hope that in the future priests would be forbidden from engaging in any political activity.[78] Following his contact with Seidler, Faulhaber wrote an extremely generous letter on behalf of Schachleiter to the Holy See's Congregation for Religious. In it he informed the Congregation's prefect that Schachleiter's suspension had served its purpose and proposed a deferment. Faulhaber also stated that he was sure Schachleiter would soon return to Leo House.[79]

On July 20, 1933, the Vatican granted Faulhaber's wish around the same time that it concluded a Concordat with the government of the German Reich. Not surprisingly, Article 32 of the Concordat specifically forbade clergy from joining or working on behalf of political parties. In August the knowledge of this legally binding treaty together with his desire to have the suspension against him lifted allegedly led Schachleiter to a change of heart.[80] He first implored Archabbot Walzer of Beuron, who still refused to lift the suspension until the Congregation for Religious had made the decision on the situation public.[81] Then he wrote Cardinal Faulhaber and promised to return to Leo House if he could visit Feilnbach one day a week. He also reminded Faulhaber that, if he had to remain silent and out of the public view, he would not be able to help the Church in its relationship with the German government.[82] Finally, Schachleiter wrote Pope Pius XI a letter in which he described the spiritual deprivation he had experienced during his suspension and promised to return to Leo House. He also described his "glorious" past work for the Church, such as his campaign against the *Los-von-Rom* movement and his pastoral work with National Socialists to keep members in the Church.[83]

Through the encouragement of his abbot primate in Rome, Simon Landersdorfer, O.S.B., the abbot of the Scheyern abbey had Schachleiter's letter delivered to Pius XI along with his own request to allow Schachleiter to preside at a mass in his monastery. Before Faulhaber even had knowledge of this development, Cardinal Pacelli, in the name of Pope Pius XI, intervened and gave permission for Schachleiter to celebrate mass once, on the Feast of the Assumption, at the Scheyern abbey, just northwest of Munich. Pacelli also informed Landersdorfer that the Congregation for Religious had sent further instructions directly to the abbot primate in regard to Schachleiter.[84] Concerned that his action might have offended Cardinal Faulhaber, Landersdorfer also wrote to the Munich archbishop to explain the circumstances of the situation so that "no misunderstanding would develop" between them.[85]

The Congregation for Religious specified what Schachleiter had to do in order to have all his suspensions lifted. He had to compose an act of

contrition, make an eight-day spiritual retreat in some abbey of his order, take up residence in Leo House, and refrain from delivering public
sermons and saying mass outside Leo House or a Benedictine abbey. By
mid-September, Faulhaber was happy to report that Schachleiter had fulfilled or would soon fulfill all the necessary stipulations to enable him to
lift the suspension.[86] Schachleiter even turned down Hitler's personal invitation to be his guest at the NSDAP's 1933 Reich Party Congress in
Nuremberg, though Schachleiter did attend rallies in Oberammergau
and Rosenheim.[87] Despite these transgressions, the turn of events had
pleased Faulhaber so much that he voluntarily sent Schachleiter twenty-
five mass requests and stipends that he had personally received. He did,
however, let the abbot know in passing that he was aware of Schachleiter's recent failure to obey the spirit of his agreement with the Holy
See when he attended rallies.[88] From his new Leo House address in Bad
Aibling, Schachleiter mailed a letter of gratitude to Faulhaber for the
greatly needed funds. In his mailing he did not mention any of his
"trespasses."[89]

By October Schachleiter was back to his old ways, spending more and
more time with the Engelhards in Feilnbach. In addition, Faulhaber had
received word that Schachleiter was out on the road again, giving
speeches on behalf of National Socialism.[90] Schachleiter realized that
these actions placed his ministry and his future with the Catholic
Church in jeopardy and started making plans in case Cardinal Faulhaber
chose to impose new suspensions on him. First and foremost, he
checked with Rudolf Hess, deputy to the Führer, to ensure that his subsidy from the party would continue. On November 6 Martin Bormann,
at the time an assistant to Hess, assured him of this fact.[91] Schachleiter
also consulted with a canon law specialist to see whether Faulhaber or
Pope Pius XI could force him into an abbey and what other canonical
recourse they might take against him.[92] He also obtained support from a
medical doctor, who advised him to remain in Feilnbach because of the
special care and diet that he received there.[93] And last, he attempted to
win Faulhaber over by praising the latter's defense of the Old Testament
during his 1933 Advent sermons.[94]

On December 20, 1933, Faulhaber confronted Schachleiter anew, reminding him that he did not have permission to say mass in Feilnbach.
Faulhaber also pointed out that the German state was in a *Kulturkampf*
with the Catholic Church and listed as evidence: persecution of Catholic clergymen, proposal of a new church tax, and the development of
a Nordic-German religion. Faulhaber boldly stated that the Reich government's "fight against the Jews and the Catholics has openly become

a fight against Christianity altogether." Then he warned Schachleiter, "I trust that every priest to whom the door to the highest Reich offices stands open does not neglect to point out, with German candor, these anti-Christian movements in our fatherland."[95]

Schachleiter took Faulhaber's last challenge to heart. According to him, his love for his Church was greater than his love for National Socialism. He also admitted candidly to his friend and fellow brown priest, Father Lorenz Pieper, that he considered "the bishops' concerns valid" and he believed they "should support the Führer and protect [Hitler] from such enemies of Christianity."[96] Since his first meeting with Hitler in the 1920s, Schachleiter viewed himself as the "unofficial" advisor to Hitler on Church matters. Consequently, after receiving Faulhaber's challenge, Schachleiter wrote Rudolf Hess to obtain an appointment with Hitler. Hess promptly acknowledged the request but intentionally delayed scheduling any meeting of the abbot with Hitler.[97] Schachleiter refused to be put off and continued to write Hess regularly with similar requests.[98] Finally, on August 10, 1934, Hess arranged for a meeting to take place between the two in Munich. After greeting each other, Schachleiter presented Hitler with a litany of concerns he had about how unfairly the state and party were treating his Church. In particular, Schachleiter complained about the confiscation and prohibition (in Munich) of the June 7, 1934, German bishops' pastoral letter that condemned neopaganism.[99] According to Schachleiter, Hitler denied any knowledge of the confiscation by throwing up his hands and saying, "I meant that the pastoral letter should be read from all pulpits."[100] Later that summer Hitler tried to pacify Schachleiter further by inviting him as a guest of honor to the National Socialist 1934 Reich Party Congress in Nuremberg.[101] Of course, this gesture was not even necessary, since Schachleiter had accepted his Führer's explanation without question, as did Cardinal Faulhaber upon learning of it.[102]

Hans Lammers, the head of Hitler's Reich chancellery, soon became Schachleiter's pseudo-pen-pal, as it were, who had to deal with the abbot's many requests to meet with Hitler over some issue or other.[103] Whenever possible, Lammers would forward the letters to the newly created Ministry of Church Affairs and request that one of its directors deal with their contents.[104] While Lammers did reply to Schachleiter, his replies were normally not to the abbot's liking, since he offered only vague promises about future meetings with Hitler.[105]

Despite his complaints, Schachleiter achieved little success in his attempt to address the tensions between the National Socialist state and his Church. However, he never made his concerns public or aired them in the press. Rather, he kept them limited to private conversations and correspondence between himself and state and party leaders. Most of these political representatives lent him a sympathetic ear, primarily because they knew of his ties to Hitler. In turn, Schachleiter realized this advantage point and used his Hitler "connection" regularly to gain favor from others or to obtain desired outcomes. In 1934, for example, tension arose in Bad Feilnbach between Hans Priller, the local NSDAP group leader, and Frau Engelhard over her leadership of the regional chapter of the National Socialist League of German Girls (BDM)—the female counterpart of the Hitler Youth. Naturally, Schachleiter sided with his protectress and caregiver against Priller. When Priller's superiors refused to remove him, Schachleiter appealed directly to Hitler to intervene.[106] In the meantime Frau Engelhard became so distraught over the situation that she resigned from the party.[107] Before the situation ended, the local NSDAP group leader underwent an investigation and hearing before a party court. Though this court declared him innocent, he eventually resigned his position to bring peace to the town.[108] The whole affair revealed how vindictive this "holy Benedictine" monk could be.

Many individuals ran afoul of Schachleiter. This included many practicing lay Catholics. In August 1935 Father Ludwig Zach pointed out this fact to the Munich chancery. According to Zach, Schachleiter had begun to receive hate mail from Catholics regarding his uncompromising pro-National-Socialist statement.[109] In particular, Schachleiter irked them when he described himself as a preeminent example of "how one could be a devout faithful Christian—in my case a Catholic—and at the same time a fighting and sacrificing, most enthusiastic National Socialist."[110] It was not that so many Catholics were opposed to the NSDAP, but rather that some Catholics resented Schachleiter's renegade approach toward the German bishops, especially when they appeared to be in a *Kulturkampf* with the German state. The SD also had little use for him and categorized him as "an old man with great ambition."[111] Such a description was not surprising, since it was difficult for anyone in the SD and SS to trust an individual who was also a Catholic priest.

Although Schachleiter was willing to challenge what he perceived to be inconsistencies between the state and the Church, he won little support from the German Catholic hierarchy. Cardinal Faulhaber and the Munich chancery continued to refuse Schachleiter's requests to say mass publicly, except in the Leo House or privately in a Benedictine abbey.[112] Yet no matter how often Faulhaber said no to Schachleiter, the abbot remained patient and tried again. To describe Schachleiter as stubborn would be an understatement. His correspondence with Faulhaber revealed that he would not think twice about going behind Faulhaber's back to contact some archdiocesan chancery official for permissions in an attempt to play them off against each other. Faulhaber soon caught on to this ploy and in March 1935 ordered Schachleiter not to call the archdiocese's vicar general with "discreet questions."[113]

In late September 1935 the situation with Faulhaber abruptly changed. On September 21 Beuron Archabbot Raphael Walzer contacted Faulhaber and asked the Cardinal if he would allow Schachleiter to preside in Bad Feilnbach in view of the abbot's failing health.[114] Out of respect for Archabbot Walzer, Faulhaber granted Schachleiter permission to say mass in Bad Feilnbach during the month of October.[115] In the middle of October the Munich chancery received a similar request, this time from Beuron's prior, Dr. Hermann Keller, O.S.B.[116] Keller, who shared Schachleiter's sympathy for Hitler and National Socialism, also showed great kindness toward Schachleiter by agreeing to pay for his health care and prescriptions.[117] Once again, the Munich chancery extended the permission through the end of the year. This pattern continued for the next two years.[118]

In 1936 the Beuron abbey's support of Schachleiter increased. In fact, 1936 became a celebratory year for Schachleiter. On January 20, his seventy-fifth birthday, the University of Munich granted him an honorary doctorate of philosophy. Representatives of the university traveled to Bad Feilnbach to present the award to him.[119] He used the occasion to renew his belief in Adolf Hitler and declared "In Hitler, God has sent us the savior."[120] Then, in mid-August, upon the invitation of Prior Keller, Schachleiter traveled to Beuron to celebrate his golden jubilee of ordination.[121] Not everyone was happy about Schachleiter's presence. One Benedictine monk from Beuron privately wrote to Cardinal Faulhaber to express his dismay, "Schachleiter comes here to Beuron for his golden jubilee of priesthood. By our invitation! Your Eminence, this invitation is not only an incrimination of our house, . . . I see in it also an indiscretion against the entire German episcopacy. Your Eminence must know that the greater part of our community thinks as I do. . . . We stand loyal and firm with you Your Eminence."[122] The will of the acting superior, Prior Keller, ruled the day, and the Beuron community had a huge celebration. After the celebratory liturgy, Schachleiter used the time allotted to him to proclaim his belief that one could be the "most enthusiastic National Socialist and at the same time the most faithful Catholic."[123] Afterward Cardinal Faulhaber wrote Keller and called the event a "politically tragic comedy" and concluded that the entire event was "embarrassing" for him.[124] Keller immediately wrote Faulhaber back to inform him that the event was "not a political celebration, but a celebration of a religious community with the entire monastery" and assured him that the only party representative, the district leader, attended in civilian clothes.[125]

Soon after attending the Beuron celebration, Schachleiter's health took a turn for the worse. His neighbor, Father Alfons Amrain, brought him communion regularly from October 1936 through January 1937 until Frau Engelhard asked the priest not to return because the visits made Schachleiter too upset.[126] Evidently Amrain was too strong a reminder to Schachleiter of his struggles with the Munich archdiocese. In February Father Benedikt Welser, a fellow brown priest, traveled far from his home diocese of Rottenburg to administer the last rites to the abbot in his Bad Feilnbach home.[127] In return, Welser received a sharply worded letter from his bishop, Johannes Baptista Sproll, who reprimanded him for traveling so far with consecrated oil and Host, especially since these were available locally.[128]

Though ill and mostly bedridden, Schachleiter did find the energy in March to send Rudolf Hess a final letter in which he asked him to deliver his "last greeting" of "loyalty . . . blessing . . . and sincere gratitude" to Hitler. In the same letter he declared, "My conscience is pure. What I have done I will answer for before my God! One can be the most devout faithful Christian and at the same time the most enthusiastic and committed National Socialist. To my death, I have proven this to the world by my actions. . . . My last greeting is Heil Hitler! And now I commend myself to God. Faithful unto death to my Führer and his wonderful movement!"[129] The strong-willed abbot lingered on for several more months before taking his last breath at 12:30 a.m. on June 20, 1937. He was 76 years old.[130]

On June 22, 1937, Joseph Goebbels, Germany's minister of propaganda, recorded in his diary, "Abbot Schachleiter deceased. An honest German priest. The Führer ordered a state funeral."[131] Indeed, Hitler held back no expense to honor his abbot. The propaganda value of the moment could not be lost for the state and party, especially when the German bishops continued to portray their Church as a victim of oppression by the state and party.[132] Schachleiter's body lay in the Court Church of All Saints while hundreds filed by the coffin to honor Hitler's friend, and an honor guard of the SS stood at command. After the funeral, presided by Abbot Raphael Molitor of St. Joseph-Gerleve Abbey, the SS honor guard accompanied Schachleiter's body, which was carried on a specially constructed coach bedecked with a swastika banner, as it traveled through the streets of Munich to its final resting place in Munich's Forest

Cemetery. The state also constructed a memorial nearby. Many church and state dignitaries attended, including the abbots of St. Bonifaz (Munich), St. Stephen (Augsburg), and Ettal; government and party representatives such as Adolf Wagner, *Gauleiter* (head of administrative district) of upper Bavaria and Bavarian minister of the interior; Ludwig Siebert, Minister President of Bavaria; and Baldur von Schirach, the Reich youth leader. However, there was one significant absence: Adolf Hitler. Instead of attending, he sent his representative Rudolf Hess who spoke at the cemetery and laid a personal wreath from Hitler near Schachleiter's grave.[133] It is unclear why Hitler did not attend. Certainly, Schachleiter was one of his greatest champions. Yet the entire affair was Church-related—something Hitler years earlier had made the decision to forgo.

In the mind of many of the brown priests Schachleiter's death was a tremendous loss. Schachleiter was someone with whom they could both share their joys and commiserate. In particular, they often shared among themselves their utter shock at how few of their fellow clergymen cared to join their side to support the policies of the NSDAP. In their minds, their task was divinely meritorious. They saw no contradiction between their support of the NSDAP and their faith. They perceived themselves to be the righteous few, while those who refused to join them were the insubordinate, confused, or disoriented clerics. In some cases they would even label those clergymen who challenged the state as treasonous. To lift their spirits and to gain support and guidance, they often turned to their brown abbot. Many also believed that Schachleiter was the Church leader who could help them strengthen their relationship with the state. For example, Fathers Friedrich Schwarz (Cologne archdiocese), Joseph Edermaniger (Passau), and Ferdinand Peter Vogt (Würzburg) all believed Schachleiter could help them obtain a chaplaincy position in the military and for that reason wrote him complimentary letters that included this request.[134] In one letter Father Vogt even revealed that the "party leadership in Berlin was very obliging so that the door was open to me. Now the Lord Bishop of Würzburg says 'no,' as he has done in all similar cases for members of the NSDAP on account of a shortage of priests. Therefore, I must abandon my beautiful dream."[135] Still later, Vogt reported that two fellow brown priests, Father Dr. Simon Pirchegger—through his letters—and Father Godehard Machens, O.S.B.—through a personal visit—had lifted his spirits.[136] Father Bernhard Weinschenk (Munich archdiocese) also wrote to Schachleiter, but with a very different request. He believed that the abbot could and should organize Catholic priests who were open to National Socialism by collecting their names and creating a kind of pastoral bureau to coordinate their efforts. Weinschenk believed that such individuals working together could "gradually strengthen National Socialist thought among the clergy."[137]

In contrast to the above, brown priests who asked something of Schachleiter, there were others, such as Fathers Hermann Fiedler (Breslau) and Nikolaus Schober (Bamberg), who simply wrote to inform him of developments in their personal lives or to offer individual support. In August 1933, for example, Fiedler contacted Schachleiter to remind him of their original meeting in the Emmaus abbey and to describe his ventures as a speaker for the NSDAP and as a member of the SA.[138] In turn, in 1936, Schober wrote to offer his heartfelt congratulations to Schachleiter on the occasion of his golden jubilee of priesthood.[139] The tone of those letters reveals the great respect and admiration the brown priests had for Schachleiter. Not only did they view him as being one of them but, even more so, viewed him as a sympathetic leader, who could make things happen for them in the Nazi Party. This belief was present not only among the brown Catholic priests, but also among some Protestant ministers. For example, in March 1936 Reverend Paul Rössger, a pastor in Pforzheim, wrote to Schachleiter and encouraged him to promote unity among their two churches; he argued that together the churches could combat the neopaganism that had crept into the National Socialist *Weltanschauung*.[140]

Not every brown priest praised Abbot Schachleiter, however. Though they had considered each other friends, in 1934 considerable disagreements arose between Schachleiter and Father Josef Roth.[141] In April of that year Roth informed Father Lorenz Pieper that Schachleiter was quite "difficult" to speak with, since he had placed himself between two opposing sides—the state and the Church. Roth attributed Schachleiter's predicament to old age, which did not allow him to follow the recent developments within National Socialism carefully. He did admit, however, that Schachleiter was "entirely devoted to the Führer."[142] It is unclear whether Schachleiter knew of Roth's concerns. Nevertheless, Schachleiter informed Cardinal Faulhaber that Roth had been working against the Church and promoting a *Weltanschauung* that was anti-Christian.[143] Faulhaber also confided to Konrad von Preysing, the bishop of Berlin, that he believed Schachleiter was fearful of losing to Roth importance in the eyes of the state and party.[144] By contrast, on August 24, 1935, Roth admitted in a letter to Schachleiter that he had not visited him in a long while and promised to visit soon. Perhaps the elderly abbot just wanted his younger friend to acknowledge his presence and visit him more often. Still, in this particular letter Roth promised to visit only sometime in the near future.[145] Clearly, Roth had not resolved the tension between the abbot and himself. So on February 7, 1936, without knowing about Roth's correspondence with Pieper, Schachleiter wrote to the latter and asked, "Is he [Roth] still Catholic? Does he still have a heart for the Church?"[146] Yet, a week later Schachleiter wrote to Pieper again and informed him that Roth and he recently had a good discussion and cleared up any misunderstandings. He also told Pieper that he did "not believe everything that had been reported about [Roth]."[147] Perhaps Schachleiter settled his disagreements with Roth out of respect for their friendship. Most probably, however, Schachleiter made amends because Roth was the rising star of the brown priests in the Nazi state and the abbot could not afford to have him as an enemy.

In 1934, the year that the tension between Roth and Schachleiter began, Roth solidified his relationship with the NSDAP and joined the SA. On Hitler's request, Roth had not up to this point joined the NSDAP in order to steer clear of any problems with his superiors. Nevertheless, his zeal for National Socialism was so strong that on April 1, 1934, he felt compelled to join the party's SA corps. Roth would remain in the SA for less than two years before withdrawing.[148]

Despite his eventual withdrawal from the SA, Roth in no way dampened his enthusiasm for National Socialism. Rather, from 1934 onward, he became even more deeply involved with the National Socialist state and party. In 1934 this engagement led the party to invite him to join the faculty of the first National Socialist German *Oberschule* at Lake Starnberg in Feldafing, in the diocese of Augsburg.[149] While Roth taught religion part time there, his archdiocese had actually assigned him to teach at the Maria-Theresia *Realschule* in Munich.[150] Roth, however, preferred to spend his time in Feldafing. In a letter to his friend Father Lorenz Pieper, Roth described the *Oberschule* as a "fantastically organized new school" that will replace the "entire school system, which is obsolete. . . . From all over Germany, Danzig, Austria, and the Saarland, about 190 students shall be brought together and taught to be leaders in the army, state, and SA. More than 7,000 have already announced their interest. . . . And the teachers, most of them very young, are brought from all over Germany."[151] In contrast to Roth, Father Lorenz Grimm, the pastor of Feldafing, did not share his fellow priest's enthusiasm for the new high school. In September 1935 he wrote the Augsburg chancery to inform them of Roth's actions. According to Grimm, a reliable witness had told him that "Roth was repeatedly present in Feldafing in his SA uniform before the summer break. The students in Feldafing never attend church and never receive the holy sacraments. The single

Church celebration in which 20 students took part was the sacrament of confirmation in Starnberg. Before the confirmation, the pastor received a report from the director of the National Socialist German *Oberschule* that about 25 students would participate in the confirmation. The religion teacher of the *Oberschule* [Roth] had prepared the students. Normally the students travel far from the school to receive the holy sacraments." Other than this, Grimm had no knowledge "about the nature of religious instruction" at the *Oberschule*.[152] It would be quite interesting to see Roth's lesson plans for his religion classes.

His work in Feldafing along with his dedicated National Socialist stance led Roth to become a rising clerical star in the new German state. It was not surprising that in August 1935 Hanns Kerrl, the minister of church affairs, invited Roth to join his newly established ministry. The month before, after dealing with increasing problems with the leadership of both the Catholic and Protestant churches, Hitler had agreed to establish this ministry and to appoint Kerrl, a loyal party member, as its minister. Kerrl sought to staff his ministry with individuals who were loyal to the state. At the same time he understood the complexities of church bureaucracy. For that reason, Roth was a natural choice. To accept this position, Roth first had to ask Cardinal Faulhaber to grant him time off from his regular diocesan duties. At first Faulhaber denied the request; however, through the encouragement of his chancery, whose officials believed Roth's assignment could prove useful for the diocese, Faulhaber relented and granted Roth permission to move to Berlin and assume the new position.[153] Considering Roth's history with the National Socialist Party, it is quite surprising that Faulhaber agreed to make such a decision. However, in 1936, upon receiving a more permanent position as head of the Catholic division, Roth requested an extension via the Berlin chancery for permission to continue his work in the Ministry of Church Affairs.[154] This time Faulhaber was not as agreeable and denied Roth's request after Roth admitted that he had not regularly presided at daily mass.[155] At this juncture, Abbot Schachleiter had contacted Cardinal Faulhaber and advised him not to give approval to Roth's new position on account of his disloyalty to Rome, his careerism, and his advocacy for a German national church.[156] Faulhaber also suspected that Roth had written and published works against the Church, but did not have the evidence to support his suspicions.[157] The cardinal was not unjustified in his intuition, since Roth regularly published articles critical of the Church throughout the Third Reich. Faulhaber kept Cardinal Pacelli in Rome informed about Roth and his work in the Ministry of Church Affairs.[158]

In the Ministry of Church Affairs Roth's co-workers referred to him as "Herr Kaplan."[159] The term might have connotations of a pastoral sort. However, in his work as a state civil servant, Roth was far from pastoral in his approach. For example, he tried endlessly to have his colleague Kurt Grünbaum, a specialist on church tax and Protestantism, dismissed from the ministry because he had a close relative who was a Jew. Every time Roth saw Grünbaum in the ministry's office building, he would address him obnoxiously as "Jew."[160]

Roth also worked against what he considered political Catholicism and the encroachment of the Catholic Church into areas of the state. In 1937 he prepared a "Plan of Action" for his superior Hanns Kerrl to deal with the "power position of the Roman Catholic Church in Germany." In the plan Roth called the Church a "political force that never recognizes the primacy of the state. It represents a universalistic *Weltanschauung* and therefore will always oppose National Socialism as well as any *völkisch Weltanschauung.*" On that account, he concluded, the "Roman Catholic Church stands in contradiction to the National Socialist state." He then suggested that the state gradually free itself from the Reich-Vatican Concordat through gradual measures of interpretation: the community school should replace the denominational school; clergymen should continue to be prosecuted for violations of currency laws and sexual misconduct; church associations should be abolished; the state should withdraw all involvement in the collection of church tax; the state should prohibit church newspapers; and the papal nuncio should be removed from the diplomatic corps and placed under the Ministry of Church Affairs.[161] In Roth's mind, as well as the view of many National Socialists, these measures would force the Church, both legally and financially, to limit itself to remaining within the walls of its worship space, with no influence over state policy.

Roth did everything possible in his job to begin the process he described in his Action Plan. As director of the Catholic division within the Reich Church Ministry, Roth had to approve the arrest of any Catholic priest whose case appeared before the Gestapo. This meant that he had a primary say in the fate of hundreds of his fellow priests whom the Gestapo had arrested regularly on charges of politically treasonous acts. Though at times some of the actions by Catholic clergymen were politically motivated, the majority came into conflict with the state over pastoral and ministerial concerns. For example, a simple phrase uttered during a homily critical of state policy affecting freedoms normally enjoyed by the Church could ultimately lead to a priest's arrest, conviction, and imprisonment. Roth also worked with the Gestapo to confiscate any "questionable" pastoral letter or Church publication. In March 1938 he ordered the confiscation of a pastoral letter by Cardinal Bertram, which the cardinal directed at children and their parents. Roth worried that this letter was "likely to disparage the values, i.e., blood and race, that unify all Germans and instead favor a specific religious denomination."[162] Last, Roth lent his services to Alfred Rosenberg by contributing entries to his *Handbook on the Roman Question,* which was meant to serve as a reference work to assist state and party officials in their dealings with the Holy See.[163]

Other priests recognized Roth's authority within the German state and at times turned to him for assistance. In September 1940 the Franciscan priest Erhard Schlund, O.F.M., wrote to Roth to seek his intercession after the Regensburg Gestapo confiscated and prohibited further distribution of his publication *Consilium a vigilantia.* In February 1928 Cardinal Faulhaber had appointed Schlund director of this internal Church news service, which observed "the book market and newspapers" and reported anything "interesting and important" on religious and Church matters. Schlund explained to Roth that the *Consilium* had always paid special attention to anything that attacked "the Catholic faith and the institution of the Church." He continued, "since January 1, 1929, this report has been exclusively sent to the German bishops and to specifically designated diocesan officials in Church offices." Schlund pleaded with Roth for assistance and swore to him that he was "not aware of having written or reported anything" that was "harmful to the state, the *Volksgemeinschaft,* and the party." Then Schlund assured Roth that he belonged "to perhaps the few theologians" who made "an effort to build bridges not only between the state and Church, but all the more between the party and the Church" and considered a "trusting cooperation to be possible and necessary." Roth, however, refused to intervene for his clerical colleague.[164]

In order to advance his work and further limit the influence of the Catholic Church on the German state, Roth also served as an informant to the SD and almost daily met his contact and friend, the former priest and SS officer Albert Hartl, over lunch to feed him any information that he had gained through his position in the Ministry of Church Affairs.[165] In June 1936 Roth even applied for admission into the SS, but Heydrich evidently did not approve his application.[166] Still, this did not deter Roth's efforts on behalf of the state. He attempted in particular to get the Reich-Vatican Concordat annulled—the first point of his "Action Plan." He thought this treaty was an outdated agreement, concluded by a state in its infancy, and, in his own words, toiled "to sabotage, to undermine, and to work for the annulment of the Concordat" through his entire professional activity.[167] Not only did he believe that the laws of the National Socialist state had surpassed the Concordat, but, under the pseudonym of Walter Berg, Roth contended in an article that the Church itself had grown ancient and ineffective and for that reason the National Socialist revolution needed to supplant it.[168]

For Roth, Christianity not only was restrictively outdated and lacking in significance, but it also was permeated by Judaism, which left it helplessly weak. As early as 1923 Roth had presented an image of Christ as a "heroic strongman," calling upon people not to mourn but to be strong in spirit.[169] In essence, Roth wanted Christianity to reclaim more manly virtues and ideals, believing that with modern Christianity's stress on charity and good work it had become effeminate. In this vein Roth argued that masculine Christian virtues "rebel against institutions and endeavors that do not fight suffering with all their might but offer only good words and support to those who suffer."[170]

By 1940 Roth had come to the conclusion that Christianity could not be saved from the influence of Judaism, which, as noted above, he believed continually crippled and distorted it. In a 1940 lecture for the Institute for the History of the New Germany, a piece published later that same year, Roth again addressed the issue he had brought up in his tract *The Catholic Church and the Jewish Question*. According to Roth, Jewish influences had penetrated the Church to its very core. This included hundreds of years of Jesuit overtures to allow Jews into its ranks. Despite a history of anti-Jewish Church law, the Church now had lost the battle against Judaism and was preaching tolerance of Jews. He concluded, "The Catholic Church will never come to a clear and determined struggle against Judaism and will never become an ally in the national ideological struggle because it would have to give up its own mission and its own spiritual substance."[171]

Roth turned his back on the Church not only because of its alleged Jewishness but also because of his own struggle with celibacy. Somehow, despite his own involvement in state measures against the Catholic Church and notwithstanding his sanctioning of the arrest of individual Catholic priests, Roth never withdrew from the Catholic priesthood. However, in 1939–1941, when he entered into a relationship with a recently divorced woman, Käthe S., Roth started to question his vow of celibacy and had to endure the pangs of conscience in deciding whether or not to marry this woman. Käthe seemed to make his decision even harder, for though she professed her love for Roth, she constantly returned to live for short periods of time with her former husband. This situation tore at his conscience and confused him even more.[172]

On July 5, 1941, before Roth could act on his feelings for Käthe and perhaps marry her, he drowned while vacationing in Rattenberg am Inn with his brother-in-law and family. Dr. Sebastian Schröcker, a colleague in the Ministry of Church Affairs and former priest of the Munich archdiocese, recorded the incident: "The Inn [River] always had a whirlpool here that was particularly strong and resulted from the pier and the high water level. This overturned Roth's folding canoe. He did not return to the surface for an abnormally long period of time. Possibly the canoe did not immediately lose its protective cover under water. That explains why he suddenly emerged next to his overturned boat. He attempted to cling to his canoe with his hand but could not pull his face from the water. The strong current tore him away from the canoe. He disappeared in the water, and his brother-in-law did not see him again. Two and a half weeks later his body turned up hanging on a grating in a branch of the Inn."[173]

Roth's untimely death caught everyone by surprise.[174] Since Roth's work for the state had affected the lives of so many clergymen, Cardinal Faulhaber informed his fellow Bavarian bishops of the *Kaplan's* death through a general mailing. There was not a hint of sympathy in the note. Instead, Faulhaber pointed out that Roth "raised both arms in the air as he went under." Then the Cardinal wrote in Latin, "Rest in peace."[175] The bureaucratic tone made the last quote seem much more like "Good riddance!" Subsequently, in September Faulhaber issued a general, two-page biography of Roth, disseminating it to dioceses throughout Germany. Through this mailing Faulhaber would once and for all be finished with Roth. To separate himself even further, the Cardinal specifically denied ever having granted Roth the *Nihil obstat,* or permission, to work for the German state.[176]

Not everyone viewed Roth's drowning as an accident. His friend Father Leonhard Wackerl reported that Roth had recently confided to him his unhappiness in Berlin. Roth supposedly told him that "if it had not been for the war, he certainly would have left Berlin and taken a parish in the archdiocese. Roth was unhappy in Berlin; he had a great opponent in Dr. Goebbels." Wackerl also reported that Roth, shortly before his death, had made a retreat to reflect on his current life and situation. However, Wackerl would not confirm this with absolute certainty.[177] Rumors persist to this day in the Munich archdiocese that Roth took his own life by venturing into a dangerous section of the Inn River.

Despite Roth's efforts against his Church and fellow clerics, he never left the Catholic Church. The archdiocese of Munich honored this fact and accorded him a Church funeral, which was held in Ottobeuren. His friend and fellow brown priest Father Philipp Haeuser of Straßberg delivered the eulogy. Haeuser took this opportunity to summarize Roth's life and work, especially his devotion to Hitler and National Socialism. For Haeuser, Roth was his "best, most reliable, and most loyal friend." He lamented that sadly they would no longer be able to join "hands in this immense development and struggle of the present as Christian and German brothers." Still, Haeuser took consolation in the fact that, though Roth's struggle had ended, his own continued onward. "Indeed," Haeuser assured himself, Roth's spirit accompanied him "on [his] paths of struggle." Then Haeuser, ever self-centered, moved to compare his life with his friend's, "The life of Josef Roth was a continual struggle. The bloody armed struggle on the front was followed by the ideological struggle for the spirit in the homeland. . . . We both fought for the things of Jesus and for those of the Führer. . . . His Jesus stood firm on the soil of reality, his Jesus was a powerful fighter whom even Alfred Rosenberg had admired, and this should not be forgotten. . . . Yes, this Jesus was his Führer."[178]

For Roth, as for Haeuser, Jesus was the Führer. In this respect both had created their own images of Christ—images that strayed far from biblical accounts. Their image of Jesus was vaguely Christian, laden with layers of Nordic mythology and imagery. This Jesus was not inclusive in his teaching of love of neighbor, but exclusive. He had a limited view of who encompassed his *Volksgemeinschaft*. Similarly, God the Father had sent into the world a new savior, named Adolf Hitler, who would save Germany from its ills and restore it to greatness. Perhaps by 1941 Roth realized that Hitler was not his savior and feared for his personal salvation. However, the record is not clear enough to come to any conclusion about this prospect. By contrast, the record of Father Philipp Haeuser's life is quite clear. Once he embraced Adolf Hitler and the National Socialist Party, he never departed from this path nor questioned its aims.

4—Antisemitism and the Warrior Priest

Next to Schachleiter, Philipp Haeuser was arguably the best known brown priest. His devotion to Hitler was so profound that he put aside his academic career as a biblical exegete and systematic theologian to focus all his attention on the NSDAP. A staunch nationalist, who abhorred the Versailles Treaty, the Weimar democratic constitution, and the Catholic Church's support of the Center Party and Bavarian People's Party, he advocated unconditional support for Hitler and the *Völkisch* movement, which he fondly called the German movement. He also professed a great disdain for Jews. Moreover, unlike many brown priests, Haeuser openly supported Hitler and his lethal antisemitism.

Foundations

Philipp Haeuser was born on April 23, 1876, in Kempten, into a family of devout Catholics.[1] His parents rigorously raised Philipp and his four siblings in the Catholic faith.[2] A bright youth, Philipp attended the Kempten gymnasium and graduated in 1895. His zealous Catholicism led him to believe that God was calling him to be a priest—a decision, he noted, he made himself. He studied philosophy and theology at the

University of Munich from 1895 to 1899 and resided at the Georgianum seminary. Though he later confessed that he did not grow spiritually in his religious and prayer life, he did enjoy his studies. His "pious exercises," however, he found tedious. "The more they were repeated," he noted, the more they became "habits devoid of meaning . . . cut off from the soul."[3] Haeuser's words describe an individual who was searching in vain for something to fill his deeper religious longings.

During his priestly formative years, one area that stimulated his interest was his studies. In particular, Haeuser fondly remembered the philologist Dr. Karl Weyman, who helped him to see that the Church was "still evolving and not a fixed, completed being" that stood "outside historical development." Gaining such insight enabled Haeuser to see that the Church, as well as its leaders, could also be subject to critique. Still Haeuser loved his Church, and on July 20, 1899, Bishop Petrus von Hötzl ordained him a priest for the Augsburg diocese.[4]

Haeuser's ordination and his subsequent appointment as associate pastor in Bertoldshofen did not mean that he relinquished his academic interests. Rather, this assignment offered him ample time to pursue them. In September 1900 this situation suddenly changed, when his bishop reassigned him to become prefect in the Royal Teacher Training College in Neuburg and simultaneously teacher and chaplain to the Catholic students at the neighboring Neuburg gymnasium. Haeuser found the students challenging and not as disciplined as he would have liked and made his Neuburg years "a time of growth."[5]

During his Neuburg tenure, Haeuser became preoccupied with the problem of suffering. He regularly asked in his sermons, "Why do people suffer?" and confessed that this was a "huge mystery that no one could truly solve." "Nevertheless," he affirmed, "the curious person finds inner calm and satisfaction if he immerses himself in the life and suffering of Jesus." To gain this peace, he exhorted his congregants in the Neuburg Hof Church to "seek Jesus in order to live!"[6] The question, however, would soon be: Who was this Jesus that Haeuser encouraged people to seek?

The Theological Exegete

After nine years of full-time teaching, Haeuser had had enough. The stress of teaching and his academic responsibilities, as well as his efforts to research and write, began to affect his health. In December 1909 Haeuser wrote to the Bavarian Ministry of Education and requested a release from his prefect position. In lieu of teaching Haeuser wanted to continue his research and writing full time. Already he had immersed himself in a study of *The Letter of Barnabas,* a late-first-century non-canonical work written by an unknown author.[7] He shared his work with Professor Georg Pfeilschifter, a church historian at the Albert-Ludwig University of Freiburg im Breisgau, who, to Haeuser's surprise, accepted it as a dissertation. In July 1911 the university awarded Haeuser a doctorate in theology. Although Haeuser was willing to accept this honor and prepare his manuscript for publication, he had a difficult time convincing his new bishop, Maximilian Lingg, of the merit of such studies. Lingg told Haeuser, "Studying makes you discontented." Haeuser shrugged off this comment by attributing it to Bishop Lingg's lack of appreciation for academic endeavors and urged the bishop to let him study anyway. Lingg finally relented and allowed Haeuser to move to the Ettal Benedictine abbey in order to concentrate on his writing.[8]

Considering his choices later on, it seems predictive that Haeuser chose *The Letter of Barnabas* as the subject matter for his first published exegetical work. *Barnabas* is a work openly hostile to Judaism, written in a time when the early Christian community was struggling for its existence. The author argues that God had rejected the Jews, redefined their institutions and rituals, and offered the covenant to the followers of Christ.[9] In his analysis Haeuser spent an inordinate amount of time juxtaposing the author's representation of Christians, who fully understood God's promises, with the author's negative sketch of Jews, who remained blind to the designs of God. Evidently the Church hierarchy, represented by Joseph Schnitz, vicar general of the Paderborn diocese, did not find anything contrary to the Church's teaching in Haeuser's interpretation and offered an imprimatur prior to its publication in 1912.[10]

After receiving positive reviews of his first work, Haeuser received an invitation to translate into German Justin's *Dialogue with Trypho, a Jew* (1917), another work of Christian apologetics that set the early Christian community in opposition to recalcitrant Jews.[11] Again, in *The Motive and Purpose of the Letter to the Galatians* (1925) Haeuser depicted Judaism and Jewish practice with antipathy.[12] He hoped to dedicate this study to Eugenio Pacelli, the apostolic nuncio to Germany (and, after 1939, Pope Pius XII, whom he claimed to know personally). Pacelli considered accepting the honor, but declined after conferring with Bishop Lingg.[13] By this time Haeuser's right-wing speeches and writings had created tensions with the diocese. In fact, every member of the bishop's priestly advisory board, the *Domvikare,* returned the publisher's gift copy of Haeuser's study.[14] It seems likely that Haeuser approached Pacelli and the *Domvikare* in order to protect himself from the criticism of his bishop.

World War I and Its Aftermath

In March 1911, Bishop Lingg appointed Haeuser at the age of thirty-four pastor of Straßberg, a tiny working-class parish with fewer than six hundred members, just outside Augsburg.[15] During the war Haeuser remained in his parish and continued to serve the people of Straßberg. Along with the majority of Germans, the loss of the Great War was devastating to Haeuser. Even more destructive, in Haeuser's mind, was the democratic republic that replaced the empire. Haeuser detested the Weimar Republic and the coalition of parties—the Social Democratic Party, the Center and Bavarian People's Party, and the German Democratic Party—that formed the first Weimar coalition. He considered all of them traitors to Germany. In 1919 he wrote a letter to Bishop Lingg and pleaded that he not support the revolution and that he take a harder line against priests who backed the democratic movement.[16]

According to Haeuser, he never desired to be active politically, but the looming threat of Marxism, the insertion of left-wing politics into the new government, and his own "enthusiasm" for his "German fatherland" changed his mind. He began to speak to small groups in his parish about "what was necessary" to solve the perceived ills plaguing Germany. "Gradually," he attested, "I was invited to collaborate with fatherland groups."[17] At first these nationalist-oriented groups brought him in contact with parties that favored a monarchical restoration, such as the Bavarian Royalist Party and the Bavarian Home and King's League. Over time, however, Haeuser developed more interest in the German National People's Party—and, finally, the NSDAP.

Haeuser volunteered to lend his name, gifted writing abilities, and speaking experience to the Right's political agenda. In January 1920 Haeuser wrote his bishop that, as a member of the state committee of the Bavarian Royalist Party, he had placed his signature on its program with the hope of integrating "the Church's aristocratic ideas also into political life and thereby to stand up for the altar as well as for the throne." For Haeuser this included demands for a restoration of the "Christian monarchy and the Christian public school." He assured Bishop Lingg that he "explicitly stressed that questions concerning the Church be considered only in consultation with Church authorities."[18] Soon thereafter he wrote several articles supporting monarchism, which he believed would unite the German people and awaken in them "the feeling of national identity." When national identity was "again awakened," he argued, "then the Bavarians, respectively the Germans, should again be sole masters in their 'house.' Strangers can remain with us as guests, but only as guests." Though he did not advocate the persecution of Jews, he did begin to speak about them in exclusionary terms.[19]

During this time Haeuser did not find a great deal of support from his local ordinary, his fellow priests, or from members of the Catholic laity when he attempted to articulate his political position. Catholic newspapers, such as the *Augsburger Postzeitung,* regularly rejected Haeuser's articles promoting monarchism.[20] Bishop Lingg began to monitor Haeuser's public activities closely, often requiring him to clarify his statements in written correspondence. When Haeuser learned that his right-wing political leanings were not favored by the Church's hierarchy, who supported the Catholic-based Bavarian People's Party, he developed an opaque writing style in order to camouflage his real intentions and activities. In early 1922, in response to an inquiry from Bishop Lingg for clarification of a sentence that Haeuser had written concerning his political activity, he responded, "I take part in a political movement as a priest only if making sacrifice is in the interest of threatened principles, . . . in contrast to the participants in a political movement, who are only out to earn honor and other profits."[21] Haeuser always portrayed himself as a humble priest, who desired no earthly riches, in contrast to the greedy politicians surrounding him. In reality Haeuser was merely using this guise to protect himself against criticism from the Church hierarchy, to make himself appear as a noble, spiritual warrior fighting for the pure *Weltanschauung* of a political movement, and, later in life, to shelter himself from the horrendous consequences of the choices that he had made earlier in his life. Though Haeuser was a well-educated man, trained in textual analysis, it appears from his life choices that he seldom if ever stopped to analyze his own life critically. Instead, he continually moved forward, heedlessly entrenching himself deeper in the right-wing movements following the Great War.

Venturing into the Political Realm

In 1922 Haeuser published *We German Catholics and the Modern Revolutionary Movements.* Written during the turmoil of postwar chaos, unemployment, and inflation, the book distinguished between those who truly defended the German cause—monarchism wedded to nationalism—and those who endeavored to destroy it. Haeuser demanded that Catholics embrace monarchism and reject the Weimar coalition with its parliamentary democracy. He firmly believed that Catholics, through their participation in the Center Party and cooperation with the Social Democratic Party, risked losing everything they had gained in society as a result of the First World War. He explained, "How often during the war did Protestant officers and Protestant and liberal newspapers publicly and joyfully concede: the Catholic too is a good soldier, who is willing to sacrifice, a good nationalist of a true German nature. . . . Our behavior during the war had erased an old accusation that tended to be made against us Catholics, wiping out every doubt of our patriotic, truly German conviction." Haeuser believed that Catholics, along with their fellow Germans, were too content to "sit back without bearing arms, exhausted like people living in slavery, as a result of non-German, Jewish machinations: the poor must sacrifice their money, the starving must sacrifice their bread." Haeuser exhorted Catholics to take up arms, enter the arena of battle "for national ideals," and struggle against "Wilson, the Freemasons, and the Social Democrats," who promoted "peace among the peoples."[22]

In *We German Catholics* Haeuser identified his foes as the Social Democrats, the Center Party supporters, the Bolsheviks, and the French—groups he loathed equally. In addition, he laced all his arguments with antisemitic rhetoric and labeled Jews as his enemies, stating, "Nationalistic thinking, willingness to sacrifice, and consistent nationalistic work is necessary if we want to vanquish the dreadful threat of the Jews and of international capitalism."[23] While Haeuser utilized economic antisemitism to attack Jews directly, he also used the word "Jew" freely, affixing it to anyone he believed had betrayed Germany, which makes it difficult to pinpoint the exact nature of his antisemitism.

We German Catholics and the Modern Revolutionary Movement immediately caused a stir. On April 7, 1922, the *Kölnische Volkszeitung* criticized it as a "scandalous denigration of the overwhelming majority of the Catholic people, of the Center and its leaders. A Catholic priest should not dare to label as unprincipled opportunists the millions of believers who share an opinion that differs from his."[24] The Center Party's indignation was so great that in August 1922 Monsignor Carl Walterbach, priest of the Bamberg archdiocese, representative of the Bavarian People's Party in the Bavarian State Parliament, and president of the South German Catholic Workers' Association, wrote *Catholics and Revolution* to refute Haeuser's claims. Walterbach challenged Haeuser's attack on democracy by arguing that it was rooted in the subjectivistic "life philosophy of Nietzsche."[25]

Not everyone, however, was outraged by Haeuser's words. In January 1922 Antonius von Henle, bishop of Regensburg, personally wrote Haeuser, "Please receive my warmest thanks for your work! If only we had a press that would offer similar thoughts as daily bread to our readers!"[26] Similarly, on February 9, 1922, Erich Ludendorff, German World War I general and right-wing political agitator, praised Haeuser, "My friend Abbot Schachleiter gave me your work. . . . I read it immediately and today cannot thank you enough. What you say, I agree with totally. I would welcome it if your ideas would be taken note of not only in Catholic, but also in Protestant circles."[27]

In December 1922, to maintain his prominence and to refute Monsignor Walterbach publicly, Haeuser published *Jew and Christian, or to Whom Does World Domination Belong?* and shortly thereafter a revised and abridged piece, "The Jewish Question from the Standpoint of the Church," with both of the publications specifically identifying Jews as Germany's enemies. In Haeuser's view, Jews controlled Walterbach and had blinded the monsignor to the wrongness of his ways. Haeuser assured his readers that this would not happen to him, for he was "strongly nationalistically oriented," endeavored "to be a good patriot," and, as a priest, stood "decidedly on the Right."[28]

Haeuser's writings strayed far from the Christian message. Their antisemitic contents also exposed to the world a perverted faith, intertwining traditional religious antisemitism with more modern, generic fallacies concerning Jews. For example, toward the beginning of *Jew and Christian,* he reinterpreted the Good Samaritan story in the New Testament to give it antisemitic overtones. Now the Jews did not even have a chance to "reject" Christ, but instead were "rejected" by Christ."[29] Likewise, in "Jewish Question" Haeuser intensified Jesus' rejection of his own people by portraying Christ as one who campaigned "against the leaders of the Jewish people, against the scribes, the Jewish preachers, the representatives of the Jewish law, and the inhabitants of Jerusalem." Consequently, Jews were profane, dissolute, sinful, depraved people, who "condemned their Messiah to death in their blindness, stubbornness, and depravity." Thus, Haeuser argued, "the Jewish people ceased once and for all to be an instrument of divine grace and mercy. Other peoples stepped into the position of the Jews to become God's people."[30]

By emphasizing Jewish responsibility for Christ's crucifixion and death, Haeuser embraced a religion-based antisemitism. At the same time he rejected a *völkisch* portrayal of Jesus by writing, "That Jesus in the flesh comes from the Jewish people should not be denied. The fairy tale that Jesus was not a Jew but rather of Aryan birth was invented for national, *völkisch* interests."[31] At this point, Haeuser's theological and exegetical training prevented him from venturing into the realm of fantasy. Still, Haeuser's emphasis on Jesus' negation of Judaism to produce Christianity suggests that he incorporated part of the ruminations of

British-born Houston Stewart Chamberlain, who was an extreme German nationalist and racist, while at the same time Haeuser retained Jesus' Jewish origins.[32] In his work *The Foundations of the Nineteenth Century*, Chamberlain had argued that Jesus was a Galilean born from an Aryan mother.[33] Many of the National Socialist writers and ideologists incorporated similar arguments into their works, but Haeuser did not.[34]

Despite his unwillingness to embrace the *völkisch* theological interpretation of Jesus' origins, Haeuser was more than willing to incorporate modern economic and politically based antisemitism into his argument. In "The Jewish Question" he identified Jews as the main force behind the Weimar Republic by writing, "The [Weimar] revolution is largely a work of the Jews. . . . What has been destroyed in terms of the people's strength and assets during the last four years since the revolution must be credited many times over to the Jews. The Jew is now definitely master of the world. In economic and political life, the Christian has become his slave. The Jew through his cleverness, his ruthlessness, his—almost exemplary—determination and tenacity has reduced almost all nations and governments to slavish obedience." In this regard, Haeuser joined his fellow antisemites and blamed Jews for the existence of everything he detested: the Weimar constitution, democracy, international conferences, separation of church and state, and the banking industry. He considered himself a noble, bold prophet, comparing himself with Stephen, the first Christian martyr, who dared to speak the truth and therefore "had to pay with his life in the fight against the Jews."[35]

Though Haeuser did not view Jews as Germans, he was still unwilling to advocate direct violence against them. In an unequivocal footnote in *Jew and Christian* Haeuser noted, "We struggle against the Jews not to fight them, but, in the final analysis, because we want to win the Jews for the cross."[36] Here Haeuser spoke in purely Catholic terms, recognizing the sacrament of baptism as effecting a profound, religious, categorical change in the convert. By recognizing this change and viewing the recently baptized person as a Christian, Haeuser revealed that he did not embrace racial antisemitism based upon unchanging blood. In "The Jewish Question" he emphasized this point even further and proclaimed, "The Jews also have the right to life; our Lord God is also the Lord God of the Jews." Nevertheless, Haeuser qualified his tolerance by writing, "In questions of national education and national government, in the important life questions of mankind, not the Jews but the Christians alone have the last word. . . . No mingling of Jewish and Christian spirit!"[37]

Reception of Haeuser's Writing

Haeuser was not alone in the beliefs that he professed in his work. Before publication, he submitted *Jew and Christian* to the Regensburg chancery, where the work was published and given an imprimatur from Father Dr. Alphons Maria Scheglmann, vicar general of Regensburg. Father Dr. Kiefl, the Regensburg cathedral rector, also reviewed the work positively: "The work is a direct hit from Haeuser's pen. It is not a matter of doubt that the Jewish question, now that the revolution stands undeniably as the work of Jews, has become a burning issue. Haeuser's work is not an antisemitic inflammatory work. . . . The author moves in an entirely new direction. . . . The presentation is gripping." Still Kiefl recognized that the work was controversial and acknowledged, "With this work the courageous and undaunted author will also come across protest from the compromise-prone and the pussyfooters."[38] Kiefl's comments reveal that centuries of Christianity-based antisemitism made it very easy for some churchmen to accept the exclusionary claims that antisemites made against Jews. As long as the demands did not specifically attack Catholics of Jewish descent and, inadvertently, the sacrament of baptism, churchmen such as Kiefl were comfortable embracing such racist thinking.

There were repercussions from the publication of this antisemitic work. In December 1922 Haeuser received an invitation from the Catholic Businessmen's Association Lätitia in Augsburg to speak further on the issue of Jews and Christians. However, a day before the scheduled lecture, Father Friedrich Müller, the Augsburg vicar general, contacted Haeuser to inform him that Bishop Lingg had forbidden it. According to Haeuser, Lingg had acted upon "the wish of Jewish Councilor of Justice Dr. Ebstein and Rabbi Dr. Grünfeld" to have the lecture cancelled.[39] In response, Haeuser immediately sent the chancery a copy of his work *Jew and Christian* along with a letter in which he proclaimed, "Fearlessly, I will continue to fight for God, truth, and fatherland, even if a member of the Church hierarchy should decide to take action against me. My life principle is taken from the words of the apostle Paul found in Galatians 1:10, 'If I would please men, I would not serve God!'"[40]

It appears that the Church hierarchy was much less concerned with the contents of Haeuser's words than with the effect the words had on the German public and their perception of the Church as an institution, so it was not surprising to see Vicar General Müller respond publicly to a *Völkischer Beobachter* article that described the Augsburg bishop as "an old man," who "immediately appropriated the line of thought of the peace-oozing Jews and enacted a ban on Dr. Haeuser."[41] Müller took particular offense at how the *Beobachter* portrayed the entire incident, and on December 21 he wrote a letter to the *Beobachter*'s editor to clarify the situation. According to Müller, the newspaper had gotten its facts wrong. Ebstein and Grünfeld had approached the Augsburg chancery to express their concern about a lecture Haeuser had delivered to the Bavarian Home and King's League before the Lätitia Association had occasion to announce his talk. In this context Müller wanted to make it clear that the bishop's prohibition against Haeuser's talk to Lätitia was not the direct result of the complaints his chancery had received from the Jewish community. In essence, Müller wanted the public to know that the Church did not take orders from Augsburg's Jews.[42] It would be interesting to know if anyone in the Augsburg chancery would have confronted Haeuser for his antisemitic activities if members of the Jewish community had not questioned the priest's activities and writings.

Such a ban on Haeuser seemed only to bring him more notoriety, and by mid-1923 Haeuser's writings had given him both celebrity and fame. Every group with right-wing leanings attempted to employ his services as a speaker and writer, although he had not yet aligned himself specifically with any particular party or movement.[43] Despite his involvement with the Bavarian Royalist Party and the Bavarian Home and King's League, he did not want to limit himself to working exclusively on behalf of these groups because he identified himself as an agitator for the general German movement.[44]

Political Agitator

In November 1923 Hitler and his followers attempted the Beer Hall Putsch in Munich. Their "bravery" and "daring" provided Haeuser with a clear example of the battle that awaited German nationalists. In January 1924 Haeuser acknowledged this fact by extolling the putsch "soldiers" in a speech to the Bavarian Home and King's League in Rosenheim. Over the course of two hours, Haeuser condemned the Reich government's ineffectiveness and justified the actions of Ludendorff and Hitler, whom he described as "great and respectable men who with the best of intentions and readiness to make the most difficult sacrifice had chosen to save the German *Volk* in its most serious crisis." He assured his audience that Hitler's action fought against the "Christian compromisers" (i.e., Center and Bavarian People's Party members), who wanted a "Jewish spirit to rule over public life." Before concluding, he predicted "a storm must come, a storm will come. If we hear it roar, then let us not be frightened. And if it violently sweeps over the land and washes away everything that is rotting and sick, then let us say with satisfaction: That is a spring storm, it is the roar of spring. If we hear this storm during this night of the German *Volk*'s history, then let us stand up bravely and undauntedly come out into the storm."[45]

When Haeuser finished his address, the crowd responded with loud applause; but on the evening of the speech Father Josef Weber, pastor in Watzling, along with a Catholic layman, both outraged at Haeuser's words, wrote to the Augsburg chancery to inform them of the day's events. The papers of Bavaria aligned with the Catholic Church also ran articles critical of Haeuser. The *Bayerischer Kurier* proclaimed it "a scandal for a Catholic priest with such views to come before the *Volk*." Even his fellow Catholic priests turned their backs on him. Father Weber used exceedingly strong language to confront his diocesan brother: "I express to you my deepest indignation over your speech in Rosenheim. Are you still unaware of the bolshevistic spirit that hides behind the Hitler movement? I am forced to see in you a very dangerous enemy of our professional concerns. Anyway, your writings have already caused enough damage." The Bavarian Catholic hierarchy felt the same way. First, Cardinal Faulhaber of Munich prohibited Haeuser "forever from any public appearance within his diocese." Then Bishop Lingg issued a prohibition against any future political appearances by his brown priest.[46]

Haeuser retaliated by publishing his speech in the East Prussian newspaper *Warmia*.[47] It is impossible to know if this was the exact text that he offered in Rosenheim. Nevertheless, before releasing his speech to *Warmia*, Haeuser did attempt to publish it with a Regensburg publishing house, Manz Verlag, which had published some of his earlier works. However, this time Monsignor Dr. Müller, the president of the Catholic Press Association, intervened and saw to it that no publishing house with Catholic connections in Bavaria would ever touch Haeuser's work.[48]

Haeuser realized that he would have to be more cautious with his public utterances. Though he had become a sought-after speaker for right-wing groups, his current precarious situation with his diocesan superiors forced him repeatedly to turn down speaking invitations, especially invitations from National Socialists.[49] Nonetheless, in the fall of 1924 Haeuser agreed to be a candidate for the German National People's Party (DNVP) in the December 7 Reichstag election.[50] He ran on a ballot including Alfred von Tirpitz, former admiral of the fleet in imperial Germany, and seven other candidates. As a priest, Haeuser needed permission from his local ordinary and from any bishop whose diocese was part of his electoral district in order to run for political office. His failure to obtain this infuriated Cardinal Faulhaber and Bishop Lingg, who immediately forbade him to accept the candidacy. Haeuser ignored their prohibition and let his name stand. In the end Faulhaber and Lingg ultimately had their decision honored when on election day the public voted against putting Haeuser into office. Haeuser seemed relieved by the outcome: "Being defeated took a load off my mind at the same time. I wanted to avoid any conflict with the diocesan authorities."[51]

Pacifism and Christianity

Losing the election probably was a great relief to Haeuser. However, it is difficult to believe that he truly wished to avoid conflict with the German bishops; immediately following the election, instead of keeping a low profile, Haeuser agreed to speak publicly to the Augsburg DNVP membership and to have his speech published under the title *Pacifism and Christianity*.[52]

In *Pacifism and Christianity* Haeuser not only attacked the German pacifist movement; he also clarified his views on the racial question in relation to the *Völkisch* movement. Oddly for a Catholic priest, Haeuser rejected pacifism because it promoted "international cooperation, brotherhood, and weakness in a society." For Haeuser, Christ too would reject such thinking because he "was not a weak, sweet pacifist. Indeed, he had the most noble, peaceful nature but still, or rather for this very reason, had a fighting spirit." German Christians had to embrace this combative nature and make it their own. Instead of focusing on international concerns, tainted by "Jewish big business" and Bolshevism, he challenged Germans to center upon national and racial concerns by embarking on a "national, healthy, racial path" that emphasized family, community, and *Volk*.[53]

In the discussion of race, however, Haeuser's views did not directly mirror those of the *Völkisch* movement, which in essence embraced National Socialist racial teaching. For Haeuser, "ethnic conceitedness, which pretends that everything good and great" in the *Volk* derived "mechanically and without spirit from German drops of blood," was pedagogically "worthless and will kill the *Völkisch* movement before long." Instead, he advocated an "ethnic and national pride that is tied to sensible cultivation of the mind and to strict schooling of the will and healthy military education." This pride, Haeuser concluded, ultimately would "give back to the *Volk* its lost honor and create the basis for a true rebuilding." According to Haeuser, "national, ethnic self-confidence" was both "good and necessary. But it must not give rise to ethnic arrogance or to disdain for other nations" because "before God no people [was] righteous and all peoples need the unending grace and mercy of God in the same way."[54]

Ultimately, in *Pacifism and Christianity,* Haeuser revealed that his eccentric thought was quite complex—a complexity that many might overlook and simplify. Haeuser also showed he was an ardent nationalist and, to some extent, an isolationist like many in the *völkisch* camp. At the same time he rejected racial theories of superiority with their overemphasis on blood. In their place, Haeuser advocated spiritual, moral, and intellectual strengthening of the German *Volk.* Despite these differences with many in the *völkisch* camp, Haeuser's argument could not hide the central fact that he detested Jews and ranked them among or even beneath those who promoted pacifism and internationalism.

Soon Haeuser's rallying cry against pacifism surfaced again. During the April 1925 Reich presidential election Haeuser lent his support to Field Marshal Paul von Hindenburg and went on the attack against the Center Party candidate, Wilhelm Marx, by proclaiming him to be a dangerous pacifist. Haeuser not only broke his speaking prohibition again by appearing and speaking at a DNVP rally for Hindenburg, but on his candidate's behalf and against Marx, he also wrote an article that appeared across the country in newspapers aligned with the DNVP and the National Socialists.[55]

Diocesan Concerns

It would seem that by this time the chancery office would have taken serious action against Haeuser. The only hint we have that his superiors criticized him at all appears in the form of brief comment in his memoirs. Here Haeuser wrote, "I was even more besmirched by certain Catholic circles."[56] One of the primary reasons Haeuser escaped stronger canonical penalties was the November 1927 appointment of Father Dr. Franz Xaver Eberle as Augsburg's vicar general. Eberle, who was Haeuser's senior by two years, had befriended him during their seminary years and used the informal German *"Du"* (you) in their discussions and correspondence. Eberle also shared many of Haeuser's convictions, but was more diplomatic in his public pronouncements.[57] Not surprisingly, time and time again Eberle would intervene to save Haeuser from harsher sanctions. Whenever possible, Eberle also would allow his friend more room to maneuver around his speaking prohibitions until the bishop finally intervened. In April 1928 Haeuser was invited to speak at several DNVP rallies in Düsseldorf in early May. On the Saturday before

Haeuser was to deliver the first speech, several newspapers announced his upcoming appearance. Immediately, Catholic clergy from Düsseldorf called the Augsburg chancery. On Saturday afternoon Eberle reluctantly called Haeuser and pleaded with him not to give the speech, but added, "I will not forbid you to speak, since I do not want to rob you of your freedom as a citizen." Naturally, Haeuser appreciated the latitude that Eberle had offered him and assured him he would talk about only cultural and religious matters and would avoid any mention of politics. However, the next day, just prior to his departure for Düsseldorf, Haeuser received a telegram from the chancery office forbidding him from speaking on any issue. Bishop Lingg had put his foot down and forced Eberle to change his position. In defiance of his bishop's wishes, Haeuser made the trip to Düsseldorf and made all his scheduled appearances. Instead of giving his planned speeches, he informed his audience that, although he had lots to say about the current dire situation of the German *Volk*, in obedience to his bishop he would refrain from uttering it.[58]

But the situation soon turned in Haeuser's favor. On May 17, 1928, after having turned down several more speaking invitations, Haeuser received an unexpected telegram from Vicar General Eberle, who lifted Haeuser's speaking prohibition for Straßberg. Eberle must have felt guilty for having taken action against his friend and assumed such an overture would restore Haeuser's confidence in him. Since Straßberg also was a small town, Eberle might have trusted that Haeuser could not cause too many problems there. In order not to lose this opportunity, Haeuser acted immediately to organize a "patriotic evening" in his parish. He even gained press coverage from the *München-Augsburger Abendzeitung*, which reported that Haeuser gave an invigorating two-and-a-half-hour speech.[59] Haeuser certainly must have had a lot to say after having been silenced.

Haeuser and National Socialism

Although Haeuser, according to his parishioners, was a caring, pastoral priest, who served them generously, at heart he was also a selfish, self-serving, egocentric man. He strategically accepted the assignment in Straßberg primarily because it would allow him ample time to continue his academic work. In addition, the inhabitants attracted him greatly. Almost 70 percent were factory workers or day-wage earners with few marketable skills.[60] Thus it was easy for a man of his education and prominence to become a central figure in the small town and serve as a father figure to the town's inhabitants. Whenever anyone questioned him, as a parishioner did in the early 1930s, Haeuser went after him with venomous prose that not only addressed the issue under dispute, but also attacked the person's character in an effort to destroy him or her.[61]

Haeuser also held grandiose ideas about his own abilities and influence. In 1925 Haeuser wrote to Cardinal Faulhaber in an attempt to have his speaking prohibition removed. The Munich NSDAP had launched a campaign to impugn Faulhaber's character. In his letter Haeuser informed Faulhaber that he had personally spoken with Hitler, who promised him that he would "make sure that all agitation against [Faulhaber] would stop." Haeuser then assured Faulhaber that "before God" his political activity was "an apologetic work for the Catholic Church in Germany." The cardinal archbishop, of course, did not buy any of Haeuser's farcical intentions.[62]

Haeuser did have personal connections with leading members of the NSDAP. In the early 1920s, when the NSDAP was in its infancy, he met Hitler several times. Naturally, it was possible for Haeuser and for any brown priest to exaggerate his connection with Hitler in order to make himself appear more important. In 1939 he sent his memoir, *My German Struggles and Development,* to Rudolf Hess, Hitler's deputy, to attest to his efforts on behalf of National Socialism.[63] Hess, who often acted as a contact person between Hitler and the brown priests, had a long-standing connection with Haeuser. In addition, the Straßberg pastor often acted as Hess's informant concerning issues pertaining to the Catholic Church.[64] Six years earlier Hess had even sought Hauser's advice on the appointment of a priest to the board of governors of the German Catholic Nurses' Association. In his reply Haeuser, of course, wholeheartedly recommended his friend and fellow brown priest Josef Roth for the position.[65] In March 1933, when the *Illustrierter Beobachter,* a NSDAP newspaper, offered a profile of priests who had supported the movement, Haeuser was one of the three priests chosen for this "honor."[66]

Though Haeuser had not spoken publicly at a NSDAP rally for a long while, it was clear that he faithfully maintained his contacts with the movement. In 1930 death suddenly removed the main obstacle that prevented Haeuser from working with the Nazi Party. On May 31 Bishop Maximilian von Lingg passed away, leaving the diocese in the hands of Haeuser's friend, Vicar General Eberle. In Augsburg the clergy expected Pius XI to name Eberle Lingg's successor. This appointment might have created an interesting turn of events for the Church in Augsburg, for the Nazi Party, and for Haeuser. Instead, the pope bypassed Eberle and named Joseph Kumpfmüller, the rector of the Regensburg Cathedral, the new bishop of Augsburg. On October 28, 1930, Kumpfmüller was consecrated a bishop.[67] This unexpected sequence of events afforded Haeuser the opportunity he needed to offer his services to the NSDAP. With Bishop Lingg out of the way, Haeuser believed he could ignore the prohibition against him and start anew with his new bishop. Already losing patience with the DNVP for its inability to unite the various factions of the *Völkisch* movement, Haeuser turned to Hitler as the individual who could bring this about.

A National Socialist Christmas

On December 14, 1930, Haeuser accepted an invitation to address the Augsburg NSDAP members during their Christmas celebration. Though free from Bishop Lingg's restrictions, Haeuser's acceptance of this engagement could not have occurred at a worse time. A few months earlier the Mainz chancery had sided with a pastor who forbade his parishioners to join the NSDAP. Other German dioceses would gradually adopt the Mainz interpretation and make it their own. With this public confrontation between the Church and the NSDAP in the forefront of German Catholics' concerns, Haeuser's Augsburg Christmas speech caused a stir both inside and outside National Socialist circles.

Playing into the Nazi slogan "Germany Awake," Haeuser entitled his speech "A Christian Message for an Awakening Germany." He designed it as a rallying cry against all those who opposed the spiritual and intellectual core of the German movement—a movement that he was now gradually and exclusively associating with National Socialism. To address this concern, he interchangeably used the terms *"Pharisäertum"* (self-righteousness; hypocrisy) and *"Pharisäer"* (pharisees) to identify the movement's opponents. Haeuser's use of these terms was varied, complex, and at times vague. They were most probably code words that right-wing adherents immediately understood. At times Haeuser would use them to refer exclusively to groups such as Jews, Church authorities, political Catholics, advocates of the Weimar government, pacifists, or Social Democrats; or he would use them collectively as a catchall term encompassing all of these groups or a combination of them.

Haeuser did not believe he was acting alone. Indeed, he held the conviction that he was continuing Jesus' mission against the Pharisees when he proclaimed, "To Jesus, the Pharisee was the target of battle; in his struggle against him he wanted to develop and reveal his superior personality. To us, the pharisee is also the target that we must fight against in order to prove ourselves as the successors of Jesus in this

battle and more and more to develop and reveal our Christian personality." With these words, Haeuser depicted a warrior Jesus. For Haeuser,
Jesus was not a pacifist. Neither was the day commemorating his birthday—Christmas—a "feast of pacifist peace." Rather, Jesus was a soldier
who wanted to engage in battle. Haeuser continued, "Without fighting, [Jesus] could never have proclaimed the truth. . . . Only because of
this will to do battle, because of this courage to do battle, was he fated
to be whipped and crucified."[68] Haeuser assured his listeners that, if
they were willing to join this battle against the pharisees, they would
have the "right to call the great sacrificial priest Jesus [their] Lord." To
this end, he invited his listeners to join with Hitler, Franz Seldte,
founder of the Stahlhelm, and Alfred Hugenberg, DNVP chairman, in
their struggle on behalf of the German movement. Haeuser's call fore-
shadowed the Harzburg Front, the name given to a failed October
1931 attempt to unite a varied group of nationalist and right-wing
groups in Bad Harzburg in order to bring about the fall of Heinrich
Brüning's government.[69] In this large-scale summons, Haeuser humbly
attested that he would play the "quiet role of a military chaplain—not
requiring much sacrifice."[70]

This affirmation of Haeuser's proposed level of commitment, of
course, caused him major problems with his religious superiors. Even before these officials acted, the Catholic press attacked Haeuser head-on.
On December 18 the *Münchener Post* declared him an "enrolled member
of the Hitler party" and at the same time challenged Bishop Kumpfmüller to enact a prohibition against Haeuser.[71] The *Schwäbische Volkszeitung* urged Kumpfmüller to act against Haeuser immediately with a
bold front-page headline reading: "Jesus not a pacifist! Bishop Joseph,
what do you say to that?!"[72] More sarcastically, the *Neue Augsburger
Zeitung* declared that Haeuser's "cassock will henceforth be the cloak in
which the anti-Rome and anti-Church writings of Rosenberg and his
cronies will be wrapped."[73]

Press coverage went much further. The National Socialist press used
the opportunity to go back and review Haeuser's past antisemitic writings. The *Westdeutscher Beobachter*, for example, published excerpts from
Haeuser's 1923 antisemitic work *Jew and Christian*.[74] *Der Stürmer* likewise
published excerpts from Haeuser's Augsburg speech by highlighting his
use of the term "pharisee." In the introduction, before examining the
text itself, a *Stürmer* writer penned, "Among the Catholic priests who do
not keep their conviction hidden belongs Father Dr. Haeuser of
Straßberg. He has become well known through his publication, in which
he deals with the Jewish question in a courageous manner."[75]

Haeuser's Church superiors viewed his speech as "a crime" and five days after his speech summoned Haeuser to the chancery.[76] Eberle confronted his friend and dispassionately challenged Haeuser to realize the problems he had created for the Church. When Haeuser refused to acknowledge that he had done anything wrong, Eberle turned to him and said, "Despite everything we still remain friends, don't we?" Bishop Kumpfmüller was not so accommodating. Upon entering the room, the bishop sternly stated, "You shall altogether no longer speak before the National Socialists, for you are the disgrace of the diocese that I just took over!" Haeuser questioned, "Your Excellency, I do not understand this remark." Kumpfmüller retorted even more forcefully, "You are the disgrace of my diocese. In fact, you are the disgrace of the entire German clergy. Period." The bishop could not have been clearer in his choice of words. Haeuser was overwhelmed. He knew the bishop might be upset, but he never imagined he would react so passionately. Distraught, Haeuser ended the conversation abruptly and fled the building. Haeuser concluded that his bishop "was not a German man who wished to understand, but a Roman lawyer who sought to destroy me."[77] In fact, Kumpfmüller did not mean to destroy Haeuser, but to silence him. On the same day as their brief meeting Kumpfmüller issued a strict speaking prohibition against Haeuser. The newspapers of Germany were filled with articles about the interdict, each speaking either for or against him, depending on political leanings.[78]

The weeks following this encounter were particularly hard for Haeuser. The Catholic press had a field day attacking his name and belittling his comments. Haeuser had become a clerical magnet for political parties and a medium through which they could fight out their differences. Naturally, he had brought this upon himself. And due to the interdict imposed by his local ordinary, Haeuser could not publicly fight back. As the weeks passed, the situation evidently became intolerable for him. On January 21, 1931, Haeuser directly disobeyed Kumpfmüller's prohibition and rebutted his critics in the *Völkischer Beobachter*, portraying himself as a persecuted prophet whom the forces of political Catholicism had attacked for speaking the truth. Through their public and open attack on him, these forces exposed their true faces and identified themselves as pharisees, he averred. Sarcastically, Haeuser added, "I thank this press for its rare honesty and frankness."[79]

Though Haeuser had strong words of criticism for the Catholic press, he was unwilling to criticize his bishop or the Church directly. Evidently he realized that such criticism might create even more serious canonical problems for him. Nevertheless, he did take the opportunity to explain why he spoke at the National Socialist Christmas celebration. Haeuser clarified, "The aim of my address was to preserve the Catholic Church from an even more serious crisis with the incipient German movement." Comparing himself then to John the Baptist, the great and last of the prophets, who prepared the way for Christ, Haeuser attested, "I wanted to rescue, and for this reason alone I called. But I am forced to realize with dismay: to those whom I wanted to warn at the last moment, I was no more than one calling in the wilderness. How can the wilderness, how can the rocks, hear? But woe to those stones that have become or will become stumbling blocks."[80] At this point Haeuser clearly was beginning to view himself (and not John the Baptist!) as the last of the great prophets, in this case called to prepare Germany for a new savior—Adolf Hitler.

Bishop Kumpfmüller responded immediately and had Vicar General Eberle write Haeuser a letter that accused the priest of disobeying "the bishop and the bishop's authority." He also added, "If you describe yourself in this [article] as a 'voice crying in the wilderness,' then, on the basis of your public activity, the only conclusion that may be drawn is that you are a voice in conflict with the Catholic Church and its leaders." Then Eberle warned him that "in the future, if you accept publishing in publications that have an ideological basis entirely different from Catholicism, then your permission to publish in newspapers and periodicals will be totally withdrawn." Furthermore, Eberle reminded Haeuser that the bishop reserved the right "to take further steps."[81]

The letter devastated Haeuser. In his memoirs he wrote, "The Sunday on which I received this letter from the bishop is unforgettable to me. It was a day of the greatest spiritual shock. My trust in the bishop, my faith in the Church's authority came fully into question." He thought, "My greatest fear was clear to me: there was more than just a warning planned against me, the aim was my destruction." Instead of dwelling on the difficult situation, Haeuser left his rectory and went for an afternoon hiking expedition into the forest that bordered the village of Straßberg. He always took refuge there when the pressures of life became too great. According to Haeuser, he saw "God's revelation much more clearly in nature than in the all-too-human Church." Soon the serenity of the forest gave him what he sought, "divine consolation and divine strength." The forest allowed him to relax by reflecting firsthand on nature and on the laws he believed God gave to all creation to guide it: fate and struggle.[82] These were natural laws that the National Socialists also believed to be of prime importance.

Though the walk in the forest might have allowed Haeuser sufficient time to calm down, it did not provide him with the fortitude to admit that he was wrong and to make amends with his bishop. Rather, Haeuser seemed even more steadfast than ever in his determination to support National Socialism and the German movement in general. Of course, Haeuser was not an unintelligent individual. He knew that if he wished to continue to be a priest in his Church, he had to make concessions to his bishop. This ultimately meant obeying the prohibition. However, now Haeuser had a major problem. Prior to receiving Eberle's letter, on Saturday, he had already sent another article to the *Völkischer Beobachter* for publication, so, the first thing Monday morning, Haeuser had to write to his friend Vicar General Eberle to inform him of the situation. Still, he revealed in his words that he was not going to give in to the wishes of the hierarchy easily. Haeuser began his letter, "If I am a voice in the conflict against the Catholic Church, God Himself will be the judge in any case. I am convinced that the day will come when His Excellency the bishop, as well as his vicar general, will appreciate me and thank me." Then he told Eberle about the article and noted that he would immediately try to have it withdrawn.[83]

It appears that Haeuser did as he promised or tried to. Despite his efforts, however, the *Völkischer Beobachter* would not pass up an opportunity to publish an article favorable to National Socialism. As a result, the newspaper published it with a disclaimer that removed from Haeuser any personal responsibility for its publication. The article ran on January 28 with the headline "The Black Terror: How the Center and the Bavarian People's Party Shift Their Own Blame to Others." In his article Haeuser explained that he never had meant to criticize the German bishops, but rather only the press of the Center Party and the Bavarian People's Party. He argued that the press of these parties "brazenly" identified itself with the German episcopacy and therefore made it appear that Haeuser had attacked the German bishops with his Christmas speech.[84] In Bishop Kumpfmüller's mind, the only way for Haeuser to redeem himself was to end his relationship with National Socialism and to make this action public. Haeuser's pathetic attempt to justify his actions, though awkward as a public account, did nothing to heal his relations with his ordinary. Nevertheless, he still had a friend in the chancery office—Franz Eberle.

On January 29, the day following the publication of his latest article in the *Völkischer Beobachter,* Haeuser accepted Eberle's invitation to join him for a conversation in the chancery. There Eberle admitted that he did "not approve of the contents of the official letter" and gave his own candid appraisal of the bishop whom he judged to be "an instrument of the Center and the Bavarian People's Party. This is why he took action against you. As a *Römling* (cleric educated at the Vatican) he cannot understand the German movement." Such a brash statement gave Haeuser sufficient ammunition to fire back at Kumpfmüller's accusations. As Haeuser's harangue heated up, Eberle cut him off abruptly by confessing that he had to intervene with the bishop in Haeuser's behalf in order to save him from expulsion from the priesthood. Not only the bishop, but all the *Domvikare*, with the exception of Eberle, had recommended Haeuser's expulsion. Haeuser looked at Eberle in disbelief. Had what he said really been that controversial for the bishop to take such drastic action?

After a long pause, Eberle divulged the main reason for Kumpfmüller's outrage: Haeuser's depiction of Christ. The bishop had accused Haeuser of scorning "the person of Jesus" in his Christmas speech. Initially dead set on ousting Haeuser, the bishop changed his mind only following a second impassioned meeting, when Eberle persuaded the bishop and the *Domvikare* to change their minds. Throughout all of these discussions there was no evidence that the bishop or any of his advisors were equally outraged by Haeuser's attack on the Catholic political parties or his indirect promotion of the National Socialist *Weltanschauung*. Rather, they solely concerned themselves with issues that touched upon Church teaching. It is of course impossible to know if Eberle was telling the truth or simply using this tactic as a means to curb his friend's proclivities. He was clearly trying to win sympathy from Haeuser. Haeuser, for his part, seemed to be aware of Eberle's ploys. Before ending the conversation, Haeuser suggested that perhaps Eberle should resign as vicar general. Then, instead of being confined in the chancery every day, Eberle could serve in a small country parish like Haeuser and "work in peace and honesty on the great problems of life and of the people." Though Haeuser might have doubted Eberle's sincerity, he did listen to his advice and decided to lower his profile, at least for a while. Haeuser also acknowledged that he owed a lot to his friend: "Eberle saved me in my support for Jesus and Hitler."[85]

Though Eberle had saved his friend from severe canonical sanctions, his warnings did not spare him from public ridicule by other members of the Church hierarchy. Soon after the publication of Haeuser's December speech, Cardinal Faulhaber dedicated the majority of his 1931 Lenten pastoral letter specifically to refuting Haeuser's "distorted" portrait of a warrior Christ. In contrast to Haeuser's depiction of Christ, Faulhaber emphasized Christ's willingness to suffer for humanity and his "endless ability to forgive."[86] Such comments angered Haeuser to no end. He believed that the Church hierarchy had lost the pulse of the nation and noted, "Increasingly I felt nauseated by the Church's politics and the Church's methods of governing and educating, and increasingly I felt myself more drawn toward Hitler, to the great Führer whose entire being and actions were built upon honor and an understanding for nature. I was tied to him emotionally. In my own quests, circles, and pursuits he was a model and leader. My strength flowed from his character. In difficult, critical hours was his ever present character the greatest source of strength to me after Jesus."[87]

The Extreme-Right-Wing Chaplain

Haeuser's speaking and writing put him into the spotlight, and soon he became the spiritual advisor to many Bavarian Catholics who were angry at their bishops for their prohibitions against the NSDAP. In most cases Haeuser counseled Catholics privately. However, in September 1931 he wrote to a National Socialist an encouraging letter that ended up gaining national attention when various newspapers reprinted it. In it Haeuser advised, "It pleases me that you are a Catholic and at the same time a National Socialist. Do not allow yourself to be led astray from your true path. Any Catholic priest who works against our German movement and wants to condemn us knows nothing about true Christianity; they do not know the *Völkisch* movement, which derives from natural law and as a result is desired by the Creator Himself. No priest has the right before God to banish a National Socialist from the Church on account of his life and loyalty for German concerns and for the German people. I am myself a Catholic priest."[88] The letter revealed that Haeuser was offering Catholics pastoral advice that contradicted the German bishops' prohibitions. At the same time, due to his previous confrontations with his bishop, Haeuser in no way meant for his advice to go public.[89]

Haeuser's letter placed his superiors in a very difficult position. In essence, his words pushed his bishop and others to be even more specific in their moral reservations concerning Catholic membership in the NSDAP. Though Kumpfmüller and his fellow Bavarian bishops had issued restrictive pastoral instructions in reference to National Socialism in order to assist priests in their ministry, they were not willing to ban Catholic National Socialists altogether from receiving the sacraments because of their party affiliation. By expressing such hesitancy, the bishops left a door open for Catholics to join the NSDAP.

On September 23 the Augsburg diocesan chancery sent Haeuser a brief letter asking him if he had actually written the letter of pastoral instruction to a National Socialist.[90] Haeuser wasted no time informing the chancery that he had previously discussed the letter's contents with Vicar General Eberle and stressed that he had never meant it to be published. He also pointed out that he had not advocated membership in a particular party but, following his own example, encouraged the individual to lend his support to the overall German movement. Haeuser argued that he had made such a recommendation in order "to preserve the faithful for the Church."[91]

On October 10 Eberle, on instruction of Bishop Kumpfmüller, replied to Haeuser. Eberle acknowledged that the bishop had placed his trust in Haeuser's "priestly honor" and accepted his explanation. However, he did request that Haeuser compose a letter, meant for public distribution, to explain his action. Eberle also told Haeuser how to compose the explanation.[92] Three days later Haeuser mailed Kumpfmüller exactly what the bishop sought: an acknowledgment that the letter was "a private matter" and the assurance that he in no way "wished to challenge the instructions of the Bavarian bishops concerning National Socialism and pastoral care."[93] Through the use of such wording, both Kumpfmüller and Haeuser avoided a serious confrontation concerning Catholic membership in the NSDAP. As a result, membership in the National Socialist Party remained in a nebulous state, subject to the interpretation of individual parish priests.

As the NSDAP quickly moved to the political fore, the questions over Catholic membership in the NSDAP would not go away. Haeuser also did nothing to help alleviate the situation. The existence of his published letter advocating acceptance of National Socialism offered Catholics justification for their membership in the NSDAP. For example, in March 1932, during a rally of National Socialists and Stahlhelm members in Ludwigsmoos, a town in the Augsburg diocese, a National Socialist Party member and state legislative representative from Munich publicly read Haeuser's letter advocating membership in the NSDAP. Present at this gathering was Franz Kraus, the town's mayor, leader of the Ludwigmoos National Socialist group, and lead singer of the Ludwigmoos Catholic Church choir.[94] Evidently Kraus was quite moved by Haeuser's letter and saw in it a justification for his own membership in the party, so he wrote to both Haeuser and the Augsburg chancery, inquiring further about the letter's contents.[95] On March 27 Haeuser replied to Kraus and encouraged him to "continue to walk quietly on the path that your conscience and your German character prescribe for you. Jesus had compassion for his people; why should we in the German movement not also have compassion for our people? Jesus was persecuted for his compassion—that is why we too will be persecuted. Your wife should be completely at ease regarding your activism. Whoever serves the fatherland also fulfills his Christian duty."[96]

Most certainly Haeuser's words assured Kraus that his work for the NSDAP would in no way conflict with the tenets of his faith. Although Haeuser was careful to avoid specific reference to the NSDAP, the tone of his letter leaves no doubt that he fully supported Kraus's political stance. Upon receiving Kraus's letter of inquiry, the Augsburg chancery wrote Haeuser and demanded to know if he was once again publicly supporting the National Socialist movement.[97] Haeuser replied, "In none of my letters do I exhort anyone to become a National Socialist, but I do indeed continually urge people, in my responses to the hundreds of letters that are sent to me, to remain true to the Catholic Church. There is a difference between the exhortation to a National Socialist not to forget his churchly obligations and the exhortation that a Catholic should become a National Socialist."[98] Though Haeuser offered this cleverly worded response, it was still easy to see, as did Father Franz Xaver Wonhaus, pastor of the Catholic parish in Ludwigmoos, that Haeuser was fundamentally supporting Hitler and the NSDAP.[99] Kraus, of course, understood Haeuser's assurances, and, though appreciating them, took into account the word game that Haeuser and the Augsburg chancery continued to play in reference to Catholic NSDAP membership. Though Kraus was a Nazi, he was also a practicing Catholic, who fully resented the fact that both sides presented their positions in less than an honest manner. He commented, "I still don't know what to make of Dr. Haeuser; without any doubt, he is a propaganda tool for the National Socialist Party with the tacit approval of the chancery. Otherwise he would not be permitted to continue to have a parish and would be ousted from the Catholic Church. I am convinced that Father Haeuser has only noble motives for his National Socialist activities, but when his bishop forbids them, he should either obey or be excluded."[100]

The Tide Gradually Turns

Though Bishop Kumpfmüller grew tired of having to discipline Haeuser and deal with the effects of his public statements and writings, by 1932 the political situation in Germany had changed drastically. On the national political scene both the NSDAP and the Communist Party fought each other, and both fought the Social Democratic and the Center Parties in an effort to dominate the Reichstag. In addition, the successive quick rise and fall of government administrations of the early 1930s heightened the political tension and unease among the German populace. By 1931 Kumpfmüller had already contemplated utilizing Haeuser's good relations with the NSDAP for the benefit of the Church if the party ever came to power in Germany.[101] Thus it would prove quite inopportune for Kumpfmüller to alienate Haeuser from his diocese. Rather, it would be much easier for the bishop to enforce limited restrictions on the priest in order to control him.

Haeuser, too, realized the unique position he held through his relationship with the *Völkisch* movement and the Nazi Party, especially as the latter gained more influence in the Reichstag and state governments. If Hitler came to power, Haeuser fully expected to wield influence on and be of importance to a NSDAP-dominated national government. Already by September 1932 he had placed his expectations solely on Hitler, after giving up all hope of reconciliation between the DNVP and the NSDAP. According to Haeuser, Alfred Hugenberg, the leader of the DNVP, had dismissed his overtures to promote cooperation between the DNVP and Hitler.[102] In the same year, it appeared that Haeuser was also beginning to give up on his Church when, under a pseudonym, he published *The Flawed Traditions of the Catholic Church.*

In *Flawed Traditions,* Haeuser's prose was more polemical. Emphasizing his great dislike for the sacrament of confession, Haeuser argued that any "church that in the confessional rummages irreverently through the purest soul for dirty garbage demanded to be viewed with a questioning and critical eye." Haeuser portrayed himself not just as a lone prophet attempting to reform the Catholic Church and awaken it to its scandalous rejection of the German movement, but as a prophet aligned with Julian the Apostate, Jan Huss, and Martin Luther, all prophets sent by God to warn the Catholic Church that it needed to mend its ways. Haeuser argued that Luther was "not a manifestation of an evil spirit against the spirit of God, but a reaction of a good force against the unhealthy humor in the Church." In Haeuser's mind the Church of the late Middle Ages had "sinned against the law of racial and national life" by creating "division within the German *Volk.*"[103]

In this context, Haeuser believed that the German bishops had betrayed the German people by issuing unwarranted prohibitions against National Socialism and causing great division among Catholics. He declared, "We foresee that the word 'betrayal' will soon hit the ears of Church leaders with a deafening sound, amid the furious screams of a German people who has been betrayed, crushed, and had the very last drop of blood sucked out of it." For Haeuser, the bishops were not acting any differently from the Jews, who, he argued, "had claimed to be the only ones who know and adore the true God. Rather, they had misused this true God in their lust for power and through this misuse had humiliated him in the eyes of the heathens so they were driven to malign the true God in the same way as his believers had done."[104]

Though many of Haeuser's fellow clergymen were nationalistic and might also have supported much of his nationalism, few would concur with his assessment of the Church. Haeuser was not blind to this fact and in July 1932 expressed his concerns to his cousin Marie R.; standing firm in his convictions, Haeuser confided, "Indeed, I can do nothing against the hatred and slander directed toward me by the entire German clergy. . . . What will I do against it, seeing that I am prohibited from speaking and writing and my ecclesiastical superiors refuse to protect my honor! There is nothing that I can do to alter my destiny."[105]

Soon, however, Haeuser could change his outlook. When Hitler came to power, Haeuser saw this event as a bright ray of sunshine breaking forth through a dark cloud of doubt and despair to shine over the "awakening" nation. He truly believed that a "savior"—Adolf Hitler—had rightfully assumed political power in his fatherland. However, he also realized that he still had to work hard to convince and educate his fellow Catholics of the importance of National Socialism.

Especially after the bishops' reversal of their prohibitions against National Socialism, Haeuser thought he would be in great demand as a speaker. Bishop Kumpfmüller and Cardinal Faulhaber also realized this fact and forbade Haeuser to speak at any National Socialist event.[106]

Frustrated and angered by these bans, Haeuser turned to his friend Eberle in an attempt to sort out the situation. Though offering a sympathetic ear, Eberle assured his longtime friend that both Kumpfmüller and Faulhaber were deadly serious in their prohibitions against him. In July 1933 Eberle repeated this warning in even stronger language by advising Haeuser to "restrain [himself] and never address National Socialists! For the bishops more than ever seek to destroy you now that the Concordat has been signed. Your greatest enemy is Cardinal Faulhaber. He repeatedly wanted to have you excommunicated, but I have always saved you from this."[107]

Haeuser found the entire situation impossible to comprehend. However, he took solace in the fact that his fellow brown priest Abbot Schachleiter also "suffered" under a similar interdict from his bishop. With that in mind, Haeuser wrote to Schachleiter and expressed his solidarity, "Honorable Monsignor, you experience the hypocritical pharisaism as the Lord himself experienced it. Important men speak pious words, but their soul does not recognize the spirit of God. Important dignitaries know your purity and honesty but nevertheless ask for your defamation and crucifixion. We may be convinced that if Jesus appeared among us today, the bishops and Rome itself would impose on him all possible Church punishments. They would work toward his downfall and after his death refuse him Church burial. No priest would stand at his grave! I write this so that we may seek and find strength in Jesus."[108]

Working for Christ and the Führer

Despite having fellow priests in whom he could confide, Haeuser still found himself in a very difficult position. He understood fully the canonical punishments that the bishops could impose on him if he disobeyed their rulings. At the same time he realized that the speaking ban deprived him of participation in the NSDAP just as its members began to form a new Germany. Naturally, he continued to hold out hope that his friend Eberle would, at the very least, persuade Bishop Kumpfmüller to rescind the speaking ban. In addition, Haeuser even contemplated secretly joining the NSDAP. To this end, he consulted Rudolf Hess, his friend and contact in the upper echelon of the Nazi Party, who in mid-September 1933, on Hitler's order, advised Haeuser to "exercise restraint 'for formal reasons' with respect to his Church" and NSDAP membership.[109] Though disappointed by the answer, Haeuser realized that Hess's advice removed a great burden from him. In early October Haeuser commented, "Naturally, it would be my wish for me as a Catholic priest to be able on this very day to speak and fight for the cause of the Führer. And clear words and speeches and honest fighting are today as necessary as ever, since the Roman spirit, which has absolutely nothing to do with Christianity or with the religion of Jesus, today leads a ruthless, secret fight against the German spirit and German will. My appearances and fighting would perhaps have demanded even the greatest sacrifice. Nevertheless, I would have been ready to make those sacrifices out of love for the German cause and the true religion of Jesus, from which the Christian churches, influenced by Jewish *Weltanschauung*, are straying more and more. Naturally, I realize that every battle, if it is to have success, must be fought at the right moment."[110]

Hitler, however, did recognize Haeuser's years of fighting in his behalf and had Hess invite him as an honored guest to the November 1933 Reich Party Day in Nuremberg. During the festivities Haeuser received a silver commemorative medal personally from Hitler. Haeuser's honored presence at Nuremberg and the particular recognition that he received from Hitler created among National Socialist Catholics an even greater demand for him as a speaker. This demand, of course, created extra work for Bishop Kumpfmüller and his chancery, who had to deal with numerous written requests for Haeuser's presence at a particular event. Until early 1934 Kumpfmüller held his ground and refused to lift his ban against Haeuser's speaking at National Socialist events. Then suddenly, on February 5, Eberle informed Haeuser that the bishop had granted him "general speaking permission, so that from now on no one will need to ask the honorable bishop or the chancery whether Dr. Haeuser may or may not deliver a speech." In the same letter Eberle also clearly warned Haeuser to "uphold the Catholic teaching, or otherwise the honorable bishop must take action against you."[111]

Once Haeuser gained the freedom to speak publicly without restrictions, he immediately began to accept invitations to address members of various National Socialist organizations.[112] Party dignitaries would regularly introduce Haeuser as "one of the few who have for more than ten years fought in public against the greatest of our enemies, the Jews . . . and thereby paved the way for National Socialism."[113] Haeuser never failed to please his audience with a lively presentation, which normally emphasized a link between the work of the Church and the goals of National Socialism. At the same time, Haeuser also continued to intensify his comparison between Christ and Adolf Hitler. Such was especially the case in May 1934, when Haeuser addressed the National Socialist Women's Organization in Kaufbeuren.

In his Kaufbeuren talk Haeuser returned to the theme of a triumphant, militant, manly Christianity that chose battle over forgiveness. For Haeuser this Christianity served not only as the foundation of honor, but also of National Socialism. In no way was National Socialism "unchristian." By contrast, National Socialism was "a distinctly Christian movement," led by a Führer whose preeminent expression of Christianity abounded with attributes on par with the divine. Indeed, Hitler was "the great German soul and the shining star in the spiritual heaven of the German *Volk*. . . . The German people have had enough occasions to learn much about ethics from Hitler. Therefore, it is above all a moral strength that speaks through him. And in him a powerful Christian person has appeared, not a Jew!" One could easily make "a marvelous comparison . . . between the struggle of Christ and the struggle of Hitler." Anyone who "poisons the German spirit by fighting against Hitler" ultimately committed a sin against Germany and God.[114]

Soon after delivering his Kaufbeuren talk, Haeuser published *The Warrior Jesus: For Searching and Struggling Germans,* in which he developed in great detail his portrait of a heroic, militant, aggressive Christ sent to earth by God in order to establish a Church purified of Jewish practices and traditions. According to Haeuser, "Jesus did not desire to establish a new kingdom peacefully based upon Jewish tradition."[115] In July 1936 he continued to address similar themes in a talk before various NSDAP organizations in Memmingen. Even before beginning his speech, Haeuser realized that his words were controversial and repeatedly told his listeners that his remarks must not be reported to the press. Although most people in attendance obeyed his request, a few did not. Those who refused to comply shared their recollections of Haeuser's talk with Father Joseph Schmid, the Catholic pastor of Memmingen, who, in turn, reported them to the Augsburg chancery. Schmid recorded Haeuser as saying, "Christ emphasizes the great law of life (I am the bread of life); he leads the struggle against inaction, against the synagogue—Hitler does the same today. His highest law is life. . . . There was never a person given so great a task as Hitler. Christ had a great task for his time, now Hitler has an equally challenging task for the present. The past political battles are a little thing compared to the struggle for *Weltanschauung,* which begins now. . . . Christ could not finish his task—he was crucified. Hitler will see the task through. The struggle was suspended for two thousand years, now it is resumed by someone as great as the former. In religious matters Hitler is authoritative for me."[116] With these words Haeuser made it clear that he believed it was now the task of the Catholic Church to take up the mission of the warrior Christ and join Hitler in his battle to rid Germany of any Jewish influence.

Chancery officials also wrote Haeuser and demanded to know if he had made the statements that witnesses had attributed to him.[117] Evidently more people had complained than Father Schmid alone. One Protestant woman even asked why Haeuser was still in public ministry, stating, "It shows a complete lack of character that this man still eats the bread of his Church."[118] Of course, Haeuser did not easily accept these criticisms and did his best to malign the witnesses. He also attempted to clarify the nature of his comments. According to him, he merely recognized that "Hitler is an entirely brilliant personality," yet at the same time he acknowledged that "Jesus is the religious source. Hitler is a human being, Jesus is God. Nevertheless, even though he is God, he did not wish to end immediately the struggle against evil by his victory but wanted to give us a chance to continue the struggle. That such truths were completely misrepresented is not my fault but rather the fault of liars."[119] Interestingly enough, nowhere in his rebuttal did Haeuser refute the accusation that he compared Hitler with Christ nor that his comments were very different from the original words attributed to him in Father Schmid's report.[120]

On August 5 the diocese came to similar conclusions and enforced a new speaking prohibition against Haeuser.[121] Haeuser, however, did not take this speaking prohibition as seriously as he had previously.[122] In June 1938, for example, he spoke at a gathering of the local National Socialist groups from Bobingen and Straßberg in celebration of the summer solstice. There he praised Hitler for making Germans more aware and appreciative of the natural world around them.[123] Perhaps he felt quite confident that the officials of the National Socialist state would intervene in his behalf if the bishop attempted to enact canonical punishments against him.

Professing Antisemitism

As if everything that Haeuser had recently stated publicly was not enough, in 1938 under the pseudonym Gottschalk, he published *The German Weltanschauung of Joy in the Most Severe Struggle against Jewish/ Ecclesiastic Pessimism*, his strongest work against Jews. Haeuser had this work privately printed, since he found it impossible to find a publisher who was willing to publish books critical of the Catholic Church. Haeuser admitted that even the NSDAP press refused to publish such works so as not to cause offense to the Church.[124] Indeed, Haeuser's superiors would have had great trouble with this publication if they had known of its existence. Similar to his friend Father Josef Roth, Haeuser essentially argued that a Jewish spirit had permeated the Catholic Church to its core. To explain the impact of this Jewish spirit, he contrasted it with the National Socialist German *Weltanschauung*. According to Haeuser, this German worldview was a "religion of joy," whereas, in contrast, Judaism was the "*Weltanschauung* or religion of fear." The latter saw in "creation and nature the curse of God and the work of the devil." This "Jewish, pessimistic *Weltanschauung*" had in turn "greatly influenced" Catholicism and Protestantism so that in this most difficult period of history they have supported "the worst enemies of Germany." Not surprisingly, Haeuser had nothing positive to say about Jews in the book, but rather portrayed them as obstinate people who stood "in the sharpest opposition to the deeply religious demands of the prophets," who, he concluded, "must have been men of entirely different blood."

In contrast he argued that Jesus had followed in the footsteps of the prophets and "preached and taught directly in contradiction to that which the Jews believe and maintain." "Thus," he concluded, "the Jewish people are according to the sermons of the prophets as well as the entirely clear, unambiguous teaching of Jesus himself not a valuable, chosen people blessed by God."[125]

Though Haeuser's anti-Jewish and antisemitic ideology had remained constant throughout the Weimar Republic and well into the Third Reich, his 1938 work was much more negative toward Judaism, Jews, and Catholicism. As for the future, he really saw hope only in National Socialism. Much of this negativity derived directly from his Church's refusal to allow him to assume an official role in the National Socialist state. For example, in April 1935 the Bavarian State Ministry of Education and Cultural Affairs attempted to appoint Haeuser as a religious instructor at the Pasing Teaching Preparatory School.[126] In order to confirm this appointment, the government needed to obtain the approval of Bishop Kumpfmüller. The bishop, however, immediately rejected Haeuser's candidacy.[127] Despite failing to obtain the Pasing teaching position, with the assistance of Father Josef Roth, Haeuser did teach part time at the National Socialist *Oberschule* at Lake Starnberg in Feldafing, near Munich.[128] Eventually, rumors spread that Haeuser was teaching in the *Oberschule,* and the diocese intervened by forcing Haeuser to resign his position.[129]

A Disillusioned Nazi?

After his forced resignation as a part-time teacher, Haeuser would never again obtain an official position within the National Socialist state or party. Instead, in 1939 local NSDAP leadership would end up harassing him for promoting Catholic instruction in the Straßberg maternity home. Since November 1935 Haeuser had served as an unofficial chaplain to the eighty to ninety women who lived in the National Socialist *Volkswohlfahrt* (NSV; people's welfare) maternity home, housed in an old castle located on the outskirts of the town.[130] Haeuser was so successful in his ministry there that even some of the Protestant women in residence were inspired to attend Sunday mass.[131] But by August 1939 the purpose of the home had changed. According to Haeuser, the former maternity home began to serve as an internment camp for "numerous pregnant women who had to flee the German-French border area." Suddenly the local leadership of the NSV prohibited Haeuser from any further contact with the women.[132] This ban followed an already tense relationship between Haeuser and the local NSV over "educational questions."[133] Haeuser immediately wrote the local NSV leaders and threatened to report them to the new Reich Ministry of Defense if they did not provide him access to the inhabitants.[134] His threats proved pointless. Haeuser soon learned that party and state leaders had no interest in promoting religion in the German state. They viewed Haeuser's means of promoting National Socialism as old-fashioned and out of date.

Haeuser gradually understood the dilemma he faced. In particular, he faced the indifference of the Augsburg *Kreisleiter* (district leader) Hermann Boch, who had no use for religion or for Haeuser. In September 1939 Boch had ordered the destruction of a local field cross. Though by nightfall the youths entrusted with the execution of this assignment had refused to carry out the order, Haeuser got wind of the plan and sent a telegram to Rudolf Hess. Haeuser still felt important. Later, in July 1940 Haeuser received the honor of addressing the military personnel at the Lechfeld air base. However, shortly before he was to give his talk, *Kreisleiter* Boch prohibited Haeuser from speaking.[135] Even before the incident, Haeuser had written to his friend Otto Merkt, mayor of Kempten and member of the Old-Catholic Church, and confided, "I fear that the Führer is mistaken if he believes in the *Volksgemeinschaft* and the unity of his party. I fight a difficult battle with party men for the cause of the Führer. In Augsburg the relationship is not good. Our task is to educate and to awaken honest, German, religiously faithful individuals. And, directly aiming at my sacrificial activity, the materialistic and egotistical party bigwigs take offense and fight against me with lies and deceit, even though I have already suffered enough from the lies and deceits of certain Catholic lords."[136]

Soon tension between Haeuser and the local NSDAP leadership increased.[137] So disgusted was Haeuser with the local NSDAP leadership that he even brought his concerns to the pulpit on a Lenten Sunday in 1943 when he preached against the ill-treatment of women in the NSV "camp." He immediately received a visit by a Gestapo agent who questioned him. Haeuser admitted that he had made several statements in defense of women and thus fulfilled his moral obligation. Luckily, for Haeuser, he knew the agent and received only a stern warning. However, the experience was threatening enough to force him to keep his criticisms of the state to himself for the remainder of the Third Reich, though he did inform his congregation of the incident on Good Friday.[138] Haeuser most probably enjoyed playing the part of the persecuted "prophet," especially on this holiest of days.

After his 1943 Good Friday homily, Haeuser chose to keep a low profile. Instead of speaking at party rallies, he busied himself with his parish ministry and with his own writing, much of which he never published. By May 1941 Haeuser had lost his main contact with the party when Rudolf Hess mysteriously flew to Scotland and was immediately imprisoned by the British. Much earlier, Hitler had removed himself from any personal contact with Haeuser. Even the local NSDAP leadership stopped using Haeuser as a speaker. Despite the party's neglect, Haeuser, like so many Germans, refused to lose faith in Adolf Hitler. No matter how slighted he may have felt by the actions of lower-level party members, Haeuser continued to see "true greatness in the person of the Führer."[139]

Haeuser perceived much more than just "true greatness" in Hitler. His written works reveal that he also attributed a messianic role to Hitler. For Haeuser, Hitler was divine, and his National Socialist ideology was God-given. He placed it nearly on the same level as Church doctrine. Like his friend Josef Roth, Haeuser came to believe that Judaism had forever tainted the Church and its teachings. For that reason, he believed National Socialism represented Christianity in its purest form, especially as a religion of conflict. He also believed that Christ was a warrior, whom God the Father sent into the world to redeem it through battle. And although Haeuser accepted that Jesus was Jewish, he essentially stripped away every element of Jewish culture and religion associated with Jesus and made him into an Aryan knight, without specifically identifying him as such.

Toward the end of Hitler's regime the problems that Haeuser encountered, especially with the younger, less church-oriented National Socialists, led him to conclude that National Socialism, similar to Christianity, had become corrupted. However, he did not directly blame Jews, the perennial National Socialist scapegoats. Instead, he blamed it on materialistic, greedy Germans who, unlike himself, did not belong to the Old Fighter generation and had never experienced the struggle for power. Still, Haeuser identified greed as a Jewish characteristic. Haeuser even feared that this greed had begun to affect also the older generation of National Socialists.

Sadly, what Haeuser failed to see was the total incompatibility of Christianity with National Socialism. In no way could an individual reconcile Jesus' command to love one's neighbor with the hate-filled ideology of National Socialism. Nevertheless, Haeuser disregarded this overarching incompatibility and instead accepted a narrowly defined understanding of "neighbor." In turn, Haeuser, like many Catholics attracted by National Socialism, emphasized the aspects and qualities of his religious tradition that intersected or mirrored those of National Socialism. Of course, this included the deicide charge and theology that portrayed Jews as the Other, unworthy of God's love, grace, and salvation. Accepting such teachings as fact made it much easier for ordinary Catholic Germans to take the next step and embrace or at least give credence to National Socialist racial ideology.

Despite the inherent contradictions between the fundamental biblical teachings of Christ and the racist, exclusivist theories of National Socialism, Father Dr. Philipp Haeuser found no problems in dedicating himself to the Hitler movement. Haeuser believed it was perfectly acceptable to be an ordained Catholic priest and an agitator for Hitler. He was not alone in this belief. Father Anton Heuberger, like Haeuser, made his National Socialist convictions public. He dared to ask, "Can a Catholic priest be a National Socialist?" Heuberger answered affirmatively. In contrast to Haeuser, a staunch nationalism and the loss of his brother in the First World War primarily drew Heuberger to National Socialism. Heuberger felt so strongly about his National Socialist beliefs that he even became a turncoat by denouncing a priestly colleague to the ruthless Gestapo. Such was the extent of his faith in National Socialism.

5—From Nationalism to National Socialism

In November 1936 Father Anton Heuberger, the pastor of the Visitation of Mary parish in Hitzhofen, sent Dr. Walter Krauß, the *Kreisleiter* of Eichstätt, a public letter that addressed the question of whether a Catholic priest could be both a faithful minister and a good National Socialist.[1] Heuberger answered in the affirmative. Indeed, he replied, a German Catholic priest could embrace the tenets of National Socialism and still be a good priest. Seizing an opportunity for Nazi propaganda, especially among Catholics, *Kreisleiter* Krauß ordered the letter printed and distributed. Copies of the letter spread like wildfire, first through the Eichstätt diocese and then to all parts of Germany. In their fervor, Heuberger and Krauß caught the diocesan chancery and Dr. Michael Rackl, bishop of Eichstätt, off guard. This is especially noteworthy, since relations between diocesan clergy and Nazi officials at the time were at best contentious.[2] Although Rackl knew from previous experiences that Heuberger could be troublesome to his Church superiors, the bishop never suspected that he would proclaim so publicly his support for the Hitler movement.

Anton Heuberger rejected the Versailles Treaty and envisioned some kind of patriotic destiny of greatness for his nation and its leaders. He was also a latent antisemite. Heuberger firmly believed in his aptitude for leadership and lamented the failure of his superiors to recognize his "inherent" gifts. Frustrated with his own career in the diocese and the alleged neglect of his Church superiors, Heuberger turned to the party for recognition and fame. This radical choice met with mixed results and ultimately led to Heuberger's estrangement from his bishop and from the majority of his fellow priests.

Born into a family of modest means on December 17, 1890, in Mörnsheim, Bavaria, in the diocese of Eichstätt, Heuberger experienced a normal childhood. From the fall of 1901 he attended the gymnasium in Eichstätt. Then suddenly in the summer of 1903 he, along with his brother Georg, decided to follow in the footsteps of their uncle, Father Joseph Heuberger, and become priests of the Eichstätt diocese.[3] With a clean bill of health from his doctor, a good recommendation from his parish priest, Father Ludwig Funk, and counsel from his priest-uncle, the bishop and seminary rectors easily accepted Anton. Soon Anton and Georg became inseparable roommates in the seminary.[4]

During his seminary study and the first year of priesthood, Heuberger experienced several events that, according to him, greatly affected his outlook on life. First, on July 7, 1909, his mother, whom he loved dearly, died after a long illness.[5] Then shortly after his ordination to the deaconate on June 7, 1914, the First World War broke out. Being in the midst of preparing for his ordination, Heuberger was not called up to serve in the army.[6] Georg, however, entered the German army as a noncommissioned officer and, on October 23, 1915, died in a battle near Belgrade.[7] Thus Anton, just ordained on May 30, 1915, by Bishop Johannes Leo von Mergel, had to deal not only with the death of a family member but also with the absence of someone who was a dear friend in whom he could regularly confide.[8]

In his memoirs Heuberger remarked how, until the death of his brother and up until the end of World War I, he was a supporter of the Catholic Center Party and, after its foundation in 1918, a supporter of its southern counterpart, the Bavarian People's Party. According to Heuberger, his brother and he closely followed politics in the bylines and articles of Catholic newspapers. Georg's death, however, caused him to view the world around him more critically. In addition, his own parish ministry that brought him into hospitals—institutions that cared for both Catholics and Protestants—gave him a different ecumenical perspective. This in turn caused Heuberger to examine more critically the political and religious rhetoric of his own Church. In an attempt to rectify the misinterpretations of his Catholic tradition, Heuberger wrote letters and articles and submitted them to various Catholic newspapers. But they were rejected outright. Then he turned to the non-Catholic *Fränk-ischer Kurier,* which published a lengthy article in which, among other things, he argued for unity among Germans. Because of this call for unity he believed the Center Party press attacked his writing. This led Heuberger only further to seek out an all-German party, one that would embrace a "Pan-German" solution to the problems facing Germany.[9]

Heuberger's search for a party that would embody and represent the interests of all Germans led him to the National Socialists. According to him, it was in 1919 or 1921 that he "heard the name Adolf Hitler for the first time." An older man had spoken "enthusiastically about a meeting in Munich at which Corporal Hitler gave a speech." This older man passionately declared to his listeners that "only *that man* will be Germany's savior." Clearly moved, Heuberger nevertheless argued that he "did not take such people and their narrow-minded grandiloquence seriously, although [he] respected their often idealistic intentions." Still, the attraction remained with him. He was not alone in this fascination. According to Heuberger, some of his fellow priests had argued that leaders like Hitler would be assets "in the struggle against Red rule." Yet he continued to hold doubts about the National Socialists because he feared that "their neopaganism and racism could become dangerous to the Church."[10] Eventually, however, curiosity led Heuberger to explore the *Weltanschauung* of the Nazi movement along with its antisemitism and anti-Catholicism.

In his writings Heuberger provides little insight into the reasons for his antisemitism. In the fourth volume of his memoirs, written some time around 1961, he admitted that he was an antisemite and blamed his father and teachers for instilling in him this negative trait. However, he made no mention of Germany's persecution and systematic murder of Jews during the Holocaust. Rather, Heuberger stated only that "all Jews should be able to return from the Diaspora to an adequate and safe Jewish land." He continued, "In this sense, it has always been our principle: Jews belong in a Jewish land where they can do honorable national work, just as other peoples do in their countries, thus competing fairly with other nations as an equal partner nation, in order to achieve at last the solution of a creeping and smoldering national and international problem." Such a quote reveals that, even in the 1960s, Heuberger still believed there was a "Jewish problem." For him, the foundation of Israel now provided a solution to this moot point and would ensure that Jews stayed far away from him and his fatherland.[11]

Though Heuberger did not discuss his own antisemitism in depth, he left enough of a paper trail to offer a clear insight into his character. In

May 1916 Bishop Leo von Mergel noted that Heuberger "seriously" needed to control his "arrogance and touchiness."[12] Yet, the 1925 report of his pastor, Father Maximilian Koeniger, who would later become his adversary, seemed to contradict the bishop's characterization of Heuberger when he described him as "a good priest," who was "industrious and conscientious in teaching catechism, in sermons, and in all other pastoral respects."[13] However, a report of the same year by Father Dr. Johannes Baptist Götz, dean of the deanery of Ingolstadt, where Heuberger served, described Heuberger as not only "enthusiastic and conscientious" but also "sneaky and conceited." Götz further offered evidence to back up his assessment of the young priest by stating that Heuberger had established a youth secretariat "without prior communication with his parish council." He also accused Heuberger of organizing a youth event without approval from his local pastor. In addition, Götz reported that during the last election Heuberger, a member of the Bavarian People's Party, caused even "more confusion among the people than had already existed." As a result of this, Heuberger resigned from the Bavarian People's Party after having reproached its chairman by telephone in a highly detailed and rather forward manner." Nevertheless, Götz concluded that in his priestly life Heuberger was "irreproachable."[14]

Little is known about Heuberger's first six years of ministry other than that he served in three different parishes—not unusual for a newly ordained priest. Finally, in August 1921, Heuberger received a more permanent assignment as a parochial vicar at St. Anton parish in Ingolstadt. In 1924 the bishop also named him a religion teacher for the parish's neighboring state schools while he continued his pastoral duties at St. Anton.[15]

While at St. Anton, Heuberger's ministry with youth caught the attention of some in the diocese. In 1925 Adolf Speinle, diocesan director for youth ministry, appointed Heuberger the district leader of the Catholic Youth and Young Men's Association. A few years later, when his colleague resigned, he assumed the position of diocesan director.[16] It is evident that Heuberger relished his new position and received praise from the adults and youth whom he served.[17] Such praise, however, caused difficulty for Heuberger in his relationship with his fellow priests, who often displayed their envy of his success in ministry.[18] In particular, his pastor, Father Koeniger, held in contempt the young priest's pompous leadership style and his lack of respect for Koeniger's authority as pastor.[19] Heuberger knew about Koeniger's negative feelings toward him and attempted several times to have the vicar general intervene in his behalf to remove him from Koeniger's authority.[20] In 1928 the situation grew difficult enough for Heuberger to write to the chancery and offer his resignation. He portrayed himself as a sacrificial lamb when he stated that a "person must sacrifice himself in order for the situation to be served."[21] The diocesan officials, however, did not take Heuberger's side in the disputes. Instead, they continually sided with Father Koeniger. As early as 1926 Dr. Klemens Wagner, the Eichstätt vicar general, wrote Heuberger and reminded him that he "should not independently carry out his parish pastoral duties and diocesan youth ministry according to his best knowledge and conscience, but perform them under the leadership of his parish council."[22] In 1928 Wagner had to remind Heuberger once again of his duty to work with the proper authorities.[23] Clearly, the bishop should have listened to Father Götz, who previously had warned that Heuberger's "appointment as director of the Catholic Youth and Young Men's association" did not appear "to be felicitous in all respects."[24]

In 1931 diocesan officials permanently intervened in Heuberger's youth ministry by forcing him to take sick leave. During his time away, the bishop filled the position with another priest. This action devastated Heuberger, who prized his position of power.[25] Clearly, the demands of his ministries and the continual pressure from the diocese had a negative impact on him. A doctor had even diagnosed Heuberger with suffering from a "nervous heart ailment and nervous dyspepsia" and prescribed "six weeks of recuperative leave."[26] Previously, Heuberger also had divulged to his diocesan superiors that he had rheumatism—a condition that would ail him throughout his life.[27] However, Heuberger's precarious health was not the sole reason for his Church superiors to change his ministry. The diocese had received numerous complaints about his behavior, which revealed that perhaps Heuberger's power had gone to his head. Thus, while attending a festival in his hometown, Heuberger had allowed himself to be driven about in "a glass chariot" as if he were a bishop. Heuberger also gained a questionable reputation in the diocese for his extremely pompous nationalistic speeches and sermons at youth rallies. Yet, when diocesan officials questioned him about these and other actions, he freely admitted that such approaches merely fulfilled his mission to integrate Catholic youths into a "grand German youth front for the purpose of breaking the chains imposed by Versailles."[28] Such bold claims concerned diocesan officials, who wondered seriously about the direction in which Heuberger was taking their Catholic youth. Ultimately, they felt compelled to remove him from his youth work.

Following his period of rest and recuperation, Heuberger applied for the pastorate of the parish in Hitzhofen, a relatively small, remote Bavarian community. As pastor, Heuberger would also be responsible for Catholics in two smaller, nearby communities, Lippertshofen and Oberzell. The latter parishioners normally traveled to Hitzhofen to attend mass. Every third Sunday, according to tradition and diocesan regulations, the parish mass was to be held in the church in Lippertshofen only. Since the government offered no objections to the appointment, on August 1, 1931, the bishop named Heuberger as pastor of the community.[29] However, after being installed as pastor, Heuberger immediately started to cause waves in the parish and the diocese by requesting faculties for bination in order to hold two masses every third Sunday so that the people of Hitzhofen would not have to walk several kilometers to Lippertshofen. Heuberger also took it upon himself to suggest to Vicar General Wagner that the diocese place the filial community of Lippertshofen under the Assumption of Mary parish in Gaimersheim.[30] On September 25, 1931, Father Wagner answered Heuberger's suggestions in a curt letter, which ordered him not to change the current order of church services "in any way." He also refused his request for bination on the express order of the bishop. Furthermore, Wagner ordered him "to carry on with his pastoral duties in his parish to the best of his knowledge, conscience, and skill as has been hitherto the tradition; and . . . to leave all other responsibilities to the higher Church authority."[31] Clearly, the diocesan authorities were not going to allow Heuberger any latitude to influence decisions normally reserved for diocesan officials.

Heuberger simply refused to obey the decision of his superiors and did as he wished. By the end of June the Catholics of Lippertshofen were complaining to the Bavarian state government about their pastor's failure to hold mass in Lippertshofen.[32] On December 6, 1933, an official from the Bavarian Ministry for Education and Culture wrote to the diocese and demanded an immediate resolution of the problem.[33] On December 20, amid the busy Advent season, Dr. Karl Kiefer, the newly appointed vicar general, replied to the state official's concerns by acknowledging that Heuberger suffered from rheumatism. He also noted that Heuberger was the first priest ever to complain about his ministry in the Hitzhofen parish. Nevertheless, Kiefer agreed to Heuberger's request for bination, which enabled him to hold an early Sunday mass in Hitzhofen on those Sundays for which mass was scheduled in the Lippertshofen church.[34] This decision still did not please Heuberger, who, throughout his ministry in Hitzhofen, continued to quarrel with the diocese and the members of the Lippertshofen community over this issue.[35]

The Lippertshofen dispute would not be the only time that Heuberger challenged the authority of his diocesan superiors. There was something in his personality that continually pushed him to seek recognition, which in turn brought him into conflict with his diocesan superiors. Even after he was made pastor of Hitzhofen, Heuberger believed he was destined for something much greater. In late 1933 and early 1934 the activities of a fellow priest, Father Willibald Johann Wanger of Gaimersheim, finally gave Heuberger the opportunity to make a name for himself.

Wanger was a priest of the Eichstätt diocese, and he had served in missions in Africa for almost twenty-five years. In 1921 he returned to Germany and his diocese.[36] His years in the missions had made him more tolerant than most of his confreres and also had imbued him with a healthy dose of skepticism he used to critique the activities of the German government. His missionary work also taught him to move beyond the traditional role of pastor and reach out to his parishioners, both spiritually and materially. The citizens of Gaimersheim highly respected and supported Wanger, especially because he was willing to offer loans or assist them in obtaining loans. He also gave advice in secular matters.[37] The deanery clergy, however, did not appreciate his popularity and often refused to invite him to their gatherings.[38] In addition, they also never forgave Wanger for undermining his pastor, Father Franz Xaver Bittner, in his attempt to win the presidency of the Catholic Worker's Association. The enmity grew so great between the two men that the chancery, upon request from the Gaimersheim mayor and his council, had to intervene.[39]

In November 1933 Wanger unwittingly gave Heuberger and other priests in the Gaimersheim deanery the opportunity to act against him. The occasion was a gathering for priests at Bittner's parish, the Assumption of the Blessed Virgin, in Gaimersheim. While passing through the church's sacristy on his way to the parish courtyard, Heuberger accidentally overheard Wanger make a derogatory comment concerning the recent Reichstag elections and referendum of November 12. According to Heuberger, Wanger told the people in the sacristy that "the best thing would be to write on the ballot 'Kiss my ass.'" Then Wanger laughed heartily "in a disdainful, contemptuous manner." When Heuberger joined his fellow priests, who had not invited Wanger to their gathering, he told them what Wanger had just said. Heuberger publicly expressed his disapproval of Wanger's statements and stated that they "should not be surprised if we priests experience more problems." An awkward silence followed, with no one daring to offer a reply.[40] Of course, Heuberger did not immediately act on this incident. However, in December 1933 two further incidents occurred. The first took place during a walk that Heuberger took with Fathers Joseph Biersack of Eitensheim and Georg Graf of Hofstetten. Graf confided to them that Wanger had accused Hitler of participating in homosexual activities. Soon thereafter someone wrote down what Wanger allegedly had said about Hitler and gave the incriminating document to Heuberger. Indignant over these statements, Heuberger denounced Wanger in early January by delivering the written statement to Kern, an SS officer in Ingolstadt.[41] The police immediately arrested Wanger, interrogated him, and placed him in so-called protective custody.[42] On January 19, 1934, Heuberger repeated his charges against Wanger to the criminal police during an interrogation conducted in Hitzhofen. He also accused Wanger of being a *Volksschädling*—destructive to the German *Volk*.[43]

A witch hunt followed, in which Father Wanger was the main target. In addition to Heuberger, the police interrogated another seven priests as well as other acquaintances of Wanger. Instead of supporting Wanger, the majority of them gave testimony that corroborated Heuberger's statements. Several of the priests also provided additional statements that further incriminated Wanger.[44] For example, Father Sebastian Speth of Etting stated that during a mid-1933 clergy meeting Wanger accused Hitler of joining Dr. Ferdinand Sauerbruch, a leading physician and supporter of the Third Reich, in sexual liaisons with a young girl.[45] At a similar clerical meeting in January 1934 Father Sebastian Ernst from Oberhaunstadt claimed he heard Wanger making statements against the government in regard to "euthanasia, sterilization, and forced abortion." According to Ernst, Wanger declared that the state mandated that "a girl who, for example, was impregnated by a Jew, must have an abortion."[46]

During the interrogations on January 23, 1934, the chancery made an appeal to the *Sonderkommissar* in Ingolstadt, promising "to transfer Wanger if that would dispense with the matter." Their appeal was of no use because Wanger, during an interrogation, had already confirmed the truth of the accounts. Wanger also stated that he took "a cautious position toward the current system"; however, he agreed that as a Catholic priest he had come to accept the state because of the signing of the Concordat."[47]

On March 31, 1934, proceedings against Wanger began in Munich. Fathers Heuberger, Graf, and Ernst, along with the sacristan and two additional parish members, served as witnesses against Wanger. On April 19, 1934, the court found Wanger guilty of an offense against the Reich president's March 21, 1933, decree to defend the government from malicious attacks and sentenced him to seven months' imprisonment and payment of all trial costs. The court, however, gave him credit for the two and a half months he had already served in protective custody prior to the trial.[48]

Heuberger's decision to denounce one of his fellow priests naturally revealed his willingness to support to the extreme the goals of the new state. Clearly, one could attribute the Wanger case to resentment among clergymen who found a convenient way to deal with one of their number whom they seriously disliked. Wanger's own popularity among the Gaimersheim population created even more animosity between him and his fellow clerics. Nevertheless, Heuberger's actions and comments during the proceedings went a step further than his confreres'. Not only did Heuberger attack Wanger's words and actions, but he also attacked his character by using the derogatory term *"Volksschädling"* to describe his clerical opponent.[49] The use of such a word also reveals how deeply National Socialist ideology had affected Heuberger's worldview. Even prior to the Wanger incident, Heuberger had begun to immerse himself in National Socialist thought by firmly convincing himself that a bridge could be built between his Church and National Socialism. He recorded this belief in his reflections on Hitler's *Mein Kampf:* "Still wary because of the opinion we had been taught regarding the dangerousness of this book, I absorbed it calmly. And when I had finished reading it, my judgment was complete as well: if its contents are genuine and honest, a reconciliation on a national and Christian basis would still be possible. I also passed on this impression to several colleagues and managed to get them to read the book as well."[50]

On November 17, 1936, Heuberger chose to make his approval of National Socialism public when he sent the Eichstätt *Kreisleiter,* Dr. Walter Krauß, an open letter that addressed the question of whether a Catholic priest could be a National Socialist.[51] This letter followed the rebuff of his diocesan superiors to appoint him pastor of the church in Gunzenhausen, a parish much larger than Hitzhofen, and their refusal to solve the contentious issue over the filial church of Lippertshofen.[52] Nevertheless, Heuberger never believed that his action compromised his priesthood or the situation of his Church in the National Socialist state. Rather, he believed his actions were perfectly justified. According to him, it was his Church superiors who were mistaken and who continually forced him to accept the role of the sacrificial lamb. He wrote, "I have always made an effort and will continue to make an effort to my dying day to serve my Church sincerely and genuinely even if I have to bear the cross and am prevented from being in any way successful."[53]

Along with his open letter, Heuberger also sent a brief cover letter that explained his reasons for writing and how he felt the candid letter should be used. He addressed the cover letter to Krauß and wrote, "I can and should no longer remain silent and, therefore, pledge my full name that this is my most sacred conviction. I put forth only one condition: print it without any changes, without any deletions, and without any additions. The mood instilled in the *Volk* is not favorable to enthusiastic cooperation with the Führer's rebuilding work; that is not as it should be, and it will be atoned for by a priest who has for years tried to promote the enthusiastic collaboration of priests. There has to be one man who sacrifices himself courageously. Heil Hitler! Yours devotedly, A. Heuberger, Pastor."[54]

Heuberger framed his open letter around a dramatic fictional dialogue between himself and his deceased brother Georg. At the beginning of the letter, Heuberger, who finds himself visiting his brother's grave in the World War I "military cemetery in Pocarevac near Belgrade," reflectively looks on his brother's tombstone and asks, "Dear brother, have I done wrong striving honestly all these years to be a good priest and a good National Socialist?" The importance of this question suddenly causes the ground to tremble, the tombstone to be uprooted, and his brother to rise from the dead "with his hand lying over his heart, which had been blown apart by a grenade." Excited at the prospect of conversing with his brother, to whom he was devoted, Anton seizes the opportunity to pose a series of questions to elicit his brother's response.[55] The remainder of the letter focuses on these questions and answers.

In his letter Heuberger first tackled the question of whether Christianity had anything to fear from National Socialism's *Weltanschauung,* especially with the latter's emphasis on blood and soil. He dismissed these fears by assuring his readers that the movement's desire to strengthen the *Volksgemeinschaft* had only a positive effect on religion and Christianity. He also reminded his readers that the state still allowed priests to continue their "work of converting people to the Church's positive Christianity from the thousands upon thousands of pulpits, from village to village, from city to city; no parishioners [were] forbidden to enter [their] houses of God, to receive [their] holy sacraments, to approach [their] sacrificial altars." He then declared what he believed had been positive accomplishments of the National Socialist state: the Winter Assistance and Reich Labor Service Programs, satisfied farmers and workers, strengthening of the family, crushing of Bolshevism, "fight against sloth in any form," and a "courageous launching of the most gigantic projects for the pride and defense and welfare of the nation." For Heuberger, these were aspects of a great "German miracle" that benefited both National Socialism and Christianity and could never have been managed by priests alone, even with the help of their "God-given strength of grace."[56]

Heuberger also addressed the claims of those who believed that the National Socialists' positive form of Christianity ignored "the dogmatic, the supernatural, the confessional Christianity." According to him, such positive Christianity meant "more religion and less creed, more agreement and less division," and ultimately "more of the positive values of Christianity to reinforce the rebuilding work of our God-given Führer!" In essence, he was calling for an end to religious divisions. Heuberger even argued that "every member of the *Volk* must be valuable" to the leader of Germany, even those who through their own fault or others' fault have "lost church-based Christianity." Consequently, Hitler had "to demand from everyone at least the positive Christianity as perceived by the National Socialist worldview." He continued, "The apostate from the Church may have to settle for this and will at least be a valuable member of the *Volksgemeinschaft,* but the faithful of the Church will exceed this state and will call forth the supernatural forces of its revelatory faith—transfiguring and enriching as they are—and like the former will be a valuable member of the *Volksgemeinschaft* as well as a valuable member of the community of the Church. It will become clear which of the two is the more valuable citizen, and the Führer will, I am sure, base his final decision on that fact."[57]

With such comments Heuberger issued a veiled warning to his fellow Catholics, especially to the Church hierarchy, that they must work more willingly with the new state or suffer the consequences. However, his words also contained expressions of hope that the Church still had time to "conform" to the new Germany. Nevertheless, Heuberger's comments regarding "blood and soil" revealed that he had already set about to unite and in some cases even replace Christian theology with Nazi ideology. According to him, the old, traditional, "theologically ordered value system" centered on God, Christ, Church, in that order. For Heuberger the new system now placed *Volk* and fatherland first. He continued, "Place your hand on your heart and ask your blood and remember that the eternal God allowed you to be born first as a child of your *Volk,* and then allowed you again to be born as a child of your Church, probably not in order to cancel the first, but to fulfill it." Heuberger then concluded that "blood is such a precious possession that even God could think of nothing better to give to his son, and soil is something so valuable that, when the great sacrificial mystery of our faith is celebrated, the eternal God resides mysteriously in the grain that grew from this soil. Tell our theologians that, while they did learn to capture the infinite God in finite concepts, the Infinite also flows beyond these limiting terms about God and allows his footprints to be seen on the beauty of our homeland and allows his countenance to shine from the face of the millions who have walked and will walk over it, following the flow of blood of the centuries."[58]

Heuberger not only embraced these basic tenets of National Socialist ideology, but he also began to reject the authority of the Church hierarchy, especially on matters regarding the relationship between church and state. He found, on the one hand, that it was not "so terrible" that the German bishops had "so often and so openly written and preached against the state," attributing this to "quite a few among them who, disappointed in their egotistical hopes and wishes" that were not "totally fulfilled, want[ed] to show pious opposition in this harmless way." On the other hand, he feared that their activities, especially by promoting "many luxuriantly sprouting forms of worship" that have been "smuggled in from effeminately sentimental southern latitudes," served to choke "the ancient, unpretentious, masculine, pithy German kind of piety." He also believed that the bishops' challenge to the state-sponsored German community school was unfounded. These schools, he fancied, would replace denominational ones. He asked, "Is it really so terrible if Catholic and Protestant Christian children sit together when studying secular subjects? . . . Indeed we have the same blood, the same language, the same Lord God in heaven, the same history on earth!"[59]

Not content to address only his concerns about the German bishops, Heuberger also used his open letter to criticize the papacy. He admitted that it was difficult to "go along with people who blaspheme the papacy and who dismiss priestly celibacy as immoral and who strive for a national church free from Rome." However, certain attacks on the papacy were justified because "some popes had disgraced the papacy by a life not appropriate to the title 'representative of God, stand-in for Christ.'" He continued, "Let us be honest: there is not only joy, there is also the burden of the papacy."[60] In this comment Heuberger revealed his sympathy for those who criticized the German Catholic Church for sending annual contributions to the Vatican. Still, he was not prepared to agree with those extreme German nationalist Catholics who called for a German National Catholic Church free from papal control. Heuberger still considered himself a son of the Church in communion with Rome. Nevertheless, his ties with National Socialism encouraged him to question some practices of his faith tradition. To this end, he challenged the vow of priests to live a life of celibacy—a life choice that went directly against the National Socialist racial policy promoting family and its role in the *Volksgemeinschaft*—by dismissing the biblical basis for the practice and directing the brunt of his complaint to the papacy.[61] He also endorsed the underlying National Socialist attack on celibacy when he stated, "This criticism is not based on hatred of religion, but on well-intended concerns for the *Volk* and for a rich growth of the *Volk*. God's Son did not venture to commit weak men to such a lifelong, heroic command; only God's representative, the pope, ventured to do so."[62]

After making these criticisms, Heuberger concluded his letter by encouraging Catholics to participate fully in the new National Socialist state. He charged Catholics to move "away from your self-dug catacombs with your sighs of persecution and yearning for martyrdom! Away from your self-created ghetto of associations. . . . Join the popular front, your *Volk*, newly formed for you by God, in genuine, honest, humble piety and find the courage to believe, to have unshakable faith in our inspired Führer and his movement, and many doubters and mistaken and embittered people will also once again find the way back to faith in you and your holy mission."[63]

Kreisleiter Krauß did not waste any time exploiting the contents of the letter. On Monday, November 30, 1936, during an evening rally of the NSDAP the *Kreisleiter* passionately read Heuberger's letter to an overflowing crowd gathered in a meeting hall in Eichstätt.[64] On December 2, 1936, the local *Eichstätter Volkszeitung* ran an article that covered Krauß's presentation of Heuberger's letter at the NSDAP gathering.[65] Realizing the discontent that his letter might cause, especially among his Church superiors, Heuberger sent a personal letter to his bishop, Michael Rackl, on December 1, assuring him of his loyalty to the Church. He told Rackl that as a "simple priest" he had to "make sacrifices in order to achieve spiritual goals" so that he "without any conflict of conscience could enthusiastically serve the Church and the new state." Heuberger expressed urgency in his letter because he believed a time would come when the people would refuse to support their priests if Church authorities continued to appear in opposition to the government and volunteered to "offer an appropriate statement" if any "misuse or misunderstanding" resulted from his public letter.[66]

Heuberger's open letter did not please his diocesan superiors. Eichstätt was a small diocese, and normally its clergymen were very tightknit and would not break rank publicly, especially against the wishes of the bishop. The difficulties that the diocese had already experienced with the Eichstätt government and local Nazi officials, especially *Kreisleiter* Krauß, made it almost impossible to imagine a member of the clergy writing such a public letter in support of a closer alliance between the Church and National Socialism. On December 2 Vicar General Kiefer decided to investigate the issue more closely and immediately wrote to Heuberger, ordering him to send an unaltered copy of his open letter to the chancery. Heuberger complied and sent Kiefer a copy of his public letter.[67] In a cover letter Heuberger compared his action to that of Bishop Alois Hudal, the Austrian rector of Anima, the Austrian-German Theological College in Rome, and an outspoken supporter of National Socialism, who in October 1936 had publicly attacked Bolshevism and praised National Socialism.[68] Heuberger explained that he wrote the letter after concluding that not even "an increase of prayers and devotions and sermons and pilgrimages" could free the Church "from its miserable situation" face to face with the state.[69] In the Hitzhofen pastor's mind, a more drastic step had to be taken to repair this broken relationship.

On December 9 diocesan officials met in Eichstätt and discussed the contents of the letter. However, they were unable to reach a unanimous decision for a response.[70] A period of inaction followed. Finally, on December 30, 1936, Bishop Rackl broke the silence. He issued a statement on the situation and ordered the declaration to be printed, distributed throughout the diocese, and read from every pulpit on Sunday, January 3, 1937.[71] By this time *Kreisleiter* Krauß already had Gestapo agents circulating copies of Heuberger's letter throughout his area of authority. Heuberger also distributed copies of his letter to those he thought would benefit from its contents.[72] For these reasons, Rackl felt compelled to act. In his statement Rackl accused Heuberger of undertaking "an arbitrary special action" that "in no way would find the approval of the bishop." Rackl sarcastically remarked that "neither the Führer and Reich chancellor nor the head of the Catholic Church or the diocesan bishop had appointed the pastor of Hitzhofen to establish peace in the church-political situation in Germany." He also accused Heuberger of heresy by "abandoning the eternal truth of Catholic dogma and the unchanging principles of Catholic moral teachings . . . in a significant way" and exhorted "the Catholic *Volk* . . . not to allow themselves to be brought into confusion by a single priest." Then he threatened Heuberger with canonical penalties, which included possible removal from the Hitzhofen parish, if he did not desist.[73]

On the same day that Rackl issued his statement to the pastors of his diocese, Heuberger wrote Rackl and assured him of his loyalty and his devotion to the priesthood. He also reminded the bishop that even "our good folks view every priest as an enemy of the Führer, to whom they are bound in fervent love." According to Heuberger, "it was this perception that forced [him] compellingly to take pen into hand." Heuberger then requested an audience with the bishop to discuss the entire situation with his "spiritual father." Although respectful of his superior, Heuberger displayed an overabundance of confidence for a priest who had just placed himself in direct confrontation with his ecclesiastical superiors. Heuberger clearly believed that state officials would continue to support him and that the bishop would feel outside pressure to endorse his written words. However, Heuberger's diocesan superiors were far from putting any stamp of approval on the priest's statements. Still, in their reply to Heuberger, his superiors seemed less concerned with his praise of National Socialism and more worried about his criticisms of celibacy and his "lack of respect for the Church and its hierarchy." They concluded that Heuberger had always been "a man in a cocoon," who had continually "isolated himself from others." They viewed him as a conceited individual who had been "slighted and now seeks to impress at the cost of his soul." They also feared that Heuberger planned to use his remark about celibacy as a "springboard for a move into world fame."[74]

By this time the bishop's concern over the affair had prompted Heuberger to make an overture of peace. On January 2, 1937, Heuberger, accompanied by his friend Father Johannes Wagner, who was also from his hometown of Mörnsheim, attempted to gain an audience with Bishop Rackl.[75] Rackl, reportedly ill, was unable to receive Heuberger. Vicar General Kiefer did agree to meet with him. The discussions during this meeting and a subsequent letter from Heuberger to the bishop convinced Rackl "sufficiently" of the priest's scandalous intentions toward the Church.[76] The chancery also continued to receive more evidence against Heuberger from dioceses throughout Germany.[77] One letter, addressed to Kiefer, was particularly alarming because the author, the above-mentioned Father Wagner, who knew Heuberger well, reported that he believed Heuberger had broken off his relationship with the Church. Wagner concluded that Heuberger was "capable of any misdeed."[78]

Heuberger still had his supporters, however. Upon hearing about the public reading of the bishop's statement from the pulpits of Catholic churches throughout the diocese, *Kreisleiter* Krauß decided to help Heuberger by inciting the people of Hitzhofen to assemble at a rally in support of their pastor. On the afternoon of January 3, 1937, Krauß, along with two of his assistants, drove to Hitzhofen and approached a leading parishioner, demanding that he call "an assembly of loyalty" for Heuberger. At first the parishioner refused, but later relented when Krauß threatened him. Krauß did not wish to call the assembly himself because he wanted it to appear as a spontaneous act on the part of Heuberger's parishioners for their pastor. For logistical reasons, the assembly was held the following evening. Amazingly, despite Heuberger's temperamental disposition, the majority of Heuberger's parishioners, including a contingent of people from Lippertshofen, the filial church that

Heuberger often ignored, attended the event. During that affair, Heuberger was compared to Abbot Alban Schachleiter, who earlier had encouraged Heuberger.[79] Heuberger was also praised for his "love of his parishioners" and dedication to pastoral work. Before the event ended, at least eighty of those present signed a document in support of their pastor.[80] Krauß also ensured that the press covered the assembly.[81]

A few days later, on January 8, Heuberger felt compelled to offer his views on the situation and decided to make them public again by sending the *Eichstätter Anzeiger* a letter that reviewed the events of the past month. In the letter he reiterated his loyalty to the Church but refused to acknowledge any wrongdoing on his part. Heuberger even claimed that he had written his bishop a letter six months prior to the publication of the November 17 letter and shared with Rackl his thoughts on the need for reconciliation between church and state. According to him, Rackl replied with a letter that supported Heuberger's concerns. In Heuberger's mind no one thus far had proven to him that he had "caused offense to the Catholic dogma," nor would it have been possible for anyone "to interpret loyalty to the Führer as disloyalty toward faith and Church." He invited "every decent member of the *Volk* to judge whether it was correct before God and conscience to insult [him] as an apostate, an unfaithful priest, a traitor, or a Judas." He ended his letter by proclaiming, "Long live the Führer!"[82]

Outraged, Rackl reacted to Heuberger's public letter with a second public statement, which he ordered to be read from every pulpit on Sunday, January 10. In this document Rackl admitted that Heuberger had written him a letter on March 9, 1936. However, Rackl argued that, unlike the November 17 public letter, this earlier draft did not contain any "prohibitive sentences about dogmas and morality." Furthermore, Rackl rejected Heuberger's attempts to redirect the issue toward nationalistic concerns over "loyalty to the Führer"—topics already addressed in the bishops' pastoral letters. For these reasons, Rackl considered Heuberger a "disobedient" priest, whom, he warned, God would not bless.[83]

Once again *Kreisleiter* Krauß came to Heuberger's aid and on January 17, in Mörnsheim and Böhmsfeld, dedicated part of his talk to the badgered cleric as a sign of support for the brown priest.[84] Krauß's attempted interventions, however, did not impress Bishop Rackl, who on January 25 sent Heuberger a long letter in which he commented in detail on the heretical nature of Heuberger's November 17 public letter. Rackl insisted that Heuberger's action was "an act of disobedience against the authority of the Church." Rackl also criticized Heuberger's comments on celibacy and the papacy. Then he invited Heuberger to resign from his parish within a week and to leave Hitzhofen for good.[85]

On January 28 Rackl's strongly worded letter, along with the invitation to resign from his parish, caused Heuberger to seek an audience with both the bishop and Vicar General Kiefer. During this three-hour meeting, Rackl took the renegade priest to task, berating Heuberger for making his private thoughts public and for causing a scandal for the Church. The bishop also criticized Heuberger's letter for a variety of reasons, not the least being the priest's audacity to have his brother "rise" from the dead. According to Heuberger's own account, Rackl disagreed with the conclusion that a priest could be a "follower of the Führer." Heuberger immediately retorted that if this were indeed the case, then he was "against the faith." This caused Rackl to rephrase his objection by stating that one could not follow Hitler "because of Hitler's opposition to the faith; National Socialism and Christianity [were] opposites like fire and water—no compromise [was] possible."[86] The bishop then accused Heuberger of having acted "from thwarted ambition on account of [his] dismissal in 1931" as director of the diocese's youth programs.[87] Heuberger denied the latter point vehemently. Clearly, neither side was prepared to budge from its entrenched position, and therefore the meeting ended abruptly at an impasse. However, one day later, on January 29, Rackl had already made up his mind as to what he expected next from Heuberger. In a letter Rackl demanded that Heuberger renounce the contents of the November 17 letter in a public statement. The bishop even spelled out for Heuberger what he wanted him to write. If Heuberger agreed to write such a letter, Rackl would rescind his decision to impose canonical penalties on him, which would have removed Heuberger from his Hitzhofen parish.[88]

Rackl's use of threats to force Heuberger to resign from his parish worked. By early February Heuberger agreed to sign a statement that the chancery had helped him to prepare.[89] In the statement Heuberger admitted that he had acted wrongly by allowing his November letter to be published and distributed and, for that reason, withdrew permission to have it circulated further. He also acknowledged that some of his statements contradicted "Catholic dogma and moral teaching" and apologized if he had "caused any anxiety to Catholics."[90]

By obtaining Heuberger's signature on the statement, Rackl could finally bring the matter to an end. On February 9 Rackl published Heuberger's signed statement in the *Pastoralblatt* of the diocese of Eichstätt so that all diocesan clergy would know that the matter had come to a conclusion. Rackl also ordered every pastor in his diocese to read Heuberger's statement from the pulpit on Sunday, February 14.[91]

For Bishop Rackl the matter had finally come to an end. However, for Heuberger it had not. On February 10 he again wrote to his bishop to suggest the possibility of issuing an additional statement concerning the proceedings. Evidently Heuberger was having second thoughts about retracting his November 17 letter. Perhaps Krauß and other party officials had pressured Heuberger to question his earlier decision. Heuberger also complained that during their interactions the bishop "had called [him] a liar and stated that [he] had acted only from ambition."[92]

Infuriated by the contents of Heuberger's latest letter, Rackl replied by refusing Heuberger the right to issue any further statements. The bishop also imposed on Heuberger a suspension that prohibited him from presiding at mass, hearing confession, preaching, and teaching religion. Furthermore, Rackl said he had initiated the canonical process to remove him from office for good.[93] Evidently, this was more of a threat than a punishment, since Heuberger continued to remain pastor of Hitzhofen. In October 1937 the issue surfaced again when Heuberger complained to his bishop that he still felt wronged by the diocese over the whole affair. Rackl refused to hear these concerns and quickly reminded his recreant priest how kind he had been toward him considering the pastor's offense.[94]

For the remainder of the Third Reich, Rackl allowed Heuberger to continue as pastor of Hitzhofen. Since it was such a small and remote parish, the bishop evidently believed it was easier to have him there than to take the chance of moving him to another parish where he might cause even greater problems. However, Heuberger was not content to remain in Hitzhofen. He realized that the bishop had publicly reprimanded him and that this action, in his own words, had affected him "deeply, very deeply."[95] Still, his pride enabled him to believe that he was destined for bigger and better things. In 1938, despite difficulties with his health, Heuberger applied for no less than four parishes whose pastorates, because of previous government agreements, were state-appointed. In each case Heuberger pledged his allegiance to Hitler and the Nazi Party in his letter of application.[96] For his part, Rackl did everything he could to prevent Heuberger from moving to a new parish. Fearing that "the party circles would stand behind" Heuberger, Rackl used personal connections to avoid having Heuberger appointed to pastorates controlled by the state.[97] Evidently Rackl did not realize that at this point Heuberger had become a disappointment to local Nazi officials for disavowing his November 17 letter. Indeed, Krauß did not do anything to help Heuberger obtain a new pastorate. Perhaps the *Kreisleiter* began to realize his own limitations in controlling the inner workings of the Catholic Church, especially in the close-knit diocese of Eichstätt, and therefore gave up on Heuberger.

For a brief period of time Heuberger had gained prominence and notoriety. He was the recipient of hundreds of letters whose authors praised him for his public avowal of National Socialism. According to Heuberger, he received "only nine dissenting ones."[98] However, his moments of notoriety were short-lived, and soon both the party and many of his confreres deserted him. Heuberger learned very quickly that restraints were put on any priest who attempted to usurp the authority normally accorded to a bishop. Similarly, *Kreisleiter* Krauß discovered how fickle a Catholic priest's allegiance could be when his bishop threatened to suspend him from priestly ministry.

Throughout the controversy Heuberger proved unwilling to sacrifice his priestly position to support the NSDAP. On March 23, 1937, he made this even clearer in a reply to Abbot Schachleiter, to whom he wrote, "For a priest who is rooted in the *Volk* with both feet and who, from there, wishes to go joyfully through the German lands by the hand of Mother Church, can there be a worse passion than having to see the world church join the horrible front of world Judaism, world Communism, and world Free Masonry in their attack on our fatherland? And there is nothing left for us to do than to pray, helplessly watching, or else to renounce the priesthood, and this I am unable to do because I wish with my entire heart to be a pastor. How easy is the daily sacrifice on the altar of the Church; how difficult the daily sacrifice on the altar of the fatherland!"[99]

Ironically, instead of bringing peace to church-state relations, Heuberger produced only greater discord. He also brought loneliness to his personal life. In 1944 he confided to his bishop that by writing his November letter he had acted "according to [his] conscience and that this was not a crime for which [he] should suffer for the rest of [his] life." He admitted that as a result of his actions the "excessively long isolation hurt" him considerably.[100] Not every brown priest, however, experienced alienation and detachment from his confreres, nor from his ministry. Father Richard Kleine of Duderstadt was greatly respected by his colleagues and by the adults and students he served. His life was not one of isolation and hurt. Rather, from Kleine's perspective, it was one of victory and growth.

6—Germanizing Catholicism

In its April 2, 1974, edition, the *Südhannoversche Volkszeitung* declared Father Richard Kleine "a good and well-respected human being and priest" who, despite "the growing terror of anti-Christian and anti-Church forces in the National Socialist regime, which wanted to remove him" from his teaching position, anchored himself "more firmly in it."[1] Born in 1891 and ordained in 1914 as a priest of the Hildesheim diocese, Kleine had labored diligently since 1919 as a religion teacher at the Duderstadt gymnasium.[2] Known affectionately as "Papa Kleine" by the thousands of students whom he taught over the years, Father Kleine was also greatly respected by his colleagues and continued to remain a presence in the gymnasium even years after his official retirement in 1957.

Though Kleine might have been a kind and dedicated priest to his "fellow Aryan Germans," he certainly did not display the same attitude toward non-Aryans. In reality Kleine was a zealous adherent of National Socialism and devoted admirer of Adolf Hitler, referring to him as "God's 'Christmas gift' to our German *Volk*."[3] At the same time he believed that the German Catholic Church was losing ground under National Socialism and for that reason needed to push for greater cooperation between church and state. Despite the urgency of his belief, Kleine preferred to shun the public spotlight and work relentlessly behind the scenes to bring together like-minded theologians, pastors, and teachers in order to create a fortified bridge between National Socialism and Catholicism.

During the Third Reich, Kleine's support for Hitler might have manifested itself in ways all too common in that time and place. Many priests, along with much of the German population, supported Hitler and held him above the party politics of the Third Reich.[4] But Kleine went much further than most Germans in his support of Hitler and National Socialism. Not only did he endeavor to create a harmonious working relationship between his Church and the National Socialist state; he also actively worked to graft National Socialism's racial teaching onto Catholicism, thus making it an integral part of Catholic teaching. Through his writing and speeches one also can detect a distinct link between Christian antisemitism and National Socialism's racial antisemitism. As Jews perished in the Holocaust, Kleine traveled around the Reich giving lectures in which he advocated the removal of Christians of Jewish descent from the Church and the expurgation of any hint of Judaism from Christian scripture and theology.

Redeeming the Church and Society

In his 1929 book *Redemption!* Kleine presented his underlying belief that both German society and German Catholicism were in need of reform. Prior to publication Father Johannes Hagemann, the Hildesheim vicar general, granted an imprimatur, and, once the book was published, leading theologians, including Father Dr. Karl Adam, professor of systematic theology at the University of Tübingen and priest of the Rottenburg diocese, greeted it positively. In *Theologische Quartalschrift* Adam wrote, "Kleine writes an exceptionally fresh, bold, realistic book. . . . Working from the firm belief that our Western development moves irresistibly toward a decision between faith and unbelief, he endeavors, in light of a conscientious recognition of our present situation, to point toward a path of 'redemption.'"[5] For Kleine this path included an active acknowledgement that Western civilization was "no longer Christian," despite the Church's claim that any Christian culture possessed this "unshakable foundation." He also thought that the Church had created too much of a divide between itself and German society to become an effective force within the nation and challenged the Church to close this gap in order to alter the course of this negative development.[6]

According to Kleine, priests were the key group within the Church to bridge this divide. They were "intimately tied to the *Volk*" and could immerse themselves in the life of their Church and, as German men, in the life of their nation by engaging in a "form of *Volk* pastoral care" that more genuinely addressed both the religious and social needs of the German people.[7]

Kleine saw this renewed path of spiritual awakening in the Church as essential to the future success of German society, especially in regard to the youth. "Ill-prepared leaders" could no longer educate the German youth carelessly in a "flag-waving patriotism in religious respects," which was an "artificial" mixture of religion and nationalism without any real substance. By contrast, the German *Volk* wanted to be properly educated. Whatever forms this education took, it would need to address both the spiritual and material concerns of his countrymen.[8]

In great earnest Kleine detailed the "life of suffering" that he believed the German *Volk* had undergone "since the Middle Ages." Despite division by class and religion, he saw the "common trait of the German *Volk*" as the "ardent desire for complete unity." Political movements such as socialism and communism hurt this unity, as did materialism and politics devoid of any religious concern. National unity could be created only by a genuine "love for homeland and for the hereditary *Volk* and enthusiasm for the kingdom of God on earth." This unity could be accomplished only if Catholics no longer viewed themselves or allowed their countrymen to view them as "nationally inferior." Such thinking was a "burning disgrace on Catholic Germany." Catholics had to reach for a "complete understanding of [their] contemporaries who [were] not Catholic" and practice ecumenism. However, Kleine's use of the word "ecumenism" did not specifically refer to the international efforts then taking place largely among Protestant Churches, but instead alluded to a new form of German religious unity based solely on national lines.[9]

In *Redemption!* Kleine's thinking was not only Germany-centered, but also exclusionary. Despite his acknowledgement that "indeed, the Spirit goes wherever he wills; even among non-Christians he has accomplished much," Kleine held that German unity ultimately "depended on grace." However, this grace could "only be given to those who are worthy." Such grace could not be fully present among Jews, whose "state of being chosen was only a preparation for the new covenant, granted in a narrow space and restricted time frame, and therefore was not a permanent distinction." Kleine believed that God bestowed grace upon the German *Volk* and would bless it by sending a prophetic figure to lead the nation.[10]

By 1932 Kleine noted that Adolf Hitler was fulfilling this prophetic role. Despite the German bishops' prohibitions toward the NSDAP, Kleine regarded the Hitler movement as the only viable group in German society that could fully address the concerns he raised in *Redemp-*

tion! Soon Kleine began to promote right-wing concerns and to develop connections among Catholics of similar political persuasion.[11] In May 1932 he wrote a supportive letter to Emil Ritter, editor of the Cologne Catholic weekly newspaper, *Der Deutsche Weg.* That publication had recently turned right, and Kleine expressed his enthusiasm for its editorial outlook. Delighted by this response, Ritter invited Kleine to submit an article entitled "Catholic Self-Assertiveness and National Responsibility," which Kleine did. Soon thereafter Kleine became a regular contributor to Ritter's weekly.[12]

In early August Kleine made his support for National Socialism more public in his *Deutscher Weg* article "Yes and No to National Socialism." Naturally, Kleine encouraged his readers to join him by declaring their support for the Hitler party. Yet, his article was much less a resounding statement of what he found attractive in National Socialism than a summary of his work *Redemption!* However, this time Kleine specifically mentioned National Socialism as the force that would "protect the Christian-German culture" and work to solve Germany's ills "from the vantage point of the national *Volksgemeinschaft.*" Kleine also attacked Communism and spoke against global ecumenism and other such "international movements." For Kleine there was only one concern: Christian love and support of his German fatherland.[13]

In early April 1933, slightly more than two months after Hitler came to power, Kleine solidified his dual concerns for Catholicism and Germany by joining Germany's vice-chancellor Franz von Papen and Emil Ritter to found the League of Catholic Germans "Cross and Eagle." The league professed to be against liberalism and promised "to deepen the Christian-conservative sentiment in the German *Volk,* to strengthen the national sense of duty of Catholic Germans, and to spiritually to foster "the building of the coming Reich." In essence, the league members' goal was to win National Socialism over to Catholicism and vice versa. However, the league did not align itself or specifically mention Adolf Hitler or National Socialism; instead, it declared itself to be "above political parties."[14]

In October 1933, following the signing of the Reich-Vatican Concordat and the disbanding of all political parties with the exception of the NSDAP, many of the league's members advocated an alignment with National Socialism. Such talk led to the league's dissolution and the establishment of the Working Group of German Catholics (AKD), which accepted as its mission the duty to strengthen the allegiance of the German Catholic population to National Socialism.[15] Kleine also remained active in the new organization.[16]

The Mislabeled Resister

In October 1933 Richard Kleine wrote to Viktor Lutze, the *Oberpräsident* (provincial governor) of Hannover, and proudly detailed his efforts "in dozens of religion classes . . . to bring the students as close as possible to the *Weltanschauung* of our Führer, particularly from a Christian faith perspective." He presented "the manly strength and greatness" of Hitler's "personality and his irreproachable, gallant honorableness as a model" for his students to emulate and regularly discussed with them "the Jewish question in its entire magnitude and urgency." In his sermons he similarly "beseeched the blessings of heaven" upon Hitler and "his difficult task" and unambiguously supported National Socialism in leading Catholic newspapers."[17]

Kleine made these bold claims so that *Oberpräsident* Lutze would know with whom he was dealing: a preeminent German citizen who worked endlessly to promote Hitler and the ideology of National Socialism. Kleine felt Lutze should seriously consider the contents of his letter because of his zeal. Kleine brought up an issue that centered around his four colleagues who had castigated an "Aryan" student and made him publicly apologize for "singing an SA song with a verse directed against the Jews close to a Jewish classmate who marched alongside him." To make matters worse, the "Aryan" student, an upperclassman, was also a member of the SA. Once the event reached the ears of local party leaders, they reacted fiercely by demanding the removal of all the teachers involved, along with the removal of the gymnasium's director.[18] What Kleine did not realize was that both the regional and district party leaders had previously questioned the loyalty of the Duderstadt gymnasium's administration and faculty and had earmarked the same director and teachers for removal. According to the party leaders, one teacher had been a member of the Stahlhelm, which in Duderstadt had opposed the NSDAP during its struggle for power. The other teachers, they argued, had belonged to political parties that at times had been in conflict with National Socialism.[19] This event now provided the Duderstadt NSDAP leaders with the necessary evidence to take this case to *Oberpräsident* Lutze for action.

The entire situation peaked in early November when the Reich Ministry of Education ordered an inquiry into the matter. A representative from this ministry, together with an official from the Hannover Department for Secondary Schools, conducted the questioning of the five accused educators, along with another fifteen individuals, of whom Kleine was one.[20] Anticipating a negative outcome, Kleine had written his letter to *Oberpräsident* Lutze several days before the inquiry began and shared his conviction that the action taken by his colleagues was "justified." For him, it was not a question of his colleagues' having dishonored "a decent German young man" and stood up for a "single, defenseless" Jew, but rather one of proper classroom demeanor and behavior among true German gentlemen. Though Kleine supported the National Socialist racial teaching, he ultimately did not want to see it implemented in a vulgar fashion.[21] After the investigation Kleine also asked his friend Franz von Papen to do whatever he could to save the jobs of his colleagues. In mid-November Papen acted by writing to Reich Education Minister Bernhard Rust to request an audience between Kleine and a ministry representative.[22] Kleine was soon on a train bound for Berlin, where he met with Martin Löpelmann, a member of Rust's staff, to whom he described the situation.[23]

Meanwhile Kleine took one further step. He wrote to Minister Rust directly to attest to the anti-Marxist spirit of his school and its efforts on behalf of Hitler. Kleine also attacked the veracity of the NSDAP faculty informant who had originally reported the incident to local party officials by recalling that the informant had hired a Jewish lawyer to represent him in a perjury case the preceding year. According to Kleine, this informant simply was trying to remove the opposition so that he could become principal of the gymnasium.[24]

By early spring of 1934 the Reich Ministry of Education finally issued its ruling on the case, which demoted the director and transferred him along with three of the teachers to other schools. After an intense investigation and debate, it finally allowed the fourth teacher, the former member of the Stahlhelm, to maintain his teaching position in Duderstadt owing to his nationalism and his efforts on behalf of Hitler during the 1932 Reich presidential campaign.[25] The entire situation did not end, however, until April 1934, when the Hannover Department of Secondary Schools appointed as director an outside candidate who had proven his loyalty to the state.[26]

Following World War II and long after, Kleine nurtured the legend that he had resisted the infiltration of National Socialism in the Duderstadt gymnasium. In reality, however, he only defended five colleagues, all of whom had never publicly opposed National Socialism nor supported Bolshevism. Though his action at the hearing involved supporting the actions of his colleagues, Kleine viewed the entire matter solely through the spectrum of proper German decorum. Believing himself an ardent supporter of National Socialism, he felt he could reason with both state and party officials. Though he was unable to prevent the transfer of four of his colleagues, the Reich Education Ministry did not force any of them into retirement. The ministry even allowed a fifth colleague to maintain his position. The event left Kleine with the belief that he had the wherewithal to bring about change in the new German state. In turn, he felt called to endeavor to make Catholicism more receptive to National Socialism.

Diocesan Concerns

By September of 1935 numerous reports, both verbal and written, were coming to the Hildesheim vicariate that Father Kleine was using prohibited books in his religion classes. These were books that the Holy See had placed on its *Index,* which meant that Catholics were not allowed to read them without explicit permission from their bishop. Concerned about the contents of Kleine's religion classes, Father Hermann Seeland, an official in the Hildesheim vicariate, asked Kleine to explain why his office had received so many complaints about his teaching.[27] Kleine responded to these concerns promptly and frankly by explaining that he fully recognized the authority of the Church's *Index.* He stated that, in fact, he regularly "drew a parallel between the *Index* of the Church and the newly established index of the state in the Third Reich in order to allow its authority to become more strongly evident." He also admitted that the complaints most probably stemmed from an incident concerning Alfred Rosenberg's *Myth of the Twentieth Century,* which he conceded was an "outrageous attack against Christianity and the Church."[28] The Vatican had placed *Myth* on the *Index* in February of the previous year.[29] According to Kleine, a student who was both a Catholic and "a leader in the Hitler Youth" and whose unit comprised several villages that were primarily Protestant, had asked "quite suddenly at the beginning of class whether he would be permitted to read the book." Kleine confessed that, as a "generally known committed National Socialist," he could "go into this matter much further than others who might easily be accused of opposition toward the Third Reich." For this reason, he instructed the student that "anyone who takes special responsibility upon himself for the sake of his faith should read it." However, he added that he was saying this only because the young man was a "splendid Catholic" who, he trusted, would turn to him with any questions that arose. Kleine concluded that "if my answer does not objectively correspond with the view of the book prohibition," then he was "naturally ready to notify this upper-level class and act accordingly in the future."[30]

Upon receiving Kleine's report of the incident, Father Seeland immediately replied by explaining the canonical definition of the book prohibition and by telling Kleine that he had acted hastily in dealing with the issue in such a public manner. He ordered Kleine to have in the future a student apply for official permission "if a real need was present to read prohibited books."[31] Interestingly, Seeland's letter never addressed Rosenberg's *Myth* by name nor challenged Kleine's National Socialist conviction, especially his comparison of the Holy See's *Index* with that of the state. One might easily criticize Father Seeland for not being more critical of Kleine. However, what the letter does not reveal was that, in early March, officers of the German Customs Investigations Office had arrested the Hildesheim vicar general, Father Otto Seelmeyer, Father Seeland's direct superior, for infractions against Germany's currency laws. This particular case involved a loan from a Dutch bank in Holland: Seelmeyer had obtained the loan to cover the building costs of a new Franciscan monastery in Hannover-Kleefeld. Though Seelmeyer had followed legal norms, it seems that the bank on the German side had mishandled the transaction. Reich Propaganda Minister Joseph Goebbels saw the negative propaganda opportunities this situation raised and used them to attack the Church. At the same time, similar cases of "financial misconduct," often involving members of Catholic religious communities, appeared throughout Germany. The international mission of the Catholic Church, which entailed having its religious orders regularly send funds from a province in one country to its generalate in another, made the members who handled these finances particularly susceptible to prosecution. In addition, the complexity of the laws and the lack of financial training among priests and members of religious communities compounded this situation. Unfortunately, Seelmeyer got caught in this quagmire and did not escape from it until his early release from the Brandenburg-Göhrden prison three years later.[32] With the process against Vicar General Seelmeyer under way, one can see why Seeland and other diocesan officials might have dealt cautiously with Father Kleine, especially since he kept reminding them of his close relationship with state and party officials.

The encounter with the Hildesheim vicariate sparked Kleine to make his views about National Socialism more explicitly known to his diocesan superiors. Up until this time, it appears that Kleine had no interaction with the diocese concerning his relationship with the NSDAP. A major factor that hindered this encounter was the October 1933 election of the Hildesheim bishop, Nikolas Bares, to the Berlin episcopacy after the death of Dr. Christian Schreiber, Berlin's first Catholic bishop.[33] Bares's successor in Hildesheim, Joseph Godehard Machens, did not officially take over the vacant seat until late July of 1934. Machens, however, was by no means foreign to the diocese, because he grew up in Hildesheim, entered the priesthood in the Hildesheim diocese, and, since 1920, had taught dogmatics, ethics, and liturgy in its seminary.[34]

On the same day that Father Seeland wrote Kleine about his teaching, Kleine sent Bishop Machens a six-page letter in which he shared his concerns about the deteriorating relationship between the Catholic Church and the National Socialist state. Kleine wrote, "As a Catholic priest I suffer indescribably from the shame that Catholicism has brought upon the Führer and his movement and has hardly made amends for so far. . . . We have sinned most severely against our Führer. And Adolf Hitler is after all the savior and great hope for our *Volk*. . . . He is a gracious gift from heaven."[35] In this letter Kleine took issue with the German bishops' annual pastoral letter, which accused the state of attempting to remove the presence of the Church and Christianity from public life.[36] Kleine feared that by making such statements the bishops had placed themselves in clear opposition to the Third Reich. In Kleine's view, the bishops' letter only hindered the possibility of ensuring the presence of Christianity in the Third Reich, most notably the development of his form of German Catholicism.[37]

Bishop Machens was fully aware of the tense relations between his Church and the German state. Already on August 29, 1935, he had written a letter of protest that detailed the difficulties his diocese had experienced with the state and sent it to the Gestapo's Berlin headquarters, in particular to Reich Ministers Hanns Kerrl (Church Affairs), Bernhard Rust (Science, Education, and Culture), and Franz Gürtner (Justice).[38] He certainly did not need Father Kleine to remind him of this troubling situation! Nor did Machens wish to hear Kleine's viewpoint, which placed blame for these problems on the Church for not being German enough. However, instead of writing to Kleine immediately and confronting him, the bishop put off meeting with him until some future date.[39] It appears that the two never met. Perhaps, Machens, like Father Seeland, proceeded carefully in his dealings with Kleine, fearful of the trouble he believed Kleine might have stirred up for the Church in Hildesheim. As a local Church figure since the time of his ordination, Machens had most probably known of or just possibly may have met Kleine in the past and had heard about his political views. On the other hand, it is also quite likely that the bishop viewed him as insignificant and unworthy of his consideration and therefore proceeded on his own with this conviction. Kleine, however, viewed himself as being far from insignificant.

Proclaiming a German Catholicism

From Kleine's perspective he was a central figure in the debate on the role of Catholicism in the National Socialist state. He fully believed that without his efforts his Church would grow further out of touch with the new realities of the German state and be brushed aside by it. In addition, he was also worried about National Socialism falling into the hands of questionable individuals who lacked any Christian orientation or grounding. In 1935, in an effort to confront this issue, Kleine came up with the idea of developing a new textbook that would address religious questions in light of the new Germany. Since Germans stood "at a turning point of Church history," he argued, his textbook had to be "a totally new creation," one that would not in any way resemble previous ones, which he judged to be of "inferior quality" and even a "disgrace for Catholicism." He believed that only individuals such as himself "who are of one mind and of one fervent love for the kingdom of God and the kingdom of the Germans" could compose a work that would fulfill the mandate arising from "the breakthrough of the National Socialist idea."[40]

In order to accomplish his goal, Kleine thought it best to seek out like-minded Catholics, especially theologians, to share in this writing task. To this end, on February 21, 1935, Kleine first wrote Joseph Lortz and invited him to join him in the task of creating this new religion textbook.[41] As the author of *Catholic Approaches to National Socialism*, which promoted a positive view of National Socialism for German Catholics, and as a member of the NSDAP Lortz was the perfect candidate for Kleine to approach.[42] Lortz's established scholarship as a noted Church historian would provide the necessary academic backing to have an impact on the theological world.

The SD would certainly have agreed with Kleine's choice as well. In an internal memorandum an agent described Lortz as a "Catholic theology professor who belongs to that group of Catholic theologians who strive for a union between Catholicism and National Socialism." Accordingly, the agent concluded, "this group can, to some extent, cause confusion in National Socialist circles that have not yet formed a clear ideological outlook. However, wherever party members have a clear ideological outlook, this group has an undermining effect on the circles of political Catholicism." "Thus," the agent stated, "neither a definitively positive nor definitely negative" judgment could be made on Lortz's "political outlook." "At any rate," he concluded, of all the Catholic theologians in Germany, Lortz was among those "who can be most positively assessed."[43]

On February 28 Lortz let Kleine know that "without any hesitation" he could "reply with a fundamental willingness to collaborate" on the task.[44] Confident in having found a worthy partner, Kleine found additional collaborators: Kuno Brombacher, a librarian, AKD representative from Baden, and NSDAP representative in the Baden state legislature; Emil Ritter, Kleine's friend, former editor of *Der Deutsche Weg* and current editor of *Germania;* and Johannes Nattermann, a priest of the Cologne archdiocese.[45]

As the authors discussed the writing task that lay ahead of them, the work gradually evolved from a textbook to a guidebook for teachers and ultimately to a general summons of all German Catholics in the form of an open letter that would exhort them to consider the current condition of church-state relations with the utmost seriousness. Kleine and Lortz also agreed that Lortz would not write an essay, but primarily serve as the work's editor.[46]

Both Kleine and Lortz soon learned that the project would prove quite challenging. In the beginning, difficulties would center around Kuno Brombacher. A zealous convert to Catholicism, Brombacher also displayed equal devotion to National Socialism. In his eyes, German Catholicism was not moving quickly enough in its acceptance and embracement of the new German state and its *Weltanschauung,* and on numerous occasions he had expressed his frustrations to Kleine.[47] Naturally, these feelings came out in his writing. The first draft of his chapter was so critical of the German Church that even Abbot Schachleiter, from whom he sought feedback, sent back the manuscript with the remark that he "could not subscribe to it without disowning his Catholic faith."[48] Lortz likewise mandated revisions.[49] Unhappy with this prospect, Brombacher complained to Kleine, "We must make Catholic revolution . . . since Christ said, 'I came to bring fire to the earth,' and how I wish it were already kindled! And therefore, since I feel a bit of that fire burning within me, I sought to express this burning."[50] In the end, through Kleine's mediation, Brombacher rewrote his contribution.[51]

By late summer of 1935, upon Lortz's recommendation and with his assistance, Kleine entered into serious negotiations with the Catholic publishing house of Aschendorff in Münster to publish the work.[52] Lortz believed that having a Catholic publisher would increase the importance and legitimacy of the work. To further these aims, he also insisted that he personally submit the completed work to Clemens von Galen, the bishop of Münster, for his support. Such approval, Lortz believed, would ensure that German Catholics would seriously consider it.[53] Though Kleine was open to this suggestion, both Brombacher and Ritter expressed their reservations. They feared Galen would insist upon major revisions that would weaken its impact.[54]

Despite the hesitation they had expressed toward Lortz's suggestion, all of these individuals operated with a genuine sense of urgency and undaunted correctness in their task. They had to reform German Catholicism and adapt it to the new German state. Between them flowed pages of correspondence that detailed the difficulties Catholics faced under National Socialism. On October 21, for example, Lortz reported to Kleine that he had been told "by a radical party member that about nine months ago *all* members of the SS *Leibstandarte* (Hitler's bodyguard regiment) were ordered to resign from the Catholic or Protestant Church, respectively, and they all did so." He lamented that "unfortunately, there are hardly any religiously faithful or any touched by Christ the Lord in the party leadership. This is a severe burden on the project and on our work. Prayer should be doubled." In subsequent letters Lortz again brought forth similar concerns, this time including the ongoing currency trials involving Catholic bishops, priests, and religious.[55]

On account of the tense situation, Lortz worked quickly to edit the manuscript, and by mid-November he confidently delivered it to Bishop Galen. For his part, Galen told Lortz that he was "open to anything that will improve the situation" and "promised to consider and inspect" the manuscript "most carefully." The bishop even added that "it might be possible to obtain a foreword" from him. Lortz informed Kleine of this positive encounter.[56]

Immediately, however, red flags went up in Kleine's mind. He asked Lortz, "Can a bishop today write anything that will agree with the deepest yearnings of our *Open Letter*?" Though Kleine had been open to sharing the work with Galen, he did not trust the bishop's ability fully to understand the depth of their appeal for some kind of cooperation between church and state.[57] Lortz agreed with Kleine's concerns but also reminded him that they had to be truthful and acknowledge that there were "monstrous things on the other side." By making such a comment, was Lortz expressing his doubts over the possibility of the Church actually being able to come to a peaceful understanding with National Socialism?[58] Certainly Kleine thought so. Thus, upon receiving the letter, Kleine wrote a strongly worded reply that reminded Lortz that "Catholicism and not the other [state] unquestionably bears the greatest blame for the present situation."[59]

Before any further exchange of letters took place, Bishop Galen summoned Lortz for a meeting about the book. Lortz reported to Kleine that "it was by far the most beautiful discussion I have ever had with him.

An honest man to the core, who made a sincere effort of adopting our viewpoint. He said he was, in effect, *immensely* impressed by the manifesto." Nevertheless, Lortz reported that Galen had found some flaws in the manuscript, but not to the extent that it would be unpublishable. Once the authors corrected these, Lortz stated, Galen would not object to publication; however, he had to inform Kleine that Galen did not want to be publicly responsible for the work and did not want any priest's name to appear in it. Instead, Galen wanted them to present it as a work written by lay Catholics. Lortz suggested Ritter as editor. Then he told Kleine that the publisher wanted to go to press immediately.[60] Though it appears that Galen was quite sympathetic toward their efforts, he was not willing to risk being alienated from his fellow bishops—most of whom were under the impression that a new *Kulturkampf* had already begun.

In early 1936 the Aschendorff publishing house released *An Open Letter of Catholic Germans to Their Volk and Fellow Christians*. On the title pages Kuno Brombacher and Emil Ritter accepted dual credit for editing the work, and the names of Fathers Lortz, Kleine, and Nattermann were found nowhere in the text.[61]

The *Open Letter*'s uncredited preface, "The Only Important Point," faithfully reflected the central concerns of all the contributors, namely, that before German Catholicism stood "the pivotal question whether it will rigidly maintain the character that the past has stamped upon it, in part even by force, or whether it will comprehend the new birth, overcoming outdated modes of thinking and breaking through the coating of random forms, and raise itself to awareness of its role in the awakening of the nation." Before German Catholicism made this decision, it had to take into account the entire German *Volksgemeinschaft*, which included all Christians as well as Aryan Germans who professed beliefs other than Christianity.[62] Thus the preface asserted that one's faith in Germany itself was of the utmost importance, even above that of anyone's denominational allegiance.

Richard Kleine's essay "German Turning Point in History" appeared next. According to Kleine, Germany had entered a new era. He proclaimed that this "German awakening" was also a "call to Christianity and the Church" to produce a change in the Church that would be "no less a blessing than this historical turning point will be for the *Volk* and the Reich." The center of this reawakening was the German *Volksgemeinschaft*, which now had "become the highest goal" of all for everyone. "The love of Christians" was certainly "not only the love for Christianity and the Church," but an "encompassing love that cannot limit the concept of 'neighbor' to the circle of brothers-in-faith."[63]

For Kleine, the relationship between state and church needed to reflect a unity similar to that experienced by the German *Volksgemeinschaft*. In order to accomplish this, Kleine suggested that church and state "achieve a closer bond beyond a more superficial, solely formal-juridical relationship with one another." The German Catholic Church and German state could accomplish this by the way they defined themselves. He explained, "The legal side of the Church will, without suffering any weakening, again become less important in the consciousness of the faithful than the community of the body of Christ. Similarly, for us Germans today, the state is less a legal institution, than the embodiment of the *völkisch* idea." He insisted, however, that a new definition of the Church should never lead into discussions for an autonomous National Church. Though Kleine loved everything German, at the root of his belief was always a desire to maintain the autonomy of his Catholic tradition within the context of German history. Still, this did not mean that Catholics and Protestants could not work together. Rather, he valued both working hand in hand to strengthen the German *Volksgemeinschaft*.⁶⁴

In their essays Ritter, Brombacher, and Nattermann offered similar arguments. In particular, in his essay "From Catholic Germany to the German *Volk*" Brombacher bluntly summarized the essence of Kleine's message by noting that Catholics ultimately had to conform to the new state or "commit suicide."⁶⁵ It seems that Lortz did not wish to dilute the potency of Brombacher's wording after all. However, what did weaken the document's impact on German Catholics was the fact that, in the end, only two rather inconsequential Catholic laymen took credit for the work. Except for a few insiders, no one knew that a prominent Catholic theologian was behind the work and that Bishop Galen had given it his "unofficial" blessing.

Eventually, most probably through an informant in Kleine's circle, SD agents learned the true identity of the authors. Originally they had high hopes for such a work, especially for its demands on Catholicism to join National Socialism in its fight against Communism. They also appreciated its emphasis on German unity, even if this emphasized "the internal condition and platform" that National Socialism created for a "reunification of all Christian confessions in Germany." Yet, they were very concerned that the work aimed "for the transformation of National Socialism in the Catholic spirit so that National Socialism should be rethought in light of Catholicism." In the SD agents' mind, "the entire danger of this work" stemmed from this attempt on the part of the Church to transform them! Interestingly, in the end the SD agents did not recommend that any action be taken against this book. Possibly they came to this conclusion after its publication, when Brombacher withdrew from the Catholic Church to join the schismatic Old Catholics. But even before this, Brombacher's essay appeared to be more the ranting of a dissatisfied and disenchanted Catholic than the thoughts of a "reformer." The SD agents concluded that Brombacher's action had "created considerable confusion and taken away the initiative for any further activity" from the circle around Kleine.[66]

Ultimately the *Open Letter* failed to create the widespread discussion and change that Kleine and his colleagues had envisioned. Nevertheless, its failure did not in the least lessen Kleine's zeal and enthusiasm for National Socialism. Nor did it dampen that of his colleagues. In fact, despite the testimony by Lortz himself that he had distanced himself from National Socialism and resigned from the party soon after the release of the *Open Letter*, he was still in contact with Kleine; in 1943 he affectionately called him "comrade" and signed his letters to him "with comradely greetings, Heil Hitler."[67]

The Austrian Connection

Despite the failure of the *Open Letter* to galvanize a change in church-state relations, Kleine desperately sought new avenues to voice his ongoing concerns. Though he had found like-minded colleagues through working on the *Open Letter*, it does not appear that they continued to work together, and the failure of the *Open Letter* to produce change caused Kleine to look elsewhere. Possibly due to the limited time that he had outside of his regular teaching duties, Kleine decided to invest his little free time only in individuals and efforts he believed could truly effect change in German Catholicism. One individual who perfectly fulfilled such a requirement was Father Johann Pircher, a priest of the archdiocese of Vienna and, like Kleine, a religion teacher. On August 19, 1953, shortly after Pircher's death, Kleine wrote the deceased's sister and described Johann as his "dear, loyal friend" with whom he had "the closest of ties." He admitted that Pircher's death had "deeply affected" him."[68] Originally their common love and support of National Socialism and Catholicism had brought them together in the late 1930s.

Born in 1886 in the South Tirolean village of Andrian, Pircher took the name Emmerich in 1906 when he entered religious life as a postulant for the Brothers of the House of St. Mary in Jerusalem, more popularly known as *Der Deutsche Orden* (German Order). In June 1911 Josef Altenweisel, the bishop of Brixen, in whose diocese *Der Deutsche Orden* served, ordained Pircher a priest. Soon thereafter Pircher's superior assigned him to serve consecutively from 1911 to 1914 as a parochial vicar in several of the order's parishes. However, by 1914 Pircher was showing signs of restlessness and requested to switch provinces. A year later he resigned from his religious community and became a parish priest in the Vienna archdiocese. After serving as a parochial vicar in several parishes, Cardinal Friedrich Gustav Piffl, the archbishop of Vienna, allowed Pircher in 1921 formally to incardinate into his archdiocese. Following his incardination, the bishop assigned Pircher to teach religion in the *Bürgerschule* in Schwechat. In 1926 he was transferred to the Neuottakring *Hauptschule* in Vienna.[69]

According to Father Franz Dutzler, a Cistercian monk and Pircher's longtime friend, Pircher whether as teacher or chaplain was "an idealist and optimist" through and through, who was "constantly intent on social justice." Such thinking, especially during the worldwide depression, led Pircher to embrace the Hitler movement and its promise to work for "social justice, to create jobs, and to bring about a better understanding between the Catholic Church and the party."[70] As Father Anton Hagenauer, pastor of the Bischofshofen parish, where Pircher lived and served after the war, recalled, Pircher quickly became known as "Nazi Pircher," a priest who worked tirelessly for "reconciliation between the Church and the NSDAP."[71]

In April 1933 Pircher's enthusiasm for National Socialism led him to join the Vienna branch of the NSDAP.[72] Soon such membership became problematic when on June 19 Engelbert Dollfuss, the Austrian chancellor, banned the Austrian National Socialist Party in order to end terrorist actions instigated by party members and to ward off impending annexation attempts, both internally and externally.[73] Despite this ban Pircher maintained his support for Hitler and eagerly waited for the day when his nation would be joined with Germany.

Father Pircher, however, had to wait almost five years before the *Anschluss* became a reality. The process began with the July 1936 agreement between Austria and Germany, which weakened the strength of Austrian Chancellor Kurt von Schuschnigg's government by making economic and political concessions to Germany. The provisions of the agreement also included the release of imprisoned National Socialists. After that, the Austrian Nazis worked to bring down Schuschnigg's government. In February 1938 Hitler single-handedly assisted in their efforts when he summoned the Austrian chancellor to his southern seat of government in Berchtesgaden and intimidated him into accepting a list of demands that included the appointment of Arthur Seyss-Inquart, a Hitler supporter, as minister of the interior. A month later, after further political pressure coupled with the threat of military invasion by Germany, Schuschnigg finally resigned and Austria's Federal President Wilhelm Miklas was obliged by the Germans to appoint Arthur Seyss-Inquart chancellor. Seyss-Inquart, who had strongly favored an *Anschluss* for many years, then schemed with Hermann Göring to have German troops "invade" Austria in order to restore order. However, instead of having to shed blood by gunfire, the German soldiers only had to maneuver carefully their "invading" vehicles and military equipment through the twists and turns of Vienna's streets in order to avoid hitting the thousands upon thousands of jubilant Austrians greeting them.[74]

Even before Pircher could begin making efforts to ensure that Austrian Catholicism had a prominent place in the newly extended Reich, on March 18 the Austrian bishops issued a "Solemn Declaration," which expressed their hopes for a positive working relationship with the government. Josef Bürckel, the *Gauleiter* of the recently created Saar-Palatinate *Gau* and now the NSDAP representative in Austria, whom Berlin had commissioned to reorganize the Austrian Nazi Party and prepare the *Anschluss* referendum, had earlier presented the bishops with the idea of issuing a declaration in support of the unification.[75] His office even drew up an initial draft of the document.[76] In the declaration's final version the Austrian bishops publicly announced their confidence that National Socialism would address their society's economic and social ills and protect the "German Reich and *Volk*" from "the danger of destructive, godless Bolshevism." In addition to pledging their faith in the NSDAP, the bishops also placed significant pressure on Catholics to vote in support of the *Anschluss* at an upcoming referendum. To this end, the bishops wrote, "On the day of the *Volk* referendum, it is for us bishops naturally a national duty as Germans to declare our support for the German Reich, and we also expect that all devout Christians know what they owe to their *Volk*."[77] A few days later the archdiocese of Vienna announced that its priests were allowed to wear publicly an item of clothing or pin bearing the swastika.[78]

To make matters worse, Cardinal Theodor Innitzer, the archbishop of Vienna, took the liberty of personally sending a copy of the bishops' declaration with a cover letter to *Gauleiter* Bürckel. In his letter Innitzer wrote, "Enclosed please find the statement of the bishops. You will gather from it that we bishops, of our own free will and without coercion, have fulfilled our national duty. I know that good cooperation will ensue from this statement." He ended it, "with the expression of great respect," and added, in pen, "Heil Hitler. Th. Card. Innitzer."[79] Even Josef Goebbels could not have created a better piece of propaganda! Bürckel seized upon this golden opportunity and plastered the streets of Vienna with facsimiles of Innitzer's letter and of the Austrian bishops' statement.[80]

Father Pircher also seized this opportunity to make public the existence of "The Association for Religious Peace" *(Arbeitsgemeinschaft für den religiösen Frieden)*, a group of Austrian priests and lay Catholics who wished to support the *Anschluss* and promote a positive relationship between the Church and German Reich.[81] Pircher, as the association's secretary, along with Karl Pischtiak, a layman and middleman for *Gauleiter* Bürckel, composed a letter that various newspapers carried, inviting their fellow priests to join their association.[82] Pircher promised that together they would work "to restore the trust between *Volk* and clergy where it had been destroyed" and "bring together both groups as Germans." He also promised that they would "remain loyal to Catholic principles," but also adhere "to the guiding principles of our great Führer and therefore be a living symbol to portray our movement accurately so that any upright Catholic could also be a good National Socialist." Moreover, Pircher argued, "membership in our association" was the "best witness for our public profession of loyalty to the Führer and *Volk*" and "for us to carry within ourselves the proud feeling of belonging to the great *Volksgemeinschaft.*"[83]

Before Pircher's group developed any real momentum, word of the Austrian bishops' "Solemn Declaration" reached Rome. This declaration pleased neither Pope Pius XI nor Eugenio Pacelli, the papal secretary of state. In no time, they summoned Innitzer to Rome. The Holy See had every right to be angry with the Austrian episcopacy. It was only a year since Pius XI had taken liberties and risked criticism by issuing the papal encyclical *Mit brennender Sorge.* Now the pope had to intervene again and deal directly with the indiscretion of an extremely high-ranking Austrian cardinal and his fellow bishops.

In an exceptionally rare move, the Holy See publicly expressed its displeasure with Innitzer and his fellow bishops. On April 1 *Osservatore Romano,* the Vatican's semiofficial newspaper, published an article that formally distanced the Holy See from the March 18 declaration, by declaring that the Austrian bishops had published their statement without permission from the Vatican. In addition, on the same evening Father Gustav Gundlach, a German Jesuit and theologian, spoke in his mother tongue over Vatican Radio and, without specifically referring to the Austrian bishops, sharply criticized any use of ecclesiastical teaching authority for secular political aims.[84] Shortly after these public reprimands and his "visit" to Rome, on April 6 Innitzer issued a second declaration in the name of the Austrian bishops. In it he confirmed their allegiance to the Holy See and also critiqued their previous "Solemn Declaration." Innitzer wrote, "The 'Solemn Declaration' of the Austrian bishops of March 18 of this year naturally was not meant to pronounce an endorsement that was and is not compatible with the laws of God and the freedom and rights of the Catholic Church. In addition, that statement shall not be understood by the state and party as conscience-binding for the faithful and utilized for propaganda."[85]

The apparent change in Innitzer's stance troubled Pircher and other like-minded Catholics. On April 8 they sent Innitzer a letter on behalf of an "Action for Religious Peace," in which they both praised him for his original stance toward Hitler and National Socialism and encouraged him not to deviate from it. Pircher, along with seventeen other Catholic priests and laymen, signed the letter.[86] By this time Innitzer realized that he had to proceed much more cautiously and judiciously in his public dealings with the German government, and he desired that his priests follow the same course of action. Thus it came as no surprise when on April 26 the Vienna *Diözesanblatt* published "directives" for priests who worked in that archdiocese. These directives made it clear that "for all times the objectives and duties of ministry unalterably and unshakably remain the proclamation of the Good News of the kingdom of God, the imparting of grace for salvation, and the salvation of souls for eternal life." In other words, the Cardinal wished his priests to concentrate on their pastoral ministry and stay out of politics.[87]

Such pastoral directives did not deter Pircher in his efforts to promote a good working relationship between church and state, and he and other like-minded clerics continued to promote their cause. However, before proceeding further, Pircher thought it best once again to clear up any misunderstandings about the work of his association with the Austrian bishops. On May 7, 1938, he and the acting chair, Father Wilhelm van den Bergh, a former Capuchin friar from Holland, who had incardinated in 1929 into the Vienna archdiocese, wrote to Cardinal Innitzer and stressed the nonpolitical nature of their association, which, they pointed out, wished to promote a "relationship based on trust between church and state and between the clergy and the broadest spectrum of the *Volk*" in order to create an "active affirmation of cooperation."[88] However, as van den Bergh soon revealed in his article "Can a Faithful Catholic Be an Even More Faithful National Socialist?," both he and Pircher were far from being apolitical clergymen.[89] Still, in their public utterances they continued to emphasize their aim for a peaceful relationship between church and state.[90]

By September church-state relations had deteriorated in Austria. On September 4 the Austrian bishops had also expressed in a pastoral letter their concerns about the state's curtailment of the Church's pastoral mission.[91] Such worries led the bishops to feel that they could not allow any group of clerics to rival their collective authority and interfere with their ongoing discussion with state and party officials. The growth and perceived influence of Pircher's association also alarmed them. According to Pircher, 525 priests had joined his association and an additional 1,844 had somehow indicated to him their sympathy for its objectives.[92] With these concerns in mind, on September 18, 1938, the Austrian bishops formally prohibited the Association for Religious Peace.[93]

Naturally Pircher had an extremely difficult time accepting the Austrian bishops' decision, and he continued to prepare newsletters that contained reports on church-state relations for former clerical members of his association. For example, in his second newsletter of January 1939 Pircher strongly expressed his frustration with the prohibition by making known his belief that "only a clergy" that was "subjectively and objectively German—*völkisch* and National Socialistically focused—can and will overcome the struggle against the unjustified Church resistance and bring the desired spiritual peace to the German *Volk*. . . . It is only too true that no one is more deprived in our state than the national-minded priest: on the part of the Church he is despised and viewed as a traitor, he is passed over, at every turn persecuted, and, on account of his *völkisch* conviction, threatened with suspension; on the part of the state he is hardly taken into account, indeed, sometimes even misjudged."[94] Fortunately for him, there were a number of Austrian and German clergymen at the time who would not rashly misjudge or easily dismiss Pircher's point of view. Among this group was Richard Kleine, who soon found a loyal comrade in Johann Pircher.

Forming a National Socialist Priests' Group

In December 1938 Kleine and Pircher met in Cologne. It is unclear whether they had met earlier. Perhaps Kleine learned of Pircher's work from the publicity surrounding the prohibition of the Association for Religious Peace and invited him to the Cologne meeting.[95] In any case, by March 1939 Kleine and Pircher had established a working relationship strong enough to address each other as comrade in arms.[96]

In early March 1939 Kleine and Pircher also shared a similar concern: whom would the College of Cardinals elect to replace the recently deceased Pius XI? On February 10, the very day of the pope's death, Kleine had already joyfully written to Pircher that owing to "the death of the Holy Father" and the upcoming election, "the era of Pacelli along with its supporters will be finished."[97] Both he and Pircher attributed the "oppositional" course of the German Catholic Church to Pacelli's influence on the German episcopacy. Almost a month later, on March 2, Kleine had to reverse his analysis of the situation when the College of Cardinals elected Eugenio Pacelli as pope. Kleine shared his deep disappointment with Pircher, writing, "The most dangerous opponent of the new Germany in our Church, Pacelli, has today already, in the third ballot, been elevated by two-thirds of the College of Cardinals to become the head of our Church, with the thunderous applause of an entire world that is set against us Germans." Kleine deemed it "the most official insult of the official Church 'leadership' against Adolf Hitler and Benito Mussolini." Still he held out hope that the German Catholic Church could overcome this obstacle. He told Pircher that "Pius XII should know that the vast majority of Catholic Germans in no way joins in the jubilant hymn of the world press, and certainly he must know that from the start, so that as the pope will not bring about a catastrophe."[98] To another confidant Kleine wrote, "Pacelli has become Pope . . . this is a catastrophe in the history of the Church. I am stunned, since I had firmly hoped that this papal election would halt the suicidal course of the Church, which is embodied particularly in this man."[99]

Though such fiery rhetoric expressed Kleine's and Pircher's frustration at recent developments in their Church, in late April the German bishops offered them and other like-minded priests a temporary reprieve from their Nazi concerns when many of them individually ordered the "celebratory ringing of bells" in their diocesan churches in honor of Hitler's fiftieth birthday. Kleine specifically expressed how much this action pleased him and also told Pircher of his joy when he saw how his diocese's newspaper "finally" carried "a nice editorial article" about Hitler.[100] Still Kleine and Pircher felt that these were only momentary awakenings of the bishops' senses, and consequently they could no longer simply share their mutual dreams and ideas but now had to work on their own to make them a reality. To this end, they agreed to establish a new priests' group that would both support National Socialism and redirect the Church from its "suicidal" course to a more harmonious relationship with the state.

In order to avoid the pitfalls of the prohibited association, Pircher also suggested that this new group have no external organizational apparatus and have a limited and exclusive membership. This time Pircher wanted only priests who were "loyal to the Church, National-Socialist-minded, academic in nature, and courageous." He also recommended that the members consistently work together and consensually agree before releasing any document or taking concrete action.[101] Such thinking made it clear that Pircher did not wish to risk any leakage of information that might cause his fellow priests or bishops to reprimand him. Thus, instead of immediately presenting the group's views in the public arena, Pircher initially advocated behind-the-scenes action that would promote change within the Church. In particular, he believed that the right moment would come eventually when Hitler would call the group's members "to the front" to take leadership roles in the church question. Then they would fulfill their duty "courageously and honorably."[102]

Kleine found Pircher's suggestions to be sound. He also insisted that they "tenaciously" preserve their "faith in our Führer despite the radical rejection of the Christian churches by influential circles . . . of the party."[103] Still, until Hitler decisively intervened, Kleine and Pircher believed that the Führer had left the overwhelming mission of strengthening the working relationship between National Socialism and Catholicism to them alone.

To organize their priests' group, Pircher first turned to clerics whom he knew well and who also had a proven track record in their support for National Socialism. Among them were Wilhelm van den Bergh, pastor of Rauchenwarth and former acting chair of the Association for Religious Peace; Dr. Alois Cloß, a priest of the Graz-Seckau diocese, who taught comparative theology briefly at the University of Vienna and then became a researcher at the Steiermark State Library until the end of the war; Dr. Ernst Kortschak, a Cistercian monk and abbot of the Rein monastery; Dr. Alois Nikolussi, a priest of the Austrian Congregation of the Canons Regular of St. Augustine, who taught New Testament studies in a college near his order's monastery, St. Florian, and served as pastor of the Asten and then St. Florian parishes; and Dr. Simon Pirchegger, a priest of the Graz-Seckau diocese and, since 1936, an instructor of Slavic studies at the University of Bonn.[104]

In addition to these individuals, Kleine and Pircher wished to include in their group academics who had significant scholarly reputations and who were also open to National Socialism. To meet this goal, they first reached out to Dr. Joseph Mayer, a priest of the Augsburg diocese and professor of moral theology at the Philosophical and Theological College in Paderborn. In 1927 the publication of Mayer's dissertation, *The Legal Sterilization of the Mentally Ill*, brought him to the fore of the sterilization and eugenics debate in Weimar Germany.[105] Surprisingly published with the Church's imprimatur and positively reviewed by many Catholic theologians, this work argued for the acceptance of the state's right to sterilize an individual for medical and security reasons under certain limited provisions.[106] Mayer also would offer a similar argument in favor of abortion. In May 1933 he altered his analysis of sterilization to follow more closely the racially based reasoning advocated by National Socialist ideology. Thus Mayer's revised interpretation supported the Reich Cabinet when on July 14 it passed the Law for the Prevention of Hereditarily Diseased Offspring, which legalized forced sterilization.[107] Mayer would continue his support of National Socialism by serving as an informant to the SD and publishing in 1939 in *Schönere Zukunft,* a leading Austrian Catholic weekly, the article "The Living Space Question of the Peoples in Light of the Christian Conception of Natural Law," which validated the National Socialist aggressive and annihilative expansionist principle of *Lebensraum* (living space).[108] There is also evidence, though not conclusive, that in 1940 the SS officer and former Munich Catholic priest Albert Hartl commissioned Mayer to write a study that supported euthanasia from the viewpoint of Catholic morality.[109]

Initially Mayer graciously accepted the offer to join the priests' group and expressed his agreement with their approach. He also added that "we"—now counting himself among their number—"must strive" to promote a "totally national, indeed National Socialist outlook among the rational part of the clergy. Furthermore, we must ensure that the princes of the Church no longer ostracize our national way of thinking, and indirectly we must bring Rome, its Vatican Radio, and the *Osservatore Romano* to a point where they no longer encroach upon our national outlook, at the minimum by reining in their hatred against Hitler."[110] Mayer's decision and attitude pleased both Pircher and Kleine. Tension developed quickly, however, when Dr. Pirchegger confided to Pircher that Mayer, along with his colleague Dr. Adolf Herte, a priest of the Paderborn archdiocese and a professor of church history and patristics, desired to make Paderborn the central place of activity for clergymen who supported the NSDAP. Of course, these ambitions did not sit well with Pircher, who viewed Vienna as the center of the endeavor. Still, he was willing to give Mayer the benefit of the doubt, though a certain level of mistrust set in.[111]

From February through October 1939 Kleine and Pircher considered a wide selection of clergymen for membership in their group. In February 1939 this even included approaching Father Philipp Haeuser's friend Franz Xaver Eberle, the auxiliary bishop of Augsburg. On December 6,

1937, through his own engineering and contacts, Eberle had met privately with Hitler in the Reich Chancellery to discuss current church-state relations. Though the two spoke frankly for ninety minutes, no concrete changes in church-state relations resulted.[112] Still, Eberle's overture to Hitler impressed Pircher a great deal, so much so that he arranged a meeting with him. According to Pircher, Eberle spoke openly about his meeting with Hitler and said that he had conveyed the contents of the meeting in a letter to Eugenio Pacelli, the cardinal secretary of state.[113] Then he shared his frustration by asking Pircher, "What do you think . . . that someone will answer me from Rome? Not one word so far!" Hearing Eberle express his frustration, Pircher exclaimed, "This leads one to conclude how little our work is valued there. Still, we will push onward until the objective is achieved."[114] Though Eberle was sympathetic to their cause, he did not join their circle.

As the work of Kleine and Pircher's group became better known, individual clergymen approached them and expressed their willingness to collaborate. In October 1943 Josef Thomé, a priest of the Aachen diocese and leader in the liturgical reform movement, had written to Kleine and expressed interest in the possibility of their two groups working together. Though this peaked Kleine's curiosity, he replied, "Concerning your group of 'Friends of Church Reform,' before I can pave the way for cooperation with my comrades, I must inquire about how this group and its individual members position themselves to the Führer and the Reich and whether possibly any individuals are tainted in one way or another through affiliation with any previous leagues or organizations. . . . We demand from everyone who wants to work with us on the great tasks for Reich and Church steadfast loyalty to the Führer and Reich and also to the Church."[115] Thomé was a bit taken aback by Kleine's politically charged attitude and especially with his request to conduct background checks on his colleagues and did not pursue further collaboration. Ever the gentleman, Thomé responded, "Both groups, yours and mine . . . work in two different areas. Therefore, it appears to me to be better if we march onward separately."[116] Despite going in different directions, Kleine's determined character and steadfastness of mission attracted Thomé, who continued to correspond with him well into 1944.[117]

Though they considered additional theologians and priests, by the end of October 1939 Pircher and Kleine had essentially completed their membership drive for the small circle of National-Socialist-minded priests, a group at times they referred to as a "community of the like-minded."[118] Pircher expressed his joy over this fact to Kleine when he wrote, "In our circle, the nobility with which mutual criticism is practiced and accepted is encouraging. When one looks closely, one can recognize the exact makeup of the co-workers. Kleine is the lightning catapult, Nikolussi the hammer, . . . Pirchegger somewhat timid, Mayer more than cautious, and van den Bergh the Flying Dutchman who is in no way definable."[119]

German Ecumenism

In the spring of 1939, while forming their group of like-minded priests to support National Socialism, Kleine and Pircher came into contact with A. Brücker, a Catholic layman, who was also an ardent National Socialist.[120] The efforts of the two priests to promote National Socialism among Catholics attracted Brücker to them. For their part, Kleine and Pircher found Brücker of particular importance because of his contacts with National Socialists who were Protestants or who practiced some form of neopaganism.

Soon after their initial meeting Brücker gave them the idea of "convening a General German Church Council with the goal of church-religious unification." Kleine explained that for Brücker this meant bringing together "Catholic, Protestant, and God-believing Germans . . . and with the help of influential personalities to recommend the event to the Führer and the pope." For Kleine this was a utopian idea, and, he argued, if Brücker pursued it, he would only "get himself into hot water."[121] Nevertheless, Kleine could not easily dismiss Brücker's idea, especially because of his personal interest in German ecumenism.[122] Kleine viewed the international ecumenical movement with suspicion. In 1940 he would even accuse it of working directly in the service of Jews and the British against the Third Reich.[123] Though needing no encouragement for his own antisemitism, Kleine made the latter accusation after the 1937 Oxford Life and Work World Conference passed certain motions that the German Reich government interpreted as hostile.[124] By that time Kleine had simply embraced the National Socialist view that the entire international ecumenical movement worked against the German Reich.[125] His personal embracing of National Socialist ideology, especially with its emphasis on German Aryan superiority, clearly made it impossible for him to be truly open to a dialogue with Christians from other nations and with the peoples whom the Third Reich deemed unworthy of consideration.

In essence Kleine agreed with Brücker's idea of creating an ecumenical movement based upon racial and national lines. However, he was extremely cautious in the manner in which he articulated his understanding of this concept. Rather than advocating a General German Church Council, which too closely mirrored the idea of a German national church, Kleine promoted "reunification in faith," which would highlight the cooperation among all Christians in the German Reich to support the goals of National Socialism and to promote a positive working relationship between the government and the German churches.[126] In contrast to the general understanding of ecumenism, which encompasses dialogue solely among Christian churches, Kleine included Aryan *gottgläubig* individuals, those who professed a belief in God but did not belong to a specific denomination.[127] Kleine could not envision any "reunification" that specifically excluded "racial comrades" who believed in God. Despite their past hostility toward Catholicism, Kleine even included some individuals associated with the neopagan German Faith movement. By May 1939 this openness led him to invite Count Ernst zu Reventlow, a former leading member of the German Faith movement and long-serving NSDAP Reichstag representative, to enter into discussions with him and his priests' group about some future means of collaboration. Kleine already had been corresponding with Reventlow for several years, even sharing with the count Brücker's proposal for a General German Church Council. Though Reventlow no longer represented any official religious group, Kleine viewed him as the spokesperson of those whom he referred to as "religious non-Christians."[128]

Though a bit skeptical about Brücker's proposal, Reventlow graciously accepted Kleine's invitation to talk with him about this issue.[129] On May 30, 1939, Kleine traveled to Potsdam and personally visited Count Reventlow at his home. Their discussion went well, though both men realistically admitted the huge obstacles that lay ahead of them.[130] In a subsequent letter Reventlow reiterated parts of their conversation, noting that he wanted to reassure Kleine that "such a convening obviously will come only at the end of a rather long and difficult development. For the time being, the theme is to be dealt with only academically, and even then there is the question whether and when such discussion can publicly take place."[131] Kleine was not taken aback by this reluctant response; rather, Reventlow had articulated Kleine's preferred method of approach: to study an issue in detail and prepare for a future summons to action.

Upon gaining Reventlow's support, Kleine decided it was time to organize a meeting among the various groups to discuss the question of collaboration. However, before he could finalize the arrangements for this meeting, Kleine still had to approach one additional group, the German Christians. Kleine was hesitant about making an overture because two years earlier he had had to "abruptly" end his correspondence with some of their members because their movement had "unmistakably evolved into a manner of combat troops against Catholicism."[132] Still, realizing the importance of having some Protestant presence at the meeting, he decided to look beyond his past experiences and invite representatives of this group to the meeting.

Once he had decided to include the German Christians in his dialogue, another dilemma arose: whom among the German Christians should he invite? To answer this question, Kleine sought counsel from his colleague Brücker, who, in turn, recommended that he contact Siegfried Leffler, a Protestant pastor in the German state of Thüringen and cofounder of one of the oldest German Christian groups.[133] Kleine first contacted Leffler by letter and stressed that "we Catholics absolutely want to take part in the solution of the religious question."[134] At the same time, in keeping with Brücker's suggestion, Kleine also wrote to Friedrich Kapferer, a former priest of the Freiburg archdiocese, who had left the priesthood in 1938, joined the German Christians, became the leader of its Catholic division, centered in Eisenach, Thüringen, and eventually married.[135]

In his private correspondence with his friend Pircher, Kleine expressed his doubts about both Leffler and Kapferer. The latter individual truly troubled him, especially since Kleine realized that he would have to work with him in his role as leader of the Catholic German Christians. Kleine warned Pircher, "We should not get involved with Kapferer any more than is absolutely necessary. I can already envision the derisive laughter and triumphant howls of our opponents within the Church as they label us before the Catholic public as 'coupled together' with 'fallen,' let alone 'married,' priests."[136] Kleine even went a step further and asked Count Reventlow's advice on whether or not he should attempt to exclude Kapferer.[137] Though Reventlow was sympathetic to Kleine's concerns, he advised against Kapferer's exclusion. He feared that such an action might destroy any possibility of a working relationship between the Catholics and the German Christians.[138] In the end, Kleine included Kapferer in his invitation. His hesitation reveals that, despite his radical stance toward National Socialism and his willingness to engage Christians and religious non-Christians in the dialogue about reunification, Kleine was still quite traditional in his view of the priesthood. In his mind, Kapferer had severely tainted the priesthood by leaving his ministry and getting married.[139]

On December 7 Kleine sent out invitations to his priests' group, to the leadership of the German Christians in Eisenach, and to the religious non-Christians centered around Count Reventlow. All were to attend an initial meeting "for joint religious reconstruction work" on December 31, 1939, in Cologne. On the day of the meeting the following were in attendance: Kleine, Pircher, and Brücker, representing German Catholics; Dr. Strassburg, representing Count Reventlow and the religious non-Christians; Walter Schultz, the Evangelical-Lutheran bishop of Mecklenburg; Pastor Siegfried Leffler; Friedrich Kapferer; and one additional, unnamed individual, representing the German Christians.[140]

According to Kleine, the members of the three groups had a positive discussion. For him, it was enough "to sit together with German comrades of different denominations who expressed [their] views in order then to feel the heartening experience of hope, . . . then to move mighty mountains." Yet, he still yearned for something concrete to result from their dialogue. At the outset Kleine and Pircher made it clear to everyone in attendance that they could "in no way make or tolerate any concessions on any point that we as Catholics are bound to represent." For Kleine this included respecting the "universal nature" of the Church and the "rejection of a national church." Kleine happily reported there was respect for the Catholic position among those in attendance, even among the German Christians whose Eisenach branch had advocated the creation of a German national church. Furthermore, Kleine noted that all in attendance agreed that their aim was not to recreate the Church "as it existed before the Reformation." According to him, those present made this clear from the beginning so that no one would attempt to "invoke the disaster of such wishful thinking." Rather, the three diverse groups would now "logically begin the work" not of "demolishing but [of] energetic building for the future." Kleine reported that they concluded their meeting agreeing on "total respect for the beliefs of their partners and the undiminished independence of every group." He then added that those present were "convinced" that they had "treaded a completely new path."[141]

Ecumenism and the "Jewish Question"

The Group for Joint Religious Reconstruction Work met again on May 4 in Weimar and May 5 in Eisenach, the latter a stronghold of the German Christian movement. Before this meeting Kleine raised the question with Pircher about whether or not they, as Catholics priests, should participate in the scheduled liturgy.[142] He was fully aware that such a practice was a severe infraction of canon law, in which a bishop could deem the participants heretics and even subject them to excommunication and loss of both clerical faculties and office.[143] Despite his voiced concerns, Kleine along with Brücker and Pircher attended the gathering and participated in the common religious service.[144] After that weekend meeting Kleine declared, "The Weimar-Eisenach experience has historical significance."[145]

While in Eisenach, Kleine's German Christian colleagues introduced him to Walter Grundmann, professor of *völkisch* theology and the New Testament at the University of Jena and academic director of the Institute for the Study and Eradication of Jewish Influence on German Church Life.[146] Though it was not an official function of the German Christians, Protestants who were involved with the German Christian movement founded the institute following the April 4, 1939, signing of the Godesberg Declaration "by representatives of eleven regional Protestant Churches." This declaration essentially asked, "What is the relation between Judaism and Christianity? Is Christianity derived from Judaism and is it its continuation and completion, or does Christianity stand in opposition to Judaism? We answer this question: Christianity is the unbridgeable religious opposition to Judaism."[147]

During their meeting Grundmann shared with Kleine his work *Jesus the Galilean and Jewry,* in which he portrayed Jesus in opposition to Judaism and argued for his non-Jewish ancestry. Grundmann also gave Kleine a copy of the institute's *The Message of God,* a compilation of excerpts from the synoptic Gospels void of any references to Jews or Judaism. The institute's members envisioned an entirely reinterpreted New Testament, entitled *The Volk Testament.*[148] Kleine immediately devoured both publications and wrote a lengthy critique. He generally praised Grundmann's *Jesus the Galilean* and found it a solid work. However, he also pointed out that Grundmann had missed an essential fact in his analysis of Christ, namely, "that Christ's monumental struggle with Jewry broke out in full force at the very beginning of his public ministry." According to Kleine, the Sermon on the Mount belonged "not in the middle, but completely at the beginning," for it "opens this battle in the most aggressive form." He continued, "One cannot completely and fully grasp the Gospel without this absolutely essential point, in the same way, for example, that future generations cannot comprehend Hitler's mission without realizing the fighting spirit in which it unfolded and was brought to fruition. If Christ had written his life's work, he would have more than likely chosen a title similar to *Mein Kampf.*"[149]

Kleine similarly reviewed *The Message of God* positively. According to him, Luther first perfected the Gospels when he translated them into his "German mother tongue." "Now," he stated, "*The Message of God* goes even further." He then asked, "Should the new *Volk Testament* replace the Gospels, taking their place and discharging their authentic character in exchange for a newly written document?" He admitted that even "after examination" he could not "give a clear answer to this," but he still considered "this question to be essential." He contemplated further, "Or should the new *Volk Testament* be only a resource in order to pave the German people's way to Christ?" He concluded, "I must assume that it will be at the same time a resource and a document."[150]

In May 1940 Kleine shared his critique with the institute. Impressed by Kleine's insights, Grundmann invited Kleine to the institute's Second National Conference, held from March 3 to 5, 1941, at the Hotel Fürstenhof in Eisenach.[151] Kleine eagerly accepted the invitation.[152] In the late afternoon of March 3 in the Wartburg castle's Great Banquet Hall, the conference began with the participants' singing Martin Luther's "A Mighty Fortress Is Our God." After local political dignitaries had formally welcomed the guests, Professor Grundmann delivered the opening address. Then two institute members presented their papers, "German, Jewish, and Christian Ideas of God" and "Racial History of the Middle East and the Study of the Old Testament." Over the course of the next two days the participants worshipped together, using *The Message of God* as their biblical text, and listened to one paper being read after the other. Apparently, all of their pseudohistorical and biblical studies worked to negate Judaism and strengthen a *völkisch* interpretation of Scripture and theology.[153]

The entire experience in the Wartburg elated Kleine. What particularly pleased him was Professor Grundmann's personal invitation to him "to assist with the work of the institute." Shortly after the meeting, Kleine contacted Grundmann and accepted his offer by including two of his articles and writing, "In case you should, on the basis of these articles, be interested in the manner in which I grapple with the Jews, I am very willing to send you further articles."[154] Though it took Grundmann almost two months to reply, Kleine's articles deeply impressed him. On May 31, 1941, he invited Kleine to help establish a study group under the auspices of the institute to examine "the question of Jewish influence and the continued effect of Germanic piety upon German Catholicism." Grundmann also asked Kleine to attend the first organizational meeting on Friday, June 6, in Weimar and agreed to reimburse Kleine for all travel costs.[155] Surprisingly, Kleine declined the offer by stating that he could not be present because of teaching obligations, but he requested minutes from the meeting and expressed his continued interest in the project.[156]

In early June the first meeting of the study group went ahead without Kleine. Afterward, in early July, Grundmann informed Kleine that Pastor Karl Dungs of Essen-Kupferdreh, an active member of the German Christians as well as of Grundmann's institute, would serve as the study group's chair and be joined by Fathers Dr. Alois Cloß of the Graz-Seckau diocese and Franz Sales Seidl of the Passau diocese. In addition, the former Freiburg diocesan priest Friedrich Kapferer, along with five other individuals, would round out this groups' membership.[157]

Even before Kleine began his work with the Catholic Study Group, Grundmann had also invited him to participate in the discussions of a separate working group that were to take place on Friday, July 18. Grundmann had formed this group to evaluate religious-education textbooks and prepare a new curriculum for German schools. Kleine's background as a religion teacher and writer made him a perfect candidate for this task.[158] This time Kleine immediately accepted the invitation. In addition, he also shared with Grundmann the "important" work of Father Karl Adam, professor at the University of Tübingen. Kleine believed that Adam might be able to contribute to the work of the institute.[159]

Kleine never forgot Adam's positive review of *Redemption!* in the *Theologische Quartalschrift*. In May 1940 Kleine finally would be able to show his appreciation for Adam's act of kindness. The previous December in Aachen Adam had delivered the lecture "The Spiritual Situation of German Catholicism," in which he had not only expressed his desire for liturgical renewal and his longing for a general, theological shift away from the Church's traditional reliance on Neo-Scholasticism, but had gone a step further by asserting that Germany possessed a uniqueness in its unmatched expression of Catholicism, which he attributed to blood and race. But, to his dismay he found that the Vatican and German Church authorities were hesitant to salute this unconventional proposition and indeed had refused to recognize it. Consequently, Adam forewarned them that their failure to endorse this Germanic uniqueness ultimately would jeopardize the future of Catholicism in Germany. To forestall such a peril, he urged the Church to promote the full participation of Catholics in both the German *Volksgemeinschaft* and the National Socialist state. For Adam this specifically meant the involvement of German Catholic seminarians in military service, the incorporation of a greater degree of German culture into Catholic theology, the use of the German language in the liturgy, and the promotion of exclusively German Catholic saints, churches, chapels, and places of pilgrimage as touchstones of the Catholic faith.[160]

In May 1940 Kleine contacted Adam at an opportune time when Adam most needed support to thank him "most sincerely" for delivering the lecture.[161] By May 1940 Adam was battling significant criticism from many German Catholics who viewed his Aachen lecture as too optimistic and conciliatory toward National Socialism.[162] In particular, Monsignor Bernhard Lichtenberg, the provost of Berlin's St. Hedwig's Cathedral, had personally written to Adam and sharply criticized him.[163] In the midst of this criticism, Kleine's letter was most welcome. Adam expressed his gratitude by writing to Kleine, "You are likely to know from experience how grateful one feels when a friendly, compassionate word is heard amid the throng of hideous retorts and uncomprehending judgments." After discussing the "ossification of . . . Catholic thinking as a whole," Adam concluded, "How important would a *closer* association for all people of the same thinking, i.e., German thinking, be. Might you not be able to initiate it? Cordial regards! Heil Hitler!"[164]

Kleine's colleague Brücker would later say that Adam "is emotionally one of us."[165] Kleine, of course, fully agreed with this assessment. Not surprisingly, on May 24, 1940, Kleine wrote to Adam and described to him the work of the priests' group, including their efforts for "reunification in faith," and invited Adam to join them.[166] At the same time, Kleine informed Pircher about this latest development and assured him that he would proceed cautiously in regard to how much information to give Adam about the various undertakings of their group.[167] Upon receiving Kleine's invitation, Adam responded in the affirmative by stating, "As Germans who have been awakened by Hitler's genius to their full self, we particularly cannot bear being permanently separated from our brothers in the deepest and holiest respects. Therefore, change *has* to be brought about—if not by the Church leadership, then by us. There is as well a holy defiance and a holy revolution. . . . For this reason, I am happy to join your group." Adam also shared his belief that everything depended on "whether we Catholics will succeed in establishing a truly German Catholicism. In my opinion, success can be hoped for *only* if the Führer issues a command to give us a German metropolitan who will possess sufficient energy to de-Romanize the entire teaching of the Church, including everything pertaining to the liturgy, catechesis, pastoral work, the education of theologians, etc., and to Germanize them." Adam did add that this metropolitan "must be as determinedly *Catholic* as German, and he must be appointed with Rome's *consent*, not in opposition to Rome."[168]

Adam's reply could not have pleased Kleine more. In late May Kleine reported with elation his "coup," as it were, to Pircher and warned him that they must not misuse Adam's membership.[169] Pircher ignored his friend's cautions and wrote to Adam directly, welcoming him into their "group of National Socialist priests."[170] Pircher's letter confused and worried Adam. Primarily, the designation of "National Socialist priests" troubled him greatly. Though he supported much within the state and National Socialism, he still did not consider himself a National Socialist but a patriotic, nationalistic German Catholic.[171] Pircher had gone too far. On June 7 Adam expressed this fact to Kleine. In no way, Adam stressed, did he want his membership in Kleine's group to mean that he had "become a member of a political and social circle." He feared that such a designation would "isolate" him "from those Catholics who have the same German attitude but are not members of any party." He then reminded Kleine that it was "our goal to provide Catholicism with a new substantial basis by means of German characteristics and German ethnicity because the old 'whole-world basis' has become brittle." This, he assured Kleine, was how he had interpreted their "comradeship."[172]

On June 10 Adam followed up his earlier letter to Kleine with an even stronger one. In it he wrote that Kleine's group was "not a loose association of like-minded persons . . . who strive, on the basis of deeply felt German ethnicity, to achieve a rapprochement of the religiously separated German denominations, but [was] instead a 'group of National Socialist priests,' and thus an eminently political group." "No matter how highly I regard Hitler's heroic figure," he concluded, "and no matter how much I believe in the providential nature of his activity, I could not and should not, as an honest individual, call myself a 'National Socialist,' since I cannot subscribe to the anti-Christian attitude of the party. I have therefore written to J[ohann] Pircher that—upon complete insight into the situation—I must revoke my joining of your circle."[173]

Upon receiving the first vacillating letter of June 7, Kleine wrote to Adam and attempted to assure him that the goal of the priests' group was "not the creation of a National Socialist cell in order to catch Catholics for National Socialism," but rather to awaken churches to the reality of the new German state. He also emphasized how the group had already begun to stand up for him against his opponents.[174] There is little evidence that the group actually attempted to fulfill that promise. Still, Kleine and Pircher did help to disseminate copies of Adam's Aachen lecture.[175] On June 19 Kleine sent a follow-up letter. This time his tone changed drastically. Instead of assuring Adam of the "altruistic," nonpolitical nature of the priests' group, Kleine now used threatening language that, in essence, pushed Adam to retain his membership. He told Adam that if he withdrew his membership, the priests' group would ultimately have to stop all intercessions in his behalf. In addition, Kleine demanded to know how Adam could say yes one minute, and no the next.[176]

Instead of ignoring Kleine's letters, Adam took them seriously. The Tübingen theologian felt compelled to defend himself by writing, "Above all, I would like to ask you to convince yourself that it is not cowardice that caused my initial yes to turn into a no, but rather fundamental considerations. There is no theologian in Germany whose life has been, from the beginning until today, as pugnacious as mine." Then Adam continued to explain that "Pircher's characterization of your circle as a 'group of National Socialist priests' startled me. As much as the driving spirit of the National Socialist movement has for years been the same as my own spirit, I cannot make friends with all (domestic political) incarnations of this spirit. But your kind letters . . . force me to go more deeply and, as it were, to bare my innermost soul to you. As a 'National Socialist group' you want to be (or become) a troop of fighters that, for the time being, prepares for the 'needed reformation' of the Church in the spirit and will of the Führer and is determined to implement it—when the Führer calls— if necessary even without the pope and the bishops, or even in opposition to them. In the light of this attitude, my Aachen lecture seemed to me nothing but harmless, . . . child's prattle. And it is only now . . . that I realize that so far I have taken too shallow a view of the entire reform question and have not thought it through sufficiently. . . . If I acknowledged that I am a 'National Socialist priest' in the sense of your group, then I would be obliged to follow [Hitler's] decision totally and submit completely to his program. Most severe conflicts of conscience will then be inevitable . . . for the time being, I cannot do otherwise than serve the National Socialist spirit, deeply though I experience it, in my own way, without a precise 'National Socialist' brand."[177]

Seeing that his previous two letters had at least been successful in persuading Adam to rethink his negative decision, Kleine wrote back to him and assured the professor that "it appears that in principle you are really one of us."[178] Pircher also followed Kleine's example by writing to Adam and assuring him that their priests' group was "not a rigid organization, but strived only for contact between like-minded priests." He assured him that there were many priests among them who were not party members and enclosed a copy of his June 1940 *Comradely Exchange of Ideas,* a newsletter about the church-state situation, which he regularly prepared and sent out to priests who shared similar interests.[179] Evidently Kleine and Pircher persuaded Adam to change his mind. On June 28 Adam wrote to Kleine, "The ice has been broken. Your dear efforts had already contributed much, even most, and the final thrust was provided today by Pircher's letter, . . . removing all my misgivings. In the *Comradely Exchange of Ideas* . . . I encountered nothing but spiritual mates or, rather, soul mates who wish to be Germans as consciously as they wish to be priests, hence 'German priests.' It must be a pleasure to be, and be active, in this circle. Therefore, please make me again a member of your comradely group." He then asked Kleine to please "forget all the annoyances that my hesitation has caused you. That hesitation was not in vain, as it introduced me more profoundly to your goals and allowed me to see many things more clearly than had been the case earlier. Heil Hitler!"[180]

From this point onward Adam and Kleine began an intense period of correspondence, in which they supported one another. In December 1940 Adam not only gave Kleine permission to use the informal German address *"du"* (you), but also asked him to rally significant party members to intercede on his behalf. According to Adam, "subterranean clerical forces" were "stirring in an effort to forestall the effect" of his Aachen lecture "upon the Catholic German public and to discredit" him and his "theological reputation." He even confessed that a colleague of his had informed him that there were "plans for holding a meeting of clergy in Würzburg" against him.[181] Kleine immediately wrote back to Adam and promised to intercede for him.[182] Despite Kleine's insinuation that he had high contacts within the NSDAP, he chose to write only a letter of concern on Adam's behalf to Cardinal Bertram of Breslau.[183]

By April 1941 Kleine felt he could trust Adam enough to reveal to him his work with the Eisenach institute and acknowledge attending its national conference the previous month.[184] This revelation did not bother Adam in the least. Rather, he confided to Kleine that he lived and died "for the conviction that Christianity viewed and realized as a life force has been and remains the only viable form for the German people. Of course, its core must be freed from all Jewish-Hellenistic and especially from all medieval feudal and canonically ossified appendages."[185] Neither Adam nor Kleine had much love for the Church's Neo-Scholastic theology. Moreover, they had no respect for Jews and Judaism at all. Therefore, Adam argued, they had to find their "way back to 'Christ's Christianity,' to the beginnings." And he believed that "to the extent that the National Socialist movement offers a most powerful impetus for a resumption of this essential Christianity, an awakening of this movement in theological circles would automatically work in favor of this necessary concentration within Christian teaching."[186]

Adam's letter assured Kleine that they were in close agreement over how they viewed the current state of the Church and theology in Germany. As a result, Kleine felt confident enough to assure Adam in his reply that the Eisenach institute's Catholic Study Group was specifically working to address the very points that he had raised, namely, uncovering the "true" roots of Christianity, which, in Kleine's view, lay far apart from Judaism. He invited Adam to join the work of their Catholic Study Group.[187] Kleine also sent him his essay "Was Jesus a Jew?," which he had been circulating since 1939.[188]

In "Was Jesus a Jew?" Kleine did not follow the path of many *völkisch* theologians, including Professor Grundmann, who argued that Jesus was not Jewish but was born of Aryan ancestry. Instead, Kleine attempted to avoid answering this question directly. According to Kleine, as the offspring of his mother, Mary, and the paternal Holy Spirit, Jesus remained free of any negative Jewish traits. He explained, "The Church expressly denies that Mary stands in the succession of sinful depravity; therefore, all the more reason that what is so hereditarily corrupting in Jewry is excluded from her and also from Jesus." Thus, even though Kleine technically did not say that Jesus was not Jewish, he did everything possible to separate him from his Jewish ancestry. For example, Kleine interpreted Jesus' scriptural rejection of the Messiah's political role as a complete rejection of Judaism and his Jewish ancestry. He also argued that figures central to the gospel narrative and Jesus' close companions, such as John the Baptist, the apostles, and Mary Magdalene were exempted from the "hereditary evils" of Judaism. Thus, for example, Kleine reasoned, "John the Baptist could not possibly have come from a succession of generations that would stand in blatant contrast to the outstanding greatness of this 'voice in the wilderness.'"[189]

In sharp contrast to these exceptional biblical figures, Kleine labeled all remaining Jews, including those who left their Jewish faith to follow Jesus, as troublesome. He wrote, "Indeed, even the baptized Jews, the Jewish Christians, by questionable behavior and, indeed, by the nature of their Jewish behavior, caused such serious dangers for the early Church that one must speak of this as the first great test of the Church; the *Acts of the Apostles* and the letters of the apostles are full of the reverberations of this struggle of life and death." Further on in the essay he clarified this point by explaining, "There were many bitter experiences for the Church . . . in cases where this precaution that a Jew remains a Jew after baptism, just as a negro remains a negro and a German a German, was not minded." Kleine quickly caught himself, however, and noted that, "of course, we cannot think poorly of the supernatural effect of grace." After all, "a beneficial effect may be expected . . . from a drastic intervention in the eastern Jewish ghettos in Poland. . . . The German *Volk* must in all circumstances be separated hermetically from Jewry, even if baptized. Also, in the Christian churches of our *Volk* the Jewish Christians are unbearable. One could bring them together in Jewish-Christian parishes. We have already experienced in the case of the Poles who live in Germany that they remain—and indeed not only on account of their native Polish language—an alien element in our parishes and feel so themselves. How much greater, then, is our distance from Jewry! Already in the early Church the Jewish-Christians and the Jewish-Christian communities led a special existence that created many and great difficulties for Christians from other peoples. . . . Only when a neat separation arose in Jewish-Christian communities could the Church there experience the strength of its mission for the peoples of this earth and be able to make itself felt."[190]

On June 24, 1941, Karl Adam sent Kleine his response to this essay and noted that "I agree with you that, in accordance with the teaching of the New Testament, Jesus was connected to Judaism only on his mother's side, and that this mother, in accordance with the dogma of the immaculate conception, was also protected from the bad influences of Jewish heredity by the first instance of her conception." Then Adam challenged Kleine to deepen his argument theologically by writing, "Perhaps one could dig even deeper by distinguishing in Jewish nature between blood and 'spirit,' i.e., differentiating the natural, ethnic being of the Jewish people and their supernatural vocation. In its ethnic substance Jewry has always been anti-God, which is also why Christ's teaching was entirely anti-Jewish in its tenor (that is why he was crucified). But that did not rule out the supernatural vocation of individuals. Precisely in contrast with the God-defying natural Jewish substance, and in fighting it, the supernatural was to prove its worth and to acquire substance (that is why the entire Sermon on the Prophets is pervaded by a rejection of Jewish mass instincts, and that is why all the prophets fell prey to these instincts as martyrs). It is only in this anti-Jewish sense that 'salvation' truly emanated from the Jews."[191]

Kleine's arguments about Jesus' Jewish origins had thus stimulated Adam's thinking. The theology professor was not content to allow the dialogue to end in a minor correspondence between two individuals. Consequently, in 1943 he wrote "Jesus, the Christ, and We Germans," in which he repeated many of Kleine's original assertions about Christ, including his emphasis on Mary's immaculate conception as the means of exempting Jesus' inheritance from any negative Jewish traits.[192] In essence, Adam put Kleine's basic argument into publishable theological language and context. Still, he needed assistance to publish such a strong piece. In February 1943 Adam approached Kleine and sought his help to find a journal willing to print the article. Through Kleine's intercession, *Wissenschaft und Weisheit* published it a few months later.[193]

Clearly, Adam's support for his theological interpretation of Jesus' origins pleased Kleine to no end. As Kleine noted, he could now rest comfortably because he had a colleague with whom he could discuss "the resolution of the Jewish question in religious respects."[194]

Despite their encouraging exchange of ideas Kleine never was able to persuade Adam to become directly involved in the work of Grundmann's institute. In July 1941, upon being informed of Adam's involvement in Kleine's priests' group, Grundmann himself showed interest in having the Tübingen professor become more involved with his institute. At best, Adam's minimal involvement meant only that Grundmann had placed Adam on the institute's mailing list to keep him well informed of its "research endeavors."[195] Nevertheless, Adam's willingness to engage himself seriously and reflectively through correspondence was enough for Kleine to deem their relationship worthwhile.

Kleine considered his relationship with Karl Adam much more significant by far than the one he shared with Professor Josef Mayer. Kleine attempted many times to bring Mayer fully into the work of the priests' group.[196] However, Mayer repeatedly gave various excuses why he could not attend meetings or work on specific projects. At times Mayer also forced Kleine to evaluate ambiguous situations realistically. In January 1940, when the priests' group joined the Group for Joint Reconstruction Work, Mayer wrote to Kleine, "Let us be clear that between the Roman Catholic Church and any German attempt at reform, a reconciliation, or even a settlement in human terms is absolutely ruled out." This, he assured Kleine, was a "realistic, sober" fact. Then he added, "If you nevertheless have the courage, I have to admit that great ideas are able to achieve the impossible."[197] Kleine naturally resisted such thinking, and his attempt to persuade Mayer to think otherwise was to no great avail.[198] He made, of course, repeated additional attempts to involve Mayer in his various efforts. Yet, at best Kleine's various overtures to Mayer only revealed to the latter Kleine's lack of trust in him. According to Mayer, his own theological research and attention to family concerns took him away from assisting Kleine further.[199] It is impossible to know the specific reasons for Mayer's hesitation. Clearly, he had previously given enough indication that he supported the aims of National Socialism and the German Reich. However, Mayer might have carved out his own path of working with the state and no longer needed to work alongside Kleine. Or Mayer might have reacted toward Kleine out of envy and did not wish to encourage him in his efforts. It is also possible that Mayer felt Kleine had gone too far in his reunification work, especially in working so closely with Protestants in Grundmann's institute.

Did Kleine, for his part, view his work at Grundmann's institute as rebellious, exceeding theological boundaries? Hardly. In fact, Kleine even
pushed Grundmann to be more aggressive at times with regard to Jews.
In October 1941, as the National Socialist state deported German Jews to
horrendous ghettos in the east, Kleine wrote to Grundmann, "The books
of the Old Testament, which we also consider to be Holy Scripture, were
written by Jews, and hence by men called upon by the Holy Spirit to
document in detail the two lines [of argument] contained in these Old
Testament texts: the positive [line], which illuminates God's paving the
way toward Christ, and the negative [line], which provides testimony of
the fate of the [positive line] being crossed even to the extent of Christ's
crucifixion. God himself saw to it that both [lines] were written down—
not cleanly separated from one another, but in their interactive, dynamic and living effect, so that—although it is difficult for us to separate the two [lines] very precisely—we find it actually easy to experience
so deeply this immense, crucial drama in the fight of light versus dark
that, from that point of view, this Judaism should really be forever finished—along with anything that might somehow threaten to, or be
tempted to, similarly cross the real meaning of the era after Christ's
birth." Nevertheless, Kleine still worried about optimists "who are of the
opinion that the banning of Juda[ism] from Germany, and now from
Europe as well, has eliminated this danger. True, the danger has been
banished to a high degree. But has it been banished completely?"
Highly pleased by Kleine's way of thinking, Grundmann responded, "I
consider your work in the Catholic area . . . extraordinarily important"
and requested to see more of his writings on this subject.[200]

By 1942 Kleine had become deeply involved in the workings of the
Institute for the Study and Eradication of Jewish Influence on German
Church Life. In June of that same year he attended the institute's national conference in Nuremberg. The conference events that he experienced and the papers he heard delivered instilled in him an urgency
greater than he had ever experienced. Upon returning home, Kleine
confided to his friend Karl Adam how "disheartened" he was to learn
how "hopeless" Catholic Germans were in the way they examined the
monumental impending religious issues of the day. This feeling compelled him to seek out like-minded individuals to join in the work of the
institute. He asked Adam, "Don't you know anyone who might be a
good fit? They would have to be men who really have something to say.
Don't we Catholic Germans have such men, not even in this historic
moment, who also address the most monumental confrontation with
the Jews?"[201]

In the following year Kleine's feeling of urgency only intensified. On January 31, 1943, following the failed battle of Stalingrad, the German army finally showed that it was not invincible when General Field Marshal Friedrich Paulus surrendered the *Wehrmacht*'s Sixth Army to the Soviets. Karl Adam lamented to his friend Kleine, "The gloomy clouds around us are beginning to get denser. My faith in Hitler alone gives me confidence that we will victoriously penetrate this cloud."[202] Days later, on February 18, in the Berlin Sport Palace, Reich Propaganda Minister Goebbels delivered a speech in which he declared a campaign of total war for Germany. Amid this chaos and almost apocalyptic atmosphere, Kleine prepared to do his part by authoring the essay "The Sermon on the Mount as a Challenge to Fight against Jewry." He believed such a publication would serve the effort of bringing a religious final solution to the "Jewish question." On April 25, 1943, Kleine wrote to Karl Dungs, the chair of the Grundmann institute's Catholic Study Group, and asked for permission to present his work at the next gathering in Vienna. Dungs consented to Kleine's request and told him to be ready to present it on August 11.[203]

The topic of the Sermon on the Mount was not new to Kleine. In 1935 he had published *The Eight Beatitudes of the Sermon on the Mount: Guidelines of the Kingdom of God for Homiletic Use*. In this purely pastoral work Kleine did not directly attack or belittle Jews. Nonetheless, he did explain that Christ's blessing of the meek was simply the act of a manly and heroic figure who was teaching his followers the virtues of living a noble life.[204] Kleine returned in 1940 to the Sermon on the Mount in a series of articles for *Der Neue Wille*, a Catholic weekly that supported National Socialism. In contrast to that found in his 1935 book, Kleine expressed in the weekly articles a distinctly negative tone toward Jews.[205] Kleine wrote in 1943 an essay that was aggressively hostile to Jews, far more hostile than anything he had written earlier.

On August 11, 1943, in Vienna, Kleine presented "The Sermon on the Mount as a Challenge to Fight against Jewry" before his colleagues. According to him, "the essential stumbling block between the National Socialist Reich and the Christian churches" was the relationship of Christianity to Judaism. The inherent hostility between the two was not an "academic question" to be pondered, but a fact intrinsic to the Gospels themselves. Now, he argued, it was the task of Christian preachers "to comprehend, in all its depth and significance, the struggle of Jesus Christ against Judaism" and to give it an "appropriate, passionate expression in our preaching." He exhorted his listeners, "It must be our most urgent task to present the Christian message from the viewpoint of the struggle of Jesus Christ against Judaism." Thus, for Kleine, in the Sermon on the Mount Jesus had first set forth on his campaign against Jews. Indeed, according to Kleine's exegesis of the well-known gospel passage, Jesus himself initiated the campaign against the Jews at the very start of his ministry.

In typical biblical exegetical style, Kleine went through the Beatitudes line by line to validate his overarching themes. An example of his anti-semitism clearly comes across in his examination of the Beatitude from Matthew's Gospel, "Blessed are you when they insult you, persecute you, and say all kinds of evil against you because of me. . . . For in the same way they persecuted the prophets before you." Kleine interpreted this passage as a literal condemnation of Jews who, he argued, always worked against Christ and his message. Furthermore, the implications of this teaching meant that a German bishop must never send a newly ordained priest to his first parish assignment with the biblical command, "'I am sending you like sheep among the wolves.' Beware your national comrades." Such an action, he argued, "would be a crime." Rather, the bishop should warn a young priest that the "adversary from the beginning is Jewry."[206]

Those in attendance received Kleine's paper positively. Dungs was so impressed that he asked Kleine for permission to copy and distribute it among the institute's membership. Of course, Kleine gave his consent. Dungs ensured that the paper received a wide distribution.[207] Through such a work Kleine had exceeded his earlier commitment to study the "evils" of Judaism and eradicate all Jewish influence in the Catholic Church. He did not display his zeal and dedication merely through writing and publishing. He traveled extensively through the Reich, meeting, speaking, and motivating like-minded individuals to work for the same cause. In April 1943 he admitted to his friend Adam that in the preceding nine months he had traveled more than 5,000 kilometers in an effort to disseminate his beliefs.[208] Through all of this, Kleine had convinced himself that something more concrete needed to result from his work. Thus, in 1943, through continued contact with a sympathetic bishop, Kleine attempted to produce something that would have a lasting effect.

Working Together against Bolshevism

By the spring of 1941 Kleine had gradually begun to make a name for himself, especially among the German Christians. Impressed by Kleine's unique willingness to engage in dialogue with Protestants, Bishop Walter Schultz, the Evangelical-Lutheran bishop of Mecklenburg and a member of the Faith Movement of German Christians, invited Kleine in

May 1941 to contact him for future collaboration.[209] The two had originally met at the initial December 1939 Cologne meeting of the Group
for Joint Reconstruction Work. It appears that Kleine accepted Bishop
Schultz's offer and remained in contact with him, though nothing immediate developed from this connection.

By the spring of 1942 Schultz and Kleine had begun in earnest to discuss the feasibility of a joint Protestant-Catholic endeavor to support the
war effort. The main impetus behind this development was the election
of Lorenz Jaeger as archbishop of Paderborn in late May 1941.[210] Jaeger
was a particularly odd choice for archbishop since, at the time, he was
serving as a military chaplain to the *Wehrmacht*'s 302d Infantry Division
in Pomerania, Mecklenburg, and Brandenburg. After he voluntarily joined
the service in 1939 the army called him for service on May 27, 1940. During his brief tenure as chaplain Jaeger worked closely with his Protestant
counterpart, Pastor Tecklenburg. Though at this time in history there normally was tension between Catholics and Protestants, the two overcame
these traditional obstacles and became good friends. Tecklenburg even attended the mass in which Jaeger was consecrated a bishop.[211]

Kleine was particularly pleased over the choice of Jaeger as bishop. Attracted by Jaeger's military service, Kleine believed he might finally gain a
sympathetic ear among the Catholic hierarchy. In order to investigate this
possibility, Kleine began in December 1941 to make inquiries into Jaeger's
background and political outlook.[212] By March 1942 Kleine felt confident
enough in Jaeger—whom he considered potentially open to his concerns
on church-state relations—to write to him. On March 17 Archbishop
Jaeger wrote back to Kleine and informed him that he had "profound em-
pathy for your concerns" and invited Kleine to write him "concretely
what in your opinion must be done by the Church in order to bring
about a more tolerable situation" between church and state. He assured
Kleine that "in all circles of the Church of Germany—by priests as well as
by laity—no more urgent desire is present than to adopt the correct outlook toward the current state leadership and to reach a trusting cooperation with it." However, in making such a statement, Jaeger also reminded
Kleine that "it would be unjust to place the blame only on our side" for
difficulties in church-state relations, "since day after day it becomes
clearer how our love for *Volk* and fatherland is met with suspicion."[213]

Though Jaeger, like many others, warned Kleine not to place the
blame for the deterioration of relations between state and church solely
on the latter, he clearly exhibited an openness to hear more about
Kleine's concerns. Unbeknownst to Jaeger, Kleine forwarded the archbishop's private letter to Bishop Schultz and encouraged Schultz to make

Hitler himself aware of Jaeger's openness. He also praised the archbishop's military record, which included infantry combat service in the Great War. Kleine concluded that "such a man must certainly be an entirely genuine German to whom one can pour out one's heart—and he has certainly not disappointed my trust in him."[214] On March 27 Schultz followed Kleine's recommendation and forwarded copies of Kleine's and Jaeger's letters to the Reich chancellery. In his cover letter Schultz recommended that since "the attitude that the archbishop displays appears to me such a notable one, I would genuinely and strongly suggest that [Hans] Lammers [chief of the Reich chancellery] inform the Führer."[215]

Despite the dissemination of Jaeger's letter, nothing resulted immediately. Still, Kleine took advantage of Jaeger's suggestion to write him a letter that fully detailed his concerns. On September 9, 1942, Archbishop Jaeger answered Kleine in a very pastoral but firm manner. From the outset Jaeger acknowledged Kleine's "concern and zeal, which without a doubt originated from genuine priestly and national concerns." He also admitted that he, too, shared Kleine's "great longing" that there be peace between church and state. According to Jaeger, all "are called upon and required to take part in the competition for the welfare of the *Volk* and homeland. Then everyone can identify how much he is able to contribute from the standpoint of reconstructing the Reich." For Jaeger, this was the common point upon which church and state must agree. Anything less would bring about "more strife."[216]

Up to this point Jaeger had been quite sympathetic in his reply to Kleine's concerns and displayed a genuine desire for reconciliation and mutual cooperation between church and state. Suddenly, however, Jaeger's argument exhibited less sensitivity to Kleine's point of view, especially when he pointed out to Kleine that he had deviated from Church teaching. Jaeger challenged Kleine, "Your presentation is based upon an erroneous concept of Church. You see in the Church . . . more or less human concerns that have to adapt to everything human, historical, political, [and] social." Jaeger reminded him that "the essence of the Church consists of that which we call the mystery of Christ." In turn, this allowed the Church to be free from and even above earthly concerns. In this context, Jaeger explained, the "Church will recognize the current state as the God-given authority and do everything to value it and happily obey it in everything that does not set itself against God's law." Jaeger also reminded Kleine that the Church had to have this reservation because it was "its task to proclaim God's truth; otherwise it would be disloyal." The archbishop then concluded by letting Kleine know for a second time that his approach was "not free from error." "Certainly," he stressed, Kleine's "viewpoint that the Church must serve the state" entailed fallacies that were "no longer reconcilable with the faith."[217]

Jaeger's frankness and criticism surprised Kleine, who contemplated giving up his pursuit of emboldening Jaeger to reach out to the state.[218] Nevertheless, Kleine did not wish to rule out Jaeger as a possible candidate with whom he could maintain a dialogue about church-state issues. After a series of letters between Kleine and Jaeger, in early January 1943 the archbishop agreed to enter into a dialogue with the state, but only if a government official initiated it. According to him, the bishops had already made their concerns well known through their pastoral letters, and now it was up to the state to make the first move to begin the process of reconciliation.[219]

Kleine viewed Jaeger's willingness to engage in a state-initiated dialogue as a window of opportunity. By the end of December he had already met with Bishop Schultz and suggested to him a joint Protestant-Catholic pastoral letter that would support the German Reich as a means of promoting reunification in the faith and reconciliation with the state. Schultz expressed his willingness to participate in such a project.[220] Then, upon receiving Jaeger's January letter, Kleine wrote back to the Paderborn bishop and emphasized the urgency of the hour and the need for action.[221] Next, in early March Kleine traveled to Schwerin to meet with Bishop Schultz. During their meeting Kleine persuaded him to take the first step and reach out to Archbishop Jaeger with the suggestion of a joint pastoral letter. On March 14, acting as a middleman for Schultz, Kleine wrote to Jaeger and requested a meeting among the three "as soon as possible" and even suggested a possible date later that month.[222] The entire idea clearly intrigued Jaeger, who did not seem put off by Kleine's forwardness. However, on March 20 Jaeger sent a telegram to Kleine to inform him that he could not make the meeting on March 24, due to previous commitments. Still, he asked him to suggest a different day and promised to send an immediate answer about his availability.[223] Jaeger followed this up with a written letter and even suggested that Kleine telephone him to arrange the meeting.[224] Finally, Kleine called him and scheduled a meeting for March 25, 1943, in Paderborn.

The time between the agreement for a meeting and its actual date was quite short. Amid his busy teaching schedule Kleine made the most of it. He prepared a list of discussion points that included a joint pastoral letter, the relationship between the National Socialist Reich and Christianity, cooperation of the churches to work toward reunification in faith, and efforts to reach out to Hitler. For Kleine the main emphasis would be on the Catholic-Protestant pastoral letter that he believed should condemn "Bolshevism, . . . Jews, . . . and enemy propaganda" and support the "homeland, *Volk*, fatherland, Führer, commitment to total war, and victory."[225]

At noon on March 25 Kleine arrived with Bishop Schultz at the archbishop's palace in Paderborn.[226] After Archbishop Jaeger had welcomed them, the three walked over to a local restaurant and enjoyed lunch together. Afterward, they returned to the palace and began their meeting at 1:00 p.m. They met for two hours. According to Kleine's notes, Schultz began the meeting by discussing the importance of the "struggle against Bolshevism" and the means to use this as a way to reach out to the state. Jaeger quickly revealed that he viewed the situation differently. He argued that no matter how much the Church reached out to the state, even by speaking out against Bolshevism, the party-state side interpreted it negatively and denigrated the effort. He emphasized that all the "honest efforts in his archdiocese to get along with all party groups . . . failed miserably." Jaeger stressed that "the attitude of the Church was unquestionably nationalistic" and should not be interpreted otherwise.[227]

Kleine could not fully agree with Jaeger's last point. He interjected that the Church's catechism and missal lacked specific references to homeland, *Volk*, and fatherland and should be more nationally oriented. In his response, Jaeger noted how challenging it was for Catholics even to feel like part of the nation. He "complained that theology students could no longer become officers," which he lamented since "the state had the best possibility to educate them to become national men." Kleine challenged this point by stating that the archbishop had to look more deeply at this situation and see that "something was not right between the Reich and the Church." Kleine had the habit of placing the blame on the Church, and surprisingly Bishop Schultz challenged him on it. Whether or not such a view was "correct" had not been "decided," but Schultz admitted that "he and his friends in Mecklenburg had enthusiastically supported National Socialism and were nevertheless experiencing very strong resistance by the party."[228]

At this point in the conversation Schultz and Jaeger noted that despite their best intentions toward the state, they had experienced only hostility from it. Jaeger also stressed that "the bishops of Paderborn and the Cologne Church provinces during their recent gathering had unanimously stressed the commitment to victory as their obvious duty and urged this within the clergy and parishes." In his mind, the danger of Bolshevism had passed, and a pastoral letter against it was not necessary.[229]

Kleine did not record much more of the conversation. He simply noted that "the rejecting outlook of the archbishop of Paderborn was striking. Even the fact that in this case both Christian churches come together in public for the first time to discuss a pastoral letter made no apparent impression." Still, the meeting ended amicably. Kleine escorted Bishop Schultz outside and gave him a tour of the cathedral. Afterward they returned for coffee with Jaeger. Suddenly, in all frankness, Schultz declared, "Your Excellency, one must be able to jump over one's own shadow." Despite the vagueness of the remark, Kleine believed that somehow Jaeger understood Schultz and saw the reality of the fact that there was an actual "threat from Bolshevism" and therefore a "joint pastoral letter must be achieved." Instead of proceeding immediately, Jaeger suggested they wait four weeks, giving him time to work on a draft of the letter. When the meeting was over, Kleine walked out with Bishop Schultz and expressed his lack of enthusiasm for the entire meeting. Schultz, however, viewed it much more optimistically.[230]

Four weeks turned into four months, and in the end Jaeger declined to collaborate with Schultz to produce a common pastoral letter against Bolshevism and in support of the war. Instead, Jaeger worked with his fellow bishops during their August 1943 meeting in Fulda to produce their annual pastoral letter to German Catholics. Often referred to as the "Decalogue Letter" because of the central role the Ten Commandments play in it, the letter addressed the situation of the Church and the rights of individuals. Though it included statements such as "Killing is in itself a wrong, even if it is allegedly committed in the interest of the general welfare" and called upon Catholics to provide assistance to those who could least help themselves, such as "the innocent people who are not of our *Volk* and blood, . . . the resettled, . . . prisoners, and foreign workers," it did not specifically mention Jews or advocate for them. It did, however, uphold the indissolubility of validly consecrated racially mixed marriages in direct contradiction to the Nuremberg laws.[231]

A contentious document from the beginning, the pastoral letter created great discord among the German bishops. Many, including Cardinal Bertram of Breslau, considered it too political in nature.[232] Once they had at last agreed on a final document, some bishops did not even order it read from the pulpit—a common practice as a means to disseminate the bishops' pastoral letter—during Sunday mass. Others, including Jaeger, altered the text by subtracting or adding to sections according to their own preferences. In Berlin Bishop Konrad von Preysing edited the letter and made additions that were much more critical of the state, whereas in Paderborn Jaeger created a tone much more sympathetic toward German suffering during the war.[233] Such a view was not uncommon for Jaeger. During the Eucharist celebrated at the conclusion of the bishops' Fulda meeting, Archbishop Jaeger delivered the sermon and even took the position that the 1943 pastoral letter had directly interfered in the area of politics. Jaeger noted that it was not up to the bishop "to take a position in the questions of world politics." Bishops, he emphasized, "received a different call from the Lord." The savior asked them "to proclaim the Gospel, to mediate his life of grace and to heal and to help in his spirit and in his strength, and to be the custodians and propagators of the faith of St. Boniface." They were, he continued, to direct their work and concern to their German brothers and sisters, with whom bishops were "united in one blood" and whose destiny they shared "so that they may participate in the temporal and eternal blessings of the kingdom of God."[234]

Though Kleine might have been proud of the stance that the Paderborn archbishop took in his Fulda homily, he lumped Jaeger together with the rest of the German hierarchy when he accused them of stabbing Germany in the back through their pastoral letter. On September 17 he composed a letter to Jaeger in which he informed him that he regarded the bishops' pastoral letter "as the episcopacy's final rejection of the New German Reich with its creator and Führer, its ideas, its mission, and its monstrous struggle in this decisive *völkisch* hour. In particular, he resented that they took the core of their message "almost exclusively from the Old Testament and unmistakably take up the cause of Jews and racially mixed marriages." Kleine then concluded, "Christ would never in a lifetime approve such writing."[235] Upon finishing the letter, Kleine read it over carefully. He could easily see that he had filled it with deadly venom—such that might lead him into significant trouble if he actually sent it. Therefore, he composed a slightly less critical version of the letter and mailed it off to Jaeger.[236]

A bit startled by Kleine's comments, Jaeger wrote to him, "If I did not know you, I would actually be offended by the tone of your criticism of what the joint episcopacy said." Nevertheless, Jaeger let him off the hook by stating, "I will attribute it to your enthusiasm for the issues." Without revealing where he stood in relation to Kleine's point of view, Jaeger explained how important the Ten Commandments were to the "path that alone leads to salvation." Thus, if Jaeger had any disagreements with the contents of the "Decalogue Letter," he certainly did not share them with Kleine.[237] After that, Kleine sent two follow-up letters to Jaeger. In the first, he again generally criticized the contents of the bishops' pastoral letter, especially the failure to mention Hitler's name even once.[238] In his second letter Kleine described his "important" work for the Eisenach institute. Then he specifically addressed the bishops' failure to address the Jewish question directly and, in his view, their continued open struggle with the government: "I have already written . . . that this open defiance of the Reich—moreover at the apex of this monstrous war, which we should continue to view as a decision against international Jewry and its henchmen—will be sure to have a most fateful effect."[239]

Kleine shared his anger over the "Decalogue Letter" more openly with his friend Brücker. He confided that he was "so annoyed by the last pastoral letter" that he had given up "all hope that anything could be accomplished with this generation of the episcopacy" and lamented that for more than a year he had "worked unremittingly with Paderborn." Still, he stated, all they could produce was "this pathetic morality sermon," in which they accused Hitler of being "guilty of the gravest deadly sins! If I were a Jew in the English or American propaganda ministry, I would open a bottle of champagne to celebrate such a treasure trove of undermining propaganda against the Reich." Then he concluded, "The Führer will never come into contact with such a group."[240] A week later Kleine wrote to his close friend Father Pircher and expressed his newfound belief that at this moment it would be impossible to make any progress with the German Catholic episcopacy.[241]

Final Thoughts

Despite frustration and anger over his failure to motivate the German bishops to write a joint Catholic-Protestant pastoral letter, and notwithstanding his disappointment over the unresolved situation of church-state relations, Kleine still attempted to press onward in his work. In particular, he continued to attend the meetings of various groups associated with the Eisenach institute.[242] However, no matter how hard he worked for this institute, the Catholic Study Group always remained a minor division within its overall structure.[243] It also appears that neither he nor Pircher had much luck accomplishing anything significant through their work and involvement with the priests' group they had founded or with the Group for Joint Reconstruction Work. For the most part their work merely served to keep other like-minded clergymen abreast of the latest developments in church-state relations.[244]

Despite the seemingly insignificant gains through their dialogue work, it could be said that Kleine and Pircher did help to influence individual state, party, or even Church leaders on certain issues, if only to the extent that as priests, as moral and articulate leaders of Catholics, they assiduously concentrated on their passionate loathing of Jews, transforming this hatred into a racist, almost annihilative antisemitism. Kleine's efforts clearly supported the work of the Institute for the Study and Eradication of Jewish Influence on German Church Life. His classroom teaching influenced the religious education of generations of Duderstadt youth.[245] And Kleine's antisemitic outlook and ideas also influenced the thought and writing of Professor Karl Adam, who was an internationally well respected Catholic theologian with a wide readership. In retrospect, however, it seems Pircher received more notice than Kleine. For example, in September 1939 a state official asked Pircher to suggest the names of priests—as possible future candidates for the episcopacy—who would be loyal to the state.[246] Pircher, of course, complied with the request. Whether his choice met with the approval of the party is uncertain. However, Pircher, like Kleine, no doubt thought that the request itself put him in the center rather than on the periphery of Nazi Party politics. Again, in March 1940, when a party official noticed Pircher's talent for producing propaganda in favor of the state, he appointed him regional propaganda director.[247] Pircher undoubtedly brimmed with pride and a sense of accomplishment after this appointment. Kleine, on the other hand, was content to remain in the background and continue to be the behind-the-scenes motivator within the various groups to which he belonged.

Ultimately Kleine's covert manner of propagating his beliefs under National Socialism allowed him to escape relatively unscathed in postwar Germany. However, he was not alone. The majority of the brown priests who were still living after the war remained in the Catholic priesthood and maintained some form of ministry. The denazification process affected only a limited few.

7—Judgment Day Brown Priests on Trial?

On October 20, 1945, Captain James Tillinghast of the United States Military Government Headquarters for Oberfranken and Mittelfranken wrote to Michael Rackl, bishop of Eichstätt, and ordered him to remove Father Anton Heuberger from his parish at Hitzhofen. According to Tillinghast, the United States Army had found Heuberger "a notorious sympathizer with National Socialism."[1] Since the surrender of the German military to Allied forces on May 7 and 8, 1945, Rackl had not called for Heuberger's resignation. His reason, which he cited over and over, was the shortage of priests in his diocese, especially due to the influx of Catholic refugees. The Allied occupying forces clearly saw the situation differently, especially in light of the recently promulgated Law no. 8, which stated that, "effective immediately, no member of the Nazi Party or of any of its affiliated organizations could legally be employed in any business enterprise in a position other than ordinary labor, unless expressly authorized by the military government."[2] Without further ado, Rackl wrote to Heuberger and asked him to resign immediately, placing all the blame on the military government. Rackl warned the pastor to heed his request because he "would be sorry if any drastic measure was taken against [him] by the military."[3] Rackl also imposed on Heuberger "a prohibition from teaching . . . and preaching."[4] By November 8 Rackl could thus write to his vicar general, Joseph Schröffer, that Heuberger had "resigned from the parish of Hitzhofen . . . effective November 16, 1945."[5]

Heuberger was one of the few Catholic clergymen affected by the denazification policy in its initial stages. The Allies' goal was to remove leading National Socialists from any positions of authority in which they might continue to influence the German population.[6] To determine who was a Nazi, the Allies created detailed *Fragebogen* (questionnaires) that asked guilty respondents to incriminate themselves by admitting to membership in the NSDAP or one of its organizations. Naturally, there were legal consequences for falsifying information. In some cases, especially for someone such as Heuberger who had not been a registered member of the Nazi Party, Allied officials had to rely on the cooperation of the local population to obtain incriminating information.[7]

Interestingly, each of the four Allied powers (Britain, France, Soviet Union, and United States) dealt in their individual zones of occupation with the issue of denazification of the churches differently.[8] In the eyes of many military commanders, churches were some of the few institutions that had not been compromised and had actively engaged in some degree of resistance against National Socialism.[9] Thus the Allied military governments initially gave Catholic Church authorities great latitude in dealing with Nazi-sympathizing priests among their clergy.[10] That is, the bishops could deal with them internally. They displayed a similar trust toward Protestants, despite the high number of party members among their clergy.[11] A general hope existed that, at least in regard to the Catholic Church, bishops would remove any suspect priest from active ministry on their own and reassign him to a highly restrictive life in a monastery.[12] Even before being given such leeway, Konrad von Preysing, the bishop of Berlin, had done this and could report to the Allied forces that he had already forthrightly removed tainted clergymen from their ministry.[13] The new political situation also gave Augsburg's bishop, Joseph Kumpfmüller, the freedom to deal with his problematic priests and begin canonical proceedings against them. Other bishops followed suit. However, in general the bishops took such action against only the most "flagrant cases" of priests and did not engage in a thorough, across-the-board examination of all diocesan clergy.[14] This bothered the Allied forces.

By February 1946 the leaders of the military government in the United States zone of occupation began to lose patience with the churches' internal cleansing process. They believed that "neither the Catholic nor Protestant Church [had] been cooperating to effect these removals, although each has a number of bad Nazis."[15] Part of the problem in Catholic circles lay with the bishops' mistrust of the denazification process itself. In August 1945 the German bishops had expressed this distrust in their annual pastoral letter by challenging any notion of "collective guilt" on the part of their fellow citizens for the crimes of the National Socialists. In this context, the bishops supported the belief that many people joined the NSDAP "knowing little of the activities and aims of the Nazi Party." They demanded that the "guilt be investigated in each individual case lest the innocent have to suffer with the guilty."[16] The German bishops felt secure taking such a stance. Two months earlier, in an address to the Sacred College of Cardinals, Pius XII had reinforced a similar stance, portraying the Catholic Church in Germany as a persecuted institution that had boldly withstood the Nazi onslaught.[17] To think otherwise, he believed, would dilute the moral weight of the Church, especially in its fight against Communism. It is important to note here that it was rare in the pre-Vatican-II Catholic Church to speak about a collective, institutional, or communal understanding of sin, especially when such shared sin often had a hidden, but controlling, theological dialectic that had never been addressed.[18] But even with this point in mind, the bishops still missed an opportunity in their pastoral letters to demonstrate moral leadership in the postwar era by publicly holding themselves, the ordained, religious, and prominent lay Catholics accountable for their actions or inactions under National Socialism.

In March 1946 a second wave of denazification began in the United States zone, after the military government promulgated the Law for Liberation from National Socialism and Militarism. This law turned much of the denazification work over to newly established tribunals staffed by Germans with proven anti-Nazi records.[19] Using *Fragebogen* as the primary means to identify individuals in need of denazification, this law acknowledged that membership in the NSDAP or its sister organizations was not the sole decisive factor, "but may be overcome, wholly or partly, by evidence to the contrary." "Conversely," the law stated, nonmembership by itself was "not decisive to absolve one of responsibility."[20] Such an understanding meant that the tribunal judges had to weigh each case individually before rendering a decision. Those cases that the tribunals had reviewed were placed in one of five categories of responsibility: (1) major offenders, (2) offenders, (3) lesser offenders, (4) followers, and (5) exonerated persons. In general the categories and sanctions corresponded to the persons' level of involvement in the Nazi Party or state and to their participation in criminal acts.[21]

Around the same time that the Americans implemented this new law, the British established a similar system of categorization, but they maintained a more direct control over the denazification tribunals until 1947. After this point they also turned the process over to the Germans. By contrast, the French concentrated their efforts less on the denazification of the general population and more on the indictment process and war crime trials of known individuals. Still, they too adopted a version of the classification system. Finally, the Soviets followed their own path by developing a unique pattern of purging well-known Nazis and rehabilitating "nominal" ones.[22]

As the second wave of denazification went forward, the Catholic Church once again remained relatively unaffected. The British and French in their respective zones of occupation advanced hardly any cases against priests.[23] The Americans, in the United States zone, which in the spring and again in the fall of 1946 promised a more aggressive examination of clergymen, likewise did little. The tribunals in the U.S. zone heard the cases of only seventeen priests out of a total of more than eight thousand.[24] Despite skirting a more thorough review of Catholic clergy, the Catholic hierarchy still criticized the process. In March 1946 the bishops of the Cologne and Paderborn church provinces issued a joint pastoral letter that was highly critical of denazification, especially the policy of dismissing from employment, before conducting a preliminary examination, those individuals suspected of working with or being a member of the National Socialist Party. Indeed, the letter was so critical in its wording that the U.S. military government requested the bishops to withdraw it, though the British military government tolerated its distribution.[25]

In general, denazification put the Catholic hierarchy on the defensive, especially with respect to the Church's rights regarding pastoral appointments—rights that, in the mind of Catholic officials, the 1933 Reich-Vatican Concordat still protected. As a result, the occupying powers received from diocesan officials a series of letters that recalled the Church's position and rights. For example, in the British zone the Paderborn diocesan vicar general, Dr. Friedrich Rintelen, reminded the local military government that although they could "issue orders for the clergy . . . within the departments for which they [were] competent" such as "admission to teaching in schools of the state," it was "different with the appointment of clergymen to purely ecclesiastical offices and dismissing them from these." Father Rintelen explained to the military authorities that in these cases the question concerned "a right that in virtue of divine mandate belong[ed] to the Church only."[26] In the

Cologne archdiocese Archbishop Josef Frings offered a similar reminder to the British military government, which earlier had moved to set up "special clerical panels" in order "to ensure that the spiritual authority" had the "determining voice in all matters of conscience affecting members of the priesthood."[27] In addition, in the Rottenburg-Stuttgart diocese, whose boundaries straddled two occupied zones (American and French), Vicar General Dr. Max Kottmann "urgently" asked the U.S. military government "to disclaim any interference with our right to appoint our officials independently" and requested that "in no case should ecclesiastics be prevented from the fulfillment of their clerical duties by the information given and gained through their *Fragebogen.*"[28]

Despite the German Catholic Church's lack of an empirical basis for an across-the-board exoneration, generally the Allied powers showed great respect for the Church's authority. Nevertheless, in September 1946 an American military official made an interesting observation. In a "brief report" on the situation of the Bavarian Catholic Church the author first lamented the fact that the denazification tribunals had made decisions in the cases of only fifteen priests (one in category 3—lesser offender—and fourteen in category 4—followers). Although this number was low, the author believed that "there certainly were Catholic priests who according to their personal view, and seemingly with the ongoing toleration of their superiors—if only in low-level functions and temporarily—participated in National Socialism."[29] Of course, the military official was correct in his observation. However, at the time it would have been next to impossible for the military governments to identify every priest who had at some time or other publicly supported the aims of the Nazi Party or state. This would be especially true without the cooperation of the German Catholic bishops. However, in the immediate postwar period the majority of the Catholic bishops agreed to the withdrawal from employment of only the most notorious Nazis and in practice followed a similar policy in regard to their priests. Generally, they removed and reprimanded only the most troublesome brown priests. The majority of those whom the bishops removed from pastoral office even eventually made their way back into full-time ministry, as shown by the postwar lives of the previously discussed brown priests.

In the case of Father Anton Heuberger the military government "demanded" that Heuberger move to a monastery, but Bishop Rackl encouraged him to apply instead for a position as an assistant to Father Josef Bengel, the pastor of the Assumption of the Blessed Virgin in Wolframs-Eschenbach.[30] On the very day that Heuberger's resignation went into effect, Rackl offered him the Wolframs-Eschenbach assignment with the stipulation that the Eichstätt vicar general could remove Heuberger from office at any time if problems arose.[31]

In 1946 Father Bengel wrote to Vicar General Joseph Schröffer to request permission for Heuberger to preach and teach religious education in his parish.[32] At this point Schröffer refused to lift the prohibition, blaming the military government for the continuation of the ban on Heuberger.[33] However, this prohibition did not last long. In August 1949 Heuberger received permission to engage once again in pastoral activities, without any restrictions. In a 1949 letter to his new vicar general, Father Joseph Heindl, Heuberger reported that a "stream of refugees" had kept the priests of the Assumption parish extremely busy with pastoral work.[34] By this time diocesan officials seemed to have totally forgotten Heuberger's actions during the Third Reich. This was not unusual, as the denazification process came to its conclusion around 1950, and many convicted and "classified" Germans returned to work.[35] In the case of Heuberger, a key factor in his return was Bishop Rackl's death in May 1948.[36] In September 1948 Joseph Schröffer, Rackl's successor as bishop of Eichstätt, took a much more lenient position toward Heuberger. In December 1949 the Eichstätt chancery even invited Heuberger to apply for the parish of St. Mauritius in Emskeim. A chancery official explained that the diocese would "take up the necessary matters with the state" if the position interested Heuberger.[37] Amazingly, Heuberger turned down the offer and attributed his decision to heart troubles. According to him, he had "found a rich field for pastoral ministry" in Wolframs-Eschenbach and, despite all the "wrongs and ingratitude" that he had suffered, he had once again the opportunity "to experience joy" as people showed "a trusting interest in [him] as a teacher, preacher, confessor, counselor to converts, minister to the sick, and counselor to children, especially the youth in their doubts and concerns."[38] Perhaps Heuberger was attempting to put his past behind him and take refuge in pastoral work.

Heuberger continued to live a relatively quiet life. In 1965 he celebrated his golden jubilee in the priesthood. To celebrate the occasion, the town of Hitzhofen made Heuberger an honorary citizen. Two years later, in 1967, Heuberger entered a hospital with a severe bladder infection. He never fully recovered and died soon thereafter.[39]

Though Heuberger had eventually made amends with his diocese and returned to full-time ministry, other priests were not as fortunate. For example, Joseph Kumpfmüller, the bishop of Augsburg, never allowed Father Johannes Müller to return to full-time ministry. As we learned earlier, Kumpfmüller's predecessor, Maximilian von Lingg, had forced

Müller from his pastorate in June 1929. The diocese never offered Müller a new parish assignment. On one occasion after the war, in May 1948, the Augsburg chancery did receive word that Müller was celebrating mass without faculties, but without any hesitation a chancery official wrote to Father Albert Schwenger, pastor of the Catholic Church in Heimenkirch within whose boundaries Müller lived, and informed him that Müller was not to celebrate mass "until he made peace with his ordinary."[40] In his reply Schwenger gave notice to the chancery that he would deny Müller permission, though, over the year, Müller had asked him for mass stipends. Upon Schwenger's refusal, Müller in typical fashion became belligerent toward the pastor.[41] After learning of these repeated difficult encounters, Father Dr. Eugen Bach, a chancery official, wrote to Müller and reminded him that he was "in fact, suspended." Bach continued, "We seriously exhort you to refrain from any celebration or other function of consecration until you are absolved, that is, granted dispensation, from censure and irregularity. Further letters from you will be answered only if they contain the imperatively necessary ecclesial declaration of obedience."[42] Before the diocese had a chance to deal with Father Müller again, he died in his sleep on Holy Saturday night in April 1949. The diocese buried him with a Church funeral.[43]

Like Father Müller, Christian Huber, formerly of the Augsburg diocese, also never returned to full-time ministry in the Catholic Church. However, he made his own decision in this regard. In October 1941 Huber had officially left the Catholic Church and a year later entered into marriage with Rosa Albert. To support himself and his wife, he continued in his archivist job in Aschaffenburg until the end of the Third Reich. Shortly before the end of the war, he did write to a pastor who had been his friend and offered his apologies for his actions under National Socialism. In his letter, however, he offered only generalizations and failed to mention any details about his contribution to the Nazi state.[44] When the Americans reached Aschaffenburg, they arrested Huber and placed him in the local prison. The American military identified him as a known district speaker for the NSDAP. Sometime later that year they transferred him to the Moosburg internment camp.[45] A Catholic chaplain in Moosburg noted that in the camp Huber did "not make any difficulties for the Church, on the contrary, he sings in the church choir."[46] While in the camp, Huber clearly underwent a deep examination of conscience, and by July he had joined the Old-Catholic Church, which also admitted him to its ministerial ranks. Upon his release in early 1948 he received a ministerial position in an Old-Catholic parish in Thalmessing.[47] Huber continued in his ministry until his retirement, at which point he moved back to Aschaffenburg with his wife. He died on February 14, 1958.[48] Upon learning of his death, an Augsburg diocesan official wrote the Würzburg diocesan chancery: "We regret that the deceased joined the Old-Catholic Church in spite of his recantation and died without reconciliation with his Church. Our special thanks to you for all of your efforts on behalf of the unfortunate priest."[49]

Similar to the treatment Father Christian Huber received, the American military personnel arrested Father Dr. Lorenz Pieper, who had been residing in Meschede since his dismissal as chaplain of the Warstein sanitarium. His own archbishop had not given him any pastoral assignment since January 15, 1933. After discussions between authorities from the American military and the Paderborn archdiocese, both agreed on Pieper's internment in the Franciscan Rietberg monastery. Pieper stayed in Rietberg until the autumn of 1946, when fellow priests and a local mayor arranged a chaplaincy for him in the small village of Berlar. Until March 1941 the Meschede Benedictines had celebrated the masses there. At that point, the Gestapo had expelled the monks and had also confiscated the monastery. Primarily out of this pastoral need, Pieper assumed the chaplaincy until the Benedictines could return. The archbishop consented to Pieper's new assignment but forbade him to preach or hear confessions. Nevertheless, those who attended his masses reported that Pieper circumvented these restrictions and offered "talks" about "the day's saint" and the talks "were strong stuff."[50] Even in the midst of defeat Pieper was determined to show his independence.

Father Pieper continued in his Berlar chaplaincy until late January 1948. By this time, the need for his services had ended. Without a ministerial position, he returned to his hometown of Eversberg and began cataloging and developing the collection of the town's history museum.[51] Pieper continued in this work without interruption until the fall of 1948. Then, unexpectedly, in October his Nazi past came back to haunt him when he was called before the Arnsberg denazification tribunal to account for his actions under National Socialism. The tribunal judges were well aware of Pieper's early work on behalf of that movement. In particular, they would recall the glowing tribute paid to Pieper in the 1938 National Socialist work *Struggle and Victory: History of the NSDAP in the Westphalia South District from the Beginning to the Takeover of Power*.[52]

In his defense Pieper cited his resistance to the state's euthanasia program. The government had instituted the secret program to reduce German state financial aid to institutionalized persons by murdering them through starvation, lethal injection, or by gassing them. Such an action taken by the state went against Pieper's Catholic moral sensibilities, in particular because it involved the killing of Aryan Germans. Pieper, however, never made a similar protest in regard to persecuted, deported, or murdered Jews. Nor did Pieper mention his decision to remove portraits of "Jewish saints" and replace them with "Aryan" ones in the Warstein sanitarium's chapel or that he greeted the mass servers with "Heil Hitler." Nevertheless, he did make his outrage over the euthanasia program known, especially since he served as a chaplain at an institution whose patients the state had targeted as "life unworthy of life." In June 1941, for example, Pieper appealed to his diocesan superiors and encouraged them to ask their fellow German bishops to speak against the euthanasia program.[53] Following this request, on July 22 Pieper wrote his own letter of protest against euthanasia and sent it to each of the doctors of the Warstein sanitarium. In this letter he quoted both Scripture and Catholic moral teaching in his opposition against the euthanasia policy.[54] The letter was soon distributed outside the Warstein sanitarium. Not long after that, on August 6, Karl Friedrich Kolbow, the leader of the Westphalian provincial government, wrote to Pieper to remind him that all patient medical information was confidential and forbade him to continue speaking publicly about patients' "medical" issues. He also informed Pieper that he had to make a choice: either follow this directive or lose his chaplain position.[55] It appears that Pieper maintained his oppositional stance, and therefore Kolbow forced him into retirement.[56]

Saddened by the loss of his job, Pieper wrote to his archbishop, Lorenz Jaeger, and informed him of the situation. He remarked that he already had passed the state's mandatory retirement age for civil servants two years earlier, but the "real basis" for his retirement, he noted, was his "energetic support for the two thousand mentally ill patients" and his effort to save them from the "known '*Aktion*.'"[57] The National Socialist euthanasia policy had the code name *Aktion* T-4 (Tiergartenstraße 4, a street address in Berlin, served as the program's headquarters). In reply, Archbishop Jaeger sent Pieper a supportive letter, in which he expressed his fear that the sanitarium would not be allowed to have another priest, yet he also confirmed that Pieper had "handled the situation correctly." Jaeger continued, "I am grateful to you that you have represented your position as a priest with such frankness and determination. . . . The best reward for you will be, however, that you have acted in keeping with your own conscience." Despite his encouraging words, Jaeger did not offer Pieper a full-time parish assignment. Rather, he encouraged him to help out with masses where needed.[58]

Pieper's defense apparently moved the denazification tribunal to judge Pieper somewhat leniently. On October 6, 1948, they declared him a lesser offender by placing him in category 3 and sentencing him to a short period of probation.[59] The denazification tribunals reserved this category for "one who would otherwise be an offender [category 2] but because of special circumstances should be less harshly treated."[60] After the denazification process, Pieper returned to Eversberg. He lived there without any specific pastoral duties until his death of anemia on January 30, 1951, in the Meschede St. Walburga hospital.[61]

Though the denazification tribunal had publicly confirmed Pieper's National Socialist ties, Pieper did his best to distance himself from his past and emphasize that during this time he was opposed to the euthanasia policy. In this way, he attempted to portray himself not as a National Socialist, but as an ardent nationalist. However, contradictions arise in this scenario. For example, in 1944, supposedly two years after he had separated himself from the state and party owing to his opposition to the euthanasia policy, Pieper was beside himself over the loss of his golden NSDAP badge. This possession was so important to him that he contacted a local NSDAP official and requested a replacement.[62] If the policy of euthanasia had truly caused him to reevaluate his relationship with National Socialism, one has to wonder why the loss of his party badge was so important to him.

Like Pieper, Richard Kleine attempted to downplay his involvement with National Socialism after the war. At first this approach did not seem to help him. Though no one from the Allied powers arrested Kleine as they had Pieper, they did immediately remove him from teaching and ensured that Kleine was no longer eligible to receive his teacher's salary or any compensatory payment.[63] The occupation authorities also identified him as a known sympathizer with National Socialism and a member of the National Socialist Teachers' Association and the NSV.[64]

Soon Kleine's unemployment brought him into a difficult financial situation. Despite this predicament, Kleine did not find himself alone. Standing by his side was the Duderstadt gymnasium's director, Dr. Johannes Hartung, whom the British military had cleared and allowed to remain in office after finding out that he had been a NSDAP member since 1937.[65] In September Hartung made a failed effort to obtain Kleine's back pay from April to July 1945.[66] Furthermore, Lorenz Jaeger, the Paderborn archbishop, did not desert him. As early as January 1946 Jaeger had made an inquiry into the priest's well-being after Kleine had contacted him to intercede on his behalf for a Protestant minister and his wife.[67] Of course, Kleine was an extremely popular teacher and must also have received assistance from his former students and Duderstadt neighbors to help him through this period.

In May 1946 the British military government allowed Kleine to return to teaching, after he signed a form pledging that in the classroom he would not glorify militarism or promote National Socialism or any of its former leaders.[68] Kleine attributed this to a "candid personal conversation with the appropriate government director and the British military head of our provincial school committee in Hannover."[69] Despite his change in status, the Hildesheim vicariate immediately attempted to intervene to prevent Kleine's reinstatement by informing the Hannover Secondary School Department that Kleine did not possess a *missio canonica* from his bishop and therefore had no right to teach religion.[70] It also informed Father Franz Ernst, the rector of St. Cyriakus in Duderstadt and dean of the Duderstadt deanery, of this fact so that Ernst would keep an eye on him.[71]

Officials of the Hildesheim vicariate soon found that they were up against a difficult challenge because Kleine had a great deal of support from his colleagues in the Duderstadt gymnasium and from the surrounding community. For example, even though Dr. Hartung had retired as the gymnasium's director in early 1946, his successor, Riemers, continued to intervene on Kleine's behalf in a manner similar to his predecessor. This meant that though Riemers obeyed the diocese's request that Kleine no longer teach religion, he did assign him to teach a variety of other subjects such as physical education, Latin, German, and music to ensure that he had a full-time teaching schedule.[72] Kleine went along with this plan for nine months. However, by early 1947 it became clear to him that he really missed teaching religion. With that, he wrote to his bishop, Dr. Josef Machens, and requested an audience with him in order to discuss the tense situation between them.[73] On March 21 Bishop Machens answered Kleine with a terse formal letter and informed him that "your attitude and your conduct in the time of distress of the Church and also afterward were regrettably such that they force me to answer negatively to your petition for a license to give Catholic religious instruction." Furthermore, Machens advised him "to get yourself transferred away from Duderstadt."[74]

Kleine was not pleased with his bishop's response. He informed Machens on March 26 that he never had a chance to defend himself and assured him that the bishop had been "completely misinformed" about his conduct under National Socialism.[75] A day later Kleine wrote to Archbishop Lorenz Jaeger and asked him for his advice and assistance.[76] By late August Jaeger had already contacted the Hildesheim vicariate and offered to grant Kleine the *missio canonica* if Kleine would accept a teaching post in the Paderborn archdiocese.[77] After this ex-change, Kleine and Jaeger would stay in contact on and off throughout the 1950s.[78] However, when the Paderborn vicariate attempted to arrange a teaching position, it quickly learned that the local government had "considerable objections against taking on teachers who somehow or other have drawn attention to themselves through National Socialist ac-tivities."[79] At the same time, the inquiry by Paderborn encouraged the Lower Saxony Education Ministry in Hannover to review Kleine's teach-ing credentials. This evaluation resulted in the ministry's sending an ulti-matum to Duderstadt gymnasium director Riemers, stating that Kleine had to obtain either the necessary teaching qualifications for the subjects that he was teaching or the *missio canonica* from his bishop before April 14, 1948. If he could obtain neither one, the ministry said it then would be forced to release Kleine from his teaching duties.[80] Before this deadline passed, however, a local denazification tribunal told Kleine that it would review his case and render a verdict sometime in the coming months.[81]

By June Kleine's situation had become quite difficult. The loss of his teaching career and the denazification hearing overwhelmed him. It ap-pears the pressure was too much for him, so Kleine made application for an extended medical leave from teaching.[82] On June 24 Kleine received approval for his leave, effective July 1 through September 30.[83] Such an arrangement also enabled the Lower Saxony Education Ministry to post-pone its decision on whether to release Kleine from teaching.

Even before Kleine began his medical leave, he received word from the Hildesheim vicariate that Bishop Machens was now willing to grant him the *missio canonica* if he would accept a teaching assignment outside Du-derstadt.[84] Perhaps Machens was anticipating a possibly lenient decision on the part of the denazification tribunal, which would place pressure on him to give Kleine permission to teach religion. If he could move Kleine before the denazification hearing, this would prevent a more difficult situ-ation from developing later. However, Kleine was resolute that his roots in Duderstadt were too deep for him to leave. Besides, the medical leave saved Kleine from having to make an immediate decision about his future.

In late August 1948 the Duderstadt denazification tribunal exonerated Kleine by placing him in category 5. The judges determined that, although Kleine was a member of the NSV and the NSLB (National Socialist Teach-ers' Association), he had never joined the NSDAP. According to them, Kleine had sympathized with National Socialism primarily to protect his Church. His "profound love of fatherland" was the cause for him "to con-sider for a time the ideas of National Socialism to be good, since in them he saw a true support of Germany and the best means to combat Bolshevism and hope for reconciliation between church and state." Stronger than his support for National Socialism was his "love of neighbor," to whom he was "always helpful." The tribunal disclosed no knowledge of Kleine's work with the Eisenach institute or of his antisemitic writings.[85]

In September, at the end of his medical leave, Kleine received word that Bishop Machens was ready to grant him the *missio canonica* for a period of one year.[86] The Duderstadt dean, Father Franz Ernst, had encouraged the bishop to make this limited overture.[87] Thereafter, on October 1, 1948, Kleine returned to full-time classroom teaching.[88] The following July Bishop Machens renewed Klein's *missio canonica* without giving him any problem.[89] Several years later the new director of the Duderstadt gymnasium, Alfred Thiel, recommended that Kleine be named a civil servant for life, an appointment that would ensure him a good income and retirement. In his recommendation the director wrote: "Kleine takes his duties as a teacher and educator extraordinarily seriously. He educates his students about religion and life more through his example, by his goodness and love, than through force and binding regulations. . . . How loved he is by the students is indicated by the fact that they elected him student proctor."[90] On April 1, 1956, the Hannover Secondary Schools Department promoted him in teaching rank, a promotion that offered Kleine further prestige and income.[91] On April 1, 1957, following civil service regulations, Kleine retired after thirty-eight years of teaching.[92] Nevertheless, he continued to teach at the Duderstadt gymnasium part time until 1964, when he ended that role after slipping on ice and suffering a fracture of his upper arm.[93] Thereafter, Kleine remained in Duderstadt until his death on April 1, 1974.[94]

After the war Kleine maintained his previous interests. As early as September 1947 he presented a lecture entitled "The Sermon on the Mount" to the Duderstadt Association of Catholic University Graduates.[95] In the 1950s he began to attend conferences on ecumenism in Germany.[96] However, instead of promoting a limited, Germanic form, he became involved in a newly established dialogue between Protestants and Roman Catholics. Though the officials in the Hildesheim vicariate originally had refused to give Kleine permission to publish, by the 1960s he was publishing again, specifically about the role of Catholics in the ecumenical movement.[97] Similarly, Kleine continued to work on new textbooks for religious catechesis. In his completed but unpublished "The Proclamation of the Good News in Secondary Schools," Kleine once again used the Sermon on the Mount as the central point from which Christians ought to depart for catechesis.[98] This time he left out his portrayal of Christ as an antisemite.

Although Kleine quickly learned after the war that it was unacceptable to use antisemitism explicitly, this did not mean that he was a changed man in this regard. Rather, in his correspondence concerning the preparation of a document that would eventually become "Declaration on the Relation of the Church to Non-Christian Religions" *(Nostra Aetate)*, which Pope Paul VI would proclaim on October 28, 1965, Kleine revealed his unaltered antisemitism. Upon learning that Cardinal Augustin Bea, S.J., president of the Vatican's newly created Secretariat for Promoting Christian Unity, was working on a "Decree on the Jews" in preparation for the Second Vatican Council, Kleine composed two letters and a statement in which he spoke sharply against any change in the Church's teaching on Jews.[99]

On August 18 Kleine wrote to Cardinal Bea and shared with him his personal view of the "Jewish question." In his letter Kleine wrote, "I hear that most recently the Jewish question has also been suggested for inclusion in the forthcoming council to the extent that it relates to the relationship with Christianity and the Church. Most particularly, this issue places 'The Trial of Jesus' at the center. This question has occupied me for decades." According to Kleine, "the high council and the high priest did not know the Trinitarian truth and the divinity of Jesus and therefore were bound to view Jesus' reply, 'Yes, I am (the son of the Living God),' as blasphemy, which was punishable by death." Despite this lack of knowledge, they still bore their "own severe guilt" for condemning Jesus. "This guilt," however, Kleine argued, was "not only inherent in this small leadership group. Again and again, the Gospel writes about the guilt of this *Volk* [the Jewish people]. The letters and the Acts of the Apostles proclaim it again and again. In Germany, particularly, a genuine solution is sought for the Jewish question because so much guilt existed here toward this *Volk*. It should be said, however, that they bore previously much guilt on their part."[100]

A day later Kleine composed a statement entitled "Judaism and Christianity." Kleine's antisemitism clearly surfaced in it when he wrote, "Why were the Jews harshly persecuted again and again? . . . Without a doubt the Jews have gained leading positions for themselves everywhere, and indeed not really through wonderful achievements but through the power of their money, which they gained in immense quantity. Their economic competition was probably always regarded as oppressive because it did not comply with the customary rules. The Jews were always rather unloved because they remained a foreign body as 'other *Volk*' and, moreover, maintained extremely strong international bonds. They themselves did not value the national worth of other peoples."[101]

After writing to Cardinal Bea and composing the above statement, Kleine also wrote to Father Thomas F. Stransky, C.S.P., a member of the Vatican Secretariat for Promoting Christian Unity, and informed him that "I have been intensely occupied with this [Jewish] question for more than three decades, particularly because it was so exaggerated here in Germany by National Socialism and was so horribly distorted." He expressed his concern that the Church had not studied this topic seriously and systematically by stating that "No correct 'diagnosis' is being made. A new complexity is established instead of a solution to the old one." Then he added, "I would like to make a modest contribution to finding an easier settlement of this problem."[102] Needless to say, Father Stransky, who was to be a firm supporter of *Nostra Aetate,* did not accept Klein's offer of assistance.

Only now is the extent of Richard Kleine's antisemitism known. His low-profile mode of operation in academic circles during the Third Reich enabled him to escape more serious postwar punishment at the hands of the denazification tribunal. By contrast, the antisemitic Father Philipp Haeuser of the Augsburg diocese had generally maintained a highly public profile, strongly supportive of National Socialism throughout the Third Reich. Not surprisingly, once the war was over, both the Allies and diocesan officials eagerly removed him from public ministry. In particular, as early as the autumn of 1945 the Augsburg chancery began a formal process to have Haeuser removed as pastor of his Straßberg parish. However, though the process began less than a month after the promulgation of Law no. 8, it is still unclear whether the U.S. military government pushed the chancery to act or if the chancery officials acted on their own.

Although a bishop has great leeway in the governance of his diocese, canon law is quite protective of the rights of a pastor.[103] In the case of Father Anton Heuberger, as noted earlier, Bishop Rackl did not have to pursue a canonical process because Heuberger willingly resigned. By contrast, Haeuser held his ground and refused to resign his pastorate voluntarily. Bishop Kumpfmüller soon discovered how difficult it was to remove this brown priest, but he was not alone in his desire to remove Haeuser from active ministry. The bishop also had the full support of his advisory clergymen. As early as 1942 Father Robert Domm, a trustworthy and faithful priest, had assumed the role of vicar general to allow Bishop Eberle more time for his diocesan pastoral obligations. Domm fully understood the significant problems that Haeuser had caused the diocese and was determined to have him removed from pastoral ministry.[104] At first his approach was quite civil. In late September of 1945

Domm asked Haeuser to resign his pastorate but insisted that he did not wish to force the priest to leave.[105] Shortly thereafter, on October 10, Mayor Günter of Straßberg informed Domm that on the previous Sunday 510 parishioners had voted positively for Father Haeuser to remain their pastor. According to Günter, "Our pastor here is held in the highest esteem, and the entire parish of Straßberg has owed him the utmost gratitude for thirty-four years. A dismissal would be the greatest ingratitude and would provoke bitterness. Through his conciliatory ways, our pastor has held the parish together in peace and quiet despite the greatest difficulties, even in the most troubled times. A dismissal would threaten the peace and quiet."[106]

Günter also informed Haeuser of the contents of his letter, which reinforced Haeuser's haughtiness and conceit. In turn, on October 16 he boldly, but irresponsibly, wrote to Domm to inform him that in no way had he planned to resign, nor did he believe that the diocese had the necessary canonical authority to remove him from office. He even threatened, "If you proceed, I will appeal to the highest Church authority and through a confidant send my letter and your letter to the Vatican." Then he added, "According to my understanding, the Catholic Church is not a Gestapo organization and not a Bolshevist institution but, in this most terrible world revolution, the sole lawful body."[107]

Domm immediately replied to Haeuser and informed him that although his superiors were unsure whether Haeuser was a member of the Nazi Party, they certainly knew that he had agitated for the cause of Hitler. Even former party members had begun to question why Haeuser had not been removed from office. Surprisingly, Domm promised Haeuser that if he would resign as pastor, the diocese would find another ministry for him. It is doubtful, however, that this offer was sincere.[108] According to Haeuser's reply on October 18, it is clear that he too did not trust the vicar general's promise. Instead of challenging Domm further, in this letter Haeuser portrayed himself as a victim who had been terrorized by the Gestapo and the NSV for his attempts to influence the German movement in a "moral, Christian" direction.[109]

Domm refused to accept Haeuser's reasoning and in early November warned him that he had taken a stance in his letter that revealed an ignorance of his situation. Furthermore, he made the priest aware that both his superiors and lay Catholics throughout the diocese knew that he had proclaimed that Hitler was "sent by God to the German people" and even compared him with Christ. Then he assured Haeuser, "The military government will no longer tolerate you in the position of pastor. At this point, it is still up to you to take the necessary steps yourself."[110]

Following this letter, it appears that seven months passed without any contact between Haeuser and the Augsburg chancery. Suddenly, on May 21, 1946, Domm wrote to Haeuser again to inform him that the diocese had begun canonical procedures to remove him as pastor. Domm called him "probably the greatest activist in the district of Schwabmünchen" for the NSDAP, "at least until the flight of Rudolf Hess." Furthermore, Domm accused Haeuser of having "no sense of responsibility for the propagandistic contributions that [he] made to the ruinous cause of the NSDAP."[111]

On October 29, 1946, before Domm had a chance to complete the canonical process, the Schwabmünchen denazification tribunal made a temporary ruling that the pastor of Straßberg could no longer preach or be involved in any public activity. The tribunal found that Haeuser had misused his authority as a priest and that, even though he was not a member of the party, he had helped to further its goals through speaking and writing, especially in the press.[112] Domm took this opportunity to act against Haeuser and on October 30 assigned Father Oskar Müller, the pastor of the nearby Bobingen parish, as church administrator of Straßberg.[113] Furthermore, in late November Domm took away Haeuser's faculties to dispense the sacraments and cut off his diocesan salary.[114] Nevertheless, Haeuser still refused to resign.

Amazingly, at first Haeuser took the temporary decision of the tribunal and subsequent actions of the diocese in stride. He filed a *pro forma* appeal with the denazification tribunal.[115] Then he sent a series of conciliatory letters to Father Müller, who seemed to lend a sympathetic ear to him.[116] Haeuser must have realized that he had no control over the situation. He soon found out how true this was when on December 1 the Schwabmünchen denazification tribunal took a further step against him by freezing all of his assets, both money and possessions.[117] The tribunal took this extraordinary action only after determining that on his *Fragebogen* Haeuser had intentionally lied about his collaboration with the Nazi Party.

After the tribunal froze his assets, Haeuser quickly became embittered and blamed his Church superiors for the tribunal's action. In late January 1947 he wrote Vicar General Domm a cynical letter in which he offered him "the greatest thanks," especially since he "had the intention to teach me to renounce all earthly goods and thus to raise me to a greater perfection" and "shape my priestly life into the poor life of an apostle." "You can take away a lot from me," he wrote, "but you will only increase my spiritual strength and inner security."[118] As a result of all this, Haeuser was left to live on the donations and support of his former parishioners, who did not forsake their "pastor." Still, the diocese allowed him to continue to live in the parish's rectory.

On May 14, 1947, Haeuser's actions under National Socialist rule finally caught up with him. The Schwabmünchen denazification tribunal declared him a major offender (category 1), a designation that placed him alongside former Gestapo agents, SS members, and the leadership corps of the NSDAP.[119] The judges sentenced him to five years in the Regensburg work camp and ordered that he never hold public office, that he lose all legal claims to pensions, and lose his eligibility to vote or be involved in politics.[120] Furthermore, he was not allowed to be a teacher, preacher, editor, writer, or radio commentator for ten years. Last, the tribunal ordered Haeuser to pay the entire cost of the proceedings.[121]

In their decision the judges concluded that Haeuser had "in extraordinary ways supported the National Socialist tyranny through propaganda. . . and exerted his religious influence on Adolf Hitler and the brown movement." They also doubted Haeuser's claim that "he believed Adolf Hitler wanted to keep the peace." Finally, the tribunal found that his writings, especially *Jew and Christian,* "provided in many sentences the basic slogans for the lethal antisemitism of *Der Stürmer.* Although the tribunal was firm in its ruling, the judges did acknowledge that Haeuser had in more recent years questioned certain actions of the state by reading from the pulpit the Mölders letter (a forged British propaganda document attributed to fighter ace Werner Mölders, which emphasized faith in Catholicism in the face of Nazi persecution) and that he had preached against the ill-treatment of women. Nevertheless, the judges concluded that Haeuser's efforts on behalf of National Socialism had overshadowed everything else through the misuse of "his influence and his priestly office in order to support Adolf Hitler and his shameful cause."[122]

The news of the judgment against Haeuser spread quickly throughout the diocese. Immediately, the pastor's supporters wrote letters requesting a reduction of sentence or lenient treatment of Haeuser in the prison camp. Over 514 parishioners from his Straßberg parish signed such a petition.[123] So, too, did his fellow priest, Father Richard Kempf of Reinhartshausen, who described himself as a "political opponent of the Nazis" and who wrote and requested "a moderation of the ruling" by stating that Haeuser was "a victim of his exaggerated idealism."[124] Even Vicar General Domm found the ruling harsh and asked for leniency. In his letter Domm recognized that Haeuser's "political outlook" and "bizarre ideology" were totally unacceptable; still, he emphasized that he had "proved himself to his parish as a cooperative, socially charitable, thoughtful priest."[125] Although Domm wanted Haeuser removed from pastoral ministry, it was clear that he did not wish this sentence upon him. Others, such as Monsignor Ulrich Müller, the director of Catholic Pastoral Care to Germans in Internment Camps, took a more reasoned approach. Recognizing the futility of requesting leniency for an individual such as Haeuser, Müller suggested that Bishop Kumpf-müller act more broadly and aggressively, as the Protestant bishop Theophil Wurm did, by pushing for clemency for those over sixty-five years of age. Müller argued that these individuals should not be placed in work camps.[126]

At this point, it might appear that Bishop Franz Eberle attempted to intercede on behalf of his friend. On May 27 Eberle wrote to assure Haeuser that he would do everything in his power to help him, since he had already learned that Haeuser was particularly concerned about the health of his sister, who had cared for him and lived in the parish rectory.[127] Haeuser trusted fully in this promise and on June 1 wrote to his sister to inform her of this fact.[128] What Haeuser did not realize, however, was that Eberle had already betrayed him. Earlier, on May 20, Eberle had written to the president of the Schwabmünchen denazification tribunal and surprisingly stated, "The ruling is absolutely fair. Haeuser is without a doubt one of the major offenders." Nevertheless, he did add, "That the ruling for the seventy-one-year-old, ill man is hard is not subject to doubt, but the ruling can pay no heed to this fact. Perhaps it will be possible later to make his stay in the camp somewhat easier."[129] Eberle deceived even Father Kempf, who had encouraged him to write to the tribunal on behalf of Father Haeuser.[130]

Despite the ruling against him, Haeuser still refused to resign as pastor of Straßberg. In his mind, the diocese, especially Bishop Kumpf-müller and Vicar General Domm, had conspired to influence the tribunal to rule against him.[131] In essence, Haeuser refused to recognize that he was complicit in his efforts to help the National Socialists gain power and spread their ideology of hate. Even though he had sought leniency for Haeuser, Domm knew that the priest should never return to pastoral ministry, and in early June, possibly believing that the experiences of the past month had helped to alter Haeuser's intransigence, Domm asked Haeuser once again to resign his pastorate.[132] But Haeuser still refused to resign. For him such a perceivedly cowardly act meant admitting that he was guilty as charged by the denazification tribunal. Instead, he portrayed himself as a sacrificial victim, like Christ, forced to wear a "crown of thorns" when all he did was to fight "for Jesus and for *Volk* and fatherland."[133]

Shortly thereafter Haeuser learned of Bishop Eberle's deceit. This betrayal deeply affected Haeuser. In correspondence with his friend August Oswald, a teacher, Haeuser referred to Eberle as a "traitor" and "this Judas."[134] Indeed, his one true friend, who had protected him so long from the wrath of Bishop Kumpfmüller, had now turned against him. Haeuser challenged Eberle, "You are not a fair judge of me. My judge is elsewhere. You harm yourself most definitely. . . . Most painfully affected and most deeply shaken, your most loyal and sincere former friend writes this to you." He signed it "Dr. Haeuser, innocent, suffering, and imprisoned priest."[135] Haeuser soon learned why Eberle was so eager to condemn him. In January 1948 a trial was about to begin against Eberle himself in connection with an investigation of Anton Scharnagl, auxiliary bishop in the Munich and Freising archdiocese. Both were accused of being SD informants. According to Haeuser, Special Minister Hagenauer intervened and had the procedures halted.[136]

Even though life in the work camp was difficult for Haeuser, he relished the opportunities and "benefits" that he received while interned. Since the tribunal had designated him a major offender, Haeuser was imprisoned with many former SS men.[137] According to Haeuser, these SS men were "pleasant comrades."[138] He even boasted, "In my room there are four comrades—all were in the SS. One left the Catholic Church. Two left the Protestant Church. One is a Protestant. But they all treat me with the highest respect."[139] It seems that, while imprisoned, Haeuser was able once again to play the role of chaplain to Nazis—the same role he had played among National Socialists prior to 1933. For example, in August 1947 Haeuser boasted to Oswald about the events surrounding a visit by Paul Althaus, a Protestant theologian who himself had been extremely nationalistic and open to National Socialism in its early years of power.[140] According to Haeuser, Althaus came "to preach Jesus to the wicked Nazis." When the audience started to "growl," Haeuser volunteered to take over the lecture from Althaus and addressed the room "full of prisoners." Although he described his words as "effective," he assured his friend that he "did not commit a folly." Instead, he "merely awakened enthusiasm among [his] comrades." Then he concluded, "Now I believe even more in new tasks for my life." In a separate letter Haeuser confided that "once free," he would "again sacrifice for a great religious and German cause."[141]

Despite his alleged enjoyment of reliving "better times," Haeuser desired to be released from the Regensburg camp. Immediately upon his conviction, Haeuser had instructed his lawyer, Otto Weinkamm, to appeal the tribunal's decision. Weinkamm worked diligently on this appeal.[142] Individuals such as Franz von Papen, the former vice-chancellor of Germany, who attested to Haeuser's dedication to providing pastoral ministry to the inmates in the Regensburg camp, aided him. During his own imprisonment, Papen had spent time with Haeuser in the camp's hospital.[143] Haeuser also wrote on his own behalf in an attempt to explain his antisemitic writings. In these appeals he refused to make any connection between his writing and preaching and the persecution and murder of European Jews. Rather, Haeuser limited his appeal to narrow theological explanations of his writings.[144]

By spring 1948 Haeuser's health had deteriorated considerably. The administration of the Regensburg camp took mercy upon the priest and released him early. He had served less than one year of his original sentence. His brief internment seemed to have lessened his stubbornness toward the requests of the diocese. Upon his release Haeuser returned to his parish and took up residency once again in his former rectory, where his sister was still living. Then Haeuser agreed to resign as pastor of Straßberg, effective May 1, 1948. The diocese also granted Haeuser a small monthly stipend that they increased over time to cover his basic living expenses and to assist him with the care of his sister.[145] Nevertheless, this act of kindness did not mean that Haeuser's diocesan superiors had totally forgotten his actions under National Socialism. On October 20, 1948, Bishop Kumpfmüller once again took away Haeuser's faculties and declared him not "emeritus," but "demeritus."[146] The latter meant that Haeuser was ineligible for any position in the diocese normally reserved for retired clergy.

Haeuser did not have any legal or canonical ground to stand upon once the bishop made this decision. He had already freely resigned his parish and for years had not been given a new assignment as pastor. Haeuser therefore responded humbly with a series of petitions that requested permission to administer the sacraments, especially the Eucharist.[147] Bishop Kumpfmüller ignored Haeuser's requests. However, at the time, Kumpfmüller had his own health problems. On February 9, 1949, the bishop's health took a turn for the worse, and he passed away. Soon after, Father Joseph Freundorfer of the Passau diocese was consecrated bishop and took Kumpfmüller's place. Yet this change of leadership did not lead to immediate improvements for Haeuser.

But eventually things did change. In early 1950 the appeals court in Munich reviewed Haeuser's denazification trial and determined that the judgment was too severe. Consequently, they reduced his categorization to group 3, designated lesser offenders. This change of status often became protocol after an individual's prison term had been completed.[148]

Then, toward the end of 1953, the diocese had a change of heart toward its rebellious priest. On November 5 the Augsburg chancery wrote to Haeuser and informed him that, effective January 1, 1954, he would receive the emeritus honor.[149]

Once reinstated, Haeuser's activities did not change a great deal and the remainder of his time in Straßberg proved uneventful. Since his release from the Regensburg work camp, Haeuser had resided in Straßberg.[150] The pastor there, Father Johann Stegmann, allowed Haeuser to maintain his apartment in the parish rectory. His new emeritus status allowed Haeuser to preside at the parish's daily liturgy. He also regularly visited parishioners in the local hospital.[151] Finally, in November 1957, after serving, in his fashion, the people of Straßberg for forty-six years, Haeuser left the parish to retire to the Cistercian Sisters' monastery Oberschönenfeld, in Gessertshausen. Before his departure, the citizens of Straßberg fêted Haeuser, upon whom they had bestowed honorary citizenship years earlier, with a farewell celebration. A huge crowd gathered in the hall of the Reichsadler Restaurant to say goodbye. One last time, he moved his congregants with his words, "Together with the citizens of Straßberg [we have] experienced many beautiful and joyful years, but also hard and bitter ones. . . . We have understood each other, and we will always understand each other, and that is why we will never forget each other." The newspaper reporter who covered the event commented, "In the old parish church that he loved and trusted he often preached from the pulpit that life is a struggle, must be a struggle, since only thus does it lead the way to the stars."[152] With that Father Haeuser left Straßberg, never to return.

Haeuser lived in Oberschönenfeld until his death on February 25, 1960. In his memoirs Haeuser stressed that he "did not need any Church to die in" and much less did he "need a Church for burial." Instead, he requested that his "dead body should not be blessed with holy water and incense," but rather "the sickliness and decay of [his] chastely kept body should turn to sacred ashes in the divine, elemental force of fire."[153] Still, it was very important for Haeuser to be remembered as he wished. Already in 1940 he wrote to his friend Otto Merkt, then the mayor of Kempten, in the hope that, following his death, he "would like to be correctly understood for the sake of the great idea for which [he had] lived, and which could never be understood by such National Socialists and such churchmen who saw only profit and business as the highest goals in life." Then he added, "I am proud of my Allgäu home region. However, the Allgäu also should not forget for what I strove sacrificially and courageously."[154]

The question remains then: what did Father Dr. Philipp Haeuser strive for? Had he been a misunderstood prophet who had endeavored to bring Christianity into the right-wing movements of Weimar Germany? Had he, like many Germans, fallen under the spell of Adolf Hitler and National Socialism? And did he truly change after the war and his denazification process? In some of his postwar correspondence with his diocesan superiors and with official state agencies Haeuser appeared repentant and humbled. However, already in his unpublished June 1943 essay, "Is the German *Volk* Being Ruined?," Haeuser lashed out against various aspects of the National Socialist movement that he believed were too extreme. This attack included a critique of the crass materialism of many state and party leaders who, he believed, had forgotten the "spiritual essence" of National Socialism. He also condemned the genocidal manner by which the Nazis attempted to solve the "Jewish question." He wrote: "The party leadership proclaims and orders the genocide of the Jewish race and in contempt of all moral law and all international agreements the 'upright SS' slaughters and shoots to death many thousands of Jewish women and children. These evil deeds scream to heaven. They cannot be concealed; the entire world knows about them. . . . This stupid and criminal battle of National Socialism and its leaders against the Jews means for the German *Volk* a loss of German honor for an unforeseeable time. And whoever takes the honor from the German *Volk* is its worst and most dangerous enemy. . . . Now also hundreds of thousands of Jewish men, women, and children are murdered, but since the party fights the battle against the Jews not in honorable battle and not in judicial judgments but through criminal methods executed by sadistic scoundrels, the Jews will possibly enjoy the compassion of the entire world and rise to a radiance never before experienced in the world. Poor German *Volk!* Through its delusions and in its madness, the party subjugates you to Jewish spirit and Jewish power."[155]

Haeuser attributed this destructive descent of the state and party to Adolf Hitler who, he argued, "liberated and rescued the German *Volk*, but who indeed has also become the destiny and ruin of the German people." Nevertheless, even in his criticism of the party and its leaders, Haeuser's words reveal his venom and hatred toward Jews. It is also interesting to see how much knowledge he had of the ongoing Holocaust. Still, for Haeuser the murder of Jews was not the most important issue. For him, the central issue primarily revolved around the matter of corruption and the bastardization of the essence and spirit of National Socialism. Haeuser believed membership in the Aryan race was not simply a matter of blood, but ultimately, he argued, the question of "whether one has Aryan blood arises above all from one's spiritual outlook."[156] By making such a statement, he revealed what some may interpret as a belief that Jews might be able to overcome their "Jewishness" and rise to a higher spiritual level, possibly alongside Aryans. At the same time he believed that leaders in his own faith tradition could be corrupted and "descend" to the depths of Judaism through their pharisaical actions and distorted spiritual worldview. By 1943, embittered by his clashes with the NSV and the Gestapo, Haeuser was able to critique, albeit distortedly, the party and leaders he so adored. Still, in his postwar correspondence and writings Haeuser refused to condemn Hitler and the NSDAP or discuss what the German nation under National Socialism, which he helped to bring to power, did to the Jews of Europe. It is possible, too, that he wrote his 1943 essay in a bizarre and distorted attempt to redeem himself for posterity.

Perhaps, to some of his fellow priests and superiors after the war, Haeuser seemed repentant. However, in his private correspondence, specifically in two letters addressed to his close friend and sympathizer August Oswald and in a written homily for a small group of Sisters, Haeuser revealed himself as an individual who stood unaltered in his belief. In September 1958 he suggested as much when he wrote to Oswald, "In German enthusiasm, I happily remembered the great German movement under Hitler and the struggle for the *Volk* against the *unvölkisch* enslavement through financial world powers. In religious enthusiasm, I immersed myself, in order to teach, ever more deeply in the great religious movement under Jesus and in the religious and spiritual struggle against Jewish and ecclesiastic paralysis and spiritual enslavement."[157] He suggested similar sentiments in a homily for the Cistercian Sisters on Christmas Day 1958, when he portrayed himself as one who had never relinquished his image of a militant Christ ready for battle against the so-called Jewish world influence. He preached, "The peaceful joys in the secluded manger in Bethlehem were the preparation for the hard and bloody life struggle of Jesus. The duty and the goal of the incarnation of Jesus was his life struggle, the struggle for the religion of the spirit and the truth against the paralysis of the Jewish Church. In this hard struggle, Jesus fell at Golgotha."[158] Finally, in a January 28, 1959, letter to Oswald, Haeuser proclaimed, "How gladly I would still, as in the time of Hitler, address large, educated, and leading audiences. How it stirs me when I think back!"[159]

Demonstrably, Philipp Haeuser is one of the clearest examples of how a "brown" Catholic priest could become a follower of National Socialism. He devoted his entire life and ministry to the cause of Adolf Hitler and the

NSDAP. While imprisoned in the Regensburg work camp, Haeuser had plenty of time to reflect on his activities of the previous twenty-five years. Fully unrepentant of his crimes under National Socialism, Haeuser blamed his diocesan superiors for his arrest and imprisonment. Embittered, he wrote to his friend Oswald and asked, "Why had Church officials not come after me earlier with canonical punishments?"[160]

Haeuser asked a perfectly valid question, since as late as 1940 four of his fellow priests had given him positive comments in a routine evaluation of his pastoral ministry. Of course, these priests did note that his preaching was "ideologically influenced," but apparently not at the expense of basic Catholic theology, and certainly not enough to expose them to the weaknesses of National Socialism, which masked as Christianity in his preaching.[161] Upon his early release from prison, he answered his question in an unpublished essay, "The Church and Denazification."[162] In this work Haeuser not only discussed the selections from his writings that the judges in the denazification tribunal used against him in their ruling; he also briefly examined the history of his Church and fellow clergymen under National Socialism. Not surprisingly, Haeuser improvised on these reflections and revealed through specific factual detail the complicity of his Church in supporting and abetting the National Socialist movement. Indeed, it was not enough for him to pass sentence upon himself; Haeuser also wanted to indict his Church, especially its bishops, and convince others that a part of German history they had not deemed true was something they had not wanted to deem true. Ultimately, Haeuser asked, "Am I the only one guilty here?"

Conclusion

As Hitler rose to power, German Catholics, both collectively and individually, found themselves facing challenging questions about their commitment to the teachings of the Church and their willingness to obey the directives of the Church hierarchy. The initial abrasive stance of their bishops toward National Socialism compelled them to choose between the Hitler movement and their Church. Of course, nationalism among many other factors played a considerable role in their decision-making process. After the bishops' reversal in March 1933 and the July signing of the Concordat, the choices became easier. Nevertheless, essential questions remained, especially between the National Socialist *Weltanschauung* and Church teaching.

In October 1967, while cataloging his letters and writings for future use by researchers, Father Richard Kleine reflected, "Since I was a child, a burning love for my German *Volk* and fatherland has been a part of me . . . the relationship between the Church and Germany has been especially important to me. I am one of those who firmly believed that the National Socialist movement stood for the national and social future of my *Volk* and was altogether the superior alternative to the Communist-Bolshevist ideology. I trusted . . . that Christian presence and cooperation in this movement could enhance Christian thought."[1]

In this reflection, Kleine identified the three traits that motivated his choices and sustained his belief in Hitler's Germany: an obsession with nationalism, a hatred of Communism, and a belief in the compatibility of Catholicism and National Socialism. These same traits motivated the majority of Kleine's fellow brown priests under National Socialism. Though these priests were not accepted by many members of their Church communities, the features that generally motivated their choices served as points of reference and mutual concern among Catholics and National Socialists alike.

The lingering effects of Bismarck's *Kulturkampf* left Catholics in a continual state of doubt about their place in German society and caused bishops and priests to view with suspicion any challenge that the German state leveled against the Church. In turn, this social and cultural uneasiness caused Catholics to overestimate and value too highly their own nationalism.[2] If the National Socialist leaders had been more savvy, they would have critiqued the Church's patriotic posture more closely instead of directly confronting its leaders and organizations, for at no time did the episcopacy wish their fellow citizens to view their Church as unpatriotic.[3] This was especially true during the Second World War, when the majority of Catholic bishops placed its full support behind the war effort.[4]

Even more significant than the Church's place in German society was the fixation of the Church's hierarchy on an impending Communist threat.[5] Such a fear served as a significant catalyst for adaptation and for the Church's accommodation to the state under National Socialism.[6] Indeed, Hitler's promise to eradicate this Bolshevik threat won Catholic clergymen's trust. At the same time, Catholic Church leaders were all too willing to concur implicitly, if not explicitly, with National Socialism's belief that Communists and Jews were of similar character and shared the goal of destroying Christian civilization.[7] However, this did not mean that the Church embraced the entirety of National Socialism's racial theory, especially its denial of the efficacy of baptism. Nevertheless, many churchmen were convinced that the moral decadence of the Weimar Republic would open up the state to Communism and tied this threat directly to liberal-leftist influences in the government and press. For their part, National Socialists were able to replace easily terms such as "liberal" and "leftist" with "Jews" and "Jewry." It therefore required no effort for many Catholics to do the same in their minds, which made them feel they had gained an "improved" understanding of Jews in relation to German politics and cultural life.

Historically, the Catholic Church tolerated discrimination against Jews, who allegedly betrayed the basic tenets of their own revealed faith by becoming obsessed with money and material goods. In turn, the

Church believed that these same unfaithful Jews, especially through the influence of the Enlightenment and modernity, had attacked and undermined Christianity and its moral and religious teaching through their "pernicious influence" on business, press, art, theater, film, and politics. Though the Church rejected the National Socialist racist form of antisemitism that preached "a struggle against the Jewish race" and made blood the sole determining factor of Jewish identity, it nevertheless, almost since its foundation, continued to promote a religion-based antisemitism, often referred to as anti-Judaism, by blaming Jews for Jesus' crucifixion.[8] Regardless of the theological logic underlying antisemitism, the negative portrayal of Jews facilitated discrimination and persecution. Even when Catholics tried to distance themselves from antisemitism or at least demonstrate moral sympathy toward Jews, it was very difficult for them to show any theological sympathy. This lack of theological sympathy led Catholics to a reductive appraisal of Jews as persistent nonbelievers, too alien and obstinate for the Church's leaders to include in the Gospel mandate to "love thy neighbor." The Catholic imagination only had to clothe these liturgical and homiletic perceptions in common and everyday antisemitic language. Consequently, priests such as Philipp Haeuser and Richard Kleine attempted to institutionalize antisemitism as a Christian mandate as well as a patriotic one. In retrospect, these priests were attempting only to rehearse earlier and more elemental antisemitic texts in the Catholic and Christian tradition, which were centuries old. From this referential perspective, much of the antisemitism in the Catholic Church was perceived as being partially in agreement with the spirit of Nazi racial teaching and National Socialism's eventual antisemitic legislation. For the ordinary Catholic, then, these various forms of antisemitism—racial, theological, economic, and cultural—became not only indistinguishable but mutually reinforcing.[9]

As a result, some Catholics, both clerics and laypersons, embraced Nazi racial theory and policy completely. For example, in 1943 Father Richard Kleine explained to his friend Father Johann Pircher how their intellectual efforts advanced in "Catholic-theological circles the settlement of the Jewish question" and "indeed in a truly positive way, though equally devastating for Judaism."[10] Kleine sanctioned a "theological final solution" to the "Jewish question," which called for the complete eradication of anything considered "Jewish" from Christianity. Such a theological mindset closely paralleled the designs and actions of the individuals who orchestrated the Holocaust and helped propel the "theological final solution" into the reality of annihilation.

Most Catholics were not willing to go as far as Kleine in their support of the state's antisemitic policies. Nevertheless, as Father Karl Adam mused in his Pentecost Sunday letter to Kleine of May 1941, only one central point prevented Catholics from directly supporting racist National Socialism. Adam conjectured, "I am convinced that the new political movement would long ago have thoroughly enriched even Church circles with its 'You will renew the face of the earth,' if the latter would not constantly encounter a profound anti-Christian instinct in certain proponents of the national movement."[11]

As Adam observed, the Church itself was an obstacle to a harmonious relationship between church and state. Any time a state official made a statement that contradicted Church doctrine or teaching, or enacted an ordinance that in any way challenged freedoms normally enjoyed by the Church, the suspicious bishops immediately assumed a combative stance. This was exactly the circumstance in which the Church found itself under National Socialism: its leaders focused solely on the survival of the institution itself and its sacramental mission. Even the brown priests realized this fact. For example, in October 1944 Johann Pircher wrote a letter to Richard Kleine complaining about a diocesan colleague. His fellow priest's eagerness to build a new rectory during World War II astonished him. Pircher lamented, "Today, these are the concerns, aren't they, while our *Volk* fights for its survival and no one knows whether or not Bolshevism will sweep everything away."[12]

Despite the cutting tone of his statement, Pircher did not mind battling for the survival of his *Volk* or the National Socialist cause. He and his fellow brown priests relished this almost apocalyptic battle. For it truly was on the terrain of a battle ground that they felt most needed by the NSDAP. Father Philipp Haeuser's writings and sermons regularly reflected this same theme. In 1936 Father Josef Roth asked his friend and priestly colleague Father Lorenz Pieper whether he would once more venture forth "to the battle field when the great days of battle finally arrive."[13] Such language put the brown priests, especially those who journeyed with Hitler as he struggled for power before 1933, back to the days when they acted as speakers and animators of National Socialism and served as chaplains to the party's right-wing troops. This mindset also allowed those priests who were not Old Fighters to feel the same camaraderie and spirit as their seasoned peers. It also heightened their own sense of self-importance —a characteristic that most of the brown priests shared.[14]

In reality, the more National Socialism permeated the German state and society, the less Nazi officials needed clerics as propagandists and speakers. Many National Socialists, particularly the younger generation, who rose to power in the latter part of the 1930s and early 1940s, saw no need at all for priests and less need for religion. The brown priests' attempt to Christianize or Catholicize National Socialism inadvertently fueled these negative feelings among younger party members, most of whom did not want to see the National Socialist message distorted through a Christian lens. This was also true of many older members. Nazis who fit these categories saw no purpose in the brown priests' ecumenical effort to reach out to Protestant Christians in order to promote the aims of the Nazi Party and the German state. If anything, party leaders believed that the party itself and its organizations could promote unity among Germans. In addition, the appearance of Catholic priests in the Nazi Party created more problems than it was worth, something Father Haeuser discovered when he could no longer find a publisher for his National Socialist theological-political writings. NSDAP leaders simply did not want to deal with the bishops' complaints concerning "sympathetic" priests who sided with the state or party against the Church.

Nineteen thirty-six was the year when many brown priests realized how distant the party had grown. In March 1936 Father Peter Vogt of the Würzburg diocese wrote to Abbot Alban Schachleiter to express these concerns. In March Vogt wrote, "I have the feeling that—at least in Lower Franconia—priests are not wanted in the party. At the very least we are being pushed to the side completely. . . . The old district leadership has completely replaced by new men. My patrons and friends no longer have any power."[15] Several months later Vogt wrote again to Abbot Schachleiter and confirmed his belief, "Priests are not wanted in the party because it is feared that they will dilute the National Socialist *Weltanschauung*."[16]

Father Vogt also lamented the lack of support for his efforts on behalf of National Socialism among the German Catholic hierarchy and the Catholic lay population. First, in March 1936, Vogt bemoaned Bishop Michael Rackl's refusal to allow him to enter the military chaplaincy. Rackl's justification was the shortage of priests needed for parish work in his diocese.[17] Then, in August, Vogt revealed to Schachleiter the animosity he felt among his parishioners because of his support of National Socialism, "Our *Volk* is faithful and strongly Catholic and is more and more emotionally alienated from the Führer. How often do I hear, 'Father, what do you have to say now? Father, have you still not had enough? You were certainly enthusiastic, can you still take part now?' This is how the Catholic people speak to their pastor. And behind all these questions lies the response, 'You are not a Catholic priest if you continue to support the party.'"[18]

Despite this lack of support for priests working on behalf of the NS-DAP, most bishops tolerated extensive disobedience from their brown priests. Of course, the bishops for the most part immediately stepped in when a priest, such as Anton Heuberger, challenged the basic tenets of the Catholic faith. In 1938 Richard Kleine experienced such a rebuke when he attempted to publish his work "The Gospel at the Turning Point of German History." The diocesan censor demanded so many changes in the manuscript that Kleine gave up trying to publish it.[19] From this, one might wish to conclude that the bishops were equally offended by a brown priest's general support of National Socialism, especially its racial antisemitism, and used a theological or canonical pretext to discipline him. Yet, the extant evidence reveals a German Catholic hierarchy oftentimes overwhelmed by a subliminal, but controlling, German nationalism, which seemed to blunt their decision making and pastoral judgment, especially in regard to disciplining brown priests. When leadership for and witness to the Gospel message of love of all people were needed most, the hierarchy seemed blindsided by purely parochial needs, clerical insularity, and the fear of a more lethal *Kulturkampf*. One example of this clerical insularity can be found in the behavior of Archbishop Lorenz Jaeger of Paderborn. Jaeger's continued willingness to communicate with Richard Kleine after the war and even to offer him a job is inexcusable. Though Jaeger might have thought he was exercising charity for Kleine, in the context of the Holocaust Jaeger's action seems more injurious in its inclination than remedial, lacking all discretion for the innocent dead. And though there is no proof that Jaeger accepted Kleine's political opinions during the war, the bishop should have distanced himself from Kleine.

Ironically, despite their allegiance to Adolf Hitler and National Socialism, most of the brown priests remained in the priesthood. Most had no problem integrating Catholic theology with National Socialist ideology or tainting Christianity with Aryan mythology. They were also able to overlook anything in National Socialism that ran counter to their Catholic faith. Moreover, these brown priests viewed their fellow clergymen who refused to act in a similar vein as misled or out of touch with modern times. In their view such "Church-minded" clergymen held an erroneous set of values that threatened the Church's downfall in the Third Reich. Interestingly, the NSDAP's anti-Christian rhetoric and allure drove only a handful of priests to desert their vocation and join state agencies or party organizations that worked directly against the Church. Among these deserters, such as the former Munich priest Albert Hartl, most could cite only personal reasons like celibacy and conflict with

Church superiors, in addition to their fervent support of National Socialism, as justification for leaving the Church.[20] However, those who carried on in the priesthood were simply unable to sever ties with their religious tradition. Catholicism had a grip on them. Though many of them attributed a messianic role to Adolf Hitler and the Nazi Party, believing that their Führer could offer them and their country the means to a better society, happiness, and life, they still found the core of their life and spiritual underpinnings anchored in the priesthood. They were pastoral ministers. Long after his death, for example, Father Haeuser's parishioners continued to attest to the exceptional pastoral care that they received from him. These Catholic men and women were readily willing to put aside their memories of Haeuser's fiery antisemitic and nationalistic rhetoric for their recollection of his unselfish caring for and attending to the dying and sick of Straßberg. Though Richard Kleine's colleagues and students knew less about his efforts on behalf of National Socialism, they too were eager to focus upon the positive image they had of their grandfatherly teacher and priest.

But another factor also came into play. In the 1930s and 1940s contesting a positive and established image of a Catholic priest was a very difficult thing to do. Catholics the world over placed priests on pedestals. The bishops had consecrated them as mediators between God and humankind and, through their ministry, they represented Jesus Christ here on earth.[21] For a dedicated and practicing Catholic it was nearly impossible to step outside the mystique of this belief system to question a priest. Such thinking also tended to inhibit bishops from either disciplining recalcitrant priests or, when facing serious breaches of conduct, taking canonical action to defrock them—stripping them of priestly privileges and functions. Following this tradition after the war, the Church and Allied powers publicly disciplined very few of them. Even priests such as Philipp Haeuser, Anton Heuberger, and Richard Kleine, whom the Allies initially forced out of office, eventually made their way back into public ministry. The death of the bishops whom some had crossed often helped to ease this transition. The German Church leaders who followed, like the German public in general, were eager to put the National Socialist past behind them. All was forgiven for the glory of God!

Appendix 1

German Catholic Ecclesiastical Structure

Roman Catholic Hierarchy and Diocesan Structure—The Catholic Church in Germany is part of the universal Roman Catholic Church. At its head is the pope (the Holy Father), the bishop of Rome, who, following the 1929 Lateran treaties between the Holy See and Italy, also serves as Vatican City's head of state. Directly beneath the pope are cardinals, whom the Holy Father appoints and who also elect a future pope. Cardinal is an honorary title that does not suggest any distinction in orders. Often they reside in the Vatican and serve in administrative positions, such as heads of the Holy See's governing congregations. Some cardinals also serve as the spiritual leaders of archdioceses. Beneath the cardinals are bishops. In select Germany dioceses the cathedral chapter *(Domkapitel)*, consisting of appointed priests *(Domkapitulare)*, elects a candidate as bishop to govern a particular diocese. The Vatican confirms such an appointment. In other dioceses the Vatican holds the right of appointment. Directly beneath a bishop are priests, who serve Catholics in a variety of ministries, especially as pastors and teachers. Priests who have performed extraordinary service to the Church often receive the honorary title of monsignor.

During the Third Reich the archbishops and bishops of all the German dioceses met in conference at least once annually in Fulda. From 1920 to 1945 Cardinal Adolf Bertram, the archbishop of Breslau, served as the head of this conference. In addition to the overarching Fulda Bishops' Conference, in the 1930s and 1940s the Catholic Church in Germany had six provinces (Bamberg, Breslau, Freiburg, Cologne, Munich and Freising, and Paderborn), overseen by metropolitans who were archbishops. The six provinces were further divided into twenty-four dioceses, which were governed by bishops. Lastly, dioceses were divided into deaneries, in which bishops appointed senior priests as deans to assist them with administrative and evaluative responsibilities.

German Ecclesiastical Titles—Due to a complex historic relation between church and state, in Germany there are more than forty different titles for priests. The official titles for a priest designate the nature of his particular appointment to a parish or chaplaincy position or identify his particular rank or status in a diocese. Unlike the ubiquitous title "Father," used to address most priests in the United States, German Catholics regularly address their clergy by their official title. The address "Father," or *Pater* in German (from the Latin), is primarily reserved for members of religious orders. However, members of religious orders who enter into diocesan ministry often use the rank and titles of the diocesan clergy. In appendix 2 I have primarily maintained the original German titles. Although there are no exact equivalents in the American Catholic Church's clerical hierarchical system, the priestly titles can be understood in general terms familiar to English-speaking readers.

In Germany a pastor of the parish is referred to as *Pfarrer* in certain dioceses or parishes. *Pfarrer* is both a title and rank among German clerics. A priest could receive the title of *Pfarrer* without the diocese appointing him to a pastorate. In some dioceses and certain parishes the state held the right to nominate a pastor. In such cases a pastor would receive the title *Stadtpfarrer*. A pastor who was also responsible for the pastoral care of soldiers or sailors stationed in his parish would be referred to as a *Standortpfarrer* (army) or *Marinestandortpfarrer* (navy). Many parishes in Germany were quite large or covered extensive areas. Often the diocesan structure would create smaller parishes that had a filial relationship with a larger parish. In such cases pastors would have a variety of titles, including *Kuratus, Benefiziat, Benefiziumsprovisor, Expositus, Provisor, Benefiziumsverwalter* or *-verweser, Schloßbenefiziat,* and *Schloßgeistlicher.* Each of these titles reflects a specific responsibility, salary, and often state-church relationship. The remaining titles generally refer to the title of parochial vicar or associate pastor. Among these titles are *Pfarrvikar, Kooperator, Kooperatorverweser, Koadjutor, Kaplan, Lokalkaplan, Benefiziumsvikar,* and *Pfarrkuratievikar.* Priests who did not have a particular parish assignment but might live or assist in a parish would be called *Aushilfsgeistlicher, Aushilfspriester,* or *Messeleser.* Priests who lived in a town, often in retirement, without a specific pastoral assignment received the title *Kommorant.* Dioceses also had other titles to confer on priests with specific parish ministries. A *Stadtprediger* or *Hofstiftsprediger* was a priest who had specific pastoral roles related to preaching, often rooted in the history of the German nobility. A *Domkapitular* was a member of the cathedral chapter and, in this role, an advisor to the bishop. *Domvikare* were also priests who served as official advisors to the bishop. In addition, *Geistlicher Rat*—a title often conferred as honorary, or *ad honores*—also served in an advisory capacity to the bishop. *Ehrenkanonikus* was an honorary title conferred on certain members of the clergy upon retirement. The term "incardinate" is used when a diocese accepts an ordained member of a religious order or a priest from a religious community or different diocese into its clergy.

Priests who served as chaplains for the *Wehrmacht* (army) held one of the following titles: *Oberdivisionspfarrer, Divisionspfarrer, Feldgeistlicher, Heerespfarrer,* and *Wehrmachtspfarrer.* Priests who served in the German navy had one of the following titles: *Marinedekan, Marineoberpfarrer,* or *Marinepfarrer.*

Priests who worked in education used the normal state titles to designate their position and rank. Such titles include *Schulrat* (state or municipal councilor on school issues); *Oberstudiendirektor* and *Studiendirektor* (school principal); *Professor* (used to designate a professor both at a college and university) and *Dozent* (instructor or assistant professor); *Studienprofessor* and *Oberstudienrat* (tenured senior high-school teacher); and *Studienrat* (tenured high-school teacher). Priests served as educators in a variety of educational institutions, including *Volksschule* and *Hauptschule* (elementary schools); *Vorbereitungsschule* (preparatory school, often for boys intending to go to a seminary); *Realschule* (trade school up to tenth grade); *Oberrealschule, Staatsrealgymnasium, Bundesrealgymnasium, Kreisoberrealschule* (schools offering languages and sciences, but not classical languages); *Höhere Töchterschule, Lyzeum* (preparatory schools for girls, grades 5–12); *Progymnasium* (high school or preparatory-level school); and gymnasium, *Missionsgymnasium* (secondary schools offering university preparatory programs, some with classical languages).

Appendix 2

The Brown Priests—Biographical Data

Statistics—The list below contains the names of 138 brown priests: 109 diocesan priests from Germany, 19 ordained members of religious orders, and 10 priests from dioceses outside Germany. The latter group either were active in Germany sometime from 1933 to 1945 or worked in close connection with priests who lived in Germany. Since degrees of "brown-ness" may vary, it is essential to call to mind the discussion from chapter 1 about the nature of brown priests. I have made every attempt to find and to identify brown priests. Of course, I am positive that I have failed to unearth the names of some of them. I will have to leave these priests for future scholars to uncover. In other cases I have left out priests' names because sufficient evidence does not exist to determine their relationship with the NSDAP. Despite these factors, I am confident that the names and biographical information provided below offer a true range of priests who publicly supported National Socialism. I realize that not everyone might agree with the inclusion or exclusion of particular priests. Though no one likes to be proved wrong, I welcome the opportunity to gain more insight into the history of any individual priest under National Socialism. There-fore, this list should in no way be viewed as final or stagnant.

A number of interesting statistics arise from this list. Among the total number, 53 became card-carrying members of the NSDAP, 42 held one or more doctorates (primarily in the fields of philosophy, theology, or history), and 28 left the priesthood, often to marry and work for the party or state in its efforts to monitor and limit the influence of the Church in German-dominated Europe.

Sources—I checked every priest's name that I encountered in my re-search against the extant membership cards and personal files of the NS-DAP and its organizations (formerly housed in the Berlin Document Center). I conducted this research using both the original records in Germany at the German Federal Archives in Berlin-Lichterfelde and mi-crofilms of the original records located in the U.S. National Archives in College Park, Maryland. If any biographical information is missing, it is because I was unable to obtain it. Some of the priests' diocesan personal files still are closed to researchers due to standard archival guidelines. Bombing raids during the war, along with the transfer of a few dioceses from German to Polish hands, also resulted in the loss of Church records. In some cases, after I had found sufficient documents in a state or church archive to determine a priest's connection with the NSDAP, I had to contact a separate archive to complete his biographical information. I regularly did this through correspondence. I have noted such instances by listing the archive abbreviation and the term "Personaldaten." The archivists used a variety of sources, such as diocesan directories *(Schematismus)*, published lists of diocesan clergy, and biographical card catalogues to provide me with this information. If the archivists provided additional documentation, I have noted it.

In the list below I have made every effort to provide basic information on a priest's background, education, assignments, and efforts on behalf of the NSDAP. In Addition, I have included known publications written in support of National Socialism. In the case of NSDAP members, I list their membership number and date of entry, along with membership in any related party organizations. I fully realize that membership in the NSDAP or related organizations does not absolutely denote support for all aspects of the National Socialist *Weltanschauung*. Nevertheless, the priests included in this list at some point publicly aligned themselves with and promoted the National Socialist Party and its *Weltanschauung*. In the cases where a priest was not a party member, I briefly identify the specific avenue by which a priest made his NSDAP convictions known. In addition, I list related primary and secondary source information at the end of each biographical entry. The latter is not meant to be exhaustive but to provide an avenue for further research for the interested reader.

Adam, Karl

born Pursruck, October 22, 1876
ordained June 10, 1900 (Regensburg)
doctorate (theology), University of Munich, 1904
Dozent, University of Munich, 1908
Professor (moral theology), University of Straßburg, 1918
Professor (dogmatics), University of Tübingen, 1919–1949
"Deutsches Volkstum und katholisches Christentum" (1933)
"Die geistige Lage des deutschen Katholizismus" (1939)
member Kleine-Pircher group of National Socialist Priests, 1940–1945
"Jesus, der Christus und Wir Deutsche" (1943/1944)
retired October 1, 1949
died Tübingen, April 1, 1966

Source: DAR NL 67 Adam, G1.7.1 no. 33 PA Adam; BArch B R53/198; Kriedler, "Karl Adam und der Nationalsozialismus"; Krieg, *Karl Adam: Catholicism in German Culture,* "Karl Adam, National Socialism, and Christian Tradition," and *Catholic Theologians in Nazi Germany,* 83–106; Scherzberg, *Kirchenreform mit Hilfe des Nationalsozialismus;* Spicer, "Last Years of a Resister in the Diocese of Berlin" and *Resisting the Third Reich,* 172–78.

Altinger, Josef, O.S.B.
born Aham, February 3, 1904
entered Benedictine order (Metten), 1924
studied theology, philology, history, pedagogy, and German language and literature, University of Munich, 1924–1930
moved to Niederaltaich monastery, 1926
ordained June 29, 1929
joined NSDAP, n.d., no. 3,611,329
left Benedictine order and joined SS March 24, 1935, no. 267,281
SD specialist on religious orders, 1936–1937
SD *Oberabschnitt* (upper section) North-East, 1937–1939
married Editha Schmorrde, December 1938
SD resettlement commission, USSR, December 1939–February 1940
died September 12, 1943
Source: NARA SSOA Altinger RG242-A3342-SSO-010; Dierker, *Himmlers Glaubenskrieger,* 551.

Arenz, Jakob Franz
born Wittlich, March 12, 1890
ordained August 1, 1914 (Trier)
Kaplan, Bildstock, Weiskirchen, Dillingen, Saarbrücken-St. Eligius, 1914–1923
Pfarrvikar, then *Pfarrer,* Schwemlingen, December 1923–1944
joined NSDAP, member 1935–1938
died Schwemlingen, February 16, 1944
Source: BAT Personaldaten; Persch, "Der Diözesanklerus und die neuen pastoralen Laienberufe," 211–12.

Bader, Benedikt
born Untergrainau near Garmisch, July 10, 1906
ordained June 29, 1931 (Munich and Freising)
Koadjutor, Vachendorf, July 1931
Kurat, Lenggries, April 1932
Kooperator, Weichs and Velden, 1934–1937 (supports NSDAP through his pastoral ministry)
Schulbenefiziat and *Kurat,* Frauenried, February 1937–January 1940

volunteered for Germany army noncombatant position, September 1939
German army, medical service, Northern France and Romania, April
   1940–November 1941
purser training course, Munich, November 1941
war administrative inspector, military hospital, Augsburg, and later
   Eastern Front, March 1942
left priesthood, March 1943, and married sometime thereafter
date of death unknown

Source: EAM NL Faulhaber 5402 and Personaldaten; NARA NSPK RG242-A3340-PK-A120; RG242 T-581, r. 98.

Barion, Hans

born Düsseldorf, December 16, 1899
infantry, WWI, 1917–1918 (POW in Great Britain, 1918–1919)
ordained August 14, 1924 (Cologne)
religion teacher, Girls' High School, Honnef, August 1924
Kaplan, Menden, August 1925
rector, St. Augustine Institute, Wuppertal-Elberfeld, August 1926
doctorate (canon law), University of Bonn, July 1929
Dozent, University of Bonn, July 1930
Dozent, then *Professor* (canon law), State Academy, Braunsberg,
   October 1931
"Kirche oder Partei? Der Katholizismus im neuen Reich" (1933)
joined NSDAP, May 1, 1933, no. 2,070,445
joined NSLB, July 1, 1933, no. 102,830
priestly faculties suspended, August 1934–October 1935
Professor (canon law), University of Munich, May 1938–February 1939
Professor (canon law), University of Bonn, April 1939
state candidate for bishop of Cologne, 1942
state candidate for bishop of Aachen, 1943
dismissed as professor by British military government, 1945
denazification, 1948, exonerated
died Bonn, May 15, 1973

Source: BArch B R58/5300 and R58/5715/A2; R5101/22534; BArch K 1516 NL
Schröcker; NARA OGK RG242-A3340-MFOK-A079; NSLB RG242-A3340-MF-A009;
Marschler, *Kirchenrecht im Bannkreis Carl Schmitts;* Preuschoff, "Zur Suspension der
Braunsberger Professoren Eschweiler und Barion im Jahre 1934"; Schröcker, "Theologische Fakultäten im Dritten Reich" and "Der Fall Barion."

Baumeister, Georg

born Berghausen April 24, 1890
ordained March 19, 1920 (Regensburg)

Kooperator, Bad Abbach, Cham, Prackenbach, Kümmersbruck, 1920–1927
Pfarrprovisor, Rieden, Rattiszell, 1927–1937
joined NSV, May 1, 1934
joined NSDAP, May 1, 1935, no. 3,636,659
Pfarrer, Reichersdorf, 1937–1958
denazification, September 20, 1946, classified as lesser offender (category 3)
died as *Kommorant,* Niederaichbach, August 28, 1962
Source: BZAR Personaldaten; BayHStA, MSo 1415; NARA NSZK RG242-A3340-MFKL-A144, OGK RG242-A3340-MFOK-A096, NSPK RG242-A3340-PK-A252.

Bergh, Wilhelm Alois van den
born Ravenstein, Holland, April 16, 1876
ordained December 21, 1900 (Order of Friars Minor Capuchin,
    O.F.M. Cap.)
Kaplan, Leopoldsdorf near Wien, 1919–1928
Benefiziat, Zwölfaxing, August 1928–May 1933
incardinated archdiocese of Vienna, August 1929
"Kann der überzeugte Katholik überzeugter Nationalsozialist sein?" (1938)
member *Arbeitsgemeinschaft für den religiösen Frieden,* 1938
member Kleine-Pircher group of National Socialist Priests, 1939–1945
Pfarrer, Rauchenwarth, June 1933–September 1955
retired, Gablitz, Waldkloster, September 1955
died Vienna, December 28, 1958
Source: DAWien Personaldaten; MIO NL Kleine; Lettl, "Die Arbeitsgemeinschaft für den religiösen Frieden 1938"; Loidl, *Religionslehrer Johann Pircher* and ed., *Arbeitsgemeinschaft für den religiösen Frieden.*

Braun, Johannes-Baptist
born Ostermünchen, August 8, 1884
ordained July 16, 1911 (Regensburg)
Kooperator, Wolfsberg (Kärnten), August 1911
Provisor, Lind, November 1912
Kooperator, Villach, September 1913
Pfarrer, Glogau, January 1915
Pfarrer, Friedlach, October 1915
religion teacher, Lam, April 1920
Expositus, Glaubendorf, November 1924
Expositus, Kläham, February 1931 (supports NSDAP through his
    pastoral ministry)
retired, Vilsbiburg, February 1939
died January 21, 1945
Source: BArch B R58/5706b; BZAR Personaldaten.

Brinkmann, Hellmuth Martin
born Ratibor, October 3, 1882
ordained February 15, 1913 (Cologne)
Kaplan, Düsseldorf, St. Paul, April 1913
Divisionspfarrer, WWI, October 1914
Kaplan, Wipperfürth, January 1919
Pfarrer, Altenberg, July 1920
Pfarrer, Bonn-Kessenich, St. Nicholas, May 1929
joined NSDAP, May 1, 1933, no. 3,133,248
named *Geistlicher Rat,* December 1951
died May 17, 1955
Source: AEK Kleruskartei; NARA NSZK RG242-A330-MFKL-D006; Brandt and Häger, eds., *Biographisches Lexikon,* 97.

Brunner, (Heinrich) Harduin, O.F.M.
born Würzburg, December 20, 1900
ordained St. Anna, Munich, February 27, 1927 (Bavarian Franciscan
    Province)
teacher, librarian, prefect, Berching, Pfreimd, Nuremberg St. Ludwig,
    Dettelbach, Tölz monasteries, 1928–1934 (preaches and writes in
    favor of NSDAP)
librarian, Munich St. Anna monastery, 1934
librarian, Eggenfelden monastery, 1936
vicar of the province, chaplain, Gößweinstein monastery, 1937–1947
religion teacher, chaplain, Munich St. Gabriel monastery, 1947–1960
religion teacher, chaplain, Munich-St. Anna monastery, 1961–1974
died Landshut, November 12, 1976
Source: ABFP Personalkataloge; NARA; RG242-T454/r. 81.

Buck, Eugen
born Guggenberg bei Schwabmünchen, July 8, 1900
infantry, WWI, June 24–August 1918
studied theology, University of Bamberg and University of Innsbruck
ordained 1925 (Bamberg)
studied canon law, Rome, 1927–1929
Pfarrer, Bamberg, 1929
supporting member of the SS, 1934–1938
joined NSV, 1934
Studienrat (religion), Vocational and Business School, Bamberg,
    1936–1940
private tutor, Bamberg, 1940–1942
Stadtpfarrer, Erlangen, 1942–1948

denazification, Erlangen, September 25, 1946, classified as follower (category 4)

Studienrat (religion), *Oberrealschule,* Bamberg, January 1948

accused of making antisemitic remarks in public, criminal trial July 21, 1949, acquitted

died December 1962

Source: BayHSta MSo 1415; MK 45818 PA Buck.

Cloß, Alois

born Neumarkt (Steiermark), Austria, October 27, 1893

ordained, March 12, 1916 (Graz-Seckau)

Kaplan, Gnas, Weizburg, Kindberg, 1916–1921

religion teacher, *Staatsrealgymnasium* Lichtenfelsgasse, 1921

doctorate (natural science)

Professor (religion), *Bundesrealgymnasium* Graz, 1932

advanced studies (religion), University of Vienna, 1933–1934

hospital chaplain, Vienna St. Josef Hospital, 1933–1934

Dozent (comparative theology), University of Vienna, 1934–1936

member Kleine-Pircher group of National Socialist Priests, 1939–1945

worked in the Catholic division of *Institut zur Erforschung und Beseitigung des jüdischen Einflusses im deutschen kirchlichen Leben,* Eisenach, 1940/1941

professor of ethnology and comparative theology, University of Graz, 1945

retired 1968

died January 9, 1984

Source: ARGS Personaldaten; MIO NL Kleine; Hofmüller, "Steirische Priester," 126–28.

Conrath, Chrysostomus (Karl M.), O.P.

born Brebach near Saarbrücken, April 4, 1880

ordained August 14, 1904 (Dominican Province Teutonia)

editor, *Mary Psalter,* 1911–1922

editor, *Rosary Calendar,* 1914–1922

military hospital chaplain, Hermsdorf St. Dominicus-Institution, 1914

member *Katholische Vereinigung für nationale Politik*

chaplain, Sanitas Hospital, Zürich, 1933

remained in Switzerland

died Zürich, April 7, 1956

Source: BArch B R5101/22314; PArcK PA Conrath; Groothuis, *Im Dienste einer über-staatlichen Macht,* 459–63; Spicer, *Resisting the Third Reich,* 143.

Drossert, Paul Arthur
born Krefeld, December 5, 1883
briefly member of the Congregation of the Holy Family, Grave,
  Netherlands
ordained Tournai, Belgium, November 23, 1913
vicar, Tertre, December 1913
Kaplan, Aachen-Burtscheid St. Johann, Mühlheim (Ruhr) St. Barbara,
  Eupen St. Nicholas, 1914–1922
Pfarrer, Sengern (Oberelsaß), October 1922
Pfarrer, Kleeburg (Unterelsaß), April 1927
suspended from ministry (claimed he was expelled by French on account of his German outlook), 1927
moved to Potsdam, then to Berlin in 1931 without any specific
  ministerial assignment
publicly declared support for Hitler in *Der Angriff* and *Völkischer
  Beobachter,* 1932
incardinated into Berlin diocese
Wehrmachtspfarrer/Wehrmachtsoberpfarrer/Divisionspfarrer, 1937–1942
Standortpfarrer and prison chaplain, Torgau and Halle a. d. Saale,
  1942–1945
Kaplan and hospital chaplain, Berlin-Gatow, June 1, 1950
retired April 1951
died Berlin-Gatow, January 24, 1969
buried Berlin-Reinickendorf, January 27, 1969, Cathedral Cemetery of
  St. Hedwig
Source: BArch D ZB 1 1035; DAB VI/1 Drossert; *Katholisches Kirchenblatt Berlin* (April 17, 1932); Brandt and Häger, eds., *Biographisches Lexikon,* 160; Spicer, *Resisting the Third Reich,* 143, 149.

Duchêne, Ferdinand, SAC
born Holzfeld, September 19, 1900
ordained June 26, 1927 (Society of the Catholic Apostolate/Pallottine Order)
left order, August 1, 1938
withdrew from Catholic Church, 1939
joined NSDAP, n.d., no. 7,251,167
joined SS
SD-OA South-West, January 1940
RSHA II, November 1940
RSHA VII B 2: Political Churches, 1943
suspended October 1943 and dismissed from the SS
date of death unknown
Source: NARA NSZK RG242-A330-MFKL-F056; Dierker, *Himmlers Glaubenskrieger,* 552.

Dümler, Hugo

born Prölsdorf, August 21, 1889
ordained August 3, 1913 (Würzburg)
Kaplan, Sulzbach, August 1913
Expositus, Leidersbach, April 1917
Lokalkaplan, Dettingen, December 1921
Pfarrer, Dettingen, October 1922–1950
joined NSDAP, May 1, 1933, no. 3,437,997
died April 13, 1950
Source: BayHStA MSo 1415; DAW PA Dümler; NARA NSZK RG242-A3340-MFKL-F060.

Edgermaniger, Joseph

born Tann, November 19, 1882
ordained June 29, 1908 (Passau)
Aushilfspriester, Dommelstadl, Roßnach, 1908–1909
Kooperator, Seebach, April 1909
Provisor, Frohnstetten, Seebach, 1911–1913
Kooperator, Tittling, February 1913
Feldgeistlicher, WWI, June 6, 1914
Kooperator, Griesbach, Tittling, Regen, 1918–1929
Provisor, then *Pfarrer,* Asbach, December 1, 1933 (supports NSDAP
    through his pastoral ministry)
Pfarrer, Mittich, July 1, 1941
Benefiziums-Verwalter, Emmersdorf, November 1, 1945
Pfarrverwalter, Weihmörting, October 15, 1948
died November 12, 1951
Source: BArch B NS 26/1330; *Schematismus Passau* 1949, 141; 1952, 109; Wurster, "Zur Geschichte des Bistums Passau im Dritten Reich," 246–47.

Elling, Georg, O.S.B.

born Wettzell, May 15, 1899
WWI, infantry, June 26, 1918–January 27, 1919
studied theology, St. Ottilien and University of Munich
ordained April 3, 1927 (Benedictine-St. Ottilien)
left order, October 1928
withdrew from Catholic Church, 1930
preacher, Free-Religious Protestant Church, Baden, then German
    Faith movement until September 1935
joined NSDAP, May 1, 1933, no. 3,461,625
joined SS, November 1, 1935, no. 233,199
race consultant, SD-OA Southwest, May 1935

married Erika Lutz, November 1937
SD-OA East, June 1939–February 1940
RSHA III, February 1940–February 1941
RSHA I and *Dozent* at the *Führerschule* for Sicherheitspolizei, February 1941
RSHA VI, June 1943 (from November 1943 onward in Rome)
German Embassy to the Holy See, January 1944
arrested by American military, 1944
denazification, classified as criminal (category 1)
denazification appeal, North-Württemberg, April 4, 1949, reduced to lesser offender (category 3)

Source: NARA NSZK RG242-A3340-MFKL-G012; NSPK RG242-A3340-PK-C54; SSOA RG 242-A3343-SSO-184; Dierker, *Himmlers Glaubenskrieger*, 552–53.

Elser, Josef

born Aalen, February 2, 1902
ordained March 12, 1933 (ordained in Augsburg diocese for the diocese of Jassy, Romania)
joined NSDAP, February 1, 1934, no. 3,401,745
Pfarrer, Emmental (German community Bessarabia, Romania), 1933–1934
arrested and deported from Romania, August 1934
appointed *Aushilfspriester*, Flochberg (Rottenburg diocese), did not assume position, October 1934
Kommorant, Dunstelkingen, October 1934–April 1936
Rottenburg bishop withdrew faculties after repeated warnings, May 1936
died June 30, 1970

Source: DAR Personaldaten; NL 67/19 Adam; NARA NSZK RG242-A3340-MFKL-G015; StA Kempten NL Haeuser.

Eschweiler, Karl

born Euskirchen, September 5, 1886
studied theology at Cologne Seminary and University of Munich
doctorate (philosophy), University of Munich, 1909
ordained March 11, 1911 (Cologne)
Divisionspfarrer, WWI
doctorate (theology), University of Bonn, 1920
Dozent, University of Bonn, 1922
Professor (apologetics and dogmatic theology), State Academy, Braunsberg, November 1928
rector, State Academy, Braunsberg, 1931–1932 and 1935–1936

joined NSDAP, May 1, 1933, no. 2,070,530
joined NSLB, July 1, 1933, no. 102,832
"Die Kirche im neuen Reich" (1933)
faculties suspended, August 1934–October 1935
died Berlin, September 30, 1936
buried in SA-uniform, Euskirchen, October 8, 1936
Source: BArch B R4901/2451; R58/5715/A2; OGK RG242-A3340-MFKL-G073; NSLB RG242-A3340-MF-A053; Brandt and Häger, eds., *Biographisches Lexikon,* 185–86; Krieg, *Catholic Theologians in Nazi Germany,* 31–55; Preuschoff, "Zur Suspension der Braunsberger Professoren Eschweiler und Barion im Jahre 1934."

Ess, Alois

born Burgberg, November 11, 1874
ordained July 23, 1898 (Augsburg)
Kaplan, Pfronten, Schwabmünchen, 1898–1900
Pfarrvikar, Schwabmünchen, 1900–1901
Benefiziat, Obertsdorf, 1901–1909
Pfarrer, Reichertshofen, June 1909
Pfarrer, Grönenbach, April 1915
denazification, September 22, 1946, classified as follower (category 4)
retired, *Kommorant,* Grönenbach, December 1, 1949
died Grönenbach, August 19, 1973
Source: ABA Personaldaten; BayHStA MSo 1414.

Etter, Josef

born Schramberg-Sulgan, February 22, 1905
ordained March 19, 1931 (Rottenburg)
vicar, Schramberg-Sulgen, Esslingen, 1931–1936
Kaplan, Buchau, April 1936
released from ministerial duties September 1936
left priesthood, February 1937
joined NSDAP, May 1, 1937, no. 5,890,077
Source: EBAF B2/NS18; NARA NSZK RG242-A3340-MFKL-G079; Bischöfliches Ordinariat Rottenburg, ed., *Das Verzeichnis der Priester und Diakone der Diözese Rottenburg-Stuttgart von 1874 bis 1983,* 48.

Fiedler, Hermann

born Guhrau, December 7, 1876
ordained June 22, 1901 (Breslau)
Kaplan, Treibnizt, 1901–1902
Administrator, Wahlstatt, 1902–1904
Administrator, then *Pfarrer,* Charlottenbrunn, 1904–1914

Pfarrer, Sprottau, 1914
joined NSDAP
date of death unknown
Source: BArch B NS 26/1330; *Schematismus Breslau; The Tablet,* "German Priests and the Nazi Party."

Fink, Anton
born Seiferts, February 25, 1910
ordained 1937 (Fulda)
Kaplan, Simmershausen and Eiterfeld, 1938–1940
in service of the Gestapo, Fulda, 1940–1945
interned in labor camp by Allies, Kassel, 1945
Source: BAF Personaldaten; Opfermann, *Das Bistum Fulda im Dritten Reich,* 17.

Flörchinger, Emil Johannes
born Dirmstein, 1892
ordained 1921 (Speyer)
Pfarrer, Bobenheim, 1929–1936 (supports NSDAP through his pastoral ministry)
Pfarrer, Ludwigshafen-Oppau, 1936–1958
died 1958
Source: ABS Personaldaten; Fandel, *Konfession und Nationalismus 1930–1939,* 482–88.

Fülle, Alois
born Augsburg, June 5, 1892
ordained July 22, 1923 (Augsburg)
Kaplan, Pfaffenhausen, September 1923
Hilfspriester, Maria Thann, December 1924
Benefiziumsvikar, Maria Thann, Illertissen, 1926–1929
Pfarrer, Pipinsried, June 1929
joined NSDAP, member from 1933 to 1937
Pfarrvikar, Lauterbrunn, August 1934
Pfarrer, Wielenbach, November 1942
died Wielenbach, June 20, 1961
Source: ABA Personaldaten; BayHStA MSo 1415.

Gehrmann, Eduard, S.V.D.
born Kirchdorf Schalmey, September 20, 1888
medical service, WWI, 1915
ordained October 1, 1915 (Society of the Divine Word)

Divisionspfarrer, Eastern and Western Fronts, 1915–1918
religion teacher, *Missionsgymnasium,* Heiligkreuz near Neisse, 1919
privy secretary of Nuncio Eugenio Pacelli, Berlin, 1925–1929
privy secretary of Nuncio Cesare Orsenigo, Berlin, 1930–1945
   (supports NSDAP through this position)
died Siegburg, December 3, 1960
Source: BArch B R58/5652; DAB VI/1-Gehrmann; Kraus, "Der Sekretär zweier Nuntien"; Preuschoff, *Pater Eduard Gehrmann SVD.*

Gigl, Josef
born Heimstetten, April 14, 1903
ordained December 21, 1930 (Munich and Freising)
Kaplan, Ismaning, January 1931
Koadjutor, Babensham, Langenpettenbach, Wartenberg, 1931–1935
Kaplan, Holy Cross Munich-Forstenried, February 1935
Kurat, St. Josef Nursing Home, Munich, September 1935
left priesthood, 1939/1940
state civil servant, 1942–1945 (works in behalf of NSDAP)
date of death unknown
Source: AEM NL Faulhaber 5402, Personaldaten.

Gött, Magnus
born Höhen, November 2, 1881
ordained July 26, 1908 (Augsburg)
Kaplan, Stadtkaplan, Pfarrvikar, Pfaffenhausen, Augsburg St. Georg,
   Altusried, Steingaden, 1908–1911
Vikar, Weiler, Lehenbühl near Legau, 1911–1913
Benefiziat, Lehenbühl, February 1913 (supports NSDAP through his
   pastoral ministry)
Pfarrer, Schrattenbach, September 1932
Pfarrer, Simmerberg, October 1938
died Simmerberg, July 21, 1944
Source: ABA Personaldaten; Hoser, "Hitler und die katholische Kirche"; Wagner, *Simmerberg—Chronik einer kleinen Pfarrei im Westallgäu,* 76–82.

Götz, Leonhard
born Mauern, October 16, 1905
studied theology, College of Philosophy and Theology, Freising
ordained May 2, 1937 (Munich and Freising)
Kaplan, Garmisch-Partenkirchen St. Martin, 1937
became involved with NSDAP, 1938

left priesthood, 1940
joined NSDAP, July 1, 1941, no. 8,779,952
Source: NARA OGK RG242-A3340-MFOK-F083, NSPK RG242-A3340-PK-D103;
Schematismus München und Freising.

Groß, Felix

born Langscheid, October 2, 1903
ordained August 8, 1926 (Trier)
Kaplan, Neunkirchen, St. Marien, Reisweiler, 1926–1933
religion teacher, Vocational Training School St. Wendel, February
  1933
joined NSLB October 1, 1933, no. 230,215
Pfarrer, Lampaden, January 1940
Divisionspfarrer, April 1940
Aushilfsgeistlicher, 1945–1948
Pfarrer, Schöneberg, April 8, 1948
died Hargesheim, November 16, 1971
Source: BAT Personaldaten; Brandt and Häger, eds., *Biographisches Lexikon,* 268;
Persch, "Der Diözesanklerus und die neuen pastoralen Laienberufe," 211–12;
NARA NSLB RG242-A3340-MF-A080.

Haase, Felix

born Protzan, August 1, 1882
ordained June 22, 1908 (Breslau)
Kaplan, Zobten, Breslau St. Bonifazius, Breslau St. Nikolaus,
  1908–1915
doctorate (theology), University of Breslau, January 1909
Privatdozent (church history), University of Breslau, April 1915
Feldgeistlicher, 1917–1918
general secretary of the East-European Institute, 1919–1923
Professor (Slavic church studies and comparative religions), University
  of Breslau, 1922/1923
joined NSDAP, May 1, 1933, no. 3,523,647
dean, faculty of theology, University of Breslau, 1933–1945
Aushilfsgeistlicher, Lindach (Augsburg diocese), 1945–1950
retired 1950
died December 25, 1965
Source: NARA OGK RG242-A3340-MFOK-G056; *Schematismus Breslau;* Brandt and
Häger, eds., *Biographisches Lexikon,* 279; Kleineidam, *Die katholisch-theologische
Fakultät der Universität Breslau,* 134–35; *The Tablet,* "German Priests and the Nazi
Party."

Haeuser, Philipp

born Kempten, April 22, 1876
ordained July 20, 1899 (Augsburg)
Kaplan, Bertoldshofen, August 1899
prefect, Neuburg Seminary, September 1900
doctorate (theology), University of Freiburg, 1911
Pfarrer, Straßberg, March 1911–May 1948
Wir deutsche Katholiken und die moderne revolutionäre Bewegung (1922)
Jud und Christ oder, Wem gebührt die Weltherrschaft? (1923)
"Die Judenfrage vom kirchlichen Standpunkt" (1923/1924)
Pazifismus und Christentum (1925)
Kampfgeist gegen Pharisäertum (1931)
Irrwege der katholischen Kirche (1932)
Der Kämpfer Jesus (1935)
Die deutsche Weltanschauung der Freude im schwersten Kampf (1938)
denazification, Schwabmünchen, May 14, 1947, classified as criminal
  (category 1), sentenced to 5 years hard labor
faculties suspended, October 1948
denazification appeal, Munich, 1950, reclassified as lesser offender
  (category 3)
retired as emeritus *Pfarrer* with restoration of faculties, January 1954
Kommorant, Straßberg, 1954
Kommorant, Oberschönenfeld-Gessertshausen, 1957
died Oberschönenfeld-Gessertshausen, February 25, 1960
Source: ABA PA 410 Haeuser; BArch B R58/5715/A2; StA Bobingen Sammlung
Haeuser; StA Kempten NL Haeuser; Blümel, "Dr. theol. Philipp Haeuser"; Lenski,
"Pfarrer Dr. Philipp Haeuser."

Häffner, Franz

born Bayreuth, September 19, 1897
ordained July 31, 1921 (Bamberg)
Kaplan, Neunkirchen and Ansbach, 1921–1928
Kuratus, Nuremberg St. Georg and Unterweilersbach, 1928–1938
  (supports NSDAP through his pastoral ministry)
Pfarrer, Unterweilersbach, October 1938
died April 9, 1963
Source: AEB Personaldaten; Breuer, *Verordneter Wandel?*, 340.

Hanner, Max

born Oberndorf near Freyung, May 26, 1910
SA member, November 1, 1933–May 1, 1934

SS member, May 1, 1934–April 1, 1935
ordained March 29, 1937 (Passau)
Kooperator, Frauenau, St. Oswald, Neuötting, Pleinting, Waldkirchen,
Prachatitz, Regen, 1937–1944
Pfarrverwalter, then *Pfarrer,* St. Oswald, October 1944–1950
denazification, August, 12, 1946, classified as offender (category 2)
Pfarrer, Holzkirchen, January 1950
Kurat, Passau-Freudenhain, July 1962
Pfarrer, Passau-Hacklberg, September 1965
Expositur-Verwalter, Passau St. Korona, October 1978
died September 13, 1983
Source: ABP Personaldaten; BayHStA MSo 1415; *Schematismus Passau* 1979, 242.

Hartl, Albert

born Roßholzen, November 13, 1904
ordained June 29, 1929 (Munich and Freising)
Kaplan, Neuaubing, 1929
prefect, Albertinum, Munich, 1930
prefect, College of Philosophy and Theology, Freising, 1932
joined NSDAP, May 1, 1933, no. 3,201,046
joined SS, April 25, 1934, no. 107,050
placed on leave by diocese, January 1934
withdrew from Catholic Church, March 1936
married Marianne Schürer-Stolle, 1937
RSHA Amt IV B Political Churches, 1939–1941
sexual misconduct, received reprimand and two-year freeze on
promotions, 1941
Kiev, Ukraine (*Einsatzgruppe* C), commissioned to write report about
spiritual life of Soviet Russia, 1942
wounded and sent to Bled, Slovenia, 1943
arrested by Americans in Kitzbühel, May 1945
denazification, November 1948, classified as criminal (category 1),
sentenced to four years in prison
died Bodman, December 19, 1982
Source: ALMU Stud.-Karte; BArch B R5101/21679, R58/5881; NSZK, NSPK, SSOA,
Reichsschrifttumskammer; BArch D ZR 204, 257, ZWN 13; BArch K 898 NL Roth;
EAM NL Faulhaber 3250, 5402, 8020, 8303; NARA RG 238-M1019/r. 24, M1270/r.
24; USHMM RG 15.007/r. 21, 37. Alvarez, *Nothing Sacred,* 51–64; Alvarez, *Spies in
the Vatican,* 164–70; Bleistein, "Überläufer im Sold der Kirchenfeinde; Denzler,
Widerstand ist nicht das richtige Wort, 144–53; Dierker, *Himmlers Glaubenskrieger,*
96–118, 554; Sereny, *Into That Darkness,* 64–71; Stehle, *Graue Eminenzen—dunkle
Existenzen,* 152–59.

Heimes, Ferdinand
born Deutnecke, July 9, 1891
studied theology, University of Freiburg and Philosophical-
Theological Academy of Paderborn
ordained March 26, 1915 (Paderborn)
Pfarrvikar, Wernigerode, May 1915
chaplain, *Leokonvikt* (college of theology student residence),
Paderborn, April 1920
doctorate (theology), University of Münster, May 1920
Dozent, Philosophical-Theological Academy of Paderborn, December
1921
Pfarrvikar, St. Boniface, Paderborn, March 1923
religion teacher, Menden *Lyzeum and Gymnasium,* April 1924
joined NSDAP, May 1, 1933, no. 3,284,142
joined NSLB, September 1, 1933, no. 246,838
Pfarrer, Berghausen, May 1939–October 1961
withdrew from NSDAP, 1942
retired October, 1, 1961
died November, 2, 1962
Source: EAP Sammlung Heimes; NARA NSZK RG242-A3340-MFKL-H038.

Hein, Josef Nikolaus
born Bad Dürkheim, 1892
ordained 1916 (Speyer)
Brasil, 1923–1934
chaplain, St. Mary's Hospital, 1934
Pfarrverweser, then *Pfarrer,* Habkirchen, 1935–1938 (supports NSDAP
through his pastoral ministry)
died Kemp-Bornhofen, 1970
Source: ABS Personaldaten; Fandel, *Konfession und Nationalsozialismus,* 492–500.

Heinen, Josef Maria
born Trier, January 15, 1899
ordained March 28, 1925 (Trier)
Kaplan, Saarbrücken St. Josef, and religion teacher, Cäcilienschule,
1925–1937
joined NSDAP, August 1, 1933, no. 2,683,712
joined NSLB, January 1, 1934, no. 252,298
faculties withdrawn, April 1937
left priesthood, May 1937
married December 1938

died Munich, December 14, 1975

Source: EBAF B2/NS18; NARA OGK RG242-A3340-MFOK-H049, NSLB RG242-A3340-MF-A094, *Rhein Front* (April 13, 1937); Persch, "Der Diözesanklerus und die neuen pastoralen Laienberufe," 211–12.

Heinsberg, Joseph

born Cologne, July 1, 1901
ordained August 14, 1924 (Cologne)
Kaplan, Viersen-Rahser, Zülpich, Düsseldorf Liebfrauen, 1924–c. 1929
doctorate (theology)
joined NSDAP, May 1, 1933, no. 1,943,678
joined NSLB, May 1, 1939, no. 401,439
withdrew from Catholic Church
date of death unknown

Source: BArch B R58/5879/A2; NARA OGK RG242-A3340-MFOK-H055; *Handbuch des Erzbistums Köln,* 23rd ed., 1933, 757.

Herte, Adolf

born Brilon, August 28, 1887
ordained August 3, 1914 (Paderborn)
religion teacher, Catholic Preparatory School, Erfurt, August 1914
doctorate (theology), University of Münster, July 1915
Bishop Karl Joseph Schulte's *Kaplan* and privy secretary, Paderborn, May 1916
Professor (church history and patristics), College of Philosophy and Theology, Paderborn, April 1922–1945 (supports NSDAP ideology through his teaching and writing)
voluntarily resigned professorship, 1945
chaplain, military hospital, Bad Salzschlirf, 1945–1949
rector, St. Petri Hospital, Warburg, February 1949
chaplain, St. Nikolai Hospital, Höxter, April 1950
named *Geistlicher Rat,* July 1963
died Höxter, March 3, 1970

Source: BArch B R58/5715/A2; USHMM 15.007/r. 4; Denzler, "Schmerzhafte ökumenische Erinnerungen"; Drobner, "Adolf Herte."

Heuberger, Anton

born Mörnsheim, December 17, 1890
ordained May 30, 1915 (Eichstätt)
Kooperator, Monheim, Ingolstadt Our Lord's, 1915–1918
Pfarrvikar, Ingolstadt Our Lord's, November 12, 1918
Kuratus, Wustenburg, Ingolstadt St. Anton, 1919–1931

Pfarrer, Hitzhofen, August 1931 (supports NSDAP through his pastoral
  ministry)
forced resignation by American military government, November 1945
Provisor, Wolframs-Eschenbach, November 1945
died Neuendetell, September 29,1967
Source: BayHStA MK 37740; DAEI, Bishofs-Archiv Heuberger, PA Heuberger, Pfarrakten Hitzhofen; SemAEI PA Heuberger; StA München ST 7763; StA Nürnberg, NS-
Mischbestand, Kreisleitung Eichstätt, Nr. 8; Hausfelder, "Die Situation der katholischen Kirche in Ingolstadt von 1918 bis 1945," 329–33 and 340–48.

Hofmann, Karl
born Straubing, June 15, 1900
member Freikorps "Oberland," 1919
joined National Socialist War Auxiliary Student Organization
ordained June 29, 1924 (Munich and Freising)
Koadjutor, Tegernsee, September 1924
Aushilfsgeistlicher, Oberwarngau, November 1924
prefect, College of Philosophy and Theology, Freising, September 1926
Kaplan, Kolbermoor, May 1927
studied University of Munich, September 1927–July 1929
chaplain, Mercy Brothers psychiatric asylum, Eglfing-Haar, November 1927
doctorate (canon law), University of Munich, July 1929
Kaplan, Marienanstalt, Munich, May 1931
Dozent, University of Munich, March 1933 (supports NSDAP in
  preaching and teaching)
visiting instructor, University of Würzburg, May 1934
visiting instructor, then *Professor,* College of Philosophy and
  Theology, Bamberg, November 1938
preacher, Holy Ghost, Munich, April 1940
sabbatical, Rome, December 4, 1940
Kaplan, Munich St. John the Baptist and *Benefiziumsverweser,* Munich
  St. Nicholas Church, March 1942
vicar, Munich St. Ludwig, Munich, June 1943
Professor (canon law), College of Philosophy and Theology, Dillingen,
  December 1945
Professor (canon law), University of Tübingen, October 1946
died January 13, 1954
Source: BArch B R5101/22526; EAM PA Hofmann.

Huber, Christian Josef
born Freising, October 7, 1888
studied theology, University of Munich and College of Philosophy

and Theology, Freising 1908–1913
ordained June 29, 1915 (Munich)
Aushilfspriester, St. Nicholas, Reichenhall, July 1915
Hilfsgeistlicher, Unterammergau, July 1916
volunteered for army service, medical orderly without pay, fall
    1917–December 1918
Kooperator, Unterammergau, Miesbach, 1918–1920
vice-president of the Catholic Central Journeymen's Association,
    Munich, February 1920
Benefiziat, Bürgersaal, Munich, February 1921
incardinated into the Augsburg diocese, February 1922
Schloßbenefiziat, Kronberg, March 1922
Pfarrer, Bühl, September 1925
Pfarrer, Sandizell, 1927
Kommorant, Munich, 1932–1935
joined NSDAP, April 1, 1933, no. 1,664,440
joined SA, April 1, 1933, no. 1,444,460
V-Mann (informant), SD-South, Munich
Hausgeistlicher, Rohesche Poor and Aged Home, Kleinwallstadt,
    1935–1941
assistant archivist, then archivist, Aschaffenburg City Archive,
    1939–1945
left priesthood, September 1941
withdrew from Catholic Church, October 1941
married Rosa Albert, January 1942
excommunicated, Church trial, June 1942
arrested and interned by Allied forces, May 1945–1947
converted to Old Catholicism, 1947
Old-Catholic *Pfarrer,* Thalmessing, 1948–1953
returned to Aschaffenburg, 1953
died Aschaffenburg, February 14, 1958
buried Aschaffenburg, February 17, 1958

Source: ABA 1467 PA Huber; BArch B NSPK, NSZK, Reichsschrifttumskammer,
R58/5715/A2, R58/5878/A1, R58/5879/A2, R58/5994/A1, SAPA; DAW BMA A22.2;
EAM NL Faulhaber 5402, PA Huber.

Hudal, Alois

born Graz, March 31, 1885
studied theology, University of Graz, 1904–1908
ordained July 19, 1908 (Graz, Austria)
Kaplan, Kindberg, 1908–1911

doctorate (theology), University of Graz, January 1911
Kaplan, Anima, Rome, 1911–1913
biblical studies, Papal Bible Institute, Rome, 1911–1913
doctorate (biblical studies), March 1913
Dozent, University of Graz, October 1914
military chaplain, WWI, 1917–1918
Professor (Old Testament), University of Graz, December 1919
vice-rector, then rector, Anima, Rome, 1923–1952
received title monsignor, June 1923
consecrated titular bishop of Ela, 1933
Die Grundlagen des Nationalsozialismus (1936)
assisted Nazis to escape postwar Germany
resigned Anima rectorship, 1952
retired to private villa Grottaferrata near Rome, 1952
died "Qui si sana" Hospital, Rome, May 13, 1963
buried German Cemetery "Campo Santo Teutonico," Rome, May 16, 1963
Source: BArch R58/5622b/A1, R58/5715/A2; R58/5726; R58/5727/A2; USHMM RG 15.007/r. 27, 41; Burkard, *Härisie und Mythus des 20. Jahrhunderts; Godman, Hitler and the Vatican;* Goñi, *The Real Odessa;* Hudal, *Römische Tagebücher;* Klee, *Persilscheine und falsche Pässe,* 32–50; Liebmann, "Bischof Hudal und der Nationalsozialismus"; Phayer, *The Catholic Church and the Holocaust,* 166–69; Rainer, "Bischof Hudal und das Wiedererwachen Österreichs 1944 in Rom"; Sanfilippo, "Archival Evidence"; Stehle, "Bischof Hudal und SS-Führer Meyer" and *Graue Eminenzen,* 111–21; Wolf, "Pius XI und die 'Zeitirrtümer.'"

Jankowski, Berthold

born Nikolai, September 23, 1884
ordained June 20, 1910 (Breslau)
Kaplan, Mikultschtz, Berlin St. Ludwig, Cosel, 1910–1922
no assignment, 1922–1925
Kurat, Freystadt, Grenzdorf, Bad Schwarzbach, 1925–1930
Pfarrer, Rogau, November 1930 (supports NSDAP through his pastoral
 ministry)
Pfarrer, Atl-Poppelau, March 1934
Pfarrer, Jungbirken, March 1941
died April 17, 1963
Source: BArch B R58/5715/A2; *Schematismus Breslau; The Tablet,* "German Priests and the Nazi Party."

Jann, Johannes

born Forcheim, November 20, 1899
ordained July 28, 1913 (Bamberg)
Kaplan, Windheim, August 1913

Feldgeistlicher, WWI, 1914–1918
Kaplan, Lichtenfels, Scheßlitz, 1918–1919
Benefiziat-Verweser, Hallstadt, March 1919 (supports NSDAP through
    his pastoral ministry)
president of the Catholic Student Association and Catholic
    Workingmen's Association, Hallstadt-Dörflein
doctorate (further information unavailable)
date of death unknown
Source: *Schematismus Bamberg;* Breuer, *Verordneter Wandel?,* 340.

Kaeufl, Georg
born Landshut, August 7, 1898
ordained June 29, 1922 (Munich and Freising)
Koadjutor, Peiting, August 1922
Pfarrvikar, Peiting, April, 1923
Kaplan, Neumarkt St. Veit, August 1935 (supports NSDAP through
    his pastoral ministry)
Koadjutor, Kiefersfeld, March 1939
Kooperator, Velden, June 1942
Pfarrer, Endlhausen, October 1943
retired Endlhausen, January 1975
died Endlhausen, April 19, 1989
Source: EAM NL Faulhaber 5401, PA Kaeufl.

Kandler, Hermann
born Weissbach, May 27, 1901
ordained June 29, 1927 (Munich and Freising)
Koadjutor, Babensham, July 1927
Aufhilfspriester, Niederaschau, April 1928
Kooperator, Frasdorf, Schwindkirchen, July 1928–1929
granted leave due to health problems, December 1929
Kooperator, Kirchdorf, Bergkirchen, February 1930–August 1930
Aushilfspriester, Rottenbuch, Großhadern, Kirchsseeon, 1930–1933
    (supports NSDAP through his pastoral ministry)
Pfarrvikar, Schwabhausen, June 1933
Aushilfsgeistlicher, Dachau, September 1933
Kooperator, Freising St. George, *Expositus,* Marzling, January 1935
Aushilfsgeistlicher, Öttingen, May 1936
Kaplan, Burgheim, August 1936
Kaplan, Altmünster, April 1937

left priesthood
date of death unknown
Source: EAM NL Faulhaber 5401; *Schematismus München und Freising.*

Kania, Franz
born Zabrze, November 30, 1888
ordained June 22, 1912 (Breslau)
Kaplan, Berlin Sacred Heart, Ostrog, Kattowitz, Sohrau, Roschow-
itzwald, Falkowitz, 1912–1927
Pfarrverweser, Rachowitz, July 1927
Kurat, Rokittnitz, September 1928
Kuratus, Nesselwitz, June 1932
Pfarrer, Leuschütz, June 1933 (supports NSDAP through his pastoral
ministry)
died April 17, 1956
Source: BArch B R58/5715/A2; *Schematismus Breslau; The Tablet,* "German Priests
and the Nazi Party."

Kapferer, Friedrich
born Ettenheim, August 29, 1891
ordained June 30, 1915 (Freiburg)
Pfarrverweser in various parishes, 1915–1928
Pfarrer, Neuhausen, 1928
left priesthood, 1938
joined National Church of the German Christians-Roman Catholic
Church branch, Eisenach, 1938
married
Pfarrer, Thüringia Protestant Church, 1941
denazification, lost title of *Pfarrer* in Protestant Church
date of death unknown
Source: MIO NL Kleine; Lautenschläger, "Der Kirchenkampf in Thüringen," 481–84;
May, *Kirchenkampf oder Katholikenverfolgung,* 391; Meier, *Der Evangelische
Kirchenkampf,* 3:681 n. 1335.

Kappel, Michael
born Baumgarten, October 21, 1884
ordained June 29, 1909 (Passau)
Koadjutor, Stammham, July 1909
Kooperator, Kellberg, November 1913
Kurat, psychiatric asylum, Hausstein, July 1917
Verwalter, Vilshofen, and director of Vilshofen *Realschule,* September 1920

Studienrat (religion), Vilshofen, November 1921
Studiendirektor, Vilshofen, 1925
retired, St. Salvator, March 1934
joined NSLB, July 1, 1934, no. 305,841
joined NSDAP, May 1, 1935, no. 3,624,093
joined NSV, member 1935–1945
denazification, October 28, 1946, classified as follower (category 4)
died St. Salvator, September 16, 1977

Source: NARA NSZK RG242-A3340-MFKL-L027, OGK RG242-A3340-MFOK-K004, NSLB RG242-A3340-MK-B017; *Schematismus Passau* 1925, 48; 1927, 15; 1977, 251; 1979, 313; Wurster, "Zur Geschichte des Bistums Passau im Dritten Reich," 246–47.

Keller, Hermann (Peter), O.S.B.
born Egesheim, June 21, 1905
student, *Oblatenschule,* Emmaus monastery, Prague, 1916–1918
studied theology in Maria Laach, 1925–1927, and St. Anselm, Rome, 1927–1932
ordained July 6, 1930 (Benedictine, St. Martin's, Beuron)
doctorate (theology), St. Anselm, Rome, 1931
lecturer of dogmatics, St. Anselm, 1931–1933
lecturer of dogmatics, *Hochschule,* Beuron, 1933–1936
prior, Beuron, November 25, 1935–1936
exiled to Sion Benedictine monastery, Jerusalem, 1936–1937
teacher, Gerleve, 1937–1938
postdoctoral studies, University of Munich, 1938–1939
drafted into *Abwehr* (German counterintelligence service), 1939
Abwehr, Paris, 1940–1944
V-Mann (informant) to SS, 1940–1945
flight to Rottach-Egern, Neuburg, 1945
Hausgeistlicher, Mariendonk Benedictine monastery, August 1946–March 1970
died Holy Ghost Hospital, Kempen, March 17, 1970

Source: AAM NL Keller; BArch B NS 26/1330, R58/5795, R5101/23312; EAM NL Faulhaber 5402; EBAF B2/NS18; USAMHI Deutsch Papers; Alvarez, *Nothing Sacred,* 28–29; Alvarez, *Spies in the Vatican,* 178–79; Deutsch, *The Conspiracy against Hitler,* 129–37; Dierker, *Himmlers Glaubenskrieger,* 371; Kaltefleiter and Oschwald, *Spione im Vatikan,* 73–82.

Kellner, Walter
born Oberglogau, April 27, 1906
ordained December 19, 1931 (Fulda)
Kaplan, Eiterfeld, March 1932–April 1934
doctorate (theology), University of Münster, June 24, 1938

withdrew from priesthood, September 16, 1938
Reich Chancellery, librarian of church collection
Soviet prisoner, sentenced to ten years (serving as chaplain)
released from Soviet prison and returned to Germany 1954/1955
died June 10, 1963
Source: BAF Personaldaten; NARA NSPK RG242-A3340-PK-F335; Opfermann, *Das Bistum Fulda im Dritten Reich*, 16–17.

Kirchberger, Alois
born Miesbach, May 10, 1886
ordained June 29, 1913 (Munich and Freising)
Kooperator, Frauendorf
became involved in NSDAP, ca. 1930
left priesthood, 1936
married
Source: EAM NL Faulhaber 5402; *Schematismus München und Freising.*

Klehr, Joseph
born Ludwigshafen, 1887
ordained 1910 (Speyer)
Pfarrer, Trulben, 1920
Pfarrer, Vinningen, 1924
Pfarrer, Dirmstein 1930–1946 (supports NSDAP through his pastoral
  ministry)
died Dirmstein, 1958
Source: ABS Personaldaten; Fandel, *Konfession und Nationalsozialismus,* 476–78.

Klein, Josef
born Würzburg, September 12, 1880
ordained August 2, 1903 (Würzburg)
Aufhilfspriester, Höchberg, September 1, 1903
Kaplan, Amorbach, Miltenberg, Würzburg St. Peter, 1903–1910
granted leave to study, August 15, 1910
research, Vatican-Library, Rome, 1910–1911
Aushilfspriester, Würzburg St. Josef, Retzbach, 1911–1912
doctorate (theology), University of Würzburg, 1912
Pfarrer, Rottenbauer, September 1913
joined NSDAP, May 1, 1933, no. 3,107,709
died October 21, 1942
Source: BArch B NS 26/1330; NARA NSPK RG 242-A3340-PK-G004, NSZK RG242-A3340-MFKL-L054, OGK RG242-A3340-MFOK-K068; DAW GA K5/4c; StA Würzburg Gestapo Akte 4003.

Kleine, Richard
born Düsseldorf, October 5, 1891
studied theology, University of Bonn and University of Tübingen,
1910–1914
ordained October 11, 1914 (Hildesheim)
Kaplan, Duderstadt, Westerode, January 1915
Merit Cross for Wartime Assistance, June 1918
religion teacher, Duderstadt gymnasium, January 1919 (named *Studienrat,* October 1921)
Erlösung! (1929)
"Ja und Nein zum Nationalsozialismus" (1932)
member national leadership board, League of Catholic Germans
Cross and Eagle, 1933
joined NSV, 1934
joined NSLB, October 1, 1936, no. 341,926
contributor to *Sendschreiben katholischer Deutscher an ihre Volks- und Glaubensgenossen* (1936)
founder, with Johann Pircher, and coleader, group of National
Socialist Priests, 1939–1945
"War Jesus ein Jude?" (c. 1939)
"Die Bergpredigt als Kampfansage gegen das Judentum" (1943)
military government removed Kleine from teaching, 1945 (reinstated 1946)
diocese withdrew *Missio Canonica,* March 1947
denazification, August 23, 1948, classified as exonerated (category 5)
reconferral of *Missio Canonica,* 1951
died Duderstadt, April 1, 1974

Source: AEGD PA Kleine; APSC Generalvikariat; BArch B NS 26/1330, NSLB, R43/178a, R58/5715/A2; BBF Personalbogen Kleine; DAR N67 NL Adam; MIO NL Kleine; GStAPK I HA Rep. 76 Kultus Z. Nr. 9 III; NSHStA 120 Hannover Acc. 164/92/74 PA Kleine; Bormann, *Keine Schule wie jede andere,* 217–23, 294–314, 352–56; Scherzberg, *Kirchenreform mit Hilfe des Nationalsozialismus,* 276–92.

Knobloch, Wilhelm
born Naumburg, February 15, 1890
ordained June 21, 1913 (Breslau/Berlin after 1930)
Kaplan, Steinau, Oels, Berlin St. Bonifatius, 1913–1923
Kuratus, Rathenow St. George, December 1923
Pfarrer, Nowawes, April 1937
forced to retire by Bishop Preysing, February 1939
died April 2, 1957
buried Berlin-Tempelhof, St. Matthias Cemetery, April 1957

Source: BArch B R5101/24279; BArch D ZB II 3689/A.14; DAB VI/1 Knobloch; Spicer, *Resisting the Third Reich,* 143, 150.

Kober, Alois

born Saarbrücken, December 17, 1901
studied theology, College of Philosophy and Theology, Bamberg
ordained December 18, 1927 (Bamberg)
Kaplan, Bayreuth, January 1928
Kaplan, Ansbach, and religion teacher, Ansbach gymnasium, March 1932
Dozent (Catholic studies and catechesis), College for Teaching
   Preparation, Pasing, January 1936
joined NSLB, February 1, 1937, no. 348,348
diocese withdrew *Missio Canonica* and suspended faculties, April 1937
joined NSDAP, May 1, 1937, no. 5,904,134
joined NSV, June 1, 1937, no. 7,530,386
suspension lifted, 1952
died October 29, 1968

Source: BArch B NS 15/475; BayStA MK 33452; EAM NL Faulhaber 5897; EBAF BS/NS18; NARA OGK RG 242-A3340-MFOK-L013, NSPK RG242-A3340-PK-G078, NSLB RG242-A3340-MF-B029; Prantl, *Die kirchliche Lage in Bayern,* 5, 169, 179.

Koch, Hugo

born Andelfingen, April 7, 1869
ordained July 19, 1892 (Rottenburg)
Kaplan, Gmünd, Ulm, 1892
tutor, *Wilhelmstift,* Tübingen, 1893
doctorate (philosophy), University of Tübingen, 1891
doctorate (theology), University of Tübingen, 1900
Stadtpfarrer, Reutlingen, April 1900
Professor (church history), State Academy (*Lyzeum* Hosianum, until
   1918), Braunsberg, April 1904
released from teaching by the state, 1912
married, and moved to Munich, 1912
"Paderborner 'Wissenschaft' und meine 'Unwissenheit'" (1936)
member of the Institute for Research on the Jewish Question, assisted
   Alfred Rosenberg with *Handbuch der Romfrage* (1940)
died Utting am Ammersee, July 26, 1940

Source: BArch N26/1330; Bischöfliches Ordinariat Rottenburg, ed. *Das Verzeichnis der Geistlichen der Diözese Rottenburg-Stuttgart von 1874 bis 1983,* 63; Dierker, *Himmlers Glaubenskrieger,* 225; Klapczynski, *Hugo Koch (1869–1940)* and "Das Wesen des Katholizmus"; May, *Kirchenkampf oder Katholikenverfolgung,* 391; Reifferscheid, *Das Bistum Ermland,* 48; Weiß, *Der Modernismus in Deutschland,* 336–43.

König, Karl

born Ilversgehofen, September 12, 1877
studied theology, College of Philosophy and Theology, Paderborn,
    and University of Freiburg, 1899–1901
ordained March 30, 1901 (Paderborn)
Kooperator, Bochum-Propstei, Dortmund Our Lady's, 1901–1910
vicar, Gelsenkirchen-Schalke, St. Joseph, August 1910
Pfarrer, Wiesenfeld, September 1913
Pfarrer, Heyerode, July 1917
vicar, Oscherleben, August 1924
Pfarrvikar, Hiltrop-Bergen, January 1925
forced to retire by diocese, moved to Bad Honnef, October 1926
stopped receiving pension from Paderborn archdiocese, May 1928
ordered to leave archdiocese of Cologne, 1930
suspended by archdiocese of Paderborn, May 1930
moved to Berlin, 1930
joined NSDAP, May 1, 1933, no. 2,460,245
suspension lifted, March 31, 1934, and pension reinstituted,
    retroactive, April 1933
withdrew from NSDAP, October 1934
reentered NSDAP February 1935
religion teacher (state-appointed), Prince Heinrich gymnasium and
    Scharnhorst School, Berlin, June 1938
died Berlin, February 18, 1939

Source: BArch B NS 6/221, NS 6/227, NS 10/109, NS 26/1239, R43 II/1636, R43
II/1636a, R58/5715/A2, R58/5879/A2, R58/5978/A1, R58/7082, R4901/4315,
R5101/22268, R5101/22341; BayHStA MA 107255, MA 107257, PrA SlgRehse 4198;
EAP Sammlung König; NARA OGK RG242-A3340-MFOK-L031; Dierker, *Himmlers
Glaubenskrieger,* 357–58; Spicer, *Resisting the Third Reich,* 154–56.

Köpf, Adam

born February 12, 1898
ordained March 20, 1922 (Augsburg)
joined NSV
Pfarrer, Ettenbeuren, November 29, 1934
local director and district propaganda director of NSV, 1935
granted emeritus status by diocese, November 1936
Pfarrvikar, Beuerbach, February 16, 1937, and religion teacher,
    Volksschule Pestenacker, May 1937
forced by diocese to retire from teaching, February 1939
Pfarrkuratievikar, Pitzling, July 1939
Pfarrer, Zuchering, January 1941

Pfarrvikar, Drößling, January 1946
declared demeritus by diocese, June 1947
denazification, Munich, October 25, 1948, classified as exonerated
  (category 5)
Pfarrvikar, then *Pfarrer,* Münster am Lech, December 1, 1948
resigned voluntarily, July 6, 1954
died September 30, 1977
Source: ABA 4425/a-e PA Köpf; BayHStA MK 49325, MSo 1415.

Kortschak, (Karl) Ernest, O.Cist.

born Graz-Graben, January 14, 1879
studied theology, University of Graz
ordained July 20, 1902 (Stift Rein, Cistercian)
doctorate (theology), University of Graz, May 2, 1906
religion teacher, *Volksschule* Graz
Pfarrer, Übelbach, March 28, 1913
chaplain, then *Divisionspfarrer,* WWI, 1914–1918
Pfarrvikar, Gratwein, 1919–1925
director, Odilien-Institute for the Blind, Graz, 1925–1931
member, Kleine-Pircher group of National Socialist Priests, 1939–1945
abbot, Stift Rein, August 19, 1931–November 15, 1945
Messeleser, Straßengel, November 16, 1945–November 8, 1957
died November 8, 1957
Source: ARGS Personaldaten; Hofmüller, "Steirische Priester," 64–75; Lettl, "Die Arbeitsgemeinschaft für den religiösen Frieden," 63; Liebmann, "Rein zur Zeit des
Nationalsozialismus."

Krawczyk, Alfons

born Ruda, July 6, 1888
ordained June 21, 1913 (Breslau)
Kaplan, Pawlowitz, June 1914
Feldgeistlicher, volunteer, WWI, 1916–1919
Kaplan, Zalenze and Cosel, 1919–1925
member of the Kattowitz diocese upon its creation in 1925
joined NSDAP, May 1, 1933, no. 2,228,307
state-appointed prison chaplain, Groß-Strehlitz (Breslau archdiocese),
  1937–1939
date of death unknown
Source: NARA OGK RG242-A3340-MFOK-M001; Brandt and Häger, eds., *Biographisches Lexikon,* 438; *The Tablet,* "German Priests and the Nazi Party."

Kreth, Werner

born Rastenburg, July 19, 1890
baptized Protestant
studied law in Munich and Berlin, 1911–1912
converted to Catholicism, 1913
studied theology, *Lyzeum Hosianum,* Braunsberg, 1913
medic, WWI, Elbing and Braunsberg, 1915–1919
returned to State Academy, Braunsberg, June 1919
ordained 1921 (Ermland)
Kaplan, Wusen, 1921
studied, Church Music College, Regensburg, 1924–1927
Kommendist (assistant to the director of Church Music College as
    organist of the Regensburg Cathedral), 1924–1927
music teacher, *Heim'sche Bauernschule* (rural school), Regensburg, and
    private music teacher, 1927
Domvikar, Ermland, 1927–1937
joined NSDAP, May 1, 1933, no. 2,287,175
V-Mann (informant) for Gastapo, District Königsberg
arrested for homosexual activity, August 24, 1936
expelled from NSDAP, November 8, 1936
suspended from priesthood after Church trial, March 18, 1937
convicted in state criminal trial, Braunsberg, May 12, 1937, of twelve of-
    fenses against §175 and eleven offenses against §175 and 20a; sen-
    tenced to twelve years of prison and ten years' loss of civil rights
unsuccessful appeal of state ruling, October 14, 1937
died Wartenburg, November 30, 1942

Source: BArch B R58/5978/A1, R5101 23337, R5101 24289; BArch D ZB I/1566, ZB
I/1751, ZB I/186; NARA OGK RG242-A3340-MFOK-M007; Directorium Diocesis
Warmiensis; Fittkau, *Biographie Maximilian Kaller;* Kather, *Von Rechts wegen,* 24–34;
Reifferscheid, *Das Bistum Ermland,* 221–22.

Kröber, Johannes

born Burrweiler, 1900
ordained 1924 (Speyer)
Pfarrer, Weidenthal, 1930
Pfarrer, Otterbach, 1935
left the priesthood, October 1, 1938
joined NSDAP, December 1, 1939, no. 7,311,966
date of death unknown

Source: ABS Personaldaten; NARA NSZK RG242-A3340-MFKL-L061; Fandel, *Konfession und Nationalsozialismus,* 472–73.

Kwastek, Richard
born Beuthen, February 15, 1882
ordained June 22, 1912 (Breslau)
Kaplan, Mikultschütz, Zabrze, Karf, Deutsch-Piekar,
Schwientochlowitz, Bobrek, 1913–1925
Pfarrer, Slawitau (after 1936, Bergkirch), July 1925 (supports NSDAP
through his pastoral ministry)
died June 14, 1957
Source: BArch B R58/5715/A2; *Schematismus Breslau; The Tablet,* "German Priests
and the Nazi Party."

Lang, Kaspar
born Waischenfeld, February 10, 1896
drafted into infantry, WWI, February 1916–April 1919
ordained April 2, 1922 (Bamberg)
Kaplan, Erlangen, April 1922
Standortpfarrer and army chaplain, Paderborn, Berlin John the Baptist,
February 1934–May 1935
Heerespfarrer, Nuremberg-Fürth (May 1935–January 1937); Munich
(January 1937–September 1939); Army group C, then D (September
1939–April 1942); Munich (April 1942–May 1942); Kassel (May
1942–July 1945) (avidly supports NSDAP and its *Lebensraum* ideology)
Pfarrer, Münchberg, April–June 1946
Pfarrer, Adelsdorf, August 1946
retired, *Kommorant,* Waischenfeld (named *Geistlicher Rat*), 1960
died Ebermannstadt, February 12, 1962
Source: AEB Personaldaten; Brandt and Häger, eds., *Biographisches Lexikon,* 461;
Breuer, *Verordneter Wandel?,* 109.

Leonards, Walter
born Rheydt, February 10, 1887
ordained Utrecht, August 15, 1910 (unidentified religious community)
Expositus, Diepenveen (Netherlands), October 1910
Hilfsgeistlicher, Düsseldorf St. Paul and Our Lady's, August 1914
military chaplain, WWI, July 1915–1918
left unidentified religious community
rector, Bitburg hospital, February 1919
rector, Elberfeld-Mirke Boarding School, March 1920
vicar and administrator, Gebenstorf (Kanton Aargau, Bistum Basel),
August 1920
Kaplan, Berlin St. Joseph, April 1922

incardinated into Breslau archdiocese, 1922 (after 1930, member of
the Berlin diocese)
Kuratus, Treptow, Rega, April 1925
Pfarrer, Prenzlau, December 1930
Standortpfarrer, Garnison Fliegerhorst, April 1935
worked with Father Anselmus Vriens, O.C.S.O., in pro-NSDAP
Netherlands Press Bureau, Berlin, 1936–1937
forced by Bishop Preysing to resign his pastorate, retires with
pension, July 1939
joined NSDAP, April 1, 1940, no. 8,011,773
Sonderführer, Wehrmacht, 1940–1945
Kooperator, Rudersdorf (Paderborn), January 1947
Pfarrverwalter, Oerlinghausen (Paderborn), appointed February 1950,
but only served there briefly
Pfarrverwalter, Sevenich (Trier), Oberfell (Trier), 1950–1965
died Oberfell, July 23, 1965

Source: BArch B NS 15/475, OGK, R58/5715/A2, RSHA (Kartei) 1703 FC 1581; BAT
Abt. 88, Nr. 112 Leonards; DAB VI/1 Leonards; EAM NL Faulhaber 8323; EAP Ruders-
dorf *Pfarrer* from 1945 on; MIO Nl Kleine; Adolph, *Geheime Aufzeichnungen;* 202;
Hürten, *Deutsche Briefe,* 1:329–33, 434–36, and 2:922–25, 930–31, 1024–26; Klein,
Berolinen Canonizationis Servi Dei Bernardi Lichtenberg, 101–2; Spicer, *Resisting the Third
Reich,* 150–53; Volk, ed., *Akten Kardinal Michael von Faulhabers,* 2:340, 618, 652.

Lindenschmit, Wilhelm

born Mainz, May 6, 1888
ordained August 11, 1912 (Mainz)
Kaplan, Gau Algesheim, Worms Our Lady's; Friedberg, Gießen,
Heusenstamm, Lampertheim, Alzey, Darmstadt St. Martin,
Mainz-Gustavsberg, 1912–1922
Pfarrkurat, Mainz-Bischofsheim, February 1923
temporarily retired due to illness, Brandenburg (Havel), Marian
Hospital, September 1932
Pfarrverwalter, then *Pfarrer,* Vendersheim, August 1933 (supports
NSDAP through his pastoral ministry)
retired March 1936
moved to archdiocese of Freiburg
Kommorant, Radozell, Zusenhofen, Rast, Dingelsdorf, Öhningen,
1936–1978
died Öhningen, October 23, 1978
buried Bichtlingen, October 26, 1978

Source: BArch B R58/5715/A2; R5101/22314; EBAF PA Lindenschmit; Hellriegel,
Widerstehen und Verfolgen, I.2: 347–50 and II.1: 9–11.

Linhardt, Robert
born Nuremberg, March 24, 1895
ordained April 13, 1919 (Munich and Freising)
Hilfspriester, Pullach, Solln, Munich-Oberföhring St. Lawrence,
    1919–1922
Benefiziat, Munich Cathedral of Our Lady, May 1922
Prediger and *Ehrenkanonikus,* Munich St. Cajetan, November 1924
doctorate (theology), University of Munich, 1931
Professor (moral theology), College of Philosophy and Theology,
    Freising, April 1, 1931 (supports NSDAP in his preaching and teaching)
not allowed to lecture from 1946 onward
forced to retire from *Hochschule,* July 1, 1950
died January 16, 1981
Source: BArch B R5101/22525; EAM NL Faulhaber 5900, 5901; *Schematismus München und Freising.*

Lintl, Oswald (Martin), O.Carm.
born 1904
studied theology, College of Philosophy and Theology, Regensburg,
    1925–1929
ordained June 1929 (Carmelite, Order of Our Lady of Mount Carmel)
assigned to novitiate staff, Carmelite monastery, Reisach, December 1930
elected prior, Carmelite monastery, Reisach, May 1936
left priesthood and religious life, January 11, 1938
Flucht aus dem Kloster (1939)
died 1969
Source: EAM NL Thalhamer Priester, abgefallene.

Löffler, Siegfried, O.F.M. Conv.
born March 27, 1905, Frankenthal
ordained August 3, 1930 (Franciscan Friars Minor Conventual,
    Province St. Elisabeth)
left the order, c. 1939/1940, and worked on behalf of NSDAP
Source: PDFM Personaldaten.

Lortz, Joseph
born Grevenmacher (Luxemburg), December 13, 1887
studied philosophy and theology, Rome, Fribourg, and Switzerland,
    1907–1913
ordained July 25, 1913 (Luxemburg)
doctorate (church history), University of Bonn, 1920

Dozent, University of Würzburg, 1923–1929
Professor (church history), State Academy, Braunsberg, 1929
Katholischer Zugang zum Nationalsozialismus (1933)
joined NSDAP, May 1, 1933, no. 2,070,748
joined NSLB, July 1, 1933, no. 102,831
Professor (church history), University of Münster, April 1, 1935
removed from professorship, 1945
Professor (history of Western religions), University of Mainz, and
  director, Institute for European History, 1950
died February 21, 1975
Source: BArch B NS 26/1330, R58/5715/A2, R58/5978/A2; MIO NL Kleine; NARA
NSLB RG242-A3340-MF-B059, OGK RG242-A3340-MFOK-N068; Conzemius,
"Joseph Lortz—ein Kirchenhistoriker als Brückenbauer"; Damberg, "Kirchengeschichte"; Krieg, *Catholic Theologians in Nazi Germany,* 56–82; Lautenschläger,
Joseph Lortz (1887–1975); Lukens, "Joseph Lortz and a Catholic Accommodation
with National Socialism."

Machens, (Heinz) Godehard, O.S.B.
born Fürstenau, July 12, 1903
studied theology, College of Philosophy and Theology, Passau,
  1923–1927
ordained July 17, 1927 (Benedictine, Schweiklberg Abbey, Vilshofen)
sent to help establish Königsmünster monastery, Meschede, April
  1928–October 1933
helped to found Hitler Youth in preparatory seminary, Schweiklberg,
  1933–1934
granted leave, May 1935 .
left Schweiklberg Abbey, November 1937
officially dismissed from Benedictine order, June 1938
married July 1938
church organist, 1966–1987
died October 30, 1988
Source: AAS PA Machens; BArch B NS 10/109, NS 12/544, NS 26/1330; R58/5008;
R58/5676/A1, R58/5700c, R58/5715/A1, R58/5715/A2, R58/5744, R58/5748/A2,
R58/5895/A1, R4901/4493; LAB Pr. Br. Rep. 57/429; Freundorfer, "Das Missionsseminar Schweiklberg"; Madl, *Pater Coelestin Maier,* 281–334, 533–58.

Machens, Wilhelm
born Hildesheim, July 30, 1910
studied theology, University of Münster, 1929–1933
studied theology, Hildesheim seminary, 1933–1935
ordained February 24, 1935 (Hildesheim)
Kaplan, Wollbrandshausen and Duderstadt, 1935–1939 (supports

NSDAP through his pastoral ministry)
Pfarrvikar, Leherheide-Bederkesa, July 1939–September 1945
Pfarrer, Bremervörde, October 1945
Pfarrer, Vienenburg, October 1953
director of the cathedral library, diocesan archive, and cathedral
    museum, October 1978
retired July 31, 1988
died Vienenburg, July 20, 2004
Source: BAH Priesterkartei; BArch B NS26/1330, R58/5715/A2; MIO NL Kleine.

Mader, Alois

born Ramsdorf, March 22, 1904
ordained June 29, 1931 (Munich and Freising)
Hilfspriester, Moosinning, July 16, 1931
Kooperator, Dachau, Peiting, 1934–1936 (supports NSDAP through his
    pastoral ministry)
Koadjutor, Peiting, April 1, 1936
Koadjutor, St. Georgen, August 16, 1936 (last known assignment)
left the priesthood sometime before 1945
Source: EAM NL Faulhaber 5402; *Schematismus München und Freising.*

Maier, Mathäus

born Ottmarschart, December 25, 1882
ordained June 29, 1907 (Augsburg)
Koadjutor, Moosen (Munich archdiocese), Schliersee, 1907–1911
Kooperator, Massenhausen, Sittenbach, 1911–1915
Pfarrer, Modelshausen, November 1915
joined NSDAP, member 1933–1943
joined NSV and Reich Colonial Association
denazification, Wertingen, October 1946
retired, *Kommorant,* Hausham-Tiefenbach, November 25, 1946
died Lindau-Reutin, July 17, 1963
Source: ABA Personaldaten; BayHStA MSo 1414.

Mayer, Joseph

born Egg an der Günz, May 23, 1886
ordained July 25, 1909 (Augsburg)
Stadtkaplan, Rain am Lech, 1909
prefect, Dillingen Junior Seminary, 1910–1913
Kaplan, Oberstdorf, September 1913
military hospital chaplain, WWI, 1915–1918

Kaplan, Berg bei Donauwörth, 1919
granted leave to study, May 1924
doctorate (theology), University of Freiburg, 1926
Gesetzliche Unfruchtbarmachung Geisteskranker (1927)
Professor (social ethics), University of Freiburg, 1930
Professor (moral theology), College of Philosophy and Theology,
    Paderborn, 1930–1945 (rector 1934–1936)
V-Mann (informant) for Gestapo
member, Kleine-Pircher group of National Socialist Priests, 1939–c. 1942
"Die Lebensraumfrage der Völker im Lichte der christlichen
    Naturrechtsauffassung" (1939)
forced to resign and left Paderborn, July 1945
moved to Munich and joined staff of *Klerusblatt* (1946–1956) and
    Pfarramtblatt (1950–1963)
died October 30, 1967

Source: BArch B, R58/5299, R58/5706b; R58/5715/A2; MIO NL Kleine; USHMM 15.004/r. 4; Benzenhöfer and Finsterbusch, *Moraltheologie pro "NS-Euthanasie"*; Dietrich, "Joseph Mayer and the Missing Memo," "Catholic Resistance to Biological and Racist Eugenics," "Catholic Eugenics in Germany," and "Nazi Eugenics"; Graham, "The 'Right to Kill' in the Third Reich"; Gruß, *Erzbischof Lorenz Jaeger,* 102–7; Richter, *Katholizismus und Eugenik;* Wollasch, "War der katholische Priester und Eugeniker Joseph Mayer ein Wegbereiter der NS-Euthanasie?"

Meier, Ludger, O.F.M.

born Bad Dürkheim, September 18, 1898
infantry, WWI, 1916–1918
ordained August 14, 1927 (Bavarian Franciscan Province)
studied University of Munich, July 1928
confessor, Quaracchi, Bad Tölz, Vierzehnheiligen, Bamberg,
    1928–1932
retreat director, Maria Rosenberg, August 1932
confessor, Vienna, Mühldorf, Miltenberg, Bamberg, Dettelbach,
    Nuremberg, 1933–1941 (supports NSDAP in pastoral ministry)
Pfarrvikar, Passau, March 1944–October 1945
confessor, Bamberg, 1945–1946
research on Duns Scotus, England, June 1949
confessor, Dettelbach, Marienweiher, 1952–1954
professor of dogmatics, Franciscan *Hochschule,* Orihuela, Spain,
    1954–1958
retired, Marienweiher, May 27, 1958
died Bamberg hospital, March 10, 1961

Source: ABFP Personaldaten; BArch B NS 15/475, NS 43/62.

Mohler, Ludwig
born Mannheim, July 16, 1883
ordained July 2, 1907 (Freiburg)
vicar, various parishes, 1910–1912
studied, Universities of Freiburg and Heidelberg
doctorate (church history), University of Freiburg, 1912
studied in Rome, 1912–1915
military chaplain, WWI, 1915–1918
doctorate (theology), University of Freiburg, 1918
Habilitation, University of Freiburg, 1920
religion and history teacher, Münster, 1920–1935
joined NSDAP, May 1, 1933, no. 2,484,314
joined NSLB, July 1, 1934, no. 293,243
Professor (church history), University of Würzburg (1935), University
    of Munich (1937), and University of Freiburg (1939)
died 1943
Source: BArch B R58/5879/A2; EBAF Personalia Mohler; NARA NSZK RG242-A3340-
MFKL-L092, NSLB RG242-A3340-MF-B078.

Mohr, Heinrich
born Lauda, September 10, 1874
ordained July 1, 1897 (Freiburg)
vicar, Mosbach, Karlsruhe St. Stefan, 1898–1900
Kaplan, Neusatzeck, 1900
Kurat, Weitenung, 1902
granted leave to write full time, 1904
doctorate (theology), University of Freiburg, 1927
V-Mann (informant) for Gestapo
died Freiburg, June 20, 1951
Source: BArch B 58/5879/A2; Dierker, *Himmlers Glaubenskrieger,* 374–75; Schwalbach, *Erzbischof Conrad Gröber und die nationalsozialistische Diktatur,* 40–42, 86,
240–41.

Müller, Johannes Baptist
born Oberhäuser, December 18, 1881
ordained July 28, 1907 (Augsburg)
Kaplan, Lechbruck, Buchenberg, Seifriedsberg, 1907–1910
vicar, Pfaffenhofen, May 1910
studied, 1911–1916
doctorate (philosophy), 1916
Pfarrer, Königsbrunn, July 1916
Pfarrer, Röfingen, October 1923

forced to resign from parish, June 1929
joined NSDAP, n.d., no. 135,978
died, *Kommorant,* Heimenkirch, April 17, 1949
Source: ABA PA 926 Müller; BayHStA StK 107255; EAM PA Müller.

Müller, Josef
born July 14, 1855
ordained November 15, 1877 (Bamberg)
Kaplan, Forchheim, Lichtenfels, Nuremberg, Mönchherrnsdorf,
    Effeltrich, 1877–1884
Pfarrerverweser, Troschenreuth, August 1884
Kaplan, Effeltrich, Eggenbach, Unterweilersbach, 1884–1886
Benefiziat, Pottenstein, March 1887
retired with medical certificate from his doctor, 1889
Kommorant, Munich, 1889
doctorate (philosophy), University of Munich, 1894
Kommorant, Bamberg, Jägersburg castle, 1907–1942
Die deutsche Ehe (1938) (advocates NSDAP racial policy)
died January 9, 1942
Source: AEB Personaldaten; Weiß, *Der Modernismus in Deutschland,* 181–96.

Murawski, Friedrich
born Cologne, March 17, 1898
converted from Protestantism to Catholicism
entered Franciscan order, novitiate name "Deodatus," left after novi-
    tiate
studied philosophy and theology, Breslau, Fulda, and Paderborn,
    1916–September 1918 and January 1919–March 1921
infantry, WWI, September 1918–January 1919
ordained March 12, 1921 (Paderborn)
vicar, Egeln, 1921
doctorate (theology), University of Breisgau, February 1924
Hausgeistlicher, Boele, February–September 1924
Die Juden bei den Kirchenvätern und Scholastikern (1925)
vicar, Paderborn Church of the Atonement, 1925
religion teacher, Paderborn Vocational School, September 1927–
    November 1928
religion teacher, Heiligenstadt, 1929
Studienassessor, Bishop's Latin School, Amöneburg, March 1933, and
    Kaplan, Amöneburg, 1933
joined NSDAP, May 1, 1933, no. 3,215,779

joined SA, July 7, 1933–August 8, 1935
forced to retire temporarily by diocese, May 1934, left priesthood
  soon thereafter
NSDAP Gau Speaker, District Fulda-Land and Frankenberg-Eder,
  June–July 1934
Studienassessor, Meppen, August 1934; also served as NSDAP district
  school director and SA school advisor for Papenburg
left teaching for full-time work in NSDAP, April 1935
joined SS, August 13, 1935, no. 272,329, stationed Frankfurt
transferred to Leipzig, September 1935
transferred to Berlin, April 1936
RSHA VII B2/VII B 3 Political Churches
co-worker on *H-Special Detachment,* Collection Historical Witchcraft
  Trials
Die politische Kirche und ihre biblischen "Urkunden" (1938)
Jesus der Nazoräer, der König der Juden (1940)
Wehrgeist und Christentum (1940)
Das Gott: Umriss einer Weltanschauung aus germanischer Wurzel (1941)
*Der Kaiser aus dem Jenseits: Bilder von Wesen und Wirken Jahwehs und
  seiner Kirche* (1942)
accused of plagiarism, released from the RSHA, April 1943
left SS on his own request, February 1944
commits suicide 1945

Source: BArch B NSPK, NSZK, OGK, SSOA; BArch D ZR 873/Akt 2; EAM NL Faulhaber 8020; EBAP Priesterkartei; Dierker, *Himmlers Glaubenskrieger,* 556; Opfermann, *Das Bistum Fulda,* 16.

Nattermann, Johannes

born Essen, February 13, 1889
ordained August 10, 1912 (Cologne)
Kaplan, Elberfeld St. Marien, Cologne-Ehrenfeld St. Peter, 1912–1920
general secretary of the Catholic Kolping Association, 1920–1934
  (supports NSDAP through his position)
doctorate (philosophy), University of Cologne, 1925
granted leave from priestly duties, 1934
contributor to *Sendschreiben katholischer Deutscher an ihre Volks- und
  Glaubensgenossen* (1936)
author and speaker
died November 6, 1961

Source: AEK Personalia-Kleruskartei; Barch B R58/5715/A2; Breuning, *Die Vision des
Reiches,* 178–79, 183–86, 189–93; Klein, *Volksverein für das katholische Deutschland,*
224–25, 317–19, 472.

Nieborowski, Hubert

born Gleiwitz, October 16, 1882
ordained June 22, 1911 (Breslau)
Kaplan, Rosdzin, Altberun, Wischnitz, Beuthen, 1911–1921
Kuratus, Pollnow, October 1921–October 1924
Pfarrer, Zawada, October 1924
Pfarrer, Klein-Lagiewnik (changed to Hedwigsruh in 1936), July 1934
"Bekenntnis zum Führer" (1934)
"Katholisch—kein Kampfruf!" (1934)
Pfarrer, Döbern, April 1939
date of death unknown

Source: BArch B NS 15/975, NS 43/62; *Schematismus Breslau; The Tablet,* "German Priests and the Nazi Party."

Nikolussi, Alois, C.R.S.A.

born Altrei, southern Tyrol, November 27, 1890
ordained July 6, 1913 (Trient)
military chaplain, WWI, 1915–1918
entered Congregation of the Canons Regular of St. Augustine
    (C.R.S.A.), St. Florian, 1919
Aushilfspriester, Attnang, 1920
Kooperator, Windhaag, 1921
studied theology, University of Vienna, 1922–1923
doctorate (theology), University of Vienna, 1923
professor of New Testament, *Lehranstalt* (educational facility), St.
    Florian, 1923
Pfarrvikar, Asten, 1938
member Kleine-Pircher group of National Socialist Priests 1939–1945
Pfarrer, St. Florian, 1941 (after January 21, 1941, in Schlagerhaus, after
    Gestapo confiscated *Stift* St. Florian)
Pfarrer, Völcklabruck, 1946
Dechant, St. Florian, 1958–1961
died St. Florian, August 17, 1965

Source: MIO NL Kleine; Lettl, "Die Arbeitsgemeinschaft für den religiösen Frieden," 21–22, 60–61, 68–71, 87–89; Riegler, "Augustiner-Chorherren," 73–84.

Patin, August Wilhelm

born Würzburg, June 25, 1879
ordained June 29, 1904 (Munich and Freising)
Koadjutor, Mittenwald, July 1904
Kuratus, Munich St. Johann Nepomuk, July 1905

Hofstiftsvikar, Munich St. Kajetan, January 1907
doctorate (theology), University of Munich, 1908
studied at University of Bamberg and University of Munich, 1916–1918
doctorate, Roman and canon law, University of Munich, 1918
professor for religious pedagogy, Munich, *Ruprecht Kreisoberrealsschule,*
  1922
professor, Munich, *Ludwigsrealschule,* 1928
joined NSDAP, April 1, 1933, no. 1,691,360
joined NSLB, October 1, 1933, no. 114,099
joined SS, n.d., no. 107,046
retired from teaching by intervention of his cousin, Heinrich
  Himmler, 1934
withdrew from Catholic Church, October 1938
married Wilhelmine Schnitzler
worked for SD and RSHA
*Beiträge zur Geschichte der Deutsch-Vatikanischen Beziehungen in den
  letzten Jahrzehnten* (1942)
died Allied detention camp, March 15, 1946

Source: BArch B NSLB, R58/5700a/A2, R58/5881/A1; BArch D ZB 1/494; ZR 918/A1; BayHStA MK 47048; EAM NL Faulhaber 5402, PA Patin; MIO NL Kleine; NARA RG242-T-581/r. 98; USHMM 15.007/r. 27; Dierker, *Himmlers Glaubenskrieger,* 52, 91, 440; Graham, "Documenti di guerra da Mosca"; Shuster, *The Ground I Walked On,* 240–41.

Pieper, Lorenz

born Eversberg, May 15, 1875
studied philosophy and theology in Paderborn and Fribourg (Switzerland)
ordained March 25, 1899 (Paderborn)
religion teacher, *Höhere Töchterschule (Progymnasium),* Wattenscheid,
  and *Kaplan,* Wattenscheid, 1899–1901
studied economics in Berlin and Munich, 1901–1903
doctorate (philosophy), University of Munich, 1903
active member *Volksverein* for Catholic Germany, 1903–1917
Kaplan, Geseke, April 1917
Kaplanverwalter, Hüsten St. Petri, August 1917
agitator *Jungdeutscher Orden*
joined NSDAP, 1922, no. 9740
NSDAP agitator in Bavaria and Württemberg, spring–October 1923
changed his NSDAP number to 15,406, August 12, 1925
Pfarrvikar, Wehrden (Weser), 1923–1928
Pfarrvikar, Halingen, 1928–1932

"Christentum und jungdeutscher Gedanke" (1924)
forced to retire by diocese, December 1932
retired Eversberg, 1933–34
Schulrat, Arnsberg district government, 1934
chaplain, State Psychiatric Asylum, Marienthal near Münster (August
    1934–March 1936) and Warstein (April 1936–February 1942)
forced to retire by state for speaking out against euthanasia,
    Meschede, March 1942–May 1945
arrested by Allies, May 1945
forced internment, Rietberg monastery, May 1945–April 1946
Eversberg, May 1946–fall 1946
acting pastor, Berlar near Ramsbeck, fall 1946–early 1948
denazification, October 6, 1948, classified as lesser offender (category 3)
retired Eversberg, 1948–1951
died St. Wallburga hospital, Meschede, January 30, 1951
buried Eversberg Cemetery

Source: AAK NL Pieper; EAP Sammlung Pieper; Tröster, "Die besondere Eigenart"; Vogel, *Katholische Kirche und national Kampfverbände*, 54–80.

Pirchegger, Simon

born Leopersdorf near Allerheiligen (Austria), September 23, 1889
studied theology, University of Graz
ordained 1914 (Graz-Seckau)
studied German philology, Indo-European languages, and classic
    philology, University of Graz, 1919–1927
studied Slavonic languages and linguistics, University of Leipzig, 1921
doctorate (philosophy), University of Graz, 1927
Dozent, University of Graz, 1927–1933
joined NSDAP, May 1, 1932, no. 901,259
Hitler und die katholische Kirche (1933)
Dozent (Slavic studies), University of Bonn, 1936
Professor (Slavic studies), University of Graz, 1943
dismissed from university teaching, 1945
returned to diocese of Graz-Seckau and served, as needed, in several
    parishes
died June 3, 1946

Source: BArch B NS15/493; R58/5557d, R58/5715/A2; R58/5727/A1, R58/5978/A1, NSPK, NSZK, OGK; MIO NL Kleine; Hofmüller, "Steirische Priester"; Lettl, "Die Arbeitsgemeinschaft für den religiösen Frieden," 63; Prunč, "Simon Pirchegger"; Spicer, *Resisting the Third Reich*, 143–44.

Pircher, Johann

born Andrian (Austria, now southern Tyrol, Italy), May 17, 1886
studied theology, Brixen Seminary, 1909–1912
ordained (as Pater Emmerich) June 29, 1911 (Deutsch-Orden)
Kooperator, Sarntal, Aldein, Vogelseifen (Schlesien), Gloggnitz,
    Atzgersdorf, and Schwechat, 1912–1923
incardinated in archdiocese of Vienna, October 1921
religion teacher, *Bürgerschule,* Schwechat, February 1923
religion teacher, *Hauptschule* for Boys, Neuottakring, Vienna,
    1926–1938
joined NSDAP April 24, 1933, no. 1,605,856 (became local *Blockwart*)
joined NSV
founder and leader, *Arbeitsgemeinschaft für den religiösen Frieden,*
    March–September 1938
founder and coleader with Richard Kleine, group of National Socialist
    Priests, 1939–1945
Kooperator, Untertauern (archdiocese Salzburg), 1945–1949
Hilfspriester and *Katechet,* Bischofshofen, 1949
died Schwarsach, August 12, 1953

Source: MIO NL Kleine; NARA NSZK RG242-A3340-MFKL-M019; Lettl, "Die Arbeit-
gemeinschaft für den religiösen Frieden"; Loidl, *Religionslehrer Johann Pircher* and
Arbeitsgemeinschaft für den religiösen Frieden.

Pohl, Johann Joseph Maria

born Cologne, 1904
ordained June 28, 1927 (Cologne)
doctorate (theology), University of Bonn, July 1929
Papal Biblical Institute, biblical studies, 1929–1932
fellow of the Middle Eastern Institute of the Görres Society,
    Jerusalem, 1931–1934
doctorate (biblical studies), Papal Biblical Institute, Rome, June 1933
left the priesthood and married Gertrud Riemer, September 1934
specialist for Hebrew literature, Prussian State Library, Berlin,
    December 1935
writes for *Der Stürmer* and other National Socialist publications
failed attempt for *Habilitation,* University of Berlin, 1939
becomes *V-Mann* (informant) to SS-*Sturmbannführer* Albert Hartl
joined NSDAP, July 1, 1940, no. 8,159,406
librarian for Alfred Rosenberg in the Frankfurt Institute for Research
    of the Jewish Question, 1941
member of Special Operation Staff of Reich Leader Rosenberg for the

Occupied Areas (ERR), active participation in confiscation and plundering of libraries of Jewish communities in occupied territories, 1941–1943

writer, *Welt-Dienst,* newspaper sponsored by Rosenberg, 1943–1945

organizer for Rosenberg of planned International anti-Jewish Congress, 1944

arrested by American military and interned, May 1945–October 1946

released without further prosecution, 1946

editor and writer, Cologne and Wiesbaden, 1946–1960

died Wiesbaden, January 30, 1960

Source: AEK Personaldaten; NARA OGK RG242-A3340-MFOK-R009; Kühn-Ludewig, *Johannes Pohl;* Piper, *Alfred Rosenberg,* 499–503.

Pollak, Josef

born Hinterdorf, March 12, 1880

ordained June 22, 1907 (Breslau)

Kaplan, Münsterber, Oberschöneweide, Waldenburg, Deutsch-Leippe, Canth, 1907–1916

Kurat, Wohlau, September 1916

Anstaltgeistlicher, Pilchowitz (after 1936, Bilchengrund), 1926 (supports NSDAP in pastoral ministry)

died February 28, 1962

Source: BArch B R58/5715/A2; *Schematismus Breslau; The Tablet,* "German Priests and the Nazi Party."

Preuß, Paul

born Landsberg, December 10, 1904

ordained, date unknown (Breslau)

parochial vicar, Danzig-Emaus

joined NSDAP, February 1, 1939, no. 7,025,651.

date of death unknown

Source: NARA NSPK RG242-A3340-PK-J193.

Rädler, Hermann

born Rieden, March 30, 1988

ordained July 25, 1912 (Augsburg)

Kaplan, Amendingen, Steinbach, 1912–1918

Benefiziumsvikar, then *Benefiziat,* Fischen, August 1918–January 1937 (supports NSDAP through his pastoral ministry)

Pfarrer, Wohnbrechts, January 28, 1937

retired August 1, 1955

Kommorant, Wohmbrechts, 1955–1959
died January 3, 1959
Source: ABA PA 1742 Rädler; BArch NS 14/475, NS43/62; Witetschek, *Die kirchliche Lage in Bayern,* 3:126.

Rarkowski, Franz Justus
born Allenstein June 8, 1873
ordained January 9, 1898 (Society of Mary, Marists)
incardinated into diocese of Brixen (Tyrol)
military chaplain, WWI, 1914
military chaplaincy, Koblenz, Königsberg, Breslau, and Berlin, 1918–1929
appointed by Fulda Bishop's Conference to oversee military chaplaincy for *Reichswehr,* August 1929
joined NSV
director of Military Bishop's Office, August 1936
appointed Catholic Military Bishop of the Army and Titular Bishop of Hierocaesarea, consecrated February 20, 1938
wartime preaching supports National Socialist ideology and war aims
retired February 1, 1945
died Munich, February 9, 1950
Source: Bergen, "German Military Chaplains in the Second World War"; Brandt, "Franz Justus Rarkowski"; Brandt and Häger, eds., *Biographisches Lexikon,* 637–40; Missalla, *Wie der Krieg zur Schule Gottes wurde;* Missalla, *Für Gott, Führer und Vaterland;* Zahn, *German Catholics and Hitler's Wars,* 143–72.

Reckenthäler, Wilhelm
born Worms, June 7, 1902
ordained August 5, 1928 (Trier)
Kaplan, Differten, Ehrang, 1928–1938
joined NSDAP, August 1, 1935, no. 3,694,719
Pfarrer, Gillenbeuren, 1938–1969
doctorate (political science), University of Bonn, 1943
retired February 1, 1969
died Gillenbeuren, October 18, 1970
Source: BArch B R58/5715/A2; BAT Personaldaten; NARA OGK RG242-A3340-MFOK-R061; Persch, "Der Diözesanklerus und die neuen pastoralen Laienberufe," 211–12.

Rempe, Karl
born Wartenburg, September 18, 1890
studied theology, University of Innsbruck and College of Philosophy and Theology, Paderborn

ordained August 7, 1921 (Paderborn)
Pfarrvikar, Bahrendorf, Hamm, August 1921–1926
Standortpfarrer, Paderborn, Berlin, Breslau, 1926–1929
Pfarrer, Berleburg, September 1929
Pfarrer, Oberhundem, April 1934
military chaplain, February 1940–October 1944
denazification, October 11, 1949, exonerated (category 5)
Pfarrer, Nieheim, May 1952–January 1967
retired (named *Geistlicher Rat*) December 1966
died Nieheim, January 14, 1970
Source: EAP XXII NSDAP 20, Sammlung Rempe; Brandt and Häger, eds., *Biographisches Lexikon,* 652.

Röder, Ernst
born Würzburg, September 29, 1900
infantry, WWI, 1918
ordained April 13, 1924 (Würzburg)
Kaplan, Wiesen, Rimpar, Aschaffenburg, April 1924–December 1926
Pfarrer, Euerbach, December 1, 1926
doctorate (history), University of Würzburg, February 1932
Benefiziat, Kitzingen, May 1932
religion teacher, *Lyzeum,* Kitzingen, fall 1932
Stadtprediger, September 1932–1938
joined NSDAP, May 1, 1933, no. 3,435,350
joined NSV
Heerespfarrer, Munich, May 1938
Wehrmachtspfarrer, January 1939
Pfarrer, Obertheres, 1946–1954
Pfarrer, Strahlungen, July 12, 1954
Pfarrer, Eßfeld, November 9, 1959
died July 31, 1961
Source: BayHStA MK 38394, MSo 1414; NARA OGK RG242-A3340-MFOK-S036, NSPK RG242-A3340-PK-K001.

Roth, Josef
born Munich, August 2, 1897
infantry, WWI, 1917–1918
studied theology, Passau and University of Munich
member *Freikorps Wachregiment* and *Bund Oberland,* 1919
ordained June 29, 1922 (Munich and Freising)
Kooperator-Verweser, Indersdorf, July 1922

Katholizismus und Judenfrage (1923)
Catechist, then *Kaplan,* Munich St. Ursula, October 1924
"Für Gott und Vaterland" (March 4, 1925)
"Katholischer Pazifismus?" (1926)
"Der Weg der Frontsoldaten" (1929)
"Gedanken zum Münchener Stahlhelmtag" (1930)
"Um die Allgemeine Wehrpflicht" (1930)
joined SA, April 1, 1934, no. 287,274 (withdrew January 1, 1936)
Studienrat (theology), Maria-Theresia-Realschule, Munich, January 1934
teacher, National Socialist *Oberschule,* Feldafing, 1934
"Die Kirche ist alt geworden" (March 27, 1935)
specialist on Catholic Church in newly formed Reich Ministry of
    Church Affairs, August 1935
temporary *Nihil obstat* from Cardinal Faulhaber, September 1935
    (withdrawn May 1936)
director of Catholic Department, Reich Ministry of Church Affairs,
    May 1937
"Die katholische Kirche und die Judenfrage" (1940)
liaison with Käthe Schirrmann, 1939–1941
died Rattenberg (boating accident), July 5, 1941

Source: ABA PA 1782 Roth; BArch B R58/5886/A2, R58/5978/A1, R4901/4314, R5101/21676, R5101/21678, R5101/24191, SAK; BArch K NL Roth 898, NL Schröcker 1516; BayHStA MK 16806; EAM NL Faulhaber 5539, 7090, 7269; Baumgärtner, "Vom Kaplan zum Ministerialrat"; Bleistein, "Überläufer im Sold der Kirchenfeinde"; Brandl, "Josef Roth"; Kreutzer, *Das Reichskirchenministerium,* 161–82; Spicer, *Resisting the Third Reich,* 156–59.

Ruland, Ludwig

born Munich, September 16, 1873
ordained June 29, 1897 (Würzburg)
prefect, Königliches Studienseminar, Bamberg, September 1897
doctorate (theology), University of Munich, 1905
Divionspfarrer, Cologne, Münster, 1905–1913
Privatdozent, University of Münster, June 1913
Professor (moral and pastoral theology), University of Würzburg,
    October 1913
"Die Katholiken und der 12. November" (1933)
joined NSDAP, May 1, 1937, no. 4,855,741
joined NSLB, n.d.
retired from teaching, October 1938
died Würzburg-Heidingsfeld, July 5, 1951

Source: BayHStA MK 44231; BArch B NSZK, RKK; DAW Personaldaten.

Sailer, Albert

born Kaisheim, January 23, 1892
ordained February 1, 1920 (Bamberg)
Kaplan, Auerbach, Schnaittach, Gaustadt, 1920–1921
Kooperator, Marktschorgast, November 1921
Pfarrverweser, Marktschorgast, December 1922
Kaplan, Waischenfeld, Eggolsheim, 1923–1926
Kuratus, Poppendorf, September 1926
Pfarrer, Enchenreuth, February 1934
joined NSDAP, May 1, 1935, no. 3,663,153
Pfarrer and prison chaplain, Bayreuth, February 1942
military government ordered his removal as prison chaplain, 1945
Kommorant, Wohlmutshüll, December 1948
died November 25, 1954

Source: AEB Personaldaten; BayHStA MSo 1413; NARA NSZK RG242-A3340-MFKL-R081.

Sandkuhl, Franz

born Minden, May 4, 1898
ordained May 30, 1926 (Paderborn)
incardinated into archdiocese of Munich, November 1926
Aushilfspriester, Gauting, November 1926
Benefiziumsverweser, spiritual director, religion teacher, Berg am Laim,
    April 1929
joined NSDAP, May 1, 1933, no. 3,213,295 (withdrew August 1934)
suspended from teaching by Cardinal Faulhaber on account of NS-
    DAP support, November 1933
Kooperator, Munich, St. Peter, December 1933
entered Benedictine order, Benediktsberg-Vaals, Holland, May 1936
withdrew from Benedictines, parish assistance, Holland, May 1937,
    and England, December 1937
associate rector, Maastricht, Marienward, May 1937
parochial vicar, Tring (Hertfordshire), December 1937
parochial vicar, Uttoxeter (Staffordshire), Painswick (Gloucester),
    Fischguard (S. Wales), 1938–1946
entered an unknown religious community in England, October 1946
remained in England until 1965
moved to St. Georgenberg-Fiecht, Austria, 1966
date of death unknown

Source: EAM Personaldaten; BArch B OGK, R58/5715/A2, R58/5879/A2, R58/5978/A1, R43/174.

Schachleiter, (Jakob) Albanus, O.S.B.

born Mainz, January 20, 1861

studied theology, Seckau

ordained August 10, 1886 (Benedictine Emaus, Prague)

chairman, Bonifatius Association, 1902

abbot, Emaus monastery, 1908–1918

forced exile to Germany, December 1918

resigned as abbot, June 1920

Holy See conferred on him title of abbot of the dissolved Benedictine
monastery Sponheim, March 1921

moved to Munich, 1921

founded *Schola Gregoriana*, October 1922

moved to Bad Aibling/Feilnbach, October 1930

suspended, July 1932–September 1933

honored guest, Nuremberg rallies, November 1933 and 1934

died Feilnbach, June 20, 1937

state funeral, Munich, June 22, 1937, buried at the Munich
Waldfriedhof cemetery (grave monument leveled with the consent
of the Benedictine congregation, summer 1987)

Source: BArch B NS26/1323-1330, NSPK, R5101/21675; R58/5715/A2; BArch Z ZA 1
11192 BayHStA NL Schachleiter; EBAF B2/NS18; EAM NL Faulhaber 5537, 5539, PA
5936 Schachleiter; Bleistein, "Abt Alban Schachleiter OSB"; Engelhard, *Abt
Schachleiter;* Haering, "Kirchenrechtliche Marginalien zum Fall Schachleiter";
Munro, *Hitler's Bavarian Antagonist,* 211–13; Šebek, "Die Äbte Alban Schachleiter
OSB und Ernst Vykoukal OSB."

Schick, Hans, O.S.Cam.

born Eitorf, April 22, 1889

ordained March 18, 1913 (Order of Saint Camillus, Vaals)

withdrew from religious order and was incardinated into archdiocese
of Cologne, 1925

doctorate (history), University of Bonn, 1931

left priesthood, October 20, 1932

private teacher

joined NSDAP, April 1, 1933, no. 1,675,565

joined NSLB, September 1, 1933, no. 185,802

withdrew from Catholic Church, March 1936

married Wilhelmine Keweloh, February 1936

joined SS, August 1, 1937, no. 229,564

SD-OA-Süd, division director II/11

Allied internment, 1945–1948

date of death unknown

Source: NARA OGK RG242-A3340-MFOK-T036; NSLB RG242-A3340-MF-C027; SSOA RG242-A3343-SSO-076B; Dierker, *Himmlers Glaubenskrieger,* 558.

Schips, Anton

born Ellwangen, August 14, 1903
ordained February 27, 1926 (Rottenburg)
Kaplan, Schramberg, Stuttgart St. Maria, 1926–1931
Pfarrer, Lauterbach, July 1931(supports NSDAP through his pastoral
  ministry)
Pfarrer, Karsee, May 1936
Pfarrer, Westhausen, March 1948
retired September 1976
died Westhausen, February 11, 1977

Source: DAR Personaldaten; Bischöfliches Ordinariat Rottenburg, ed., *Das Verzeichnis der Priester und Diakone der Diözese Rottenburg-Stuttgart von 1922 bis 1992,* 25.

Schmidtke, Friedrich

born Würzen, May 3, 1891
ordained August 12, 1916 (Breslau)
doctorate (theology and philosophy), 1925
Privatdozent, Breslau, and hospital chaplain, 1926
Die Einwanderung Israels in Kanaan (1933), placed on Index by Holy See
joined NSLB, October 1, 1933, no. 227,835
joined NSDAP, May 1, 1937, no. 5,652,025
remainder of his career unknown
date of death unknown

Source: DAB VI/1 Doberschütz; NARA NSLB RG242-A3340-MF-C034, OGK RG242-A3340-MFOK-U005; *Schematismus Breslau; The Tablet,* "German Priests and the Nazi Party."

Schober, Nikolaus

born Rattelsdorf, March 11, 1879
ordained July 26, 1903 (Bamberg)
Kaplan, Bühl, Trunstadt für Viereth, Lichtenfels, 1903–1904
Pfarrverweser, Hirschaid, Seußling, 1904–1905
Kuratus, Rehau, Oberkotzau, 1905–1918
Pfarrer, Steinwiesen, February 1918
Pfarrer, Hausen, October 1931 (supports NSDAP through his pastoral
  ministry)
Kommorant, Hausen
denazification, Forchheim, 1945 (fined)
died November 15, 1948

Source: AEB Personaldaten; BArch B NS26/1330, Breuer, *Verordneter Wandel?,* 340.

Scholz, Anton
born Graase, July 13, 1891
ordained Breslau, April 23, 1922 (Breslau/Berlin)
Kaplan, Breslau St. Michael, Brockau, Berlin St. Petrus, Nowawes,
    Berlin St. Pius, 1922–1928
Kuratus, Zossen, September 1928
joined NSDAP, March 1, 1933, no. 1,545,459
Kuratus, Strasburg, December 1935
V-Mann (informant), SD-East, May 1936
Strafanstaltspfarrer, Brandenburg, March 1937
Kuratus, Birkenwerder, April 1951
retired October 1957
moved to Neu-Zittau, 1957
moved to Eggstetten near Simbach am Inn, Bavaria, 1961
died Zwiesel, December 21, 1980
Source: BArch B NSZK, OGK, R5101/22384, R58/5978/A1; BLHA Pr. Br. Rep. 2A II
Pdm. 525; DAB VI/I Scholz; Spicer, *Resisting the Third Reich*, 149–53.

Schröcker, Sebastian
born Munich, September 1, 1906
ordained June 29, 1932 (Munich and Freising)
Aushilfspriester, Königliches Erziehungsinstitut der Englischen
    Fräulein, July 1932
Kuratus, Planegg psychiatric asylum, October 1932
doctorate (law), University of Munich, December 1931
doctorate (theology), University of Munich, December 1934
Habilitation (canon law), University of Munich, June 1936
Dozent (canon law), University of Munich, June 1938
advisor, Reich Ministry for Church Affairs, October 1938
Dozent (canon law), University of Vienna, November 1939
military service, April 1940
joined NSDAP, January 1941, no. 8,289,138
joined NSV
married Margarete Wiedemann, May 1943
named *Regierungsrat* (mid-level civil servant), October 1943
denazification, Munich, exonerated (category 5)
administrative court councilor *(Verwaltungsgerichtsrat)*, Braunschweig,
    December 1952
higher administrative court councilor *(Oberverwaltungsgerichtsrat)*,
    Lüneburg, July 1953
judge *(Bundesrichter)*, Federal Administrative Court, Berlin, April 1955

retired September 1974
died Berlin, April 5, 1992

Source: ALMU Stud.-Karte; BArch B MFOK, NSPK, R5101/22462 BArch D DOK/
P8130; BArch K NL Schröcker 1516; BayHStA MK 35718; EAM NL Faulhaber 5402;
Boberach, "Organe der nationalsozialistischen Kirchenpolitik," 324–25; Kreutzer,
Das Reichskirchenministerium, 182–85.

Schürmeister, Wilhelm

born Munich, December 21, 1899
ordained May 30, 1926 (München)
Kooperator, Freising St. Georg, July 1, 1926 (supports NSDAP through
his pastoral ministry)
Expositus, Gröbenzell, September 16, 1936
Pfarrkurat, Gröbenzell, February 1, 1938
date of death unknown

Source: ALMU Studenten-Karte, EAM NL Faulhaber 5402; *Schematismus München.*

Schwarz, Friedrich Joseph Jakob

born Oberhausen, March 22, 1895
infantry, WWI (wounded June 1918)
ordained August 13, 1922 (Cologne)
Kaplan, Essen-Unterfrintrop Sacred Heart, Essen-Rüttenscheid St.
Andreas, Cologne-Birkendorf St. Rochus, Essen-Stoppenberg St.
Nikolaus, 1922–1938 (supports NSDAP through his pastoral ministry)
Marinestandortspfarrer, Kiel, January 1, 1938
Marinestandortspfarrer, Gotenhafen, December 19, 1939
Marinepfarrer, Norway and Denmark, April 1942
Marinestandsortspfarrer, Wesermünde, December 1942
Marineoberpfarrer, Wesermünde, Cuxhaven, February 1944
Marinedekan, May 1945
discharged from navy, December 1947
chaplain to refugees, Bremerhaven-Lehe-Land, December 1947
Pfarrvikar, Bremerhaven-Lehe-Land, January 1948
lived in Essen, 1958
died October 16, 1970

Source: AEK Personalia-Kleruskartei; BArch B NS26/1330; Brandt and Häger, eds.
Biographisches Lexikon, 758–59.

Seidl, Franz Sales

born Passau, January 12, 1904
ordained April 9, 1938 (Passau)
Kooperator, Waldkirchen, Frauenau, Winzer, Pocking, Altötting,

1928–1938

Expositus, Hohenwart, June 1938

involved in Catholic division, *Institut zur Erforschung und Beseitigung des jüdischen Einflusses im deutschen kirchlichen Leben,* Eisenach, 1940/1941

Pfarrer, Landau a. d. Isar, February 1943

retired Landau a. d. Isar, September 1971

died Landau a. d. Isar, May 28, 1994

Source: ABP Personaldaten; MIO NL Kleine; *Schematismus Passau* 1933; Hehl, *Priester unter Hitlers Terror,* 1270.

Seiller, Bernhard Johann, O.S.B.

born Wolfsberg, January 6, 1863

ordained July 25, 1889 (Benedictine order St. Stefan)

doctorate (philology), University of Würzburg, July 1892

teacher (anthropology, history, and science), St. Stefan gymnasium, 1891–1937

novice master, St. Stefan, 1896–1920

Konrektor, St. Stefan gymnasium, 1916–1937 (in contact and working with other brown priests, such as Philipp Haeuser)

promoted to *Oberstudienrat,* 1920

retired 1937 (endeavors to promote harmonious relationship between church and state through letter-writing campaign)

died Augsburg, October 22, 1942

Source: AAStS NL Seiller; BArch B R43II/178a; BayHStA File Number; MIO NL Kleine; StA Kempten NL Haeuser.

Senn, Wilhelm Maria

born Hemsbach, October 15, 1878

ordained July 5, 1905 (Freiburg)

vicar, Walldürn, Mannheim St. Joseph, Heidelberg-Handschuhsheim, 1905–1911

Pfarrverweser, Heidelberg-Handschuhsheim, 1911

Pfarrer, Flehingen, 1917

Pfarrer, Sickingen, 1930

"Das Komplott des Schweigens in der Judenfrage" (1930)

Katholizismus und Nationalsozialismus (1931)

faculties suspended, August 1931–October 1931

Halt! Katholizismus und Nationalsozialismus (1932)

faculties suspended, July 1932–December 1932

diocesan-granted sabbatical for writing, May 1934–March 1936

returned to Sickingen, March 1936
died Sickingen, January 23, 1940

Source: BArch B R58/5715/A2, R58/5879/A2; EBAF PA Senn; Weis, *Würden und Bürden,* 35–38.

Springer, Josef

born Steinkirchen a. d. Ihm, August 12, 1902
ordained June 29, 1928 (Munich and Freising)
Koadjutor, then *Pfarrvikar,* Langenpettenbach, July 1928
Aushilfspriester, then *Koadjutor,* Holzkirchen, December 22, 1928
Kooperator, Ebersberg, Grassau, 1929–1935
joined NSDAP, February 1, 1932, no. 874,126 (withdrew May 13, 1943)
retired temporarily due to illness, March 1935
moved to Leipzig, 1936
date of death unknown

Source: EAM Personaldaten; NARA OGK RG242-A3340-MFOK-W002.

Stempfle, Bernhard, O.S.H.

born Munich, April 17, 1882
ordained November 1904 (Poor Hermits of St. Hieronymus of the
    Congregation of St. Peter of Pisa)
stationed at *Sant'Onofrio,* Rome
returned to Munich to live with his family, 1918
editor of *Miesbacher Anzeiger,* 1922–1925
joined NSDAP, January 1, 1934
murdered July 2, 1934

Source: ACIVC, Apostolic Visits, September 1932; BArch B NSPK; BayHStA NL Stempfle; LofCong 3983G; Heiden, *The Führer,* 304-308, 600; Heiden, *Hitler: A Biography,* 193, 384.

Stempfle, Hubert

born Spandau near Berlin, August 12, 1905
ordained June 29, 1934 (Berlin)
chaplain, Frutillar (Chile), 1934–1946 (avid promoter of NSDAP)
chaplain, Chilean police, 1946–1962
Kaplan, Freutsmoos, 1962–1968
Kaplan, Brannenburg, 1968–1979
died June 24, 1982

Source: BArch R5101/22530.

Stern, Johannes

born Straubing, March 31, 1885
ordained July 28, 1912 (Bamberg)
Kaplan, Schlüsselau, August 1912
Pfarrvikar, Drosendorf, June 1913
Kooperator, Drosendorf, July 1917
Kuratus, Appenfelden, Stappenbach, Kornhöfstadt, Friesen, 1920–1929
Pfarrer, Buttenheim, 1929 (supports NSDAP through his pastoral ministry)
forbidden to preach by diocese, 1939
Kommorant, Friesen
died June 3, 1950

Source: AEB Personaldaten; Breuer, *Verordneter Wandel?,* 339–40; Witetschek, *Die Kirchliche Lage in Bayern,* 2:282, 294, 314.

Stipperger, Georg

born Munich, December 30, 1881
ordained June 29, 1905 (Munich and Freising)
Stadtkaplan, Pasing, 1905–1907
Kurat, Munich, 1907–1909
Kaplan and religion teacher, Royal School for Girls of the Congregation of Jesus (Königliches Erziehungsinstitut der Englischen Fräulein), Munich-Nymphenburg, 1909–1910
Stadtpfarrprediger, Munich St. Ludwig, and chaplain for university students, Munich, 1910
Hofstiftsprediger, St. Cajetans Royal Parish Church *(Hofkirche),* Munich
Ehrenkanonikus, Royal Residential Foundation *(Königliches Hofstift),* Munich, 1913
Feldgeistlicher, WWI, August 1914–September 1916 (Belgium, France, and Serbia)
Hofprediger, All Saints Church, located within the royal residence *(Hofkirche),* Munich, 1916
religion teacher, Luitpold *Kreisoberrealschule,* Munich, 1918–1920
left priesthood, June 1921
married Edith Aswaldt, 1921
doctorate (theology), University of Munich, n.d.
Habilitation (history), University of Munich, July 1929
NSDAP *Gauredner* (district speaker), 1933
reconciled with Catholic Church, 1949–1952

Source: BayHStA MK 38700; EAM NL Faulhaber 5407, 5409; NARA OGK RG242-A3340-MFOK-W044, NSPK RG242-A3340-PK-M018; *Schematismus München.*

Stonner, Anton
born Starkstadt (Böhmen), August 2, 1895
ordained December 3, 1922 (Society of Jesus, Jesuit, Austria)
chaplain, University of Vienna, 1923–1927
Boniface House near Emmerich, 1927
left Jesuit order, 1928
incardinated into Breslau archdiocese; after 1930, member of Berlin
    diocese
doctorate (philosophy), University of Munich, 1930
doctorate (theology), University of Munich, 1932
Dozent (catechesis and pedagogy), University of Munich, September
    1935 (supports NSDAP through teaching, preaching, and writing)
university preacher, University of Munich, March 1937
acting chair for Christian philosophy, University of Prague, 1940
acting chair for pastoral theology, University of Munich, 1948
professor of pastoral theology, University of Bonn, 1951
emeritus professor, University of Bonn, 1963
designated monsignor, April 21, 1970
died Bonn, January 22, 1973

Source: AJO Personaldaten; BDM Personaldaten; DAB Personaldaten; EAM Personaldaten; Alzheimer and Brückner, "Volkstumsaffinitäten"; Denzler, *Widerstand ist
nicht das richtige Wort*, 74–82; Dierker, *Himmlers Glaubenskrieger*, 211.

Strehl, Johannes
born Berlin, August 2, 1887
ordained June 18, 1914 (Breslau/Berlin)
Kaplan, Ossig, Neusalz (Oder), Ziegenhals, Brieg, Forst, Steinau,
    Berlin-Tegel Sacred Heart, 1914–1927
Kuratus, Berlin-Lichterfelde St. Anna, April 1931
joined NSDAP, May 1, 1933, no. 2,658,955
Pfarrer and *Standortpfarrer*, Potsdam St. Peter und Paul, May 1933
Potsdam leader, *Katholische Vereinigung für nationale Politik*
V-Mann (informant) for SD-East
forced to resign his pastorate by Bishop Preysing, March 1936
chaplain, Berlin-Spandau-Hakenfelde, May 1937
granted leave, moved to Königshausen
died Konstanz, May 18, 1951

Source: BArch B OGK; R43II/174, R5101/22301, R5101/22312, R58/5879/A2,
R58/5978/A1; BLHA Pr. Br. Rep. 2A Regierung Potsdam II Pdm./525, Pr. Br. Rep. 2A
Regierung Potsdam II Gen./283, /287; DAB VI/1 Strehl; Spicer, *Resisting the Third
Reich*, 144–50.

Sturm, Totnan, O.F.M. Conv.

born Mundenheim, October 19, 1883

ordained 1906 (Franciscan Friars Minor Conventual, Province St. Elisabeth)

Pfarrverweser, Kaiserslautern, October 16, 1933 (supports NSDAP through his pastoral ministry)

Source: PDFM Personaldaten; Fandel, *Konfession und Nationalsozialismus,* 489–92.

Trogemann, Bonifatius (Franz), O.P.

born Buer-Resse, October 16, 1889

ordained February 24, 1926 (Dominican Province Teutonia)

Warburg, 1932

Kaplan, Wörishofen, 1933 (supports NSDAP through his pastoral ministry)

mission preacher, Dominican House St. Paulus, Berlin, 1934

Kaplan, St. Joseph's House, Berlin-Reinickendorf

mission preacher, Dominican House, Maria Victoria, Berlin

Kaplan, Wilhelminenhof, Berlin, 1936

Kaplan, Berlin-Südende, St. Anna Institute, 1937

incardinated into Berlin diocese, 1938

Kaplan, Tegel prison, Berlin 1938

died Berlin, July 26, 1939

Source: BArch R5101/22530; Groothuis, *Im Dienste einer überstaatlichen Macht,* 463–65.

Vogl, Theodor

born Munich, April 3, 1902

ordained June 29, 1927 (Munich and Freising)

Aushilfspriester, Grosshadern, July 1927

Kaplan, Oberammergau, September 1927

Koadjutor, Tegernsee, September 1929

prefect, Hansaheime, Munich, May 1930

Hausgeistlicher, St. Alfonsusheim, Munich, December 1930

Katechet, Munich St. Benedikt, November 1933 (supports NSDAP through his pastoral ministry)

left the priesthood (works actively in NSDAP)

married 1941

date of death unknown

Source: EAM NL Faulhaber 5402; *Schematismus München und Freising.*

Vogt, Peter Ferdinand
born Weisnau, September 9, 1876
ordained July 29, 1900 (Eichstätt)
Kaplan, Berngau near Neumarkt, 1900
Schloßgeistlicher, Laudenbach, 1902
Benefiziums-Verweser, Klingenberg, September 1903
Divisionspfarrer, WWI, 1914–1918
Benefiziums-Verweser, Haßfurt and Wonfurt, May 1919
incardinated into Würzburg diocese, March 1921
Benefiziat, Steinsfeld, September 1921
Pfarrer, Eibelstadt, April 1923
Pfarrer, Obertheres, December 1932
joined NSDAP, May 1, 1933, no. 3,434,554
joined SA, February 1, 1934, number unknown
died Schweinfurt, July 30, 1938
Source: DAW Personaldaten; NARA OGK RG242-A3340-MFOK-X076, SAK RG242-A3341-SA-Kartei-291B.

Vriens, Anselmus, O.C.S.O.
born Oirschot (Netherlands), July 4, 1880
ordained December 1, 1907 (Cistercian Order of the Strict Observance)
chaplain, St. Vincent Home, Berlin-Steglitz, October 1926
pastor of Danish and Dutch Catholics in Berlin
director, pro-NSDAP Netherlands' Press Bureau
date of death unknown
Source: BArch B NS 15/475; Volk, *Akten Kardinal Michael von Faulhabers,* 2:340.

Weinschenk, Bernhard
born Falkenberg, April 11, 1892
ordained July 8, 1917 (Strasbourg)
vicar, Bitschweiler, Herlisheim, Bergheim, 1918–1920
Koadjutor, Flintsbach, Olching, 1920–1922
Benefiziumsverweser, Munich, St. Ludwig, May 1922
religion teacher, St. Ursula, Munich, May 1927
Kooperator, Eitting, September 1925
religion teacher, *Fortbildungsschulen,* Munich, May 1926
incardination into Munich and Freising archdiocese, December 1930
Expositus, Jakobsbaiern, March 1931 (supports NSDAP in his pastoral
    ministry)
Pfarrkurat, Tuntenhausen, May 1941
Pfarrer, Mettenheim, September 1944
Pfarrer, Götting, December 1945

voluntary resignation, *Kommorant,* Götting, June 1946
Emeritenbenefiziumsverweser, Landshut, Precious Blood, August 1946
Pfarrer, Margarethenried, June 1947
Pfarrer, Berbling, September 1953
retired and appointed *Kommorant,* Lengdorf, 1963
Kommorant, Tuntenhausen, September 1966
Kommorant, Feilnbach, April 1970
chaplain, *Klostergut* Osterwald, March 1977
Theresianum Nursing Home, Fürstenfeldbruck, 1984–1990
died Fürstenfeldbruck, 1990
Source: AEM Personaldaten; BayHStA NL Schachleiter.

Weis, Jakob
born Ommersheim, 1879
ordained 1901 (Speyer)
chaplain, Zweibrücken prison, 1909
Feldgeistlicher, WWI, 1914–1918
Red Cross delegate, Bucharest, November 1918–May 1920
Pfarrer, Pirmasens, March 1, 1921
doctorate, n.d.
Studienprofessor, Zweibrücken gymnasium, April 1, 1925
supporting member, SS
joined NSLB, July 3, 1933, no. 81,162
V-Mann (informant) for the SD
denazification
died Zweibrücken, 1948
Source: NARA NSLB RG242-A3340-MF-C091; Dierker, *Himmlers Glaubenskrieger,* 367–68; Fandel, *Konfession und Nationalsozialismus,* 500–505.

Welser, Benedikt
born Sulmingen, October 18, 1891
ordained 1921 (Rottenburg)
Kaplan, Ochsenhausen, August 1921
chaplain, Heggbach psychiatric asylum, August 1923
Pfarrverweser, Pommertsweiler, Laubach, 1929–1931
Pfarrer, Walpertshofen, July 1931
religion teacher, Ehingen gymnasium, September 1936
joined NSLB, November 1, 1936, no. 343,372
retired from teaching, June 1943
died April 11, 1978
Source: DAR Personaldaten; NARA NSLB RG242-A3340-MF-C092; Bischöfliches Ordinariat Rottenburg, ed. *Das Verzeichnis der Geistlichen der Diözese Rottenburg-Stuttgart von 1874 bis 1983,* 193.

Willimsky, Karl Marco
born Hindenburg-Biskupitz, Upper Silesia, March 27, 1898
ordained April 23, 1922 (Breslau/Berlin)
Kaplan, Mikultschütz, Berlin-Lichtenberg St. Mauritius, Frankfurt
  (Oder), Berlin-Lichterfelde Holy Family, 1922–1929
Pfarrer, Bergen (Rügen), 1929 (supports NSDAP through his pastoral
  ministry)
Kuratus, Gransee, 1942
took leave, 1947
retired Limburg, 1954
died July 14, 1973
Source: BArch R5101/22277; DAB VI/1 Willimsky.

Wirth, Josef
born Munich, October 8, 1891
studied theology, Canisianum, Innsbruck, 1913–1917
ordained May 27, 1916 (Cistercian, Stams monastery)
medic, WWI, August 1917
Feldgeistlicher, August 1918
Kooperator, Sautens, March 1919
expelled from Cistercian Order Stams monastery, August 1921
returned to parents' home in Munich, 1921
civil servant, *Finanzamt* (Internal Revenue Office) Munich II,
  September 1922–April 1925
entered Benedictine Ettal monastery, April 1925 (stayed until July
  1927)
chaplain, Mercy Brothers, Neuburg, October–December 1927
chaplain, Franciscan Sisters, Wittibsmühl near Moosburg, December
  1927–June 1930
incardinated into diocese of Berlin, 1930
Kaplan, Berlin St. Bonifatius, June 1930–September 1932
Hausgeistlicher, St. Josefsheim, Berlin, September 1932–May 1933
Kurat, Treptow, May 1933–December 1935
Pfarrer, Treptow, December 1935–1939
V-Mann (informant) for Gestapo
joined NSDAP, 1936
Berlin diocese suspended faculties after mass stipend scandal, 1944
Berlin diocese ordered him to Springborn penal monastery, East Prus-
  sia, May 1939–January 1940
"Christkönighaus" (Catholic boarding house), 1940–early 1942
Pension Schunke, Berlin-Schöneberg, early 1942–December 1942

lived with friends, Berlin, December 1942–August 1944
moved to diocese of Regensburg, Alteglofsheim, August 1944
denazification, December 9, 1946, classified as criminal (category 1),
   sentenced to five years' work camp
internment and work camp, Regensburg, November 1946–June 1948
Berlin diocese renewed suspension of faculties, April 1947
denazification appeal, February 17, 1949, category reduced to
   follower (category 4)
died January 13, 1956
Source: BZAR PA 4250 Wirth, PA 4269 Wirth.

Wolf, Edgar

born Ratibor-Plania, August 28, 1882
ordained June 22, 1907 (Breslau)
Kaplan, Rauden, Liegnitz, 1907–1910
religion teacher, Royal Catholic Teacher Training College,
   Preiskretscham, April 1910
Pfarrer, Markowitz, March 5, 1912
DNVP, Reichstag representative, Catholic division, 1922–1929
Pfarrer, Benkowitz, June 1932
joined NSDAP, May 1, 1933, no. 2,288,070
Pfarrer, Schnwald, April 1934
died interment camp, Schwientochlowitz, August 1945
Source: NARA OGK RG242-A3340-MFOK-Z038; *Schematismus Breslau; The Tablet,*
"German Priests and the Nazi Party."

Würzburger, Wilhelm

born Külsheim, January 2, 1870
ordained July 30, 1893 (Bamberg)
Kaplan, Königsfeld, Auerbach, Döringstadt, Viereth-Trunstadt, Sein-
   sheim, 1893–1896
Kuratus, Bellershausen, Mönchherrnsdorf, 1896–1900
Pfarrverweser, Herzogenaurach, December 1900
Pfarrer, Kleukheim, December 1905 (supports NSDAP through pastoral
   ministry)
retired October 1, 1936
Kommorant, Würzburg
Kommorant, Külsheim
died September 28, 1950
Source: AEB Personaldaten; BArch R5101/21675; Breuer, *Verordneter Wandel?,* 47,
66–68, 339.

Zeimet, Johann Kornelius

born Trier, August 19, 1890
ordained August 1, 1914 (Trier)
Kaplan, Ahrweiler, 1914–1915
director, Helenenberg; rector, Cochem hospital; Franziska-Stift, Bad
   Kreuznach, 1915–1920
Kaplan, Daun, April 1920
Pfarrvikar, Namedy, 1923
doctorate, University of Würzburg, February 1928
Pfarrer, Münster near Bingen, January 1932
Dozent, Teacher Training College, Trier, 1936
Professor, Koblenz, February 1938
joined NSDAP, May 1, 1933, no. 3,441,956
joined NSLB, April 1, 1937, no. 351,383
left priesthood and Catholic Church, 1941
married 1941
joined Old-Catholic Church, active as *Dozent* and *Pfarrer*
reconciled with the Catholic Church shortly before his death
died Karlsruhe, July 9, 1979

Source: BAT Personaldaten; NARA OGK RG242-A3340-MFOK-Z070, NSLB RG242-A3340-MF-C106; Persch, "Der Diözesanklerus und die neuen pastoralen Laienberufe," 211–12.

Zenger, Wolfgang

born Weiden, December 20, 1896
doctorate (history), University of Würzburg, November 9, 1921
ordained June 24, 1928 (Bamberg)
Kaplan, Hof, August 1928
granted leave, December 1928
Kaplan, Bühl, March 1929
Pfarrverweser, Giech, September 1929
Kaplan, Rothenkirchen, Auerbach, 1929–1931
Kurat, Kirchenbirkig, Hohenberg, 1931–1935
joined NSLB, July 1, 1933, no. 48,960
joined NSDAP, May 5, 1935, no. 3,663,128
Kuratus, Rehau, November 1935
Stadtpfarrer, Rehau, October 1938
Pfarrer, Hersbruck, July 1941
named *Geistlicher Rat,* December 1963
died April 25, 1972

Source: BArch B NSLB; NSPK; NARA NSPK RG-A3340-PK-A019 (Johann Albrecht), OGK RG242-A3340-MFOK-Z073; Spindler to Denzler, December 27, 1983 (copy in possession of author); Breuer, *Verordneter Wandel?*, 244, 339–40.

Notes

Introduction

1. In 1930 the NSDAP went from 12 (2.6% of the vote) to 107 (18.3% of the vote) Reichstag delegates. Kirk, *Longman Companion to Nazi Germany*, 22.

2. Haeuser, *Kampfgeist gegen Pharisäertum*, 5.

3. Murphy to Matthews, May 23, 1945, NARA RG84, box 1.

4. Ziegler, "Die deutschen katholischen Bischöfe"; and Bendel-Maidl and Bendel, "Schlaglichter auf den Umgang der deutschen Bischöfe."

5. Phayer, *Catholic Church and the Holocaust*, 133–83; and Brown-Fleming, *Holocaust and Catholic Conscience*.

6. Neuhäusler, *Kreuz und Hakenkreuz.*

7. Böckenförde, "Der deutsche Katholizismus im Jahre 1933"; and Lewy, *Catholic Church and Nazi Germany.*

8. Spicer, *Resisting the Third Reich*, 161, 164–65.

9. Lenz, *Der katholische Geistliche im weltlichen Recht,* esp. 7–15.

10. *Amtsblatt des Bischöflichen Ordinariats Berlin,* September 22, 1933, 73–74.

11. Dierker, *Himmlers Glaubenskrieger.*

12. Priests who supported the movement were sometimes referred to as "brown Father" or "brown pastor" *(braune Pfarrer)*. At times, opponents of the Hitler party used the term "brown" to identify those who supported or were members of the NSDAP. Fandel, *Konfession und Nationalsozialismus*, 479–89.

13. Childers, *Nazi Voter*, 262–69; and Merkl, *Political Violence under the Swastika.*

14. May, *Kirchenkampf oder Katholikenverfolgung?*, 309.

15. SD-Bericht, c. 1936/1937, BArch B R58/5237, ff. 9–10.

16. Kerrl to Goebbels, November 21, 1935, BArch B R5101/22314.

17. Greive, *Theologie und Ideologie,* 41, 76; and Breuning, *Die Vision des Reiches,* 21.

18. Wagener, "Unterdrückungs- und Verfolgungsmaßnahmen," 56.

19. Cardinal Bertram's Hirtenbrief, January 1, 1931; Kundgebung der Fuldaer Bischofskonferenz, March 28, 1933, in Müller, *Katholische Kirche und Nationalsozialismus,* 15–21, 76–78; and Kaller, *Unser Laienapostolat,* 264–67.

20. Spicer, *Resisting the Third Reich,* 120–38.

21. Müller, *Katholische Kirche und Nationalsozialismus,* 21–37.

22. Zentralstelle des Volksvereins für das katholische Deutschland, ed., *Der Nationalsozialismus und die deutschen Katholiken.*

23. Steigmann-Gall, *Holy Reich,* esp. 13–50.

24. Heilbronner and Mühlberger, "Achilles' Heel of German Catholicism."

25. Anderson, "Kulturkampf," 82–115; Griech-Polelle, *Bishop von Galen,* 23–41; Gross, *War against Catholicism;* Krieg, *Catholic Theologians in Nazi Germany,* 21–27; Martin, *Der katholische Weg ins Reich;* Repgen, "Christen im Widerstand"; Spicer, *Resisting the Third Reich,* 18–19.

26. *Katholisches Kirchenblatt für das Bistum Berlin,* June 12, 1932; and Notiz Gröbers, n.d., EBAF B2/NS 51.

27. *Kölnische Volkszeitung,* March 29, 1933, BArch B R5101/21675, f. 108.

28. The Vatican did sign concordats with the German state governments of Bavaria (1924), Prussia (1929), and Baden (1932). Coppa, ed., *Controversial Concordats;*

Hughes, "Reich Concordat 1933"; Rhodes, *Vatican in the Age of the Dictators;* Volk, *Das Reichskonkordat vom 20. Juli 1933;* and Zeender, "Genesis of the German Concordat of 1933."

29. Münch, ed., *Gesetze des NS-Staates,* 79–82; Frei, *National Socialist Rule in Germany,* 83–90; and Krausnick et al., *Anatomy of the SS State.*

30. Baumgärtner, *Weltanschauungs-Kampf im Dritten Reich;* and Burkard, *Häresie und Mythus des 20. Jahrhunderts.*

31. Kershaw, *'Hitler Myth,'* 105–20.

32. Gründer, "Rechtskatholizismus im Kaiserreich"; and Jones, "Catholic Conservatives," and "Franz von Papen."

33. SD-Bericht, c. 1936/1937, BArch B R58/5237, ff. 5–7, 10.

34. Bergen, *Twisted Cross,* 7.

35. Banki and Pawlikowski, eds., *Ethics in the Shadow of the Holocaust;* Baum, *Is the New Testament Anti-Semitic?,* and *Christian Theology after Auschwitz;* Bergen, "Catholics, Protestants, and Antisemitism," 329–48; Carroll, *Constantine's Sword;* Dietrich, *God and Humanity in Auschwitz;* Flannery, *Anguish of the Jews;* Greive, *Theologie und Ideologie;* Hürten, *Deutsche Katholiken,* 425–40; Littell, *Crucifixion of the Jews;* Nicholls, *Christian Antisemitism;* Reuther, *Faith and Fratricide;* Spicer, ed., *Antisemitism, Christian Ambivalence, and the Holocaust;* and Tal, *Christians and Jews in Germany.*

36. Kertzer, *Popes against the Jews.*

37. Commission for Religious Relations with the Jews, *We Remember;* and Benedict XVI, "Pope's Address in Synagogue of Cologne."

1—Adapting Catholic Teaching to Nazi Ideology

1. Third Army Report, May–June 1945, in Ziemke, *U.S. Army in the Occupation of Germany,* 147, 380–81.

2. Schmidt to Informationsoffizier, n.d., EAM NL Faulhaber 8552.

3. Lortz, *Katholischer Zugang;* and Schmaus, *Begegnungen zwischen katholischem Christentum.*

4. Adam, "Theologisches Volkstum," *Theologische Quartalschrift* 114 (1933): 40–63, and pt. 2 (unpublished), DAR N67/34.

5. Recker, *"Wem wollt ihr glauben?"* 59–63.

6. Berning, *Katholische Kirche und deutsches Volkstum.*

7. Recker, *"Wem wollt ihr glauben?"* 89–92.

8. Heydrich to Rosenberg, April 8, 1935, BArch B NS 8/150, f. 195.

9. Helmreich, *German Churches under Hitler,* 246.

10. *Das Deutsche Führerlexikon 1934/35,* 32, USAMHI, Donovan Papers, box 37B.

11. Preysing to the Fulda Bishops' Conference, May 31, 1933, in Stasiewski, ed., *Akten deutscher Bischöfe,* 1:238.

12. *Württemberg Zeitung,* January 10, 1934, BArch B NS 8/256, f. 79.

13. Babel to Ordinariat Freiburg, April 17, 1946; Gröber to Babel, June 7, 1946, EBAF B2/NS10; Gröber to Governor, July 6, 1945, EBAF B2/NS51; Buchheim, "Fördernde Mitgliedschaft bei der SS."

14. *AKD Mitteilungsblatt,* 1 (November 22, 1933), BArch B NS 8/130.

15. Bertram to Praschma, November 13, 1933, DAR G1.5/138.

16. *Kölnische Volkszeitung,* April 27, 1933; quoted in Schwalbach, *Erzbischof Conrad Gröber,* 38.

17. Erlaß Gröbers, June 28, 1933, in Müller, *Katholische Kirche und Nationalsozialismus,* 167.

18. See *Pastoralblatt des Bistums Eichstätt,* June 27, 1933, insert; and *Würzburger Diözesanblatt,* July 6, 1933, insert.

19. Rede Gröbers, October 10, 1933, in Müller, *Katholische Kirche und National-sozialismus,* 207.

20. Schwalbach, *Erzbischof Conrad Gröber,* 65–78.

21. Hürten, *Deutsche Briefe,* 2:797–798; Maier, *Schulkampf in Baden,* 123–24; and Weis, *Würden und Bürden,* 113–14.

22. Pohl to Himmler, January 19, 1938, and SS-Gruppenführer to Pohl, January 29, 1938, NARA RG242 T580, reel 42.

23. *Germania,* June 26, 1933.

24. *Germania,* September 18, 1933.

25. NSDAP Groß-Berlin Gaupropagandaleitung to Reichskanzlei, August 23, 1933, BArch B R43 II/174, f. 85; and Kupper, ed., *Staatliche Akten,* 346 n.3.

26. Vetter sermon, Cologne, July 4, 1937, PArcK, PA Vetter.

27. *Mainzer Anzeiger,* November 16, 1940; reported in SD-Bericht, Darmstadt, November 21, 1940, BArch B BA R58/5809, f. 116.

28. Hartl/SD Berlin to SS Berlin, December 12, 1940, BArch B BA R58/5809, f. 115.

29. Kershaw, *Hitler 1889–1936: Hubris,* 590.

30. Spruchkammer Aichach to Minister für Sonderaufgaben München, June 14, 1948, BayHStA MSo 1413.

31. Erklärung Schultes zur Abstimmung, March 19, 1936, in Stasiewski, *Akten Deutscher Bischöfe,* 3:303.

32. *Amper Bote,* November 20, 1934, EAM, PA-P III 1316 Pfanzelt; and Pfanzelt to Burk, February 25, 1946, BayHStA MSo 1413.

33. Erklärung Ludwig Wirth, April 21, 1948, EAM, PA-P III 1316 Pfanzelt.

34. NSDAP Kreisleiter Dachau to Bayerisches Staatsministerium für Unterricht und Kultus, October 24, 1934, EAM, PA-P III 1316 Pfanzelt.

35. Schober Berichte, July 6 and 19, 1934, BayHStA MK 38287.

36. Pfanzelt to Ordinariat München, October 24, 1934, BayHStA MK 38287; Müller to Hagenauer, July 19, 1948; Klageschrift Pfanzelt, June 14, 1948; Haaser to Spruchkammer Dachau, July 21, 1948; Haaser to Bayerisches Staatsministerium für Sonderaufgaben, July 27, 1948, BayHStA MSo 1413.

37. *Dachauer Zeitung,* January 19 and 20, 1932; and *Amper Bote,* January 22, 1932, EAM, PA-P III 1316 Pfanzelt.

38. Pfanzelt to Generalvikar, January 22, 1932, EAM, PA-P III 1316 Pfanzelt.

39. Pfanzelt to Ordinariat München, May 3, 1949, EAM, PA-P III 1316 Pfanzelt.

40. Krose, *Kirchliches Handbuch,* 21, 291.

41. "Land Baden: List of clergymen indicating political reliability." Nazi Party records, 1937–38, NARA RG 260, box 171.

42. Hehl, *Priester unter Hitlers Terror,* 599–661; and EBAF PA Baumann, Beugel, Gütle, Hettich, Kirchgessner, Krems, Lehrmann, Marbe, Reisterer, Uihlein, and Winkel.

43. Baumann, Gütle, and Lehrmann, EBAF PA.

44. Beugel, Frei, Krems, and Uihlein, EBAF PA.

45. Assorted correspondence, EBAF PA Riesterer.

46. Jahresbericht 1936, January 20, 1937, EBAF PA Riegelsberger.

47. Benz to Gröber, October 15, 1940, EBAF PA Riegelsberger.

48. Dreher to Gröber, April 3, 1936, EBAF PA Sigi.

49. NSDAP Ortsgruppenleiter to Gröber, April 9, 1936, EBAF PA Sigi.

50. Hirt (Ordinariatsrat) Bericht, April 16, 1936, EBAF PA Sigi.

51. Dreher to Ordinariat Freiburg, June 17, 1936, EBAF PA Sigi.

52. Obituary, *Konradsblatt,* September 15, 1963, EBAF PA Sigi.

53. Baumann, Bleichroth, Gihr, Haas, Henn, Hettich, Hofmann, Market, Öchsler, Sigi, Spitzmüller, Voegelbacher, and Winkel, EBAF PA.

54. Beck, Ebner, Lehrmann, and Schaak, EBAF PA.

55. Aktennotiz, January 1941, EBAF PA Riesterer.

56. Schweizer to Ordinariat Freiburg, July 4, 1940, EBAF PA Schweizer.

57. Senn, *Katholizismus und Nationalsozialismus,* 58, 61, *Halt! Katholizismus und Nationalsozialismus,* and "Das Komplott des Schweigens."

2—In the Trenches for Hitler

1. *Völkischer Beobachter,* Munich ed., April 12, 1933.

2. Sandkuhl to Staebe, April 12, 1933, BArch R58/5994/A1, f. 507.

3. Sandkuhl, NSZK, BArch B.

4. Staebe to Sacher, April 20, 1933, BArch R58/5994/A1, f. 508.

5. Huber to Staebe, n.d., BArch R58/5994/A1, f. 517.

6. Bormann to Lammers, April 30, 1940, BArch B R58/5809, f. 86.

7. Anderson, *Windthorst: A Political Biography;* Blackbourn, *Class, Religion, and Local Politics;* Evans, *German Center Party;* Gross, *War against Catholicism;* Lepper, ed. *Volk, Kirche und Vaterland;* and Morsey, *Die deutsche Zentrumspartei.*

8. Neumann, *Die Parteien der Weimarer Republik;* and Stachura, *Political Leaders in Weimar Germany.*

9. Rösch, *Die Münchner NSDAP.*

10. Allen, *Nazi Seizure of Power;* Bergerson, *Ordinary Germans in Extraordinary Times;* Grill, *Nazi Movement in Baden;* and Rinderle and Norling, *Nazi Impact on a German Village.*

11. Kershaw, *Hitler 1889–1936: Hubris,* 189, 259.

12. Jablonsky, *Nazi Party in Dissolution;* and Kershaw, *Hitler 1889–1936,* 223–53.

13. Cancik and Puschner, eds., *Antisemitismus, Paganismus, Völkische Religion;* Puschner, *Handbuch zur 'völkischen Bewegung' 1871–1918;* Puschner, *Die völkische Bewegung im wilhelminischen Kaiserreich;* and Schmitz and Vollnhals, eds., *Völkische Bewegung, konservative Revolution, Nationalsozialismus.*

14. Kershaw, *Hitler 1889–1936,* 238–39, 262–63.

15. Huber to Staebe, n.d., BArch R58/5994/A1, f. 517.

16. In the 1928 election the NSDAP received 2.6 percent of the vote. In 1930 this increased to 18.3 percent. Kirk, *Longman Companion to Nazi Germany,* 22.

17. "Winke betr. Aufgaben der Seelsorger," in Corsten, ed. *Sammlung kirchlicher Erlasse,* 619–24.

18. "Zur Frage einer Stellungnahme," in *Verordnungen des Fürstbischöflichen Ordinariats in Breslau,* March 5, 1924; and Vogel, *Katholische Kirche und nationale Kampfverbände,* 50–52.

19. "NSDAP Party Platform," in Noakes and Pridham, eds., *Nazism,* l:16.

20. Scholder, *Churches and the Third Reich,* 1:88–98; and Rißmann, *Hitlers Gott,* 34–40.

21. *Völkischer Beobachter,* May 20–21, 1923; and Hastings, "How 'Catholic' Was the Early Nazi Movement?" 403–4.

22. *Vörwarts,* July 11, 1923.

23. Held to Faulhaber, October 6, 1923, in Volk, *Akten Kardinal Michael von Faulhabers,* 1:315.

24. *Völkischer Beobachter,* August 12/13, 1923.

25. "Dr. Ottokar Kernstock, ein völkischer Priester," newspaper clipping, n.d., n.p., AAK NL Pieper.

26. Grollegg-Edler, *Die wehrhaft Nachtigall Ottokar Kernstock,* 139–48; Liebmann, "Ottokar Kernstock, der missbrauchte Dichter," 389–93; Liebmann, "Ottokar Kernstock, Gefeierter," 26–35; and Roschnik, *Die nationale Gefühls- und Gedankenwelt.*

27. Bayerische Benediktinerakademie, ed., *Bibliographie der deutschsprachigen Benediktiner 1880–1980,* 412–13.

28. Conradi, *Hitler's Piano Player.*

29. Hanfstaengl, *Zwischen Weißem und Braunem Haus,* 107–8; Hanfstaengl, *Unknown Hitler,* 87; and Hastings, "How Catholic Was the Early Nazi Movement?" 403.

30. Hanfstaengl, *Zwischen Weißem und Braunem Haus,* 107–8.

31. Hanfstaengl, *Unknown Hitler,* 87.

32. "Zum Stammbaum der Familie Schachleiter," BArch NS26/1323; and Schmid-Egger, *Klerus und Politik in Böhmen um 1900.*

33. Smith, *German Nationalism and Religious Conflict,* 206–32.

34. Weissenberger, *Das Benediktinische Mönchtum,* 71–72.

35. Cohen, *Politics of Ethnic Survival;* and Šebek, "Die Äbte Alban Schachleiter OSB," 31–32.

36. *Kölnische Volkszeitung,* July 7 and 9, 1923, BArch B NS 26/1323.

37. Rehberger, "Die Stifte Oberösterreichs unter dem Hakenkreuz," 245.

38. Weissenberger, *Das Benediktinische Mönchtum,* 87; and Haering, "Kirchenrechtliche Marginalien zum Fall Schachleiter," 947.

39. "Apostolisches Breve," March 21, 1921, EAM NL Faulhaber 5537; and Weissenberger, *Das Benediktinische Mönchtum,* 88.

40. Heiden, *Führer,* 305; and Kershaw, *Hitler 1889–1936,* 242, 515–16.

41. Hoffmann, *Hitler was my friend,* 52; Hanfstaengl, *Unknown Hitler,* 142; and Phelps, "'Before Hitler Came,'" 255.

42. *Völkischer Beobachter,* November 4/5 and 7, 1923, BayHStA NL Stempfle 6.

43. Stempfle to Pfeiffer, September 21, 1929, BayHStA NL Stempfle 5.

44. Stempfle's invitation to Thanksgiving mass, November 20, 1904, LofCong Prints and Photographs Division, lot 3983 G.; and Stempfle to Pfeiffer, September 21, 1929, BayHStA NL Stempfle 5.

45. Heimbucher, *Die Orden und Kongregationen der katholischen Kirche,* 2:660.

46. Stempfle to Pfeiffer, September 21, 1929, BayHStA NL Stempfle 5.

47. Apostolic visit report, September 15–30, 1932, ACIVC.

48. *Deutsche Presse,* May 7, 1924, BayHStA PrASlgRehse 235 and *Neue Zeitung,* January 23, 1926, BayHStA NL Stempfle 6, identified him as "Pater Stempfle."

49. *Augsburger Postzeitung,* February 19, 1920, addressed him as "Herr Gymnasialprofessor Dr. Stempfle," BayHStA NL Stempfle 5.

50. In 1918 Stempfle did produce a twenty-four-page study entitled *De Scriptis Editis Doctoris Philisophiae Maximiliani Fastlinger Monacensis,* which is primarily a bibliography of the works of Father Max Fastlinger, priest and archivist of the Munich and Freising archdiocese.

51. *Münchener Post,* October 20, 1926, BayHStA PrASlgRehse 235, refers to Stempfle as "ex-priest."

52. Stempfle to Girolamo, March 20, 1932, BayHStA NL Stempfle 5.

53. *Mühldorfer Tageblatt,* January 8, 1919, BayHStA NL Stempfle 6.

54. *Freilassinger Zeitung,* February 12, 1919; and *Reichenhaller Grenzbote,* February 15, 1919, BayHStA NL Stempfle 6.

55. "Gedenktag," BayHStA NL Stempfle 8.

56. Franz, "Munich: Birthplace and Center," 332.

57. Stempfle, press release, n.d., BayHStA NL Stempfle 8.

58. "Der Fall Stempfle," newspaper article, n.d., n.p., BayHStA PrASlgRehse 235.

59. *Miesbacher Anzeiger,* November 12, 1922, BayHStA PrASlgRehse 235; and *Münchener Beobachter,* August 16, 1919, BayHStA NL Stempfle 6.

60. *Völkischer Beobachter,* November 20, 1919, BayHStA NL Stempfle 6.

61. Huber to his parents, June 28, 1912, ABA PA 1467 Huber.

62. "Sacrorum Antistitum," in *Acta Apostolicae Sedis* (1910), 2:669–692; and *American Catholic Quarterly Review* 35 (1910): 712–731.

63. Widmann to Bettinger, September 22, 1913, ABA PA 1467 Huber.

64. *Miesbacher Anzeiger,* October 9 and 10, 1919, ABA PA 1467 Huber.
65. *Schematismus Augsburg* 1932, 271; and Huber to Ordinariat Munich and Freising, August 25, 1921, ABA PA 1467 Huber.
66. Excardination letter, February 17, 1922, EAM PA Huber.
67. Huber to Buchberger, December 9, 1921; and Vequel to Niedermair, December 11, 1921, ABA PA 1467 Huber.
68. Mitteilung des Bezirksamtes Memmingen to Regierung von Schwaben, September 1923, ABA PA 1467 Huber.
69. Hoser, "Hitler und die katholische Kirche," 475.
70. Ibid., 475–478.
71. Ibid., 478–479.
72. Ibid., 478 n.52.
73. Mitteilung des Bezirksamtes Memmingen to Regierung von Schwaben, September 1923, ABA PA 1467 Huber.
74. Hoser, "Hitler und die katholische Kirche," 479.
75. Brandl, "Josef Roth," 742.
76. SA-Führer Fragebogen, June 15, 1935, BArch SAPA Roth.
77. Jones, *Brief History;* Koch, *Der deutsche Bürgerkrieg;* and Waite, *Vanguard of Nazism.*
78. Roth, "X Jahre Reichskonkordat," BArch K NL 898 Roth.
79. Brandl, "Josef Roth," 742.
80. *Völkischer Beobachter,* June 6, 7, and 8, 1923.
81. Roth, *Katholizismus und Judenfrage,* 2, 4, 6.
82. Ibid., 10.
83. Ibid., 8, 11.
84. Mitteilung "Josef Roth," September 10, 1941, EAM NL Faulhaber 7269.
85. Bleistein, "'Überläufer im Sold der Kirchenfeinde,'" 74–75.
86. Brunnert, *Vielfalt des Lebens,* 19, 23.
87. Heitzer, *Der Volksverein für das katholische Deutschland im Kaiserreich;* and Klein, *Der Volksverein für das katholische Deutschland 1890–1933.*
88. Brunnert, *Vielfalt des Lebens,* 21–23.
89. Tröster, "'. . . die besondere Eigenart des Herrn Dr. Pieper!'" 46.
90. Brunnert, *Vielfalt des Lebens,* 48.
91. Pieper diary, November 15, 1918, AAK NL Pieper.
92. Pieper diary, November 24, 1919, AAK NL Pieper.
93. Ganyard, *Rebels and Revolutionaries;* Schlund, *Neugermanisches Heidentum,* 50; Wolf, *Die Enstehung des Jungdeutschen Ordens, Der Jungdeutsche Orden in seinen mittleren Jahren, 1922–1925,* vol. 1, and *Der Jungdeutsche Orden in seinen mittleren Jahren, 1925–1928,* vol 2.
94. Pieper diary, July 23, 1921, and June 22, 1922, AAK NL Pieper.
95. Pieper diary, February 21, 1922, AAK NL Pieper.
96. Pieper diary, July 26, 1922, AAK NL Pieper.
97. Lohalm, *Völkischer Radikalimsus,* 246–51.
98. Pieper diary, August 16, 1922, AAK NL Pieper.
99. Pieper diary, October 8, 1922, AAK NL Pieper.
100. Pieper diary, October 25, 1922, AAK NL Pieper.
101. Pieper diary, November 9. 1922, AAK NL Pieper.
102. Pieper diary, November 16, 1922, AAK NL Pieper.
103. Pieper diary, August 16, 1922, AAK NL Pieper.
104. *Miesbacher Anzeiger,* January 18, 1923, BayHStA NL Stempfle 6.
105. Haerendel, ed., *München—"Hauptstadt der Bewegung,"* esp. 105–17; and Large, *Where Ghosts Walked.*
106. Fischer, *Ruhr Crisis.*
107. Baird, *To Die for Germany,* 13–40.

108. Ordinariat Munich to Schachleiter, September 15, 1922, in Engelhard, *Abt Schachleiter*, 35.

109. Hanfstaengl, *Zwischen Weißem und Braunem Haus*, 108–9, and *Unknown Hitler*, 88–89.

110. *Völkischer Beobachter*, June 12, 1923.

111. Hinkel, *Einer unter Hunderttausend*, 99.

112. *Völkischer Beobachter*, June 12, 1923.

113. *Völkischer Beobachter*, July 10, 1923.

114. *National-Zeitung*, September 30, 1934.

115. Tröster, "'. . . die besondere Eigenart des Herrn Dr. Pieper!'" 54; and Vogel, *Katholische Kirche und nationale Kampfverbände*, 58.

116. Pieper diary, July 5, 1923, and August 9, 1923, AAK NL Pieper; *Völkischer Beobachter*, August 1, 26/27, 28, 1923.

117. *Völkischer Beobachter*, August 24, 1923.

118. Bericht of the City Police Bureau, Nuremberg-Fürth, September 18, 1923, in Deuerlein, ed., *Der Hitler-Putsch*, 170; "Der Deutsche Tag in Nürnberg," *Bayern und Reich*, n.d., BArch K NL 898 Roth; and Kershaw, *Hitler 1889–1936*, 199.

119. Bericht of the City Police Bureau, Nuremberg-Fürth, September 18, 1923, in Deuerlein, ed., *Der Hitler-Putsch*, 170.

120. "Fahneneide der Wehrbereiten," *Bayern und Reich*, September 4, 1923, BArch K NL 898 Roth 1.

121. "Der Deutsche Tag in Nürnberg," *Bayern und Reich*, n.d., BArch K NL 898 Roth 1.

122. Kershaw, *Hitler 1889–1936*, 205–19.

123. Pieper diary, November 10, 1923, AAK NL Pieper.

124. Tröster, "'. . . die besondere Eigenart des Herrn Dr. Pieper!'" 54; and Vogel, *Katholische Kirche und nationale Kampfverbände*, 58.

125. "Winke betr. Aufgaben der Seelsorger" and "Stellung der Kirche," in Corsten, *Sammlung kirchlicher Erlasse*, 619–625.

126. "Zur Frage einer Stellungnahme," in *Verordnungen des Fürstbischöflichen Ordinariats in Breslau*, March 5, 1924.

127. Vogel, *Katholische Kirche und nationale Kampfverbände*, 75.

128. Ibid., 126–34, 144; and Kreutzer, *Das Reichskirchenministerium*, 172 n.321.

129. Pieper, OGK BArch B.

130. Vogel, *Katholische Kirche und nationale Kampfverbände*, 165.

131. November 4 and 13, 1925, Pieper diary, AAK NL Pieper.

132. May 20, 1928, Pieper diary, AAK NL Pieper.

133. Hoser, "Hitler und die katholische Kirche," 479–480.

134. Hanfstaengl, *Unknown Hitler*, 142; and Heiden, *Hitler: A Biography*, 193.

135. *Bayerischer Kurier*, November 13, 1925; and *Neue Zeitung*, January 23, 1926, BayHStA NL Stempfle 6.

136. *Münchener Zeitung*, February 3–4, 1932, BayHStA PrASlgRehse 235; and Heiden, *Führer*, 305.

137. Various correspondence Kanzler and Stempfle, June–July 1932, BayHStA NL Stempfle 3.

138. NSDAP Reichsleitung Munich, Amt für Rechtsverwaltung, to Bayerisches Staatsministerium des Innern, June 21, 1937, EAM PA Müller.

139. Roßteuscher to Neuhäusler, April 14, 1948, ABA PA 926 Müller.

140. Bergen, *Twisted Cross*, 61–81; and Padberg, "Reinhard Heydrich und das Beichtgeheimnis."

141. Roßteuscher to Neuhäusler, April 14, 1948, ABA PA 926 Müller.

142. Various correspondence and trial verdicts, ABA PA 926 Müller and EAM PA Müller.

143. Engelhard, *Abt Schachleiter*, 37.

144. *Münchener Neueste Nachrichten*, March 27, 1926, EAM NL Faulhaber 5936.

145. Faulhaber to Geschäftsstelle des Priestervereins Pax, Cologne, May 3, 1926, EAM NL Faulhaber 5936.

146. *Völkischer Beobachter*, April 9, 1926.

147. Faulhaber to Schachleiter, June 11, 1927, EAM NL Faulhaber 5537.

148. Schachleiter to Faulhaber, June 15, 1927, EAM NL Faulhaber 5537.

149. Protokoll der Konferenz des bayerischen Episkopats, September 10–11, 1929, in Volk, *Akten Kardinal Michael von Faulhabers*, 1:473; and Munro, *Hitler's Bavarian Antagonist*, 211–13.

150. Faulhaber to Schachleiter, September 16, 1929, EAM NL Faulhaber 5537.

151. Protokoll der Konferenz des bayerischen Episkopats, September 10–11, 1929, in Volk, *Akten Kardinal Michael von Faulhabers*, 1:473.

152. Faulhaber to Walzer, September 16, 1930, EAM NL Faulhaber 5537.

153. Engelhard, *Abt Schachleiter*, 37.

154. Faulhaber to Walzer, September 16, 1930, EAM NL Faulhaber 5537.

155. Faulhaber to Vassallo, February 14, 1931, EAM PA Schachleiter.

156. *Völkischer Beobachter*, January 21, 1931; and *München-Augsburger Abendzeitung*, January 19, 1931.

157. Faulhaber to Nuncio Vassallo, February 14, 1931, EAM PA Schachleiter.

158. Heuschkel to NSDAP Ortsgruppe Feilnbach, January 7, 1933, BArch B NSPK Schachleiter.

159. Faulhaber to Bishop Gföllner, February 4, 1933, EAM NL Faulhaber 5539.

160. Various correspondence, BArch B NSPK Schachleiter.

161. Zach to Faulhaber, January 22, 1931, EAM NL Faulhaber 5537.

162. Faulhaber to Zach, February 16, 1931, EAM NL Faulhaber 5537.

163. Zach to Faulhaber, April 8, 1932, EAM NL Faulhaber 5537; and Gendarmerie Station Feilnbach to Bezirksamt Aibling, April 6, 1932, EAM PA Schachleiter.

164. Flugblatt zur Präsidentenwahl, Easter Sunday 1932, in Engelhard, *Abt Schachleiter*, 89–90.

165. Ordinariat Munich to Schachleiter, April 19, 1932, EAM NL Faulhaber 5537.

166. Schachleiter to Hindringer, May 17, 1932; and Mitteilung, June 15, 1932, EAM NL Faulhaber 5537.

167. Apostolisches Breve, Benedict XV to Schachleiter, March 21, 1921, in Engelhard, *Abt Schachleiter*, 84–85.

168. Faulhaber to Schachleiter, June 24, 1932, EAM PA Schachleiter.

169. Schachleiter Entwurf, August 1932; and Roth to Schachleiter, August 10, 1932, BArch B NS 26/1324.

170. Schachleiter to Faulhaber, February 5, 1933, EAM NL Faulhaber 5539.

171. Schachleiter to Hitler, October 6, 1932, BArch NS26/1323.

172. Rösch, *Die Münchener NSDAP*, 171.

173. *Warmia*, March 3, 1925, EAM NL Faulhaber 7269.

174. Roth, "Für Gott und Vaterland," 9, 12, 14–16.

175. *Warmia*, March 3, 1925, EAM NL Faulhaber 7269.

176. Roth, "Katholischer Pazifismus."

177. Roth, "Der Weg der Frontsoldaten."

178. Haeuser, "Mein deutsches Ringen und Werden," StA Kempten, NL Haeuser, 178.

179. "Katholizismus und Judenfrage," *Antisemitische Zeitung*, February 8, 1929.

180. Deutsche Liga für Menschenrechte to Faulhaber, March 20, 1929, EAM NL Faulhaber 7090.

181. Hindringer to Roth, April 4, 1929, EAM NL Faulhaber 7269.

182. Roth to Hindringer, April 5, 1929, EAM NL Faulhaber 7269.

183. Hindringer to Deutsche Liga für Menschenrechte, April 15, 1929, EAM NL Faulhaber 7090.
184. Roth, "Gedanken zum Münchener Stahlhelmtag," 117.
185. Roth, "Feminismus im öffentlichen Leben der Gegenwart," 442–445.

3—The Old Fighters under Hitler's Rule

1. Huber to Kumpfmüller, August 30, 1936, ABA PA 1467 Huber.
2. Gött to Hitler, December 4, 1926, in Wagner, *Simmerberg*, 76–78.
3. Hitler to Gött, February 4, 1927, in Hoser, "Hitler und die katholische Kirche," 486–87.
4. Gött to Hitler, February 10, 1927, in Wagner, *Simmerberg*, 80.
5. Hitler to Gött, March 2, 1927, in Hoser, "Hitler und die katholische Kirche," 487–88.
6. Hoser, "Hitler und die katholische Kirche," 481.
7. Stempfle, *Staatsanwalt!*, esp. 21–22, 27–28, 31–32.
8. BArch B NSPK Stempfle; Heiden, *Hitler: A Biography*, 384, and *Führer*, 308.
9. "Vorgänge vor dem Tod des Professors B. Stempfle," 1934, LofCong 3983G.
10. Heiden, *Führer*, 304–8.
11. Waffenschein, March 6, 1930, BArch B SAPA Huber.
12. Ordinariat Augsburg to Bayerisches Staatsministerium für Unterricht und Kultus, January 7, 1931, ABA PA 1467 Huber.
13. Bayerisches Staatsministerium für Unterricht und Kultus to Huber, January 14, 1931, ABA PA 1467 Huber.
14. Ärzliches Zeugnis, January 23, 1931, ABA PA 1467 Huber.
15. Huber to Kumpfmüller, March 9, 1932; and Ruhestand-Notiz, November 15, 1932, ABA PA 1467 Huber.
16. BArch B OGK and SAPA Huber.
17. *Bayerischer Kurier*, November 14, 1933, BArch B R58/59947/A1, f. 519.
18. Huber to Ordinariat Augsburg, June 11, 1935, ABA PA 1467 Huber.
19. Ordinariat Würzburg to Ordinariat Augsburg, September 18, 1936, ABA PA 1467 Huber.
20. Ehrenfried to Huber, April 3, 1936, ABA PA 1467 Huber.
21. Huber to Kumpfmüller, August 30, 1936, ABA PA 1467 Huber.
22. Hartl to SD Munich, May 28, 1936, and June 4, 1936, BArch R58/5978/A1, ff. 782–783.
23. Miltenberger to Huber, September 21, 1936, ABA PA 1467 Huber.
24. Stephen Huber to Eberle, February 9, 1937, ABA PA 1467 Huber.
25. Eberle to Stephen Huber, February 15, 1937, ABA PA 1467 Huber.
26. Eberle to Christian Huber, November 20, 1936, ABA PA 1467 Huber.
27. Ordinariat Regensburg to Ordinariat Augsburg, May 28, 1937; and Ordinariat Augsburg to Ordinariat Regensburg, June 3, 1937, ABA PA 1467 Huber.
28. Ehrenfried to Bayerisches Staatsministerium für Unterricht und Kultus, March 22, 1937, DAW BMA A22.2.
29. Spangenberger to Ordinariat Würzburg, January 12, 1938, ABA PA 1467 Huber.
30. Ordinariat Augsburg to Ordinariat Würzburg, January 27, 1938, ABA PA 1467 Huber.
31. Spangenberger to Ordinariat Würzburg, February 2, 1938, ABA PA 1467 Huber.
32. Antrag, March 31, 1942, BArch B RKK Huber.
33. Kumpfmüller to Huber, January 28, 1942, ABA PA 1467 Huber.
34. Strafsache Huber, June 24, 1942, ABA PA 1467 Huber; and Peters, *Pio-Benedictine Code of Canon Law*, 735, 756.

35. Ordinariat Würzburg to Ordinariat Augsburg, February 28, 1958, ABA PA 1467 Huber.

36. "Die Trägodie des katholischen Geistlichen," newspaper article, n.p., n.d., AAK NL Pieper; and Generalvikariat Paderborn, December 30, 1932, EBAP Sammlung Pieper.

37. "Lorenz Pieper," newspaper article, n.p., January 5, 1933.

38. *Rote Erde am Sonntag,* January 31, 1933, and February 26, 1933, AAK NL Pieper.

39. Tröster, "'. . . die besondere Eigenart des Herrn Dr. Pieper!'" 46–47.

40. Reprint, in "Die Nationalsozialistische Freiheitsbewegung," BArch 26/1326.

41. *Völkischer Beobachter,* February 1, 1933, BayHStA NL Schachleiter.

42. Faulhaber to Vassallo, February 4, 1933, EAM PA Schachleiter; and Haering, "Kirchenrechtliche Marginalien zum Fall Schachleiter."

43. *Vossische Zeitung,* February 4, 1933, BArch R5101/21675, f. 90; and *Bayerischer Kurier,* February 4 and 7, 1933, EAM NL Faulhaber 5539.

44. *Münchener Neueste Nachrichten,* February 6, 1933; and Schachleiter to Ordinariat Munich, February 5, 1933, EAM NL Faulhaber 5539.

45. Decree of the Reich president, February 28, 1933, in Noakes and Pridham, *Nazism,* 1:142.

46. *Der Alemanne,* February 7, 1933, EBAF B2/NS18.

47. *Germania,* February 5, 1933, EAM NL Faulhaber 5539.

48. *Linzer Volksblatt,* February 9, 1933, EAM NL Faulhaber 5538.

49. Albrecht to Ordinariat Munich, March 2, 1933, EAM PA Schachleiter.

50. *Aiblinger Pfarrblatt,* February 1933, BayHStA NL Schachleiter.

51. *Bayerischer Kurier,* February 26, 1933, BayHStA PrASlgRehse 1885; and *Völkischer Beobachter,* March 4/5, 1933, BayHStA NL Schachleiter.

52. Faulhaber to Muhler, October 26, 1936; and *Bayerischer Kurier,* March 2, 1933, EAM NL Faulhaber 5539.

53. Hehl, *Priester unter Hitlers Terror,* 1:961.

54. Amrain to Ordinariat Munich, March 12, 1933, EAM PA Schachleiter.

55. Amrain to Buchwieser, March 22, 1933, EAM PA Schachleiter; and Engelhard, *Abt Schachleiter,* 123.

56. Schachleiter to Hitler, October 6, 1932, BArch B NS26/1323.

57. Lammers to Schachleiter, March 25, 1933, BArch NS26/1326 and R43II/174.

58. "Ministerbesprechung," March 7, 1933, in Minuth, ed., *Die Regierung Hitler,* 163; Samerski, "Der geistliche Konsultor"; and Spicer, *Resisting the Third Reich,* 33–35.

59. Bleistein, "Abt Alban Schachleiter," 178.

60. Ibid.

61. Spicer, *Resisting the Third Reich,* 29.

62. *Fränkischer Kurier,* March 23, 1933, BayHStA PrASlgRehse 1885; and *Völkischer Beobachter,* March 26/27, 1933, BArch B R5101/21675, f. 113.

63. *Münchener Zeitung,* March 25/26, 1933; and *Trostberger Tageblatt,* March 25, 1933, EAM PA Schachleiter.

64. Amrain to Buchwieser, March 22, 25, 1933, EAM PA Schachleiter.

65. Schachleiter to Faulhaber, April 28, 1933, BayHStA NL Schachleiter.

66. Schachleiter to Hitler, March 30, 1933, BArch Z ZA 1 11992/A13.

67. *Völkischer Beobachter,* April 6, 1933.

68. *Völkischer Beobachter,* April 9/10, 1933.

69. Pacelli to Faulhaber, May 22, 1933, EAM NL Faulhaber 5539.

70. Faulhaber to Stotzingen, March 4, 1933, EAM NL Faulhaber 5539.

71. Stotzingen to Schachleiter, March 12, 1933, EAM PA Schachleiter.

72. Faulhaber to Walzer, April 18, 1933, in Volk, *Akten Kardinal Michael von Faulhabers,* 1:713.

73. Walzer to Faulhaber, April 19, 1933, EAM NL Faulhaber 5539.
74. *Berliner Börsen-Zeitung,* May 16, 1933, BArch R5101/21675.
75. *Völkischer Beobachter,* Munich ed., May 26, 1933.
76. Schachleiter to Haeuser, June 18, 1933, StA Kempten NL Haeuser.
77. Seidler to Faulhaber, June 12, 1933, EAM NL Faulhaber 5539.
78. Faulhaber to Seidler to Faulhaber, July 16, 1933, EAM NL Faulhaber 5539.
79. Faulhaber to Congregation for Religious, June 20, 1933, EAM PA Schachleiter.
80. Seidler to Faulhaber, July 29, 1933, EAM NL Faulhaber 5539.
81. Walzer to Schachleiter, August 5, 1933; and Seidler to Faulhaber, August 8, 1933, EAM NL Faulhaber 5539.
82. Schachleiter to Faulhaber, August 9, 1933, EAM NL Faulhaber 5539.
83. Schachleiter to Pope Pius XI, August 8, 1933, EAM NL Faulhaber 5539.
84. Pacelli to Landersdorfer (telegram), August 13, 1933, EAM NL Faulhaber 5539.
85. Landersdorfer to Faulhaber, August 14, 1933, EAM NL Faulhaber 5539.
86. Faulhaber to Stotzingen, September 19, 1933, EAM NL Faulhaber 5539.
87. Seidler to Faulhaber, September 9, 1933, EAM NL Faulhaber 5539.
88. Faulhaber to Schachleiter, September 14, 1933, EAM NL Faulhaber 5539.
89. Schachleiter to Faulhaber, September 17, 1933, EAM NL Faulhaber 5539.
90. Faulhaber to Schachleiter, October 7, 1933, EAM NL Faulhaber 5539.
91. Bormann to Schachleiter, November 6, 1933, BArch B NS26/1329.
92. Schachleiter to Eichmann, December 5, 1933, BArch B NS26/1324.
93. Dr. Auer, note, December 16, 1933, BArch B NS26/1324.
94. Schachleiter to Faulhaber, December 17, 1933, EAM NL Faulhaber 5539.
95. Faulhaber to Schachleiter, December 20, 1933, BayHStA NL Schachleiter.
96. Schachleiter to Pieper, December 12–13, 1933, in Brunnert, *Vielfalt des Lebens,* 161.
97. Hess to Schachleiter, November 4, 1933, BArch B NS26/1329.
98. Ibid., March 7, 1934, BArch B NS26/1329.
99. Fulda Hirtenbrief, June 7, 1934, in Stasiewski, ed., *Akten deutscher Bischöfe über die Lage der Kirche,* 1:704–15.
100. Faulhaber to Pacelli, September 1, 1934, in Volk, ed. *Akten Kardinal Michael von Faulhabers,* 895.
101. "Der festliche Einzug," n.p., September 4, 1934, EAM PA Schachleiter.
102. Referat Faulhabers, January 30, 1935, in Volk, ed., *Akten Kardinal Michael von Faulhabers,* 2:12.
103. Various correspondence, BArch B NS26/1326.
104. Lammers to Kerrl, August 3, 1935, BArch B R5101/21676.
105. Lammers to Schachleiter, October 13, 1935, and March 29, 1935, BArch B NS26/1326.
106. Schachleiter to Hitler, n.d., BArch B NS26/1329.
107. NSDAP Gaugericht München-Oberbayern, June 26, 1934, BArch B NSPK Schachleiter.
108. Nippold to Freiherr von Holzschuher, September 19, 1934; and Nippold to Schachleiter, September 19, 1934, BArch B NSPK Schachleiter.
109. Zach to Ordinariat Munich, August 12, 1935, EAM PA Schachleiter.
110. *Völkischer Beobachter,* July 24, 1935, EAM NL Faulhaber 539.
111. SD Berlin Berichte, c. 1936, BArch B R58/5237.
112. Buchwieser to Schachleiter, December 18, 1934, BArch NS 26/1324.
113. Faulhaber to Schachleiter, March 23, 1935, EAM NL Faulhaber 5539.
114. Walzer to Faulhaber, September 21, 1935, EAM NL Faulhaber 5539.
115. Buchwieser to Schachleiter, September 30, 1935, BArch B NS26/1324.

116. Keller to Ordinariat Munich, October 10, 1935, EAM PA Schachleiter.

117. Engelhard to Vykoukal, June 26, 1937, BArch B NS26/1324.

118. Ordinariat Munich to Keller, October 30, 1935, EAM PA Schachleiter; and Ordinariat Munich to Schachleiter, April 20, 1936, BArch B NS 26/1324.

119. *Münchener Neueste Nachrichten,* January 21, 1936, EAM PA Schachleiter; and "Abt Schachleiter Ehrendoktor der Münchner Universität," *Zeitschrift für Musik* (February 1936), BayHStA NL Schachleiter.

120. *Aiblinger Zeitung,* January 29, 1936, EAM NL Faulhaber 5538.

121. Weissenberger, *Das Benediktinische Mönchtum,* 112.

122. Deninger to Faulhaber, June 21, 1936, EAM NL Faulhaber 5538.

123. "Ehrentag," n.p., August 16, 1936, BArch NS26/1325.

124. Faulhaber to Keller, September 7, 1936, EAM NL Faulhaber 5539.

125. Keller to Faulhaber, September 12, 1936, EAM NL Faulhaber 5539.

126. Zach to Faulhaber, January 14, 1937, EAM NL Faulhaber 5539.

127. Bleistein, "Abt Alban Schachleiter," 186; and Engelhard, *Abt Schachleiter,* 180.

128. Sproll to Welser, February 16, 1937, BArch B NS26/1326; and Engelhard, *Abt Schachleiter,* 180.

129. Schachleiter to Hess, March 8, 1937, BArch B NS26/1326.

130. *Völkischer Beobachter,* June 21, 1937, BArch B NS26/1323.

131. Goebbels diary, June 22, 1937, in Fröhlich, ed., *Die Tagebücher von Joseph Goebbels* I:3, 181.

132. Läpple, "Adolf Hitler, Psychogramm einer katholischen Kindheit."

133. *Völkischer Beobachter,* northern Germany ed., June 23, 1937; and *Völkischer Beobachter,* Munich ed., June 22 and 23, 1937, BayHStA PrASlgRehse 1885.

134. Weinschenk to Schachleiter, September 6, 1933, BayHStA NL Schachleiter; Schwarz to Schachleiter, April 7, 1936; Edermaninger to Schachleiter, August 20, 1936; and Vogt to Schachleiter, March 4, 1936, BArch B NS26/1330.

135. Vogt to Schachleiter, March 4, 1936, BArch B NS26/1330.

136. Ibid., August 3, 1936, BArch B NS26/1330.

137. Weinschenk to Schachleiter, September 6, 1933, BayHStA NL Schachleiter.

138. Fiedler to Schachleiter, August 26, 1933, BArch NS26/1330.

139. Schober to Schachleiter, August 28, 1936, BArch B NS26/1330.

140. Rössger to Schachleiter, March 2, 1936, BArch B NS26/1330.

141. Schachleiter to Roth, January 30, 1933, in Engelhard, *Abt Schachleiter,* 105.

142. Roth to Pieper, April 15, 1934, in Brunnert, *Vielfalt des Lebens,* 179.

143. Rundschreiben 22, attachment 2, August 28, 1935, EBAF B2/NS18 and EAM NL Faulhaber 5539.

144. Faulhaber to Preysing, September 16, 1935, EAM NL Faulhaber 7269.

145. Roth to Schachleiter, August 24, 1935, BArch B R5101/21676, f. 220.

146. Schachleiter to Pieper, February 7, 1936, in Brunnert, *Vielfalt des Lebens,* 163.

147. Schachleiter to Pieper, February 12, 1936, in Brunnert, *Vielfalt des Lebens,* 164.

148. BArch N SAK Roth and Brandl, "Josef Roth," 743.

149. Roth to Pieper, April 15, 1934, in Brunnert, *Vielfalt des Lebens,* 179.

150. *Schematismus München und Freising* 1934.

151. Roth to Pieper, April 15, 1934, in Brunnert, *Vielfalt des Lebens,* 178.

152. Grimm to Ordinariat Augsburg, September 22, 1935, ABA PA 1782 Roth.

153. Various correspondence, Faulhaber, Ordinariat Munich, and Roth, EAM NL Faulhaber 7269.

154. Steinmann to Neuhäusler, April 23, 1936, EAM NL Faulhaber 7269.

155. Roth to Faulhaber, May 17, 1936; and Faulhaber to Roth, May 28, 1936, EAM, NL Faulhaber 7269.

156. Rundschreiben 22, attachment 2, August 28, 1935, EBAF B2/NS18 and EAM NL Faulhaber 5539.

157. Faulhaber to Roth, May 7, 1936, EAM NL Faulhaber 7269.

158. Faulhaber to Pacelli, June 1, 1936, in Volk, *Akten Kardinal Michael von Faulhabers*, 2:139.

159. Ausarbeitungen von Dr. Sebastian Schröcker, n.d., BArch K NL 898 Roth.

160. Schröcker, "Aufsätze und Ausarbeitungen von Josef Roth," BArch K NL 898 Roth.

161. Roth, "Kirchenpolitischer Aktionsplan," May 7, 1937, BArch B R5101/21678; and Roth to Goebbels, December 9, 1937, BArch R5101/24191, f. 133.

162. Roth to Gestapo Berlin, March 28, 1938, R4901/4314, f. 181.

163. Dierker, *Himmlers Glaubenskrieger*, 225.

164. Schlund to Roth, September 4, 1940, NL 1516 Schröcker.

165. Hartl Final Interrogation Report CI-FIR/123, January 9, 1947, NARA RG238/M1020/r.24, f. 795; and Dierker, *Himmlers Glaubenskrieger*, 370.

166. Letter to SS-Hauptamt Berlin, author unknown, June 15, 1936, BArch B R58/5978/A1, f. 735.

167. "X Jahre Reichskonkordat," BArch K NL 898 Roth.

168. Roth, "Die Kirche ist alt geworden."

169. "Fahneneide der Wehrbereiten," *Bayern und Reich*, September 4, 1923, BArch K NL 898 Roth.

170. Baumgärtner, "Vom Kaplan zum Ministerialrat," 227.

171. Roth, "Die katholische Kirche und die Judenfrage," 175.

172. Roth diary fragments, BArch K NL 898 Roth.

173. Narrative from Ausarbeitungen von Dr. Sebastian Schröcker, n.d., BArch K NL 898 Roth.

174. Kerrl to Bayer, July 25, 1941, BayHStA MK 16806.

175. Faulhaber to Bavarian bishops, July 27, 1941, in Volk, ed. *Akten Kardinal Michael von Faulhabers*, 2:768.

176. Faulhaber, "Josef Roth," September 10, 1941, EAM NL Faulhaber 7269.

177. Zech to Bischöfliches Sekretariat Augsburg, September 16, 1941, ABA PA 1782 Roth.

178. Haeuser Eulogy for Josef Roth, July 29, 1941, EAM NL Faulhaber 7269.

4—Antisemitism and the Warrior Priest

1. Haeuser, "Mein deutsches Ringen," 1.

2. Lenski, "Pfarrer Dr. Philipp Haeuser," 1.

3. Haeuser, "Mein deutsches Ringen," 2.

4. Ibid., 3; and Haeuser Karte, ABA PA 1410 Haeuser.

5. Haeuser, "Mein deutsches Ringen," 11–12.

6. Ibid., 20.

7. *Letter of Barnabas.*

8. Haeuser, "Mein deutsches Ringen," 23–24.

9. Jefford, *Reading the Apostolic Fathers*, 20–22.

10. Haeuser, *Der Barnabasbrief,* esp. 13–16, 27, 91, 98.

11. Haeuser, trans., *Justinus Dialog.*

12. Haeuser, *Anlass und Zweck des Galaterbriefes.*

13. Haeuser, "Mein Werden," 9; and Pacelli to Lingg, March 28, 1925, ABA PA 1410 Haeuser.

14. Haeuser, "Mein Werden," 9–10.

15. *Schematismus Augsburg 1933.*

16. Haeuser to Lingg, August 5, 1919, ABA PA 1410 Haeuser.

17. Haeuser, "Mein Werden," 13.

18. Haeuser to Lingg, January 16, 1920, ABA PA 1410 Haeuser.

19. Philipp Haeuser, "Die Königstreuen," ABA PA 1410 Haeuser.

20. Haeuser to Lingg, February 27, 1920, ABA PA 1410 Haeuser.

21. Ibid., January 4, 1922, ABA PA 1410 Haeuser.

22. Haeuser, *Wir deutsche Katholiken,* 7, 32, 47.

23. Ibid., 49–50.

24. *Kölnische Volkszeitung,* April 7, 1922.

25. Walterbach, *Katholiken und Revolution,* 45.

26. Henle to Haueser, January 9, 1922, StA Kempten, NL Haueser.

27. Ludendorff to Haeuser, February 9, 1922, StA Kempten, NL Haeuser.

28. Haeuser, *Jud und Christ,* 15.

29. Ibid., 18–19.

30. Haeuser, "Die Judenfrage," 442–43.

31. Ibid., 443.

32. Davies, *Infected Christianity,* 37; and Heschel, "When Jesus Was an Aryan."

33. Chamberlain, *Die Grundlagen des neunzehnten Jahrhunderts;* and Field, *Evangelist of Race.*

34. Steigmann-Gall, *Holy Reich,* esp. 13–50.

35. Haeuser, "Die Judenfrage," 442–45.

36. Haeuser, *Jud und Christ,* 39.

37. Haeuser, "Die Judenfrage," 445–46.

38. Kiefl, "Jud und Christ," StA Kempten, NL Haeuser.

39. Haeuser, "Mein deutsches Ringen," 116–17.

40. Haeuser, "Mein Werden," 17.

41. *Völkischer Beobachter,* December 13, 1922.

42. Ibid., January 24, 1923.

43. *Neue Preußische Zeitung/Kreuz-Zeitung,* March 21, 1922; and *Jungdeutsche,* 1925, StA Kempten, NL Haeuser.

44. Haeuser, "Mein deutsches Ringen," 180.

45. Ibid., 165–69.

46. Ibid., 170–77.

47. *Warmia,* March 22, 1924, StA Kempten, NL Haeuser.

48. Haeuser, "Mein deutsches Ringen," 176.

49. Ibid., 181.

50. Jones, "Catholics on the Right."

51. Haeuser, "Mein deutsches Ringen," 237–42.

52. Ibid., 242.

53. Haeuser, *Pazifismus und Christentum,* 7, 17, 19.

54. Ibid., 24, 30.

55. Haeuser, "Mein deutsches Ringen," 249–50.

56. Ibid., 250.

57. Denzler, *Widerstand ist nicht das richtige Wort,* 165–77; and Groll, "Franz Xaver Eberle."

58. Haeuser, "Mein deutsches Ringen," 253–56.

59. Ibid., 257.

60. Blümel, "Dr. theol. Philipp Haeuser," 1, 5.

61. Various correspondence, January–March 1932, ABA PA 1410 Haeuser.

62. Haeuser to Faulhaber, August 22, 1925, EAM NL Faulhaber 8040.

63. Haeuser to Merkt, November 6, 1939, StA Kempten, NL Haeuser.

64. Haeuser to Hess, August 1933 and July 22, 1940, StA Kempten, NL Haeuser.

65. Ibid., October 17, 1933, BArch D ZB 1/1411, 790.

66. *Illustrierter Beobachter,* March 4, 1933.

67. Hetzer, *Kulturkampf in Augsburg,* 15–16; and Rummel, "Joseph Kumpfmüller," 420.

68. Haeuser, *Kampfgeist gegen Pharisäertum,* 5–6, 12.
69. Jones, "Nationalists, Nazis, and the Assault against Weimar."
70. Haeuser, *Kampfgeist gegen Pharisäertum,* 13–15.
71. *Münchener Post,* December 18, 1930, BayHStA PrASlgRehse 3757.
72. *Schwäbische Volkszeitung,* December 18, 1930, StA Kempten NL Haeuser.
73. *Neue Augsburger Zeitung,* December 20, 1930, StA Kempten NL Haeuser.
74. *Westdeutscher Beobachter,* January 2, 1931, BayHStA PrASlgRehse 3757.
75. *Der Stürmer,* December 1930, BayHStA PrASlgRehse 3757.
76. Haeuser, "Mein deutsches Ringen," 192; Ehrenfried to Faulhaber, December 19, 1930; Faulhaber to Bavarian Episcopate, January 26, 1931; and Buchberger to Faulhaber, January 29, 1931, in *Akten Kardinal Michael von Faulhabers,* 1:531, 535–39.
77. Haeuser, "Mein deutsches Ringen," 194.
78. *Augsburger Postzeitung,* December 24, 1930; *Bayerischer Kurier,* December 20, 22, and 23, 1930; *Völkischer Beobachter,* December 23 and 24, 1930, BayHStA PrASlgRehse 3757.
79. *Völkischer Beobachter,* Janary 21, 1931, StA Kempten, NL Haeuser.
80. *Völkischer Beobachter,* Janary 21, 1931, StA Kempten, NL Haeuser.
81. Haeuser, "Mein deutsches Ringen," 204.
82. Ibid., 204–5.
83. Ibid., 205.
84. *Völkischer Beobachter,* January 28, 1931, BayHStA PrASlgRehse 3757.
85. Haeuser, "Mein deutsches Ringen," 206–7.
86. Faulhaber, *Rufende Stimmen in der Wüste,* 194.
87. Haeuser, "Mein deutsches Ringen," 212.
88. *Bayerischer Kurier,* September 27, 1931; *Neue Nationalzeitung,* September 21, 1931; and *Traunsteiner Tageblatt* to Ordinariat Augsburg, September 18, 1931, ABA PA 1410 Haeuser.
89. Haeuser, "Mein deutsches Ringen," 215.
90. Ordinariat Augsburg to Haeuser, September 23, 1931, ABA PA 1410 Haeuser.
91. Haeuser to Ordinariat Augsburg, September 28, 1931, ABA PA 1410 Haeuser.
92. Eberle to Haeuser, October 10, 1931, ABA PA 1410 Haeuser.
93. Haeuser to Ordinariat Augsburg, October 6, 1931, ABA PA 1410 Haeuser.
94. Wonhaus to Ordinariat Augsburg, March 22, 1932, ABA PA 1410 Haeuser.
95. Augsburg chancery to Pfarramt Ludwigsmoos, March 26, 1932, ABA PA 1410 Haeuser.
96. Haeuser to Kraus, March 27, 1932, ABA PA 1410 Haeuser.
97. Ordinariat Augsburg to Haeuser, March 24, 1932, ABA PA 1410 Haeuser.
98. Haeuser to Ordinariat Augsburg, March 29, 1932, ABA PA 1410 Haeuser.
99. Wonhaus to Ordinariat Augsburg, March 29, 1932, ABA PA 1410 Haeuser.
100. Kraus to Ordinariat Augsburg, July 30, 1932, ABA PA 1410 Haeuser.
101. Haeuser to Ordinariat Augsburg, September 28, 1931, ABA PA 1410.
102. Haeuser, "Mein deutsches Ringen," 267–68.
103. Haeuser, *Irrwege,* 1, 5.
104. Ibid., 8–9.
105. Haeuser to Marie R., July 22, 1932, StA Kempten, NL Haeuser.
106. *Völkischer Beobachter,* May 24, 1933; and *Rheinisch-Westfälische Zeitung,* May 24, 1933, EAM NL Faulhaber 8040.
107. Haeuser to Hess, August 3, 1933, StA Kempten NL Haeuser.
108. Haeuser to Schachleiter, February 5, 1933, BayHStA NL Schachleiter.
109. Haeuser, "Mein deutsches Ringen," 234.
110. Ibid., 234–35.
111. Ibid., 232–33, 235.
112. *Allgäuer Anzeigeblatt,* May 25, 1934; Deutscher Arbeitsdienst (Franken) to

Haeuser, April 24, 1934, and June 2, 1934, StA Kempten NL Haeuser; Roth to Pieper, April 15, 1934, in Brunnert, *Vielfalt des Lebens,* 179.

113. *Kaufbeurer Nationalzeitung,* May 29, 1934, StA Kempten, NL Haeuser.

114. Ibid.

115. Haeuser, *Der Kämpfer Jesus,* 16.

116. Schmid to Ordinariat Augsburg, July 19, 1936, ABA PA 1410 Haeuser.

117. Ordinariat Augsburg to Haeuser, July 22, 1936, ABA PA 1410 Haeuser.

118. Ordinariat Augsburg to Schmid, July 22, 1936, ABA PA 1410 Haeuser.

119. Haeuser to Ordinariat Augsburg, July 24, 1936, ABA PA 1410 Haeuser.

120. Landesversicherungsanstalt Schwaben to Kumpfmüller, May 5, 1936, ABA PA 1410 Haeuser.

121. Eberle to Haeuser, August 5, 1936; and Ordinariat Augsburg to Haeuser, February 15, 1937, ABA PA 1410 Haeuser.

122. Haeuser to Ordinariat Augsburg, January 16, 20, 1937; and Ordinariat Augsburg to Haeuser, February 15, 1937, ABA PA 1410 Haeuser.

123. *Schwabmünchen Nationalzeitung,* June 24, 1938, StA Kempten, NL Haeuser.

124. Haeuser to Merkt, December 12, 1940, StA Kempten NL Haeuser.

125. Haeuser, *Die deutsche Weltanschauung,* 3, 5, 23–30.

126. Boepple to Haeuser, April 1, 1935, StA Kempten, NL Haeuser.

127. Ordinariat Augsburg to Görlitz, December 9, 1935; and Eberle to Haeuser, December 19, 1935, ABA PA 1410 Haeuser.

128. Roth to Haeuser, June 6, 1935, StA Kempten NL Haeuser.

129. Eberle to Haeuser, November 5, 1936, ABA PA 1410 Haeuser.

130. Haeuser to Ordinariat Augsburg, November 11, 1935, ABA PA 1410 Haeuser.

131. Ibid., October 12, 1936, ABA PA 1410 Haeuser.

132. Ibid., August 31, 1939; and Haeuser to leadership of NSV Home in Castle Straßberg, August 31, 1939, ABA PA 1410 Haeuser.

133. Haeuser to Ordinariat Augsburg, September 1, 1939, ABA PA 1410 Haeuser.

134. Ibid., August 31, 1939, ABA PA 1410 Haeuser.

135. Haeuser to Hess, July 22, 1940, StA Kempten, NL Haeuser.

136. Haeuser to Merkt, March 19, 1940, StA Kempten, NL Haeuser.

137. NSDAP Kreisleitung Augsburg-Land to Haeuser, July 22, 1941, StA Kempten, NL Haeuser.

138. Karfreitag 1943 Predigt, StA Kempten, NL Haeuser.

139. Haeuser to Merkt, January 20, 1942, StA Kempten, NL Haeuser.

5—From Nationalism to National Socialism

1. Heuberger to Krauß, November 17, 1936, BArch B NS 43/62, ff. 58–59.

2. Roth, *Parteikreis und Kreisleiter der NSDAP,* 376–98.

3. Heuberger, "Wiedervereinigung im Glauben," I:9, 16.

4. Ärztliches Zeugnis, July 12, 1903; Pfarramtliches Zeugnis, July 11, 190; Heuberger to Leonrod, July 18, 1903, SemAEI PA Heuberger.

5. Heuberger, "Wiedervereinigung im Glauben," I:16.

6. Priesterkartei Heuberger, DAEI.

7. Heuberger to Polizeivorschule Eichstätt Werbestelle, May 4, 1931, SemAEI DJK.

8. Heuberger, "Wiedervereinigung im Glauben," I:53.

9. Ibid., I:36, 62–63.

10. Ibid., I:63, 70.

11. Ibid., IV:50–51.

12. Heuberger to Generalvikariat Eichstätt, May 3, 1916, DAEI PA Heuberger.

13. Relatiostatus, July 21, 1925, DAEI PA Heuberger.

14. Götz, Osterbericht 1924/25, DAEI PA Heuberger.

15. Priesterkartei Heuberger, DAEI; and Heuberger, "Wiederveinigung im Glauben," I:69.

16. Heuberger, "Wiedervereinigung im Glauben," I:69.

17. Various correspondence, SemAEI DJK.

18. Heuberger, "Wiedervereinigung im Glauben," I:164–65.

19. Heuberger to Ordinariat Eichstätt, September 15, 1928; Heuberger to Mergel, November 9, 1928; Heuberger to Mergel, January 10, 1929; Heuberger to Mergel, January 16, 1929, SemAEI DJK.

20. Heuberger to Ordinariat Eichstätt, n.d.; Bayerisches Staatsministerium für Unterricht und Kultus to Heuberger, February 23, 1925; Heuberger to Ordinariat Eichstätt, June 19, 1928; Heuberger to Ordinariat Eichstätt, July 1, 1928; Heuberger to Mergel, June 10, 1929, DAEI PA Heuberger.

21. Heuberger to Generalvikariat Eichstätt, July 1, 1928, DAEI PA Heuberger.

22. Generalvikariat Eichstätt to Heuberger, c. June 1926, DAEI PA Heuberger.

23. Heuberger to Generalvikariat Eichstätt, June 19, 1928, DAEI PA Heuberger.

24. Götz, Osterbericht des Stadtdekanats Ingolstadt 1924/25, DAEI PA Heuberger.

25. Heuberger to Generalvikariat Eichstätt, April 9, 1932, DAEI Pfarrakten Hitzhofen VIa.

26. Dr. Kramer, Zeugnis, June 10, 1931, DAEI PA Heuberger.

27. Heuberger to Generalvikariat Eichstätt, August 22, 1926, DAEI PAHeuberger.

28. Heuberger, "Wiedervereinigung im Glauben," I:69, 157, 162.

29. Regierung von Mittelfranken Kammer des Innern to Ordinariat Eichstätt, July 14, 1931; Regierung von Mittelfranken Kammer des Innern to Bezirksamt Eichstätt, October 28, 1931; and Protokoll, August 23, 1931, DAEI Pfarrakten Hitzhofen X.

30. Heuberger to Generalvikariat Eichstätt, September 14 and 15, 1931, DAEI PA Heuberger.

31. Generalvikariat Eichstätt to Heuberger, September 25, 1931, DAEI PA Heuberger.

32. Niederschrift, June 26, 1933, DAEI Pfarrakten Hitzhofen VIa.

33. Bayerisches Staatsministerium für Unterricht und Kultus to Ordinariat Eichstätt, December 6, 1933, DAEI Pfarrakten Hitzhofen VIa.

34. Kiefer to Bayerisches Staatsministerium für Unterricht und Kultus, December 20, 1933; Kiefer to Heuberger, December 22, 1933, DAEI Pfarrakten Hitzhofen VIa.

35. Anfragen der Gemeinde Lippertshofen to Ordinariat Eichstätt, January 31, 1935; Bürgermeister Lippertshofen to Ordinariat Eichstätt, January 11, 1936; Heuberger to Rackl, January 29, 1936; Ordinariat Eichstätt to Heuberger, October 31, 1936, DAEI Pfarrakten Hitzhofen VIa.

36. Vorführungs-Notiz, January 24, 1934, SM, ST 7763; and Hausfelder, "Die Situation der katholischen Kirche in Ingolstadt," 329–33.

37. Testimony of Bittner, January 20, 1934, StA München ST 7763.

38. Testimony of Heuberger, January 19, 1934, StA München ST 7763.

39. Gendarmeriestation Gaimersheim to Bezirksamt Ingolstadt, February 26, 1934, StA München ST 7763.

40. Testimony of Heuberger, January 19, 1934, StA München ST 7763.

41. Hauptkammer München Außenstelle Nürnberg, Prozeß gegen Heuberger, December 8, 1950, StA München ST 7763.

42. Warmuth to Vorsitzender des Sondergerichtes München, April 4, 1934, StA München ST 7763.

43. Testimony of Heuberger, January 19, 1934, StA München ST 7763.

44. Testimony of Biersack, January 22, 1934; Testimony of Graf, January 20, 1934; Testimony of Bittner, January 20, 1934; Testimony of Engelhardt, January 23, 1934; Testimony of Rotter, January 22, 1934, StA München ST 7763.

45. Testimony of Speth, January 22, 1934, StA München ST 7763.

46. Testimony of Sebastian, January 23, 1934, StA München ST 7763.

47. Vorführungs-Notiz, Ingolstadt, January 24, 1934, StA München ST 7763.

48. Warmuth to Vorsitzender des Sondergerichtes München, April 10, 1934, StA München ST 7763.

49. Schmitz-Berning, *Vokabular des Nationalsozialismus,* 671–73.

50. Heuberger, "Wiedervereinigung im Glauben," I:188.

51. Krauß to Landesstelle Franken of Reichsministerium für Volksaufklärung und Propaganda Nürnberg, March 12, 1937, StA Nürnberg, NS-Mischbestand, Kreisleitung Eichstätt, Nr. 8.

52. Heuberger to Ordinariat Eichstätt, June 20, 1936, DAEI Pfarrakten Hitzhofen VIa; and Heuberger to Rackl, November 11, 1936, DAEI Bischofs-Archiv Heuberger.

53. Heuberger to Rackl, November 11, 1936, DAEI Bischofs-Archiv Heuberger.

54. Heuberger to Krauß, November 17, 1936, BArch B NS 43/62, f. 58.

55. Ibid.

56. Ibid.

57. Ibid.

58. Ibid., ff. 58–59.

59. Ibid., f. 59.

60. Ibid.

61. Burleigh and Wippermann, *The Racial State, Germany 1933–1945;* and Pine, *Nazi Family Policy 1933–1945.*

62. Heuberger to Krauß, November 17, 1936, BArch B NS 43/62, f. 59.

63. Ibid.

64. Flugblatt für Großen Sprechabend der NSDAP, November 30, 1936, SemAEI PA Heuberger; Bericht über Großen Sprechabend, November 30, 1936, DAEI NL Krauß, *Kreuz gegen Hakenkreuz,* vol. 1, document 60.

65. *Eichstätter Volkszeitung,* December 2, 1936, DAEI Pfarrakten Hitzhofen VIa.

66. Heuberger to Rackl, December 1, 1936, DAEI Bischofs-Archiv Heuberger.

67. Kiefer to Heuberger, December 2, 1936, DAEI Pfarrakten Hitzhofen VIa.

68. *Ermländische Zeitung,* October 17/18, 1936.

69. Heuberger to Generalvikariat, December 6, 1936, DAEI Bischofs-Archiv Heuberger.

70. Notiz Kiefers, December 2, 1936, DAEI Pfarrakten Hitzhofen VIa.

71. Monatsbericht für Dezember 1936, January 7, 1937, BayHStA MK 37740 Heuberger.

72. Neuhäusler to Rackl, January 8, 1937, DAEI Bischofs-Archiv Heuberger.

73. Bischöfliche Erklärung, December 30, 1936, SemAEI PA Heuberger.

74. Heuberger to Rackl, December 30, 1936, DAEI Bischofs-Archiv Heuberger.

75. Wagner to Kiefer, January 4, 1937, DAEI Pfarrakten Hitzhofen VIa.

76. Rackl to Heuberger, January 25, 1937, in *Pastoralblatt des Bistums Eichstätt,* February 9, 1937, 26–32.

77. Various correspondence, DAEI Bischofs-Archiv Heuberger.

78. Wagner to Kiefer, January 11, 1937, DAEI Pfarrakten Hitzhofen VIa.

79. Schachleiter to Heuberger, February 24, 1937; Herberger, "Wiedervereinigung im Glauben," I:207.

80. Vertrauenskundgebung, January 4, 1937, DAEI Pfarrakten Hitzhofen VIa.

81. *Eichstätter Anzeiger,* January 5, 6, and 7, 1937, DAEI Bischofs-Archiv Heuberger.

82. *Eichstätter Anzeiger,* January 8, 1937, DAEI Bischofs-Archiv Heuberger.

83. Bischöfliche Erklärung, January 8, 1937, SemAEI PA Heuberger.

84. Krauß (speech), January 17, 1937, DAEI NL Kraus, *Kreuz gegen Hakenkreuz,* vol. 1, document 26.

85. Rackl to Heuberger, January 25, 1937, in *Pastoralblatt des Bistums Eichstätt,* February 9, 1937.

86. Herberger, "Wiedervereinigung im Glauben," I:205–6.

87. Heuberger to a friend, September 22, 1937, DAEI Bischofs-Archiv Heuberger.

88. Rackl to Heuberger, January 29, 1937, in *Pastoralblatt des Bistums Eichstätt,* February 9, 1937, 32.

89. Heuberger to Rackl, February 2 and 5, 1937, DAEI Bischofs-Archiv Heuberger.

90. *Pastoralblatt des Bistums Eichstätt,* February 9, 1937.

91. Ibid.

92. Heuberger to Rackl, February 10, 1937, DAEI Bischofs-Archiv Heuberger.

93. Rackl to Heuberger, February 6, 1937, DAEI Bischofs-Archiv Heuberger.

94. Heuberger to Rackl, October 13, 1937; Rackl to Heuberger, October 24, 1937; and Heuberger to Rackl, October 26, 1937, DAEI Bischofs-Archiv Heuberger.

95. Heuberger to a friend, September 22, 1937, DAEI Bischofs-Archiv Heuberger.

96. Kiefer to Heuberger, n.d., DAEI PA Heuberger; Heuberger to Bürgermeister of Ingolstadt, September 11, 1938; Heuberger to Rackl, November 11, 1938; Heuberger to Stadtpfarrer of Freystadt, 1938, DAEI Bischofs-Archiv Heuberger.

97. Rackl to Grabmann, January 23, 1938, DAEI Bischofs-Archiv Anton Heuberger.

98. Herberger, "Wiedervereinigung im Glauben," I:207.

99. Heuberger to Schachleiter, March 23, 1937, BayHStA NL Schachleiter.

100. Heuberger to Rackl, January 12, 1944, DAEI Bischofs-Archiv Heuberger.

6—Germanizing Catholicism

1. *Südhannoversche Volkszeitung,* obituary, April 2, 1974 (reprint, Duderstadt gymnasium newsletter, "Oberstudienrat i.R. Richard Kleine zum Gedenken"), AEGD PA Kleine.

2. Generalvikariat Hildesheim to Kleine, January 14, 1919, AEGD PA Kleine, f. 10.

3. Kleine to Witowski, December 11, 1935, MIO NL Kleine.

4. Kershaw, *'Hitler Myth.'*

5. Adam, *"Erlösung!," Theologische Quartalschrift* 4 (1929), MIO NL Kleine.

6. Kleine, *Erlösung!,* 13–14.

7. Ibid., 19, 65, 68.

8. Ibid., 62, 66.

9. Ibid., 26, 55, 99–199, 115, 159, 187–89.

10. Ibid., 83, 125, 176, 178.

11. Kleine to Brauer, April 29, 1935, MIO NL Kleine.

12. Ritter to Kleine, May 26, 1932; and Kleine to Ritter, June 5, 1932, MIO NL Kleine.

13. *Der Deutsche Weg,* August 5, 1932, BAH PA Kleine.

14. "An die katholischen Deutschen," in Breuning, *Die Vision des Reiches,* 326–27, 235.

15. Breuning, *Die Vision des Reiches,* 225–38, 326–46.

16. Kleine to Reich Minister Rust, November 19, 1933, GStAPK I HA Rep. 76 Kult. z. Nr. 9/III.

17. Kleine to Lutze, October 27, 1933, GStAPK Rep. 76 Kult. z. Nr. 9/III.

18. Oberpräsident Hannover, Abteilung für das höhere Schulwesen, to Rust, November 13, 1933, GStAPK I HA Rep. 76 Kult. z. Nr. 9/III.

19. Kommission für höhere Schule, Oberpräsidium Hannover, to Rust, August 19, 1933, GStAPK I HA Rep. 76 Kult. z. Nr. 9/III.

20. Oberpräsident Hannover, Abteilung für das höhere Schulwesen, to Rust, November 14, 1933, in Bormann, *Keine Schule wie jede andere*, 287–90.

21. Kleine to Lutze, October 27, 1933, GStAPK Rep. 76 Kult. z. Nr. 9/III.

22. Papen to Rust, November 17, 1933, GStAPK Rep. 76 Kult. z. Nr. 9/III.

23. Kleine to Löpelmann, November 19, 1933, GStAPK Rep. 76 Kult. z. Nr. 9/III.

24. Kleine to Rust, December 17, 1933, GStAPK Rep. 76 Kult. z. Nr. 9/III.

25. Votum des Generalreferenten, n.d.; and Rust to Oberpräsident Hannover, Abteilung für das höhere Schulwesen, GStAPK Rep. 76 Kult. z. Nr. 9/III.

26. Bormann, *Keine Schule wie jede andere*, 223–25.

27. Generalvikariat Hildesheim to Kleine, September 9, 1935, MIO NL Kleine.

28. Kleine to Generalvikariat Hildesheim, September 11, 1935, MIO NL Kleine.

29. Burkhard, *Häresie und Mythus des 20. Jahrhunderts*, 34.

30. Kleine to Generalvikariat Hildesheim, September 11, 1935, MIO NL Kleine.

31. Generalvikariat Hildesheim to Kleine, September 13, 1935, MIO NL Kleine.

32. Nowak, "Der Devisenprozeß Dr. Seelmeyer," esp. 507–17; and Hoffmann and Janssen, *Die Wahrheit über die Ordensdevisenprozesse 1935/36.*

33. Clauss and Gatz, "Nikolaus Bares," 25.

34. Aschoff, "Joseph Godehard Machens," 468.

35. Kleine to Machens, September 9, 1935, MIO NL Kleine.

36. Hirtenbrief an die deutsche Katholiken, *Amtsblatt Berlin,* September 4, 1935, 70–75; and Gruber, *Katholische Kirche und Nationalsozialismus,* 198–264.

37. Kleine to Machens, September 9, 1935, MIO NL Kleine.

38. Machens to Gestapo, Kerrl, Rust, Gürtner, and Berning, August 29, 1935, in Stasiewski, ed., *Akten Deutscher Bischöfe,* 2:388–90.

39. Machens to Kleine, September 30, 1935; Kleine to Machens, October 1, 1935; and Machens to Kleine, October 3, 1935, MIO NL Kleine.

40. Kleine to Lortz, February 21, 1935, MIO NL Kleine.

41. Ibid.; Conzemius, "Joseph Lortz"; Krieg, *Catholic Theologians in Nazi Germany,* 56–82; and Luckens, "Joseph Lortz."

42. Lortz, *Katholischer Zugang zum Nationalsozialismus.*

43. SD Berlin to I, n.d., BArch B R58/5978/A2, f. 475.

44. Lortz to Kleine, February 28, 1935, MIO NL Kleine.

45. SD-Bericht, c. 1936, BArch B R58/5237, ff. 5–6.

46. Lautenschläger, *Joseph Lortz,* 311–12.

47. Brombacher to Kleine, June 5, 1935, and October 8, 1935, MIO NL Kleine.

48. Brombacher to Ritter, September 14, 1935, MIO NL Kleine.

49. Lortz to Brombacher, October 27, 1935, MIO NL Kleine.

50. Brombacher to Kleine, October 30, 1935, MIO NL Kleine.

51. Kleine to Brombacher, November 1, 1935; Brombacher to Kleine, November 2, 1935; and Brombacher to Lortz, November 7, 1935, MIO NL Kleine.

52. Aschendorff to Kleine, August 13, 1935, and September 6, 1935, MIO NL Kleine.

53. Lortz to Kleine, September 15, 1935, MIO NL Kleine.

54. Lautenschläger, *Joseph Lortz,* 314.

55. Lortz to Kleine, October 21, 24, 26, 1935, MIO NL Kleine.

56. Ibid., November 16, 1935, MIO NL Kleine.

57. Kleine to Lortz, November 17, 21, 1935, MIO NL Kleine.

58. Lortz to Kleine, December 2, 1935, MIO NL Kleine.

59. Kleine to Lortz, December 3, 1935, MIO NL Kleine.

60. Lortz to Kleine, December 14, 1935, MIO NL Kleine.

61. Brombacher and Ritter, eds., *Sendschreiben katholischer Deutscher.*

62. Ibid., 11–12.

63. Ibid., 15–16, 21–22.

64. Ibid., 31–32.

65. Ibid., 68.

66. SD-Bericht, c. 1936, BArch B R58/5237, ff. 6–7.

67. Lortz to Kleine, January 12, 1943, MIO NL Kleine; and Lautenschläger, *Joseph Lortz*, 330–31.

68. Kleine to Geschwister Pircher, August 19, 1953, in Loidl, *Religionslehrer Johann Pircher*, 22–23.

69. Loidl, *Religionslehrer Johann Pircher*, 1–5.

70. Dutzler to Loidl, January 15, 1971, in Loidl, *Religionslehrer Johann Pircher*, 24–27.

71. Hagenauer to Loidl, January 21, 1971, in Loidl, *Religionslehrer Johann Pircher*, 27–28.

72. Pircher, NSZK NARA RG242–A3340–MFKL–M019.

73. Bukey, *Hitler's Austria*, 13; and Pauley, *Hitler and the Forgotten Nazis*, 107–9.

74. Bukey, *Hitler's Austria*, 15–16, 25–39; Luža, *Austro-German Relations*, 34–53; Pauley, *Hitler and the Forgotten Nazis*, 163–66, 193–215.

75. Schütz and Kosiek, eds., *Deutsche Geschichte im 20. Jahrhundert*, 60; and Deniffel, "Josef Bürckel."

76. Hürten, *Deutsche Katholiken*, 400–424; Liebmann, *Theodor Innitzer und der Anschluß*, 61–119; Luža, "Nazi Control of the Austrian Catholic Church," 541–547; and Reimann, *Innitzer, Kardinal zwischen Hitler und Rom*, 102–15.

77. "Feierliche Erklärung!" March 18, 1938, DAW NL Leier Kasten 1 Faszikel 5.

78. *Wiener Diözesanblatt*, March 22, 1938, in Loidl, *Arbeitsgemeinschaft für den religiösen Frieden*, 1:3.

79. Innitzer to Bürckel, March 18, 1938, DAW NL Leier Kasten 1 Faszikel 5.

80. Hürten, *Deutsche Katholiken*, 407–8.

81. Lettl, "Die Arbeitsgemeinschaft für den religiösen Frieden 1938"; Liebmann, *Kardinal Innitzer und der Anschluss*, 116–18, 126–38; Loidl, *Religionslehrer Johann Pircher*, 6; Scholz and Heinisch, ". . . alles werden sich die Christen nicht gefallen lassen," 99.

82. Pircher to Press, n.d., in Loidl, *Arbeitsgemeinschaft für den religiösen Frieden*, 1:12; and Loidl, *Religionslehrer Johann Pircher*, 6.

83. Pircher to "Hochwürdiger Mitbruder," n.d., in Loidl, *Arbeitsgemeinschaft für den religiösen Frieden*, 1:6.

84. Hürten, *Deutsche Katholiken*, 408.

85. Erklärung, April 6, 1938, in Volk, ed., *Akten Kardinal Michael von Faulhabers*, 2:559 n.4.

86. Pircher et al. to Innitzer, April 8, 1938, in Reimann, *Innitzer, Kardinal zwischen Hitler und Rom*, 346–47.

87. "Weisungen an die Seelsorger," *Wiener Diözesanblatt*, April 26, 1938, in Loidl, *Arbeitsgemeinschaft für den religiösen Frieden*, 1:18.

88. Pircher and van den Bergh, May 7, 1938, in Loidl, *Arbeitsgemeinschaft für den religiösen Frieden*, 1:28.

89. Moritz, *Grüß Gott und Heil Hitler*, 46, 284 n.104.

90. *Korrespondenzblatt für den katholischen Klerus*, May 10, 1938, in Loidl, *Arbeitsgemeinschaft für den religiösen Frieden*, 1:30–34.

91. Joint pastoral letter of the Austrian hierarchy, September 4, 1938, in *The Catholic Mind* 36 (1938): 429–36.

92. Johann Pircher, interview, October 22, 1938, in Loidl, *Religionslehrer Johann Pircher*, 12–13; and Hürten, *Deutsche Katholiken*, 630 n.96.

93. Information II über die kirchenpolitische Lage in Großdeutschland, January 1939, MIO NL Kleine.

94. Ibid.

95. Kleine to Pircher, May 11, 1939, MIO NL Kleine.

96. Pircher to Kleine, March 21, 1939, MIO NL Kleine.

97. Kleine to Pircher, February 10, 1939, MIO NL Kleine.

98. Ibid., March 2, 1939, MIO NL Kleine.

99. Kleine to a friend, March 2, 1939, MIO NL Kleine.

100. Kleine to Pircher, April 26, 1939, MIO NL Kleine.

101. Pircher to Kleine, April 4, 1939, MIO NL Kleine.

102. Pircher to Brücker, May 2, 1939, MIO NL Kleine.

103. Kleine to Pircher, April 26, 1939, MIO NL Kleine.

104. Pircher to Kleine, September 29, 1939, MIO NL Kleine; Wilhelm Alois van den Bergh and Alois Cloß, DAWien Personaldaten; Hofmüller, "Steirische Priester," 64–75, 93–101, 126–28; Liebmann, "Rein zur Zeit des Nationalsozialismus," 252–64; Riegler, "Augustiner-Chorherren," 73; and Spicer, *Resisting the Third Reich*, 143–44.

105. Mayer, *Gesetzliche Unfruchtbarmachung Geisteskranker*.

106. Dietrich, "Catholic Eugenics in Germany"; Graham, "Right to Kill"; Richter, *Katholizismus und Eugenik*, 207–27; and Wollasch, "Eugeniker Joseph Mayer."

107. Richter, *Katholizismus und Eugenik*, 143, 320–30.

108. SD Düsseldorf to Himmler, November 5, 1938, USHMM 15.007–4, f. 37; Mayer, "Die Lebensraumfrage der Völker"; and Dierker, *Himmlers Glaubenskrieger*, 374–75, 531 n.189.

109. Dierker, *Himmlers Glaubenskrieger*, 114–16; Dietrich, "Joseph Mayer and the Missing Memo" and "Catholic Eugenics in Germany"; Benzenhöfer and Finsterbusch, *Moraltheologie pro "NS-Euthanasie"*; Richter, *Katholizismus und Eugenik*, 507–9.

110. Pircher to Kleine, October 7, 1939, MIO NL Kleine.

111. Ibid., October 19, 1939, MIO NL Kleine.

112. Aufzeichnung Faulhabers über eine Unterredung mit Eberle, December 22, 1937; Eberle to Pacelli, January 14, 1938, in Volk, ed., *Akten Kardinal Michael von Faulhabers*, 2:457–59, 490–92; Gross, "Franz Xaver Eberle," 448–50; and Hetzer, *Kulturkampf in Augsburg*, 60–66.

113. Eberle to Pacelli, January 14, 1938, in Volk, ed., *Akten Kardinal Michael von Faulhabers*, 2:490–92.

114. Pircher to Kleine, February 12, 1939, MIO NL Kleine.

115. Kleine to Thomé, October 20, 1943, in Wolf and Arnold, eds., *Der Rheinische Reformkreis*, 2:196.

116. Thomé to Kleine, October 24, 1943, in Wolf and Arnold, eds., *Der Rheinische Reformkreis*, 2:197.

117. Ibid., July 28, 1944, and August 13, 1944, MIO NL Kleine.

118. Kleine to Reventlow, May 19, 1939, MIO NL Kleine.

119. Pircher to Kleine, October 29, 1939, MIO Kleine.

120. Brücker to Kleine, September 22, 1941; and Brücker to Jaeger, April 18, 1943, MIO NL Kleine.

121. Kleine to Pircher, June 8, 1939, MIO NL Kleine.

122. Faith and Order to Kleine, June 8, 1929; and Faith and Order to Kleine, June 24, 1929, MIO NL Kleine.

123. *Der Neue Wille*, September 8, 1940, MIO NL Kleine.

124. Kleine, "Union im Dienste des Empires," *Der Neue Wille*, September 8, 1940, MIO NL Kleine; Besier, *Die Kirchen und das Dritte Reich*, 431–655; and Boyens, *Kirchenkampf und Ökumene*, 144–70.

125. Jasper, *George Bell*, 223–44.

126. Kleine, *Erlösung!*, 99–100, 159; and Kleine, "Wiedervereinigung im Glauben," March 26, 1944, MIO NL Kleine.

127. Helmreich, *German Churches under Hitler*, 179, 502 n.71.

128. Kleine to Reventlow, February 6, 1939, May 19, 1939, June 8, 1939; Kleine to Leitung der Deutschen Christen, Eisenach, December 7, 1939, MIO NL Kleine;

Boog, *Graf Ernst zu Reventlow;* and Schumacher, *Die Reichstagsabgeordneten,* 1225.

129. Reventlow to Kleine, May 22, 1939, MIO NL Kleine.

130. Kleine to Pircher, June 6, 1939, MIO NL Kleine.

131. Reventlow to Kleine, June 10, 1939, MIO NL Kleine.

132. Kleine to Pircher, December 13, 1939, MIO NL Kleine.

133. Kleine to Leitung der Deutschen Christen, Eisenach, December 7, 1939, MIO NL Kleine.

134. Kleine to Pircher, December 13 and 15, 1939, MIO NL Kleine.

135. Kleine to Pircher, November 29, 1939, MIO NL Kleine; Lautenschläger, "Der Kirchenkampf in Thüringen," 481–484; May, *Kirchenkampf oder Katholikenverfolgung?,* 391; and Meier, *Der Evangelische Kirchenkampf,* 3:681 n.1335.

136. Kleine to Pircher, November 29, 1939, MIO NL Kleine.

137. Kleine to Reventlow, December 7, 1939, MIO NL Kleine.

138. Reventlow to Kleine, December 8, 1939, MIO NL Kleine.

139. Kleine to Pircher, September 28, 1939; and Pircher to Kleine, October 20, 1939, MIO NL Kleine.

140. Kleine to Leitung der Deutschen Christen, Eisenach, December 7, 1939; memorandum, n.d.; and Kleine to Pircher, January 9, 1940, MIO NL Kleine.

141. Memorandum, n.d.; and "Ist ein gemeinschaftliches Arbeiten notwendig?" December 20, 1939, MIO NL Kleine.

142. Kleine to Pircher, April 24, 1940, MIO NL Kleine.

143. Peters, *Pio-Benedictine Code of Canon Law,* 426, 735–36.

144. Pircher to Kleine, April 29, 1940, MIO NL Kleine.

145. Kleine to Brücker, May 21, 1940, MIO NL Kleine.

146. Heschel, "Nazifying Christian Theology," 591.

147. Ibid.

148. Head, "Nazi Quest for an Aryan Jesus," 79–85.

149. Kleine to Brauer, Eisenach, May 6, 1940, NL Kleine.

150. Ibid.; and Institut zur Erforschung des jüdischen Einflusses auf das deutsche kirchliche Leben, ed., *Die Botschaft Gottes.*

151. Grundmann to Kleine, January 17, 1941; and Pich to Kleine, February 15, 1941, MIO NL Kleine.

152. Kleine to Institut zur Erforschung des jüdischen Einflusses auf das deutsche kirchliche Leben, Eisenach, February 14, 1941, MIO NL Kleine.

153. Second major conference of Institut zur Erforschung des jüdischen Einflusses auf das deutsche kirchliche Leben, Eisenach, March 3–5, 1941, program, MIO NL Kleine.

154. Kleine to Grundmann, April 4, 1941, MIO NL Kleine.

155. Grundmann to Kleine, May 31, 1941, MIO NL Kleine.

156. Kleine to Grundmann, June 3, 1941, MIO NL Kleine.

157. Grundmann to Kleine, July 7, 1941, MIO NL Kleine.

158. Ibid., July 2, 1941, MIO NL Kleine.

159. Kleine to Grundmann, July 3, 1941, MIO NL Kleine.

160. Adam, *Die geistige Lage des deutschen Katholizismus.*

161. Kleine to Adam, May 17, 1940, MIO NL Kleine; and Ernesti, *Ökumene im Dritten Reich,* 231–38.

162. Adam to Kleine, June 7, 1940, MIO NL Kleine.

163. Spicer, "Last Years of a Resister."

164. Adam to Kleine, May 22, 1940, MIO NL Kleine.

165. Brücker to Kleine, February 16, 1941, MIO NL Kleine.

166. Kleine to Adam, May 24, 1940, MIO NL Kleine.

167. Kleine to Pircher, May 27, 1940, MIO NL Kleine.

168. Adam to Kleine, May 29, 1940, MIO NL Kleine.

169. Kleine to Pircher, May 31, 1940, MIO NL Kleine.

170. Pircher to Adam, June 5, 1940, DAR NL 67 Adam, Nr. 33, f. 324.

171. Adam to Kleine, May 31, 1940, MIO NL Kleine.

172. Kleine to Adam, June 7, 1940, MIO NL Kleine.

173. Adam to Kleine, June 10, 1940, MIO NL Kleine.

174. Kleine to Adam, June 9, 1940, MIO NL Kleine.

175. Kleine to Kapferer, October 31, 1940, MIO NL Kleine.

176. Kleine to Adam, June 19, 1940, DAR NL 67 Adam, Nr. 33, f. 317.

177. Adam to Kleine, June 24, 1940, MIO NL Kleine.

178. Kleine to Adam, June 28, 1940, MIO NL Kleine.

179. Pircher to Adam, June 27, 1940; and *Kameradschaftlicher Gedankenaustausch,* June 1940, DAR NL 67 Adam, Nr. 33, ff. 306–10.

180. Adam to Kleine, June 28, 1940, MIO NL Kleine.

181. Ibid., December 10, 1940, MIO NL Kleine.

182. Kleine to Adam, December 12, 1940, DAR NL 67 Adam, Nr. 33, f. 79.

183. Ibid., May 9, 1941, DAR NL 67 Adam, Nr. 33, f. 7.

184. Ibid., April 6, 1941, DAR NL 67 Adam, Nr. 33, f. 28.

185. Adam to Kleine, May 12, 1941, MIO NL Kleine.

186. Ibid., May 12, 1941, MIO NL Kleine.

187. Kleine to Adam, June 3, 1941, MIO NL Kleine.

188. Kleine to Pircher, November 12, 1939, MIO NL Kleine; and Hübner/*Der Neue Wille* to Kleine, March 28, 1940, MIO NL Kleine.

189. Kleine, "War Jesus ein Jude?" c. 1939, MIO NL Kleine, ff. 4, 9, 12.

190. Ibid., ff. 7, 9–10.

191. Adam to Kleine, June 24, 1941, MIO NL Kleine.

192. Adam, "Jesus, der Christus und wir Deutsche," pt. 2, 91; and Krieg, *Catholic Theologians in Nazi Germany,* 102–3.

193. Adam to Kleine, February 6, 1943; and Kleine to Adam, February 14 and 18, 1943, MIO NL Kleine.

194. Kleine to Adam, June 29, 1941, MIO NL Kleine.

195. Grundmann to Kleine, July 7, 1941, MIO NL Kleine; and Pich to his colleagues at the institute, "Grundsätzliches zur Arbeit des Institutes," attached, October 9, 1941, DAR NL 67 Adam, Nr. 2, ff. 10–16.

196. Kleine to Mayer, January 14, 1940, MIO NL Kleine.

197. Mayer to Kleine, January 17, 1940, MIO NL Kleine.

198. Kleine to Mayer, February 10, 1940, MIO NL Kleine.

199. Mayer to Kleine, April 25, 1940, MIO NL Kleine.

200. Kleine to Grundmann, October 29, 1941, MIO NL Kleine; and Grundmann to Kleine, October 30, 1941, and December 4, 1941, MIO NL Kleine.

201. Kleine to Adam, July 7, 1942, MIO NL Kleine.

202. Adam to Kleine, February 6, 1943, MIO NL Kleine.

203. Kleine to Dungs, April 25, 1943; and Dungs to Kleine, May 31, 1943, MIO NL Kleine.

204. Kleine, *Die acht Seligpreisungen der Bergpredigt,* 19.

205. *Der Neue Wille,* February 4, 1940; May 19, 1940; June 16, 1940; and August 4, 1940, MIO NL Kleine.

206. Kleine, "Die Bergpredigt als Kampfansage," Vienna, August 1943, MIO NL Kleine.

207. Kleine to Dungs, August 19, 1943; Dungs to Kleine, October 22, 1943; Waag to Dungs, June 30, 1944; and Kleine to Waag, July 28, 1944, MIO NL Kleine.

208. Kleine to Adam, April 20, 1943, MIO NL Kleine.

209. Ibid., May 9, 1941, DAR NL 67 Adam Nr. 33, f. 7.

210. Gatz, "Lorenz Jaeger," 345.

211. Gruß, *Erzbischof Lorenz Jaeger als Kirchenführer,* 73–75.

212. Adam to Bagus, December 7, 1941, MIO NL Kleine.

213. Jaeger to Kleine, March 17, 1942, MIO NL Kleine.

214. Kleine to Schultz, March 19, 1942, BArch B R43II/178a, f. 205.

215. Schultz to Kritzinger, March 27, 1942; and Kritzinger to Schultz, March 31, 1942, BArch B R43II/178a, ff. 204–5.

216. Jaeger to Kleine, September 9, 1942, MIO NL Kleine.

217. Ibid.

218. Kleine to Brücker, March 3, 1943, MIO NL Kleine.

219. Jaeger to Kleine, January 5, 1943, MIO NL Kleine.

220. Kleine to Brücker, March 3, 1943, MIO NL Kleine.

221. Kleine to Jaeger, January 13, 1943, MIO NL Kleine.

222. Ibid., March 14, 1943, MIO NL Kleine.

223. Jaeger to Kleine (telegram), March 19, 1943, MIO NL Kleine.

224. Jaeger to Kleine, March 20, 1943, MIO NL Kleine.

225. Kleine, Entwurf, March 25, 1943, MIO NL Kleine.

226. Gruß, *Erzbischof Lorenz Jaeger als Kirchenführer,* 267–68; and Stüken, *Hirten unter Hitler,* 160–62.

227. Kleine, minutes, April 9, 1943, MIO NL Kleine.

228. Ibid.

229. Ibid.

230. Ibid.

231. Pastoral letter of the German episcopacy, August 19, 1943, in Volk, *Akten deutscher Bischöfe,* 6:178–84, 197–205.

232. Leugers, *Gegen eine Mauer bischöflichen Schweigens,* 275–93.

233. Spicer, *Resisting the Third Reich,* 69–70; and Stüken, *Hirten unter Hitler,* 166–67.

234. Leugers, *Gegen eine Mauer bischöflichen Schweigens,* 292; and Stüken, *Hirten unter Hitler,* 165–66.

235. Kleine to Jaeger, September 19, 1943, MIO NL Kleine.

236. Kleine's handwritten notes on Kleine to Jaeger, September 19, 1943, MIO NL Kleine.

237. Jaeger to Kleine, September 25, 1943, MIO NL Kleine.

238. Kleine to Jaeger, October 6, 1943, MIO NL Kleine.

239. Ibid., November 1, 1943, MIO NL Kleine.

240. Kleine to Brücker, September 21, 1943, MIO NL Kleine.

241. Kleine to Pircher, September 30, 1943, MIO NL Kleine.

242. Dungs to Kleine, October 20, 1943, MIO NL Kleine.

243. Institut-Berichte, May 13, 1943, MIO NL Kleine.

244. Assorted *Kameradschaftlicher Gedankenaustausch,* MIO NL Kleine.

245. Festgottesdienst der Staatlichen Oberschule für Jungen, Duderstadt, April 20, 1939, MIO NL Kleine.

246. Pircher to Kleine, September 29, 1939, MIO NL Kleine.

247. Ibid., March 11, 1940, MIO NL Kleine.

7—Judgment Day—Brown Priests on Trial?

1. Tillinghast to Rackl, October 20, 1945, DAEI Bischofs-Archiv Heuberger.

2. Griffith, "Denazification Program," 94; and Vollnhals, ed., *Entnazifizierung,* 100–101.

3. Rackl to Heuberger, November 2, 1945, DAEI Bischofs-Archiv Heuberger.

4. Rackl to Heuberger, November 3, 1945, DAEI Bischofs-Archiv Heuberger.

5. Rackl to Schröffer, November 8, 1945, DAEI PA Heuberger.

6. Vollnhals, ed., *Entnazifizierung*, 7–9.

7. Jarausch, *After Hitler*, 48–49; and Peterson, *American Occupation of Germany*, 143.

8. Cohen, "Transitional Justice in Divided Germany"; Melis, "Katholische Kirche und politische Säuberungen" and *Entnazifizierung in Mecklenburg-Vorpommern;* Tischner, *Katholische Kirche in der SBZ/DDR 1945–1951;* Vogt, *Denazification in Soviet-Occupied Germany;* and Vollnhals, ed., *Entnazifizierung.*

9. Boyens, "Die Kirchenpolitik," 14, 22, 33; Lehmann, *Katholische Kirche und Besatzungsmacht,* 84–87; and Spotts, *Churches and Politics,* 54.

10. Religious Affairs to director, Office of Military Government for Bavaria, Baden-Württemberg, and Greater Hessen, n.d., NARA RG260, box 943; Melis, "Der katholische Episkopat und die Entnazifizierung," 50; and Spotts, *Churches and Politics,* 108.

11. Melis, "Der katholische Episkopat und die Entnazifizierung," 49–51.

12. Kurzbericht für den Herrn Staatsminister über die katholische Kirche in Bayern, n.d., BayHStA MSo 1413.

13. Preysing to Dengler, December 18, 1945, NARA RG260, box 154.

14. Headquarters U.S. Forces, European Theater, G-5 Division, to commanding general, Seventh U.S. Army, July 11, 1945, NARA RG260, box 158.

15. Headquarters Office of Military Government U.S. Zone to General Adcock, February 7, 1946, NARA RG260, box 158.

16. "German Bishops at Fulda," August 23, 1945, in *Catholic Mind* 43 (1945): 693.

17. "Pius XII: Nazism and Peace," June 2, 1945, in *Catholic Mind* 43 (1945): 449–57.

18. Neuner and Dupuis, *Christian Faith,* 457–65.

19. Cohen, "Transitional Justice in Divided Germany after 1945," 74.

20. Griffith, "Denazification Program," 190.

21. Ibid., 195–227.

22. Boyes, "Die Kirchenpolitik der amerikanischen Besatzungsmacht, 49–51; and Cohen, "Transitional Justice in Divided Germany after 1945," 72–82.

23. "German Priests and Nazism," *Catholic Mind* 45 (1947): 483.

24. Denazification of Clergy, statistical summary, OMGUS Education and Religious Affairs Branch, May 15, 1946, NARA RG260, box 158; U.S. Office of Military Government for Bavaria to Prime Minister Högner, September 26, 1946, BayHStA MSo 1413; Hürten, "Kirchen und amerikanische Besatzungsmacht," 572; and Melis, "Der katholische Episkopat und die Entnazifizierung," 50.

25. "On Right and Justice," March 27, 1946, *Catholic Mind* 44 (1946): 385–88.

26. Rintelen to Military Government Westfalen, Region Münster, July 1946, EBAP XXII 20 Entnazifizierung.

27. Macmillian to Frings, July 30, 1946, EBAP XXII 20 Entnazifizierung.

28. Kottmann to the Ministry for Political Liberation Stuttgart, October 10, 1947, NARA RG260, box 942.

29. Kurzbericht für den Herrn Staatsminister über die katholische Kirche in Bayern, n.d., BayHStA MSo 1413.

30. Rackl to Heuberger, November 8, 1945, DAEI Bischofs-Archiv Heuberger.

31. Rackl to Schröffer, November 16, 1945, DAEI PA Heuberger; and Rackl to Heuberger, November 16, 1945, DAEI Bischofs-Archiv Heuberger.

32. Bengel to Bischöfliches Ordinariat Eichstätt, December 2, 1946, DAEI Bischofs-Archiv Heuberger.

33. Schröffer to Bengel, January 9, 1947, DAEI Bischofs-Archiv Heuberger.

34. Heuberger to Bischöfliches Ordinariat Eichstätt, August 29, 1949, DAEI PA Heuberger.

35. Cohen, "Transitional Justice in Divided Germany after 1945," 87; and Grif-

fith, "Denazification Program," 516–52.

36. Ludwig Brandl, "Michael Rackl," 153–56.

37. Bischöfliches Ordinariat Eichstätt to Heuberger, n.d., DAEI PA Heuberger.

38. Heuberger to Bischöfliches Ordinariat Eichstätt, December 6, 1949, DAEI PA Heuberger.

39. *St. Willibalds Bote,* June 13, 1965; and Ritter to Bischöfliches Ordinariat Eichstätt, March 14, 1967, DAEI PA Heuberger.

40. Ordinariat Augsburg to Schwenger, May 7, 1948, ABA PA 926 Müller.

41. Schwenger to Ordinariat Augsburg, May 31, 1948, ABA PA 926 Müller.

42. Ordinariat Augsburg to Müller, October 19, 1948, ABA PA 926 Müller.

43. Weiler to Ordinariat Augsburg, April 22, 1949, ABA PA 926 Müller.

44. Huber to "Herrn Pfarrer," April 9, 1945, ABA PA 1467 Huber.

45. Ordinariat Würzburg to Ordinariat Augsburg, February 28, 1958, ABA PA 1467 Huber.

46. Dekan für katholische deutsche Lagerseelsorge to Ordinariat Augsburg, June 13, 1947, ABA PA 1467 Huber.

47. Müller to Ordinariat Würzburg, August 11, 1947, ABA PA 1467 Huber.

48. Ordinariat Würzburg to Ordinariat Augsburg, February 28, 1958, ABA PA 1467 Huber.

49. Ordinariat Augsburg to Ordinariat Würzburg, March 5, 1958, ABA PA 1467 Huber.

50. Tröster, "'. . . die besondere Eigenart des Herrn Dr. Pieper!'" 82–83.

51. Ibid., 84.

52. Beck, *Kampf und Sieg,* 24, 537–39.

53. Tröster, "'. . . die besondere Eigenart des Herrn Dr. Pieper!'" 70, 73, 76

54. Pieper to Petermann, Kordes, Engelmann, Stolze, Fabry, and Hamacher, July 22, 1941, EBAP Sammlung Pieper.

55. Kolbow to Pieper, August 6, 1941, EBAP Sammlung Pieper.

56. Ibid., December 31, 1941, EBAP Sammlung Pieper.

57. Pieper to Jaeger, January 12, 1942, EBAP Sammlung Pieper.

58. Jaeger to Pieper, January 14, 1942, EBAP Sammlung Pieper.

59. Der Sonderbeauftragte für die Entnazifizierung im Lande Nordrhein-Westfalen to Generalvikariat Paderborn, November 9, 1948, EBAP XXII NSDAP, 20 Entnazifizierung.

60. Griffith, "Denazification Program," 207.

61. Fischer to Generalvikariat Paderborn, January 30, 1951, EBAP Sammlung Pieper.

62. Ahrends to Reichsschatzmeister der NSDAP, Munich, June 24, 1944; and Reichsschatzmeister der NSDAP, Munich, to Ahrends, November 9, 1944, BArch B NSPK Pieper.

63. Landrat des Kreises Duderstadt to Kleine, August 2, 1945; Oberstudiendirektor of Oberschule Duderstadt to Oberpräsident Hannover, Abteilung für höheres Schulwesen, September 22, 1945; and Oberpräsident Hannover, Abteilung für höheres Schulwesen, to Oberstudiendirektor of Oberschule Duderstadt, October 6, 1945, AEGD PA Kleine, ff. 16, 18–19.

64. Kleine, NSLB BArch B, and Höhere Schulen Personalblatt A, AEGD PA Kleine.

65. Bormann, *Keine Schule wie jede andere,* 341.

66. Oberstudiendirektor of Oberschule Duderstadt to Oberpräsident Hannover, Abteilung für höheres Schulwesen, September 6, 1945, AEGD PA Kleine, f. 17.

67. Jaeger to Kleine, January 22, 1946, and April 18, 1946, Jaeger to Kleine, MIO NL Kleine.

68. Erklärung, May 8, 1946; and Oberstudiendirektor of Oberschule Duderstadt

to Oberpräsident Hannover, Abteilung Wissenschaft, Kunst und Volksbildung, May 8, 1946, AEGD PA Kleine, ff. 20, 23.

69. Kleine to Jaeger, n.d., MIO, NL Kleine.

70. Generalvikariat Hildesheim to Oberpräsident Hannover, Abteilung für höheres Schulwesen, June 7, 1946, NSHStA 120 H.A. 164/92/74 PA Kleine.

71. Generalvikariat Hildesheim to Ernst, July 19, 1946, APSC Generalvikariat.

72. Oberstudiendirektor of Oberschule Duderstadt to Oberpräsident Hannover, Abteilung für höheres Schulwesen, June 25, 1946, AEGD PA Kleine, f. 26.

73. Kleine to Machens, January 29, 1947, MIO NL Kleine.

74. Machens to Kleine, March 21, 1947, MIO NL Kleine and BAH PA Kleine.

75. Kleine to Machens, March 26, 1947, MIO NL Kleine and BAH PA Kleine.

76. Kleine to Jaeger, March 28, 1947, MIO NL Kleine.

77. Generalvikariat Hildesheim to Verwaltung der höheren Schulen beim Niedersächsischen Kultusministerium in Hannover, August 28, 1947, NSHStA 120 H.A. 164/92/74 PA Kleine, f. 15.

78. Jaeger to Kleine, February 13, 1958, MIO NL Kleine.

79. Brockmann to Machens, February 19, 1948, NSHStA 120 H.A. 164/92/74 PA Kleine, f. 23.

80. Verwaltung der höheren Schulen beim Niedersächsischen Kultusminister to director of Duderstadt gymnasium, April 5, 1948, AEGD PA Kleine.

81. Entnazifizierungs-Haupt-Ausschuss Duderstadt to Verwaltung der höheren Schulen beim Niedersächsischen Kultusminister, May 29, 1948; and Kleine to Verwaltung der höheren Schulen beim Niedersächsischen Kultusminister, May 30, 1948, NSHStA 120 H.A. 164/92/74 PA Kleine, ff. 36–39.

82. Kleine to Verwaltung der höheren Schulen beim Niedersächsischen Kultusminister, June 15, 1948, NSHStA 120 H.A. 164/92/74 PA Kleine, f. 44; and Oberstudiendirektor of Duderstadt gymnasium to Staatliches Gesundheitsamt Duderstadt, June 14, 1938, AEGD PA Kleine, f. 38.

83. Verwaltung der höheren Schulen beim Niedersächsischen Kultusminister to director of Duderstadt gymnasium, June 24, 1948, AEGD PA Kleine, f. 40.

84. Generalvikariat Hildesheim to Kleine, June 10, 1948, NSHStA 120 H.A. 164/92/74 PA Kleine, f. 48.

85. Entnazifizierung, August 26, 1948, BAH PA Kleine.

86. Generalvikariat Hildesheim to Kleine, September 11, 1948, NSHStA 120 H.A. 164/92/74 PA Kleine, f. 56.

87. Ernst to Machens, April 23, 1948, BAH PA Kleine.

88. Oberstudiendirektor of Duderstadt gymnasium to Verwaltung der höheren Schulen beim Niedersächsischen Kultusminister, September 15, 1948, AEGD PA Kleine, f. 41.

89. Generalvikariat Hildesheim to Kleine, June 25, 1949, NSHStA 120 H.A. 164/92/74 PA Kleine, f. 69.

90. Oberstudiendirektor of Duderstadt gymnasium to Verwaltung der höheren Schulen beim Niedersächsischen Kultusminister, December 13, 1951, AEGD PA Kleine, f. 52.

91. Staatliche Verwaltung der höheren Schulen in Hannover to direktor of Duderstadt gymnasium, June 22, 1956, NSHStA 120 H.A. 164/92/74 PA Kleine, f. 71.

92. Kleine to Staatliche Verwaltung der höheren Schulen in Hannover, January 17, 1957, NSHStA 120 H.A. 164/92/74 PA Kleine.

93. Oberstudiendirektor of Duderstadt gymnasium to Niedersächsisches Landesverwaltungsamt der höheren Schulen, February 4, 1964, AEGD PA Kleine.

94. Obituary, Duderstadt gymnasium, n.d., AEGD PA Kleine.

95. Flyer advertising speech of Studienrat Kleine on September 9, 1947, Katholische Akademiker-Vereinigung, Ortsgruppe Duderstadt, BAH PA Kleine.

96. Kleine to Staatliche Verwaltung der höheren Schulen in Hannover, April 25, 1952, AEGD PA Kleine, f. 54; and Jaeger to Kleine, September 13, 1959, MIO NL Kleine.

97. Generalvikariat Hildesheim to Kleine, February 15, 1950, BAH PA Kleine; Kleine, "Das Ringen um die Einheit," *Rheinischer Merkur*, April 13, 1962; and various articles in *Anzeiger für die katholische Geistlichkeit*, 1961–1963, MIO NL Kleine.

98. Kleine, *Die Verkündigung der Frohbotschaft*, "Die grundlegende Bedeutung der Bergpredigt," and "Die Mission im Religionsunterricht der höheren Schulen."

99. Rynne, *Third Session*, 24–61; Soetens, "Ecumenical Commitment of the Catholic Church," esp. 275–88 and 275–76; and Vereb, *"Because he was a German!"*

100. Kleine to Bea, August 18, 1962, MIO NL Kleine.

101. Kleine, "Judentum und Christentum," August 19, 1962, MIO NL Kleine.

102. Kleine to Stransky, August 23, 1962, MIO NL Kleine.

103. Peters, ed., *Pio-Benedictine Code of Canon Law*, 683–87.

104. Haeuser to Staatsminister Loritz, May 25, 1947, StA Kempten NL Haeuser.

105. Domm to Haeuser, September 29, 1945, ABA PA 1410 Haeuser.

106. Günter to Ordinariat Augsburg, October 10, 1945, ABA PA 1410 Haeuser.

107. Haeuser to Ordinariat Augsburg, October 16, 1945, ABA PA 1410 Haeuser.

108. Ordinariat Augsburg to Haeuser, October 17, 1945, ABA PA 1410 Haeuser.

109. Haeuser to Ordinariat Augsburg, October 18, 1945, ABA PA 1410 Haeuser.

110. Ordinariat Augsburg to Haeuser, November 8, 1945, ABA PA 1410 Haeuser.

111. Ordinariat Augsburg to Haeuser, May 21, 1946, ABA PA 1410 Haeuser.

112. Spruchkammer Schwabmünchen Anordnung, October 29, 1946, StA Kempten, NL Haeuser.

113. Domm to Haeuser, October 30, 1946, ABA PA 1410 Haeuser.

114. Ordinariat Augsburg to Haeuser, November 26, 1946, ABA PA 1410 Haeuser.

115. Haeuser to Spruchkammer Schwabmünchen, November 4, 1946, StA Kempten, NL Haeuser.

116. Haeuser to Müller, November 25 and 28, 1946, and December 1, 1946, ABA PA 1410 Haeuser.

117. Spruchkammer Schwabmünchen, December 1, 1946, ABA PA 1410 Haeuser.

118. Haeuser to Ordinariat Augsburg, January 25, 1947, ABA PA 1410 Haeuser.

119. Ordinance no. 79, Table of Categories, Penalties, and Sanctions, NARA RG 260, box 596.

120. Horn, *Die Internierungs- und Arbeitslager in Bayern 1945–1952*.

121. Spruchkammer Schwabmünchen, May 14, 1947, StA Kempten NL Haeuser.

122. Ibid.

123. Domm to Leitung des Internierungslagers Regensburg, May 31, 1947, ABA PA 1410 Haeuser.

124. Kempf to Ministerium für Sonderaufgaben, May 15, 1947, StA Bobingen Haeuser Sammlung.

125. Domm to Leitung des Internierungslagers Regensburg, May 31, 1947, ABA PA 1410 Haeuser.

126. Müller to Ordinariat Augsburg, May 22, 1947, ABA PA 1410 Haeuser.

127. Eberle to Haeuser, May 27, 1947, StA Kempten NL Haeuser.

128. Haeuser to his sister, June 1, 1947, StA Kempten NL Haeuser.

129. Eberle to Vorsitzender der Spruchkammer Schwabmünchen, May 20, 1947, StA Kempten NL Haeuser.

130. Kempf to Oswald, May 23, 1947, StA Bobingen Haeuser Sammlung.

131. Haeuser to Staatsminister Loritz, June 18, 1947, StA Kempten NL Haeuser; and Haeuser to Oswald, August 5, 1947, StA Bobingen Haeuser Sammlung.

132. Ordinariat Augsburg to Haeuser, June 13, 1947, ABA PA 1410 Haeuser.
133. Haeuser to Ordinariat Augsburg, June 18, 1947, StA Kempten NL Haeuser.
134. Haeuser to Oswald, August 5, 1947, StA Bobingen Haeuser Sammlung.
135. Haeuser to Eberle, August 14, 1947, StA Kempten, NL Haeuser.
136. Haeuser to Oswald, January 3, 1948, StA Bobingen Haeuser Sammlung; and Groll, "Spruchkammerverfahren."
137. Haeuser to Frau Oswald, July 11, 1947, StA Bobingen Haeuser Sammlung; and Peterson, *American Occupation of Germany,* 146–47.
138. Haeuser to Oswald, July 18, 1947, StA Bobingen Haeuser Sammlung.
139. Ibid., August 15, 1947, StA Bobingen Haeuser Sammlung.
140. Ericksen, *Theologians under Hitler,* esp. 79–119.
141. Haeuser to Oswald, August 29, 1947, and June 19, 1947, StA Bobingen Haeuser Sammlung.
142. Weinkamm to Berufungskammer Regensburg, June 2, 1947, StA Kempten NL Haeuser.
143. Papen to Kumpfmüller, December 31, 1948, StA Kempten NL Haeuser.
144. Haeuser to Berufungskammer Regensburg, August 2, 1947, StA Kempten NL Haeuser.
145. Stegmann to Ordinariat Augsburg, April 17, 1948, and November 8, 1948; Domm to Haeuser, April 23, 1948; Ordinariat Augsburg to Haeuser, May 11, 1948; and Bischöfliche Finanzkammer Augsburg to Haeuser, July 11, 1952, ABA PA 1410 Haeuser.
146. Ordinariat Augsburg chancery to Bischöfliche Finanzkammer Augsburg, November 1, 1948, ABA PA 1410 Haeuser.
147. Haeuser to Kumpfmüller, December 1, 1948; Haeuser to Ordinariat Augsburg, December 4, 1948; Haeuser to Domm, December 4, 1948; Haeuser to Kumpfmüller, December 8, 1948; Haeuser to Kumpfmüller, December 25, 1948; and Bürgermeister der Gemeinde Straßberg to Kumpfmüller, December 28, 1948, ABA PA 1410 Haeuser.
148. Berufungskammer München, February 28, 1950; and Haeuser to Merkt, March 5, 1950, StA Kempten NL Haeuser; Ordinance no. 79, Table of Categories, Penalties, and Sanctions, NARA RG 260, box 596.
149. Ordinariat Augsburg to Haeuser, November 5, 1953, ABA PA 1410 Haeuser.
150. Stegmann to Ordinariat Augsburg, February 26, 1956, ABA PA 1410 Haeuser.
151. Stegmann to Bischöfliche Finanzkammer Augsburg, March 26, 1956, ABA PA 1410 Haeuser.
152. *Schwabmünchener Zeitung,* November 20, 1957.
153. Haeuser, "Mein deutsches Ringen," f. 371.
154. Haeuser to Merkt, March 27, 1940, StA Bobingen Haeuser Sammlung.
155. Haeuser, "Geht das deutsche Volk zu gründe?" StA Kempten NL Haeuser, ff. 10–11.
156. Haeuser, "Geht das deutsche Volk zugrunde?" StA Kempten NL Haeuser, ff. 15, 21.
157. Haeuser to Oswald, September 1, 1958, StA Bobingen Haeuser Sammlung.
158. "Meine Weihnachtsansprache 1958 in Oberschönenfeld," StA Bobingen Haeuser Sammlung.
159. Haeuser to Oswald, January 28, 1959, StA Bobingen Haeuser Sammlung.
160. Ibid., December 13, 1947; and Haeuser to Oswald, January 28, 1959, StA Bobingen Haeuser Sammlung.
161. Qualification Sheet, 1940, ABA PA 1410 Haeuser.
162. Haeuser, "Kirche und Entnazifizierung oder, War ich Hauptschuldiger?" StA Kempten NL Haeuser.

Conclusion

1. Richard Kleine, "Wie stehen wir zu einem geläuterten Verständnis?" October 17, 1967, MIO NL Kleine.

2. Amery, *Capitulation;* and Kopf, *Franz Weiß—Für Deutschland und Christus.*

3. Griech-Polelle, *Bishop von Galen;* and Wolf, *Clemens August Graf von Galen.*

4. Missalla, *Wie der Krieg zur Schule Gottes wurde,* and *Für Gott, Führer und Vaterland;* and Zahn, *German Catholics and Hitler's Wars.*

5. Graham, *Vatican and Communism during World War II;* Kent, *Lonely Cold War of Pope Pius XII;* and Stehle, *Eastern Politics of the Vatican.*

6. Bendel, ed., *Die Katholische Schuld?;* Conzemius, "Zwischen Anpassung und Widerstand"; Dirks, "Katholiken zwischen Anpassung und Widerstand"; Hehl, "Die Kirchen in der NS-Diktatur"; and Rhodes, *Vatican in the Age of the Dictators,* esp. 131–40.

7. Besier, "Anti-Bolshevism and Antisemitism."

8. Blaschke, *Blaming the Victim,* 19–21; Kauders, "Jews in the Christian Gaze," 29–30; and Spicer, *Resisting the Third Reich,* 121–22.

9. On the effects of Christian antisemitism on Germans, see Bauer, *Rethinking the Holocaust,* 105.

10. Kleine to Pircher, May 10, 1943, MIO NL Kleine.

11. Adam to Kleine, May 31, 1941, MIO NL Kleine.

12. Pircher to Kleine, October 8, 1944, MIO NL Kleine.

13. Roth to Pieper, January 17, 1936, in Brunnert, *Vielfalt des Lebens,* 179.

14. Kleine to Bertram, August 26, 1924; and Machens to Kleine, August 25, 1924, MIO NL Kleine.

15. Vogt to Schachleiter, March 4, 1936, BArch B NS26/1330.

16. Ibid., August 10, 1936, BArch B NS26/1330.

17. Ibid., March 4, 1936, BArch B NS26/1330.

18. Ibid., August 10, 1936, BArch B NS26/1330.

19. Various correspondence on "Das Evangelium in der deutschen Zeitenwende," BAH PA Kleine and MIO NL Kleine.

20. Bleistein, "'Überläufer im Sold der Kirchenfeinde.'"

21. Stockums, *Das Priestertum.*

Sources Cited

Archival Sources

Archiv der Abtei Königsmünster, Meschede (AAK)
    Nachlaß Lorenz (NL) Pieper

Archiv der Abtei Mariendonk, Grefrath bei Kempen (AAM)
    Nachlaß Hermann Peter Keller, O.S.B.

Archiv der Abtei Schweiklberg, Schweiklberg (AAS)
    Personalakte Godehard Machens, O.S.B.

Archiv der Abtei St. Stephan, Augsburg (AAStS)
    Nachlaß Bernhard Seiller, O.S.B.

Archiv der Bayerischen Franziskanerprovinz, München (ABFP) (per correspondence)
    Personalkataloge

Archiv des Bistums Augsburg, Augsburg (ABA)
    Personalia
    Personaldaten

Archiv des Bistums Passau, Passau (ABP) (per correspondence)
    Personaldaten

Archiv des Bistums Speyer, Speyer (ABS) (per correspondence)
    Personaldaten

Archiv des Eichsfeld-Gymnasiums, Duderstadt (AEGD)
    Personalakte (PA) Richard Kleine

Archiv des Erzbistums Bamberg, Bamberg (AEB) (per correspondence)
    Personaldaten

Archiv der Jesuiten in Österreich, Vienna (AJO) (per correspondence)
    Personaldaten

Archiv der Ludwig-Maximilians-Universität, München (ALMU)
    Studentenkartei

Archiv der Propstei St. Cyriakus, Duderstadt (APSC)
    Generalvikariat

Archive, Congregatio pro Institutis Vitae Consecratae et Societatibus Vitae Apostolicae, Vatican City (ACIVC) (per correspondence)
    Apostolic Visits

Bayerisches Hauptstaatsarchiv, München (BayHStA)
Abteilung II: Neuere Bestände 19./20. Jahrhundert
MInn   Ministerium des Innern
MA   Ministerium des Äußern
MK   Ministerium für Unterricht und Kultus
MSo   Ministerium für Sonderaufgaben, Minister für
            Politische Befreiung
StK   Staatskanzlei
Abteilung V: Nachlässe und Sammlungen
            Nachlaß Abt Alban Schachleiter
            Nachlaß Bernhard Stempfle
PrASlgRehse   Presseausschnittsammlungen Rehse

Bibliothek für Bildungsgeschichtliche Forschung des Deutschen Instituts für Internationale Pädagogische Forschung (BBF) (per correspondence)
            Personalbogen Richard Kleine

Bischöfliches Zentralarchiv Regensburg, Regensburg (BZAR)
4250   Personalakte Josef Wirth
            Personaldaten

Bistumsarchiv Dresden-Meißen (BDM) (per correspondence)
            Personaldaten

Bistumsarchiv Fulda, Fulda (BAF) (per correspondence)
            Personaldaten

Bistumsarchiv Hildesheim, Hildesheim (BAH)
            Personalakte Richard Kleine
            Priesterkartei

Bistumsarchiv Trier, Trier (BAT)
Abt. 88, Nr. 112   Walter Leonards
            Personaldaten

Brandenburgisches Landeshauptarchiv, Potsdam (BLHA)
Pr. Br. Rep. 2A Regierung Potsdam I Pol.
Pr. Br. Rep. 2A Regierung Potsdam II Pdm.
Pr. Br. Rep. 2A Regierung Potsdam II Gen.

Bundesarchiv, Koblenz (Barch K)
898   Nachlaß Josef Roth
1516   Nachlaß Sebastian Schröcker

Bundesarchiv, Lichterfelde-Berlin (BArch B)
            Personenbezogene Unterlagen aus der NS-Zeit:
            NSDAP Korrespondenz (NSPK)
            NSDAP Ortsgruppenkartei (OGK)
            NSDAP Zentralkartei (NSZK)
            NS-Lehrerbundkartei (NSLB)
            Reichskulturkammer (RKK)
            SA Kartei (SAK)
            SA Personalakte (SAPA)

	SS Offiziersakte (SSOA)
NS 6	Partei-Kanzlei
NS 8	Kanzlei Rosenberg
NS 10	Persönliche Adjudantur des Führers und Reichskanzlers
NS 12	Hauptamt für Erzieher/NS-Lehrerbund
NS 15	Der Beauftragte des Führers für die Überwachung der gesamten geistigen und weltanschaulichen Schulung und Erziehung der NSDAP
NS 22	Reichsorganisationsleiter der NSDAP
NS 26	Hauptarchiv der NSDAP
R 43	Reichskanzlei
R 53	Stellvertreter des Reichskanzlers
R 58	Reichssicherheitshauptamt
R 4901	Reichsministerium für Wissenschaft, Erziehung und Volksbildung
R 5101	Reichsministerium für kirchliche Angelegenheiten

Bundesarchiv, Zwischenarchiv, Dahlwitz-Hoppegarten (BArch D)
Dok/P
ZA
ZB I
ZB II
ZR
ZWM

Diözesanarchiv Berlin, Berlin (DAB)
V/16   Nachlaß Konrad von Preysing
VI/1   Dokumentationsgut: Personen A–Z
         Personaldaten

Diözesanarchiv Eichstätt, Eichstätt (DAEI)
         Anton Heuberger
         Bischofs-Archiv
         Nachlaß Johannes Krauß
         Personalakten
         Pfarrakten
         Priesterkartei

Diözesanarchiv Graz-Seckau (ARGS) (per correspondence)
         Personaldaten

Diözesanarchiv Rottenburg, Rottenburg (DAR)
G 1.5   Nationalsozialismus
G 1.7.1, Nr. 33 Personalakte Karl Adam
N 67   Nachlaß Karl Adam
                Personaldaten

Diözesanarchiv Wien, Vienna (DAWien) (per correspondence)
         Personaldaten

Diözesanarchiv Würzburg, Würzburg (DAW)
         Bischöfliche Manualakten (BMA)
         Gestapo-Akten (GA)
         Nachlaß Heinrich Leier
         Personalakten Priester
         Personaldaten

Erzbischöfliches Archiv Freiburg, Freiburg im Breisgau (EBAF)
B2/NS   Nationalsozialismus
                Personalia

Erzbischöfliches Archiv München und Freising, München (EAM)
                Nachlaß Cardinal Michael Faulhaber
                Nachlaß Joseph Thalhamer
                Personalakten Priester
                Personaldaten

Erzbistumsarchiv Paderborn, Paderborn (EBAP)
XXII 19   NSDAP
XXII 20   Entnazifizierung
                Priesterkartei
                Rudersdorf Pfarrer, ab 1945
                Sammlung zum Pfarrer Ferdinand Heimes
                Sammlung zum Pfarrer Karl König
                Sammlung zum Pfarrer Lorenz Pieper
                Sammlung zum Pfarrer Karl Rempe

Geheimes Staatsarchiv, Preußischer Kulturbesitz, Berlin (GStAPK)
I HA Rep. 76   Kultusministerium
I Rep. 90 Annex P Geheime Staatspolizei

Historisches Archiv des Erzbistums Köln, Köln (AEK)
Generaka II, 23e Entnazifizierungsakten
Personalia   Kleruskartei

Johann Adam Möhler Institute für Ökumenik, Paderborn (MIO)
                Nachlaß Richard Kleine

Landesarchiv Berlin, Berlin (LAB)
Pr. Br. Rep. 57   Stadtpräsident der Reichshauptstadt Berlin

Library of Congress, Prints and Photographs Division, Washington, DC (LofCong)
3983 G   A Case History: Bernhard Rudolf Stempfle

Niedersächsisches Hauptstaatsarchiv, Hannover (NSHStA)
120 H.A. 164/92/74 Personalakte Richard Kleine

Provinzarchiv der Dominikanerprovinz Teutonia, Köln (PArcK) (per correspondence)
                Personalakte Chrysostomus Conrath, O.P.
                Personalakte Marianus Vetter, O.P.

Provinzialat Deutsche Franziskaner-Minoriten Provinz St. Elisabeth (PDFM) (per correspondence)
                Personaldaten

Seminararchiv Eichstätt, Eichstätt (SemAEI)
                Deutsche Jugendkraft (DJK)
                Personalakte Anton Heuberger

Staatsarchiv München, München (StA München)
ST   Staatsanwaltschaften

Staatsarchiv Nürnberg (StA Nürnberg) (per correspondence)
    NS-Mischbestand

Staatsarchiv Würzburg, Würzburg (StA Würzburg)
    Gestapo-Akten

Stadtarchiv Bobingen, Bobingen (StA Bobingen)
    Philipp Haeuser Sammlung

Stadtarchiv Kempten, Kempten (StA Kempten)
    Nachlaß Philipp Haeuser

United States Army Military History Institute, Carlisle, PA (USAMHI)
    Harold C. Deutsch Papers
    William J. Donovan Papers

United States Holocaust Memorial Museum, Washington, DC (USHMM)
    15.007   Records of the Reichssicherheitshauptamt (Microfilm copies of re-
                cords in Fond 362, Institute of National Memory, Main Commission
                for the Investigation of Crimes against the Polish Nation, Warsaw)

United States National Archives, College Park, MD (NARA)
    RG 84   Foreign Service Posts of the United States
    RG 238   Microfilm Copies of World War II War Crimes Records
    RG 242   Microfilm Copies of General Records of the NSDAP and Related
                Organizations (See BArch B above for abbreviations)
    RG 260   Records of the Office of the Military Governor, United States

Contemporary Newspapers, Newsletters, and Journals

Aiblinger Zeitung
AKD Mitteilungsblatt
Der Alemanne
Allgäuer Anzeigeblatt
Amper Bote
Amtsblatt des Bischöflichen Ordinariats Berlin
Antisemitische Zeitung
Augsburger Postzeitung
Bayerischer Kurier und Münchener Fremdenblatt
Bayern und Reich
The Catholic Mind
Dachauer Zeitung
Deutsche Freiheit
Deutsche Presse
Ecclesiastica
Eichstätter Anzeiger
Eichstätter Volkszeitung
Ermländische Zeitung
Fränkischer Kurier
Der Freiheitskampf
Freilassinger Zeitung
Germania
Illustrierter Beobachter

Der Jungdeutsche
Katholisches Kirchenblatt für das Bistum Berlin
Kaufbeurer Nationalzeitung
Kölnische Volkszeitung
Legauer Anzeiger
Linzer Volksblatt
Mainzer Anzeiger
Miesbacher Anzeiger
Mühldorfer Tageblatt
München-Augsburger Abendzeitung
Münchener Beobachter
Münchener Neuste Nachrichten
Münchener Post
Münchener Zeitung
National-Zeitung
Neue Augsburger Zeitung
Neue Nationalzeitung
Neue Preußische Zeitung/Kreuz-Zeitung
Der Neue Wille
Neue Zeitung
Pastoralblatt des Bistums Eichstätt
Reichenhaller Grenzbote
Rhein-Front
Rheinisch-Westfälische Zeitung
Rheinischer Merkur
Schönere Zukunft
Schwäbische Volkszeitung
Schwabmünchener Zeitung
Schwabmünchen Nationalzeitung
St. Willibalds Bote
Der Stürmer
Verordnungen des Fürstbischöflichen Ordinariats in Breslau
Völkischer Beobachter
Volksparole
Vorwärts
Vossische Zeitung
Warmia
Westdeutscher Beobachter
Württemberg-Zeitung
Würzburger Diözesanblatt
Zeitschrift für Musik
Zentrum Spiegel

Published Sources

Adam, Karl. "Deutsches Volkstum und katholisches Christentum." *Theologische Quartalschrift* 114 (1933): 40–63.
———. "Die geistige Lage des deutschen Katholizismus." Aachen, December 10, 1939. (BArch B NS43)
———. "Jesus, der Christus und wir Deutsche." *Wissenschaft und Weisheit* 1/2, no. 10 (1943): 73–103; and 3, no. 11 (1944): 10–23.
Adolph, Walter. *Geheime Aufzeichnungen aus dem nationalsozialistischen Kirchenkampf 1935–1943*. Ed. Ulrich von Hehl. 4th ed. Mainz: Matthias Grünewald, 1987.

Allen, William Sheridan. *The Nazi Seizure of Power: The Experience of a Single German Town, 1922–1945*. Rev. ed. New York: Franklin Watts, 1984.

Alvarez, David. *Spies in the Vatican: Espionage and Intrigue from Napoleon to the Holocaust*. Lawrence: University Press of Kansas, 2002.

Alvarez, David, and Robert A. Graham. *Nothing Sacred: Nazi Espionage against the Vatican, 1939–1945*. London: Frank Cass, 1997.

Alzheimer, Heidrun, and Wolfgang Brückner. "Volkstumsaffinitäten: Anton Stonner und das Dritte Reich." *Jahrbuch für Volkskunde* 14 (1991): 115–20.

Amery, Carl. *Capitulation: The Lesson of German Catholicism*. Trans. Edward Quinn. Freiburg: Herder and Herder, 1967.

Anderson, Margaret Lavinia. *Windthorst: A Political Biography*. Oxford: Clarendon Press, 1981.

———. "The Kulturkampf and the Course of German History." *Central European History* 19 (1986): 82–115.

Aschoff, Hans-Georg. "Joseph Godehard Machens." In *Die Bischöfe der deutschsprachigen Länder 1785/1803 bis 1945: Ein biographisches Lexikon*. Ed. Erwin Gatz. Berlin: Duncker & Humblot, 1983, 467–70.

Baird, Jay W. *To Die for Germany: Heroes in the Nazi Pantheon*. Bloomington: Indiana University Press, 1990.

Banki, Judith H., and John T. Pawlikowski, eds. *Ethics in the Shadow of the Holocaust: Christian and Jewish Perspectives*. Chicago: Sheed & Ward, 2001.

Barion, Hans. "Kirche oder Partei? Der Katholizismus im neuen Reich." *Europäische Revue* 9 (1933): 401–9. In *Kirche und Kirchenrecht: Gesammelte Aufsätze*. Ed. Werner Böckenförde. Reprint, Munich: Ferdinand Schöningh, 1984, 453–61.

Bauer, Yehuda. *Rethinking the Holocaust*. New Haven, CT: Yale University Press, 2001.

Baum, Gregory. *Is the New Testament Anti-Semitic? A Re-evaluation of the New Testament*. Glen Rock, NJ: Paulist Press, 1965.

———. *Christian Theology after Auschwitz*. London: Council of Christians and Jews, 1976.

Baumann, Schaul. *Die Deutsche Glaubensbewegung und ihr Gründer Jakob Wilhelm Hauer (1881–1962)*. Marburg: Diagonal, 2005.

Baumgärtner, Raimond. *Weltanschauungs-Kampf im Dritten Reich: Die Auseinandersetzung der Kirchen mit Alfred Rosenberg*. Mainz: Matthias Grünewald, 1977.

———. "Vom Kaplan zum Ministerialrat: Josef Roth—eine nationalsozialistische Karriere." In *Politik—Bildung—Religion*. Hans Maier zum 65. Geburtstag. Ed. Theo Stammen, Heinrich Oberreuter, Paul Mikat. Paderborn: Ferdinand Schöningh, 1996, 221–34.

Bayerische Benediktinerakademie, ed. *Bibliographie der deutschsprachigen Benediktiner 1880–1980*. 2 vols. St. Ottilien: EOS Verlag, 1985/1987.

Beck, Friedrich Alfred, ed. *Kampf und Sieg: Geschichte der Nationalsozialistischen Deutschen Arbeiterpartei im Gau Westfalen-Süd von den Anfängen bis zur Machtübernahme*. Dortmund: Westfalen-Verlag, 1938.

Bendel, Rainer, ed. *Die katholische Schuld? Katholizismus im Dritten Reich—Zwischen Arrangement und Widerstand*. Münster: LIT, 2002.

Bendel-Maidl, Lydia, and Rainer Bendel. "Schlaglichter auf den Umgang der deutschen Bischöfe mit der nationalsozialistischen Vergangenheit." In *Die katholische Schuld? Katholizismus im Dritten Reich—Zwischen Arrangement und Widerstand*. Ed. Rainer Bendel. Münster: LIT, 2002, 221–47.

Benedict XVI. "Pope's Address in Synagogue of Cologne." Zenit News Agency, August 19, 2005. http://www.zenit.org/english/visualizza.phtml?sid=75136.

Benzenhöfer, Udo, and Karin Finsterbusch. *Moraltheologie pro "NS—Euthanasie": Studien zu einem "Gutachten" (1940) von Prof. Joseph Mayer mit Edition des Textes*. Hannover: Laurentius, 1998.

Bergen, Doris L. "Catholics, Protestants, and Antisemitism in Nazi Germany." *Central*

European History 27 (1994): 329–48.

———. *Twisted Cross. The German Christian Movement in the Third Reich.* Chapel Hill: University of North Carolina, 1996.

———. "German Military Chaplains in the Second World War and the Dilemmas of Legitimacy." In *The Sword of the Lord: Military Chaplains from the First to the Twenty-First Century.* Ed. Doris L. Bergen. Notre Dame, IN: University of Notre Dame Press, 2004, 165–86.

Bergerson, Andrew Stuart. *Ordinary Germans in Extraordinary Times: The Nazi Revolution in Hildesheim.* Bloomington: Indiana University Press, 2004.

Bergh, Wilhelm Alois van den. "Kann der überzeugte Katholik überzeugter National-sozialist sein?" Unpublished manuscript, 1936.

Berning, Wilhelm. *Katholische Kirche und deutsches Volkstum.* Munich: Georg D. W. Callwey, 1934.

Besier, Gerhard. "Anti-Bolshevism and Antisemitism: The Catholic Church in Ger-many and National Socialist Ideology, 1936–37." *Journal of Ecclesiastical History* 43 (1992): 447–56.

———. *Die Kirchen und das Dritte Reich: Spaltungen und Abwehrkämpfe 1934–1937.* Mu-nich: Propyläen, 2001.

Bischöfliches Ordinariat Rottenburg, ed. *Das Verzeichnis der Geistlichen der Diözese Rottenburg-Stuttgart von 1874 bis 1983.* Rottenburg, 1984.

———. *Das Verzeichnis der Priester und Diakone der Diözese Rottenburg-Stuttgart von 1922 bis 1992.* Rottenburg, 1993.

Blackbourn, David. *Class, Religion, and Local Politics in Wilhelmine Germany: The Centre Party in Württemberg before 1914.* New Haven, CT: Yale University Press, 1980.

Blaschke, Olaf. *Blaming the Victim: Jewish Attitudes towards Catholics and their Anti-semitism.* Lincoln: University of Nebraska Press/The Vidal Sassoon International Center for the Study of Antisemitism, forthcoming.

Bleistein, Roman, S.J. "Abt Alban Schachleiter, OSB: Zwischen Kirchentreue und Hitlerkult." *Historisches Jahrbuch* 115 (1995): 170–87.

———. "'Überläufer im Sold der Kirchenfeinde' Josef Roth und Albert Hartl: Priesterkarrieren im Dritten Reich." *Beiträge zur Altbayerischen Kirchengeschichte* 42 (1996): 71–109.

Blümel, Jutta. "Dr. theol. Philipp Haeuser, ein Pfarrer im Nationalsozialismus." Zulas-sungsarbeit, University of Augsburg, 1986.

Boberach, Heinz. "Organe der nationalsozialistischen Kirchenpolitik: Kompetenz-verteilung und Karrieren in Reich und Ländern." In *Staat und Parteien.* Festschrift für Rudolf Morsey zum 65. Geburtstag. Ed. Karl Dietrich Bracher, Paul Mikar, Konrad Repgen, Martin Schumacher, and Hans-Peter Schwarz. Berlin: Duncker & Humblot, 1992, 305–31.

Böckenförde, Ernst-Wolfgang. "Der deutsche Katholizismus im Jahre 1933: Eine kritis-che Betrachtung." *Hochland* 53 (1961): 215–39.

Boog, Horst. *Graf Ernst zu Reventlow (1869–1943): Eine Studie zur Krise der deutschen Geschichte seit dem Ende des 19. Jahrhunderts.* Heidelberg, 1965.

Bormann, Irene. *Keine Schule wie jede andere: Geschichte des Staatlichen Gymnasiums in Duderstadt 1876–2001.* Duderstadt: Mecke, 2001.

Boyens, Armin. *Kirchenkampf und Ökumene 1933–1939: Darstellung und Dokumentation.* Munich: Chr. Kaiser, 1969.

———. "Die Kirchenpolitik der amerikanischen Besatzungsmacht." In *Kirchen in der Nachkriegszeit: Vier zeitgeschichtliche Beiträge.* Ed. Hannelore Braun. Göttingen: Vandenhoeck & Ruprecht, 1979, 7–57.

Brandl, Ludwig. "Josef Roth." *Biographisch-Bibliographisches Kirchenlexikon.* Vol. 8. Ed. Friedrich Wilhelm Bautz. Herzberg: Traugott Bautz, 1994, 742–44.

———. "Michael Rackl." In *Die Bischöfe der deutschsprachigen Länder 1945–2001: Ein bi-

ographisches Lexikon. Ed. Erwin Gatz. Berlin: Duncker & Humblot, 2002, 153–56.

Brandt, Hans-Jürgen. "Franz Justus Rarkowski." In *Die Bischöfe der deutschsprachigen Länder 1785/1803 bis 1945: Ein biographisches Lexikon.* Ed. Erwin Gatz. Berlin: Duncker & Humblot, 1983, 594–95.

Brandt, Hans-Jürgen, and Peter Häger, eds. *Biographisches Lexikon der katholischen Militärseelsorge Deutschlands 1848 bis 1945.* Paderborn: Bonifatius, 2002.

Breuer, Thomas. *Verordneter Wandel? Der Widerstreit zwischen nationalsozialistischem Herrschaftsanspruch und traditioneller Lebenswelt im Erzbistum Bamberg.* Mainz: Matthias Grünewald, 1992.

Breuning, Klaus. *Die Vision des Reiches: Deutscher Katholizismus zwischen Demokratie und Diktatur (1929–1934).* Munich: Max Hueber, 1969.

Brombacher, Kuno, and Emil Ritter, eds. *Sendschreiben katholischer Deutscher an ihre Volks- und Glaubensgenossen.* Münster: Aschendorff, 1936.

Brown-Fleming, Suzanne. *The Holocaust and Catholic Conscience: Cardinal Aloisius Muench and the Guilt Question in Germany.* Notre Dame, IN: University of Notre Dame Press in association with the United States Holocaust Memorial Museum, 2006.

Brunnert, Clemens, O.S.B. *Vielfalt des Lebens: Dr. Lorenz Pieper, 1875–1951.* Königsmünster. N.p., n.d. (AKK NL Pieper)

Buchheim, Hans. "Fördernde Mitgliedschaft bei der SS." In *Gutachten des Instituts für Zeitgeschichte.* Munich: Institut für Zeitgeschichte, 1958, 350–51.

Bukey, Evan Burr. *Hitler's Austria: Popular Sentiment in the Nazi Era 1938–1945.* Chapel Hill: University of North Carolina Press, 2000.

Burkard, Dominik. *Härisie und Mythus des 20. Jahrhunderts: Rosenbergs nationalsozialistische Weltanschauung vor dem Tribunal der römischen Inquisition.* Paderborn: Ferdinand Schöningh, 2005.

Burleigh, Michael, and Wolfgang Wippermann. *The Racial State: Germany 1933–1945.* Cambridge, MA: Cambridge University Press, 1991.

Cancik, Hubert, and Uwe Puschner, eds. *Antisemitismus, Paganismus, völkische Religion.* Munich: K. G. Saur, 2004.

Carroll, James. *Constantine's Sword: The Church and the Jews. A History.* New York: Houghton Mifflin, 2001.

Chamberlain, Houston Stewart. *Die Grundlagen des neunzehnten Jahrhunderts.* 10th ed. Munich: F. Bruckmann, 1912.

Childers, Thomas. *The Nazi Voter: The Social Foundations of Fascism in Germany, 1919–1933.* Chapel Hill: University of North Carolina Press, 1988.

Clauss, Manfred, and Erwin Gatz. "Nikolaus Bares." In *Die Bischöfe der deutschsprachigen Länder 1785/1803 bis 1945: Ein biographisches Lexikon.* Ed. Erwin Gatz. Berlin: Duncker & Humblot, 1983, 23–26.

Cohen, David. "Transitional Justice in Divided Germany after 1945." In *Retribution and Reparation in the Transition to Democracy.* Ed. Jon Elster. Cambridge, MA: Cambridge University Press, 59–88.

Cohen, Gary B. *The Politics of Ethnic Survival: Germans in Prague, 1861–1914.* 2d rev. ed. Princeton, NJ: Princeton University Press, 2006.

Commission for Religious Relations with the Jews. *We Remember: A Reflection on the Shoah.* http://www.vatican.va/roman_curia/pontifical_councils/chrstuni/documents/rc_oc_chrstuni_doc_16031998_shoah-en.html.

Conradi, Peter. *Hitler's Piano Player: The Rise and Fall of Ernst Hanfstaengl, Confidant of Hitler, Ally of FDR.* New York: Carroll & Graf, 2004.

Conway, John S. *The Nazi Persecution of the Churches 1933–45.* New York: Basic Books, 1968.

Conzemius, Victor. "Joseph Lortz—ein Kirchenhistoriker als Brückenbauer." *Geschichte und Gegenwart* 9 (1990): 247–78.

———. "Zwischen Anpassung und Widerstand: Die Christen und der Nationalsozialismus." *Internationale katholische Zeitschrift* 23 (1994): 483–502.

Coppa, Frank J., ed. *Controversial Concordats: The Vatican's Relations with Napoleon, Mussolini, and Hitler*. Washington, DC: Catholic University of America Press, 1999.

Corsten, Wilhelm, ed. *Sammlung kirchlicher Erlasse, Verordnungen und Bekanntmachungen für die Erzdiözese Köln*. Cologne: Bachem, 1929.

Damberg, Wilhelm. "Kirchengeschichte zwischen Demokratie und Diktatur. George Schreiber und Joseph Lortz in Münster 1933–1950." In *Theologische Fakultäten im Nationalsozialismus*. Ed. Leonore Siegele-Wenschkewitz and Carsten Nicolaisen. Göttingen: Vandenhoeck and Ruprecht, 1993, 145–64.

Davies, Alan. *Infected Christianity: A Study of Modern Racism*. Montreal: McGill-Queen's University Press, 1988.

Deniffel, Monika. "Josef Bürckel." *Biographisches Lexikon zum Dritten Reich*. Ed. Hermann Weiß. Frankfurt: S. Fischer, 1998.

Denzler, Georg. "Schmerzhafte ökumenische Erinnerungen: Neugefundene Briefe des Paderborner Kirchenhistorikers Adolf Herte an den Erlanger Kirchenhistoriker Walther von Loewenich." *Zeitschrift für bayerische Kirchengeschichte* 71 (2002): 187–200.

———. *Widerstand ist nicht das richtige Wort: Katholische Priester, Bischöfe und Theologen im Dritten Reich*. Zürich: Pendo, 2003.

Deuerlein, Ernst, ed. *Der Hitler-Putsch: Bayerische Dokumente zum 8./9. November 1923*. Stuttgart: Deutsche Verlags-Anstalt, 1962.

Deutsch, Harold C. *The Conspiracy against Hitler in the Twilight War*. Minneapolis: University of Minnesota Press, 1968.

Dierker, Wolfgang. *Himmlers Glaubenskrieger: Der Sicherheitsdienst der SS und seine Religionspolitik 1933–1941*. Paderborn: Ferdinand Schöningh, 2001.

Dierks, Margarete. *Jakob Wilhelm Hauer 1881–1962: Leben, Werk, Wirkung*. Heidelberg: Lambert Schneider, 1986.

Dietrich, Donald J. "Joseph Mayer and the Missing Memo: A Catholic Justification for Euthanasia." In *Remembering for the Future: Working Papers and Addenda*. vol 2. Ed. Yehuda Bauer, Alice Eckardt, Franklin H. Littell, and Robert Maxwell. Oxford: Pergamon Press, 1989, 38–49.

———. "Catholic Resistance to Biological and Racist Eugenics in the Third Reich." In *Germans against Nazism: Nonconformity, Opposition, and Resistance in the Third Reich*. Ed. Francis R. Nicosia and Lawrence D. Stokes. New York: Berg, 1990, 137–55.

———. "Nazi Eugenics: Adaptation and Resistance among German Catholic Intellectual Leaders." In *Medicine, Ethics, and the Third Reich: Historical and Contemporary Issues*. Ed. John J. Michalczyk. Kansas City, MO: Sheed & Ward, 1994, 50–63.

———. "Catholic Eugenics in Germany, 1920–1945: Hermann Muckermann, S.J., and Joseph Mayer." *Journal of Church and State* 34 (1994): 575–600.

———. *God and Humanity in Auschwitz: Jewish-Christian Relations and Sanctioned Murder*. New Brunswick, NJ: Transaction, 1995.

Directorium Dioecesis Warmiensis (Schematismus Ermland).

Dirks, Walter. "Katholiken zwischen Anpassung und Widerstand." In *Widerstand und Verweigerung in Deutschland 1933 bis 1945*. Ed. Richard Löwenthal and Patrick von zur Mühlen. Bonn: J. H. W. Dietz, 1982, 140–42.

Drobner, Hubertus. "Adolf Herte." In *Biographisch-Bibliographisches Kirchenlexikon*. Vol. 24. Ed. Traugott Bautz. Nordhausen: Traugott Bautz, 2005, 833–35.

Dröder, Johannes. "Angriffe auf den Jungdeutschen Orden und deren Widerlegung." In *Jungdeutscher Orden, Katholizismus und Zentrum*. Kassel: Jungdeutscher Verlag, 1924, 8–13

Engelhard, Gildis. *Abt Schachleiter, der deutsche Kämpfer*. Munich, 1941.

Ericksen, Robert P. *Theologians under Hitler: Gerhard Kittel/Paul Althaus/Emanuel Hirsch.* New Haven, CT: Yale University Press, 1985.

Ernesti, Jörg. *Ökumene im Dritten Reich.* Paderborn: Bonifatius, 2007.

Eschweiler, Karl. "Die Kirche im neuen Reich." *Deutsches Volkstum, Monatsschrift für das deutsche Geistesleben* 15 (1933): 451–58.

Evans, Ellen Lovell. *The German Center Party 1870–1933: A Study in Political Catholicism.* Carbondale: Southern Illinois University Press, 1981.

Fandel, Thomas. *Konfession und Nationalsozialismus: Evangelische und katholische Pfarrer in der Pfalz 1930–1939.* Paderborn: Ferdinand Schöningh, 1997.

Faulhaber, Michael von. *Rufende Stimmen in der Wüste der Gegenwart: Gesammelte Reden, Predigten, Hirtenbriefe.* 2d ed. Freiburg: Herder, 1932.

Field, Geoffrey G. *Evangelist of Race: The Germanic Vision of Houston Stewart Chamberlain.* New York: Columbia University Press, 1981.

Fischer, Conan. *The Ruhr Crisis, 1923–1924.* New York: Oxford University Press, 2003.

Fittkau, Gerhard. "Biographie Maximilian Kaller." Manuscript, n.d.

Flannery, Edward H. *"The Anguish of the Jews": Twenty-Three Centuries of Antisemitism.* Rev. ed. Mahwah, N.J.: Paulist Press, 1985.

Franz, Georg. "Munich: Birthplace and Center of the National Socialist German Workers' Party." *Journal of Modern History* 29 (1957): 319–34.

Frei, Norbert. *National Socialist Rule in Germany: The Führer State, 1933–1945.* Trans. Simon B. Steyne. Oxford: Blackwell, 1993.

Freundorfer, Martin. "Das Missionsseminar Schweiklberg." In *O Lux Beata Trinitas: Hundert Jahre Kloster Schweiklberg 1904–2004.* Passau: Dietmar Klinger, 2005, 251–34.

Fröhlich, Elke, ed. *Die Tagebücher von Joseph Goebbels, sämtliche Fragmente.* I:3. Munich: K. G. Saur, 1987.

Gatz, Erwin. "Lorenz Jaeger." In *Die Bischöfe der deutschsprachigen Länder 1785/1803 bis 1945: Ein biographisches Lexikon.* Ed. Erwin Gatz. Berlin: Duncker & Humblot, 1983, 344–46.

Gaynard, Clifton Greer. "Rebels and Revolutionaries: Artur Mahraun and the Young German Order: A Study in Germanic Ideology." Ph.D. diss., State University of New York at Buffalo, 2000.

Godman, Peter. *Hitler and the Vatican: Inside the Secret Archives That Reveal the New Story of the Nazis and the Church.* New York: Free Press, 2004.

Goñi, Uki. *The Real Odessa: Smuggling the Nazis to Perón's Argentina.* London: Granta, 2002.

Graham, Robert A., S.J. "The 'Right to Kill' in the Third Reich: Prelude to Genocide." *Catholic Historical Review* 62 (1976): 56–76.

———. "Documenti di guerra da Mosca: Spionaggio nazista antivaticano." *La Civiltà Cattolica* 144 (1993): 542–50.

———. *The Vatican and Communism during World War II: What Really Happened?* San Francisco: Ignatius Press, 1996.

Greive, Hermann. *Theologie und Ideologie: Katholizismus und Judentum in Deutschland und Österreich, 1918–1935.* Heidelberg: Lampert Schneider, 1969.

Griech-Polelle, Beth A. *Bishop von Galen: German Catholicism and National Socialism.* New Haven, CT: Yale University Press, 2002.

Griffith, Williams E. "The Denazification Program in the United States Zone of Germany." Ph.D. diss., Harvard University, 1950.

Grill, Johnpeter Horst. *The Nazi Movement in Baden.* Chapel Hill, NC: University of North Carolina Press, 1983.

Groll, Thomas. "Franz Xaver Eberle (1874–1951)." *Jahrbuch des Vereins für Augsburger Bistumsgeschichte* 39 (2005): 433–55.

———. "Spruchkammerverfahren Weihbischof Dr. Franz Xaver Eberle Februar 1947 bis

März 1948." *Verein für Augsburger Bistumsgeschichte* 40 (2006): 549–605.

Grollegg-Edler, Charlotte. *Die wehrhaft Nachtigall Ottokar Kernstock (1848–1928): Eine Studie zu Leben, Werk und Wirkung.* Graz: Leykam-Grazer Universitätsverlag, 2006.

Groothuis, Rainer Maria. *Im Dienste einer überstaatlichen Macht: Die deutschen Dominikaner unter der NS-Diktatur.* Münster: Regensburg, 2002.

Gross, Michael B. *The War against Catholicism: Liberalism and the Anti-Catholic Imagination in Nineteenth-Century Germany.* Ann Arbor: University of Michigan Press, 2004.

Gruber, Hubert. *Katholische Kirche und Nationalsozialismus: Ein Bericht in Quellen.* Paderborn: Ferdinand Schöningh, 2006.

Gründer, Horst. "Rechtskatholizismus im Kaiserreich und in der Weimarer Republik unter besonderer Berücksichtigung des Rheinlandes und Westfalens." *Westfälische Zeitschrift* 134 (1984): 107–55.

Gruß, Heribert. *Erzbischof Lorenz Jaeger als Kirchenführer im Dritten Reich: Tatsachen—Dokumente—Entwicklungen—Kontext—Probleme.* Paderborn: Bonifatius, 1995.

Haerendel, Ulrike, and Bernadette Ott, eds. *München—"Hauptstadt der Bewegung."* Munich: Münchener Stadtmuseum, 1993.

Haering, Stephen. "Kirchenrechtliche Marginalien zum Fall Schachleiter." In *Für Euch Bischof—mit Euch Christ.* Festschrift für Friedrich Kardinal Wetter zum siebzigsten Geburtstag. Ed. Manfred Weitlauff and Peter Neuner. St. Ottilien: EOS, 1998, 945–59.

Haeuser, Philipp. *Der Barnasbrief neu untersucht und neu erklärt.* Paderborn: Ferdinand Schöningh, 1912.

———. *Wir deutsche Katholiken und die moderne revolutionäre Bewegung oder, Los vom Opportunismus und zurück zur Prinzipientreue!* Regensburg: G. J. Manz, 1922.

———. *Jud und Christ oder, Wem gebührt die Weltherrschaft?* Regensburg: G. J. Manz, 1923.

———. "Die Judenfrage vom kirchlichen Standpunkt." *Das Neue Reich* 5 (1923/1924): 442–46.

———. *Anlass und Zweck des Galaterbriefes: Seine Logische Gedankenentwicklung.* Münster: Aschendorff, 1925.

———. *Pazifismus und Christentum.* Augsburg: Schlosser/F. Schott, 1925.

———. *Kampfgeist gegen Pharisäertum: Nationalsozialistische Weihnachtsrede eines katholischen Geistlichen.* Munich: Franz Eher, 1931.

———. [Von einem katholischen Historiker, pseud.]. *Irrwege der katholischen Kirche.* Berlin: Deutschkirche, 1932.

———. [Father Willibald, pseud.]. *Der Kämpfer Jesus: Für suchende und ringende deutsche Menschen.* Stuttgart: Wilhelm Schöberl, 1935.

———. "Mein deutsches Ringen und Werden." Manuscript, 1936–1939. (StA Kempten NL Haeuser)

———. [Gottschalk, pseud.]. *Die deutsche Weltanschauung der Freude im schwersten Kampf mit dem jüdisch-kirchlichen Pessimismus.* Self-published, 1938.

———. "Mein Werden." Manuscript, 1942. (StA Kempten NL Haeuser)

———, trans. *Des Heiligen Philosophen und Martyrers Justinus Dialog mit dem Juden Tryphon.* Kempten: Kösel, 1917.

Handbuch des Erzbistums Köln. 23d ed. 1933.

Hanfstaengl, Ernst. *Zwischen Weißem und Braunem Haus: Memoiren eines politischen Außenseiters.* Munich: R. Piper, 1970.

———. *The Unknown Hitler.* Introduction by Richard J. Evans. London: Gibson Square, 2005.

Hastings, Derek. "How 'Catholic' Was the Early Nazi Movement? Religion, Race, and Culture in Munich, 1919–1924." *Central European History* 36 (2003): 383–433.

Hausfelder, Edmund. "Die Situation der katholischen Kirche in Ingolstadt von 1918 bis 1945." In *Ingolstadt im Nationalsozialismus: Eine Studie. Dokumentation zur Zeitgeschichte.* Ingolstadt: Stadtarchiv, 1995, 310–50

Head, Peter M. "The Nazi Quest for an Aryan Jesus." *Journal for the Study of the Historical Jesus* 2 (2004): 55–89.

Hehl, Ulrich von. "Die Kirchen in der NS-Diktatur: Zwischen Anpassung, Selbstbehauptung und Widerstand." In *Deutschland 1933–1945: Neue Studien zur nationalsozialistischen Herrschaft.* Ed. Karl Dietrich Bracher, Manfred Funke, and Hans Adolf Jacobsen. Düsseldorf: Droste, 1992, 153–81.

Hehl, Ulrich von, Christoph Kösters, Petra Stenz-Maur, and Elisabeth Zimmermann. *Priester unter Hitlers Terror: Eine biographische und statistische Erhebung.* 2 vols. 3d enl. ed. Paderborn: Ferdinand Schöningh, 1996.

Heiden, Konrad. *Hitler: A Biography.* Trans. Winifred Ray. New York: Alfred A. Knopf, 1936.

———. *The Führer.* Trans. Ralph Manheim. 1944. Reprint, Edison, NJ: Castle Books, 2002.

Heilbronner, Oded, and Detlef Mühlberger. "The Achilles' Heel of German Catholicism: 'Who Voted for Hitler?' Revisited." *European History Quarterly* 27 (1997): 221–49.

Heimbucher, Max. *Die Orden und Kongregationen der katholischen Kirche.* Vol. 2. Paderborn: Ferdinand Schöningh, 1933, 660.

Heitzer, Horstwalter. *Der Volksverein für das katholische Deutschland im Kaiserreich 1890–1918.* Mainz: Matthias Grünewald, 1979.

Hellriegel, Ludwig, ed. *Widerstehen und Verfolgung in den Pfarreien des Bistums Mainz 1933–1945.* Vol. 1, *Rheinhessen.* Pt. 2, Dekanate Bingen, Gau-Bickelheim, Oppenheim, Worms. Mainz: Bischöfliches Ordinariat, 1990.

———, ed. *Widerstehen und Verfolgung in den Pfarreien des Bistums Mainz 1933–1945.* Vol. 2, *Starkenburg.* Pt. 1, Dekanate Mainz-Land (rechtsrheinisch), Bensheim, Darmstadt, Dieburg. Mainz: Bischöfliches Ordinariat, 1990.

Helmreich, Ernst Christian. *The German Churches under Hitler: Background, Struggle, and Epilogue.* Detroit: Wayne State University Press, 1979.

Heschel, Susannah. "Nazifying Christian Theology: Walter Grundmann and the Institute for the Study and Eradication of Jewish Influence on German Life." *Church History* 63 (1994): 587–605.

Hetzer, Gerhard. *Kulturkampf in Augsburg 1933–1945: Konflikte zwischen Staat, Einheitspartei und christlichen Kirchen, dargestellt am Beispiel einer deutschen Stadt.* Augsburg: Hieronymus Mühlberger, 1982.

Heuberger, Anton. [Spectator, pseud.]. "Die Voraussetzungen hüben und drüben für die Wiedervereinigung im Glauben in der von Christus gebotenen Una Sancta." Pt. I, "Unter Brüdern." Unpublished memoir, n.d. (DAEI)

———. "Die Voraussetzungen hüben und drüben für die Wiedereinigung im Glauben in der von Christus gebotenen Una Sancta." Pt. IV, "Nachlese: Priesterliche Gedanken an der Schwelle des Siebzigers," February–June, 1961. Unpublished memoir, 1961. (DAEI)

Hinkel, Hans. *Einer unter Hunderttausend.* Munich: Knorr & Hirth, 1942.

Hoffmann, Ernst, and Hubert Janssen. *Die Wahrheit über die Ordensdevisenprozesse 1935/36.* Bielefeld: Hausknecht, 1967.

Hoffmann, Heinrich. *Hitler was my friend.* Trans. R. H. Stevens. London: Burke, 1955.

Hofmüller, Harold Anton. "Steirische Priester befürworten den Nationalsozialismus und den Anchluss an das Deutsche Reich Adolf Hitlers." University of Graz, 1997.

Horn, Christa. *Die Internierungs- und Arbeitslager in Bayern 1945–1952.* Frankfurt: Peter Lang, 1992.

Hoser, Paul. "Hitler und die katholische Kirche: Zwei Briefe aus dem Jahr 1927."

Vierteljahrshefte für Zeitgeschichte 42 (1994): 473–92.

Hudal, Alois C. *Die Grundlagen des Nationalsozialismus.* 5th ed. Leipzig and Vienna: Johannes Günther, 1937.

————. *Römische Tagebücher: Lebensbeichte eines alten Bischofs.* Graz and Stuttgart: Leopold Stocker, 1976.

Hughes, John Jay. "The Reich Concordat 1933: Capitulation or Compromise." *Australian Journal of Politics and History* 20 (1974): 164–75.

Hürten, Heinz. "Kirchen und amerikanische Besatzungsmacht in Deutschland: Die OMGUS-Papiere als kirchengeschichtliche Quelle." In *Kirche, Staat und katholische Wissenschaft in der Neuzeit.* Festschrift für Heribert Raab zum 65. Geburtstag am 16. März 1988. Ed. Albert Portmann-Tinguely. Paderborn: Ferdinand Schöningh, 1988, 565–81.

————. *Deutsche Katholiken 1918–1945.* Paderborn: Ferdinand Schöningh, 1992.

————, ed. *Deutsche Briefe 1934–1938: Ein Blatt der katholischen Emigration.* Vol. 1, 1934–1935. Mainz: Matthias Grünewald, 1969.

————, ed. *Deutsche Briefe 1934–1938: Ein Blatt der katholischen Emigration.* Vol. 2, 1936–1938. Mainz: Matthias Grünewald, 1969.

Institut zur Erforschung des jüdischen Einflusses auf das deutsche kirchliche Leben, ed. *Die Botschaft Gottes.* Leipzig: Georg Wigand, 1940.

Jablonsky, David. *The Nazi Party in Dissolution: Hitler and the Verbotzeit, 1923–25.* London: Frank Cass, 1989.

Jarausch, Konrad H. *After Hitler: Recivilizing Germans, 1945–1995.* Trans. Brandon Hunziker. New York: Oxford University Press, 2006.

Jasper, Ronald C. D. *George Bell, Bishop of Chichester.* London: Oxford University Press, 1968.

Jefford, Clayton N., with Kenneth J. Harder and Louis D. Amezaga Jr. *Reading the Apostolic Fathers: An Introduction.* Peabody, MA: Hendrickson Publishers, 1996.

Jones, Larry Eugene. "Catholic Conservatives in the Weimar Republic: The Politics of the Rhenish-Westphalian Aristocracy, 1918–1933." *German History* 18 (2000): 60–85.

————. "Franz von Papen, the German Center Party, and the Failure of Catholic Conservatism in the Weimar Republic." *Central European History* 38 (2005): 191–217.

————. "Catholics on the Right: The Reich Catholic Committee of the German National People's Party, 1920–1933." *Historisches Jahrbuch* 126 (2006): 221–67.

————. "Nationalists, Nazis, and the Assault against Weimar: Revisiting the Harzburg Rally of October 1931." *German Studies Review* 29 (2006): 483–94.

Jones, Nigel H. *A Brief History of the Birth of the Nazis: How the Freikorps Blazed the Trail for Hitler.* New York: Carroll & Graf, 2004.

Kaller, Max. *Unser Laienapostolat: Was es ist und wie es sein soll.* Leutesdorf am Rhein: Johannesbund, 1927.

Kaltefleiter, Werner, and Hanspeter Oschwald. *Spione im Vatikan. Die Päpste im Visier der Geheimdienste.* Munich: Pattloch, 2006.

Kather, Linus. *Von Rechts wegen? Prozesse.* Esslingen: Bruno Langer, 1982.

Kauders, Anthony. "Jews in the Christian Gaze: Munich's Churches before and after Hitler." *Patterns of Prejudice* 34 (2000): 27–45.

Kent, Peter C. *The Lonely Cold War of Pope Pius XII: The Roman Catholic Church and the Division of Europe, 1943–1950.* Montreal: McGill-Queen's University Press, 2002.

Kershaw, Ian. *The 'Hitler Myth': Image and Reality in the Third Reich.* Oxford: Oxford University Press, 1989.

————. *Hitler 1889–1936: Hubris.* New York: W. W. Norton, 1999.

Kertzer, David I. *The Popes against the Jews: The Vatican's Role in the Rise of Modern Anti-Semitism.* New York: Knopf, 2001.

Kirk, Tim. *The Longman Companion to Nazi Germany.* New York: Longman, 1995.

Klapczynski, Gregor. "Hugo Koch (1869–1940): Skizze einer Modernisten-Biographie." University of Münster, 2005.

———. "Das Wesen des Katholizismus-oder: Warum Paulus in Korinth kein Pontifikalamt hielt. An sichten des Kirchenhistorikers Hugo Koch (1869–1940)." *Rottenburger Jakrbuch für Kirchengeschichte* 25 (2006): 251–69.

Klee, Ernst. *Persilscheine und falsche Pässe: Wie die Kirchen den Nazis halfen.* Frankfurt: Fischer, 1991.

Klein, Gotthard. *Berolinen Canonizationis Servi Dei Bernardi Lichtenberg: Sacerdotis Saecularis in Odium Fidei, Uti Fertur, Interfecti (1875–1943).* Vol. 2, *Summarium-Documenta.* Rome: Congregation de Causis Sanctorum, 1992.

———. *Der Volksverein für das katholische Deutschland 1890–1933: Geschichte, Bedeutung, Untergang.* Paderborn: Ferdinand Schöningh, 1996.

Kleine, Richard. *Erlösung!* Munich: Josef Kösel and Friedrich Pustet, 1929.

———. "Ja und Nein zum Nationalsozialismus." *Der Deutsche Weg,* August 5, 1932.

———. *Die acht Seligpreisungen der Bergpredigt: Die Richtlinien des Reiches Gottes als Predigtreihe.* Paderborn: Ferdinand Schöningh, 1935.

———. "War Jesus ein Jude?" (c. 1939). (MIO NL Kleine))

———. "Die Bergpredigt als Kampfansage gegen das Judentum." Vienna, August 1943. (MIO NL Kleine)

———. *Die Verkündigung der Frohbotschaft in der höheren Schule.* Duderstadt, 1950.

———. "Die grundlegende Bedeutung der Bergpredigt." *Die Kirche in der Welt* 6 (1953): 5–10.

———. "Die Mission im Religionsunterricht der höheren Schulen." *Zeitschrift für Missionswissenschaft und Religionswissenschaft.* N.d., 25–34. (MIO NL Kleine)

Kleineidam, Erich. *Die katholisch-theologische Fakultät der Universität Breslau 1811–1945.* Cologne: Weinand, 1961.

Koch, Hugo. "Paderborner 'Wissenschaft' und meine 'Unwissenheit.'" *Nationalsozialistische Monatshefte* 7 (1936): 417–25.

Koch, H. W. *Der deutsche Bürgerkrieg: Eine Geschichte der deutschen und österreichischen Freikorps, 1918–1933.* Trans. Klaus Oelhaf and Ulrich Riemerschmidt. Dresden: Antaios, 2002.

Kopf, Paul. *Franz Weiß—Für Deutschland und Christus.* Ostfildern: Schwabenverlag, 1994.

Kraus, Johann. "Der Sekretär zweier Nuntien Pater Eduard Gehrmann, SVD." In *In Verbo Tuo.* Festschrift zum 50 jährigen Bestehen des Missionspriesterseminars St. Augustin bei Siegburg, Rheinland, 1913–1963. Ed. St. Augustin editors. St. Augustin: Steyl, 1963.

Krausnick, Helmut, Hans Buchheim, Martin Broszat, and Hans-Adolf Jacobsen. *Anatomy of the SS State.* Trans. Richard Barry, Marian Jackson, and Dorothy Long. New York: Walker, 1968.

Kreidler, Hans. "Karl Adam und der Nationalsozialismus." *Rottenburger Jahrbuch für Kirchengeschichte* 2 (1983): 129–40.

Kreutzer, Heike. *Das Reichskirchenministerium im Gefüge der nationalsozialistischen Herrschaft.* Düsseldorf: Droste, 2000.

Krieg, Robert Anthony. *Karl Adam: Catholicism in German Culture.* Notre Dame, IN: University of Notre Dame Press, 1992.

———. "Karl Adam, National Socialism, and Christian Tradition." *Theological Studies* 60 (1999): 432–56.

———. *Catholic Theologians in Nazi Germany.* New York: Continuum, 2004.

Krose, Hermann A., ed. *Kirchliches Handbuch für das katholische Deutschland.* Vol. 21, 1939–1940. Köln: Bachem, 1940.

Kühn-Ludewig, Maria. *Johannes Pohl (1904–1960): Judaist und Bibliothekar im Dienste Rosenbergs: Eine biographische Dokumentation.* Hannover: Laurentius, 2000.

Kupper, Alfons, ed. *Staatliche Akten über die Reichskonkordatsverhandlungen 1933.* Mainz: Matthias Grünewald, 1969.

Läpple, Alfred. *Adolf Hitler: Psychogramm einer katholischen Kindheit.* Stein am Rhein: Christina, 2001, 173–78.

Landkreis Augsburg, ed. *Landkreis Schwabmünchen: Landschaft, Geschichte, Wirtschaft, Kultur.* 2d rev. ed. Augsburg: Landratsamt Augsburg, 1975.

Large, David Clay. *Where Ghosts Walked: Munich's Road to the Third Reich.* New York: W. W. Norton, 1996.

Lautenschläger, Gabriele. *Joseph Lortz (1887–1975): Weg, Umwelt und Werk eines katholischen Kirchenhistorikers.* Würzburg: Echter, 1987.

———. "Der Kirchenkampf in Thüringen." In *Nationalsozialismus in Thüringen.* Ed. Detlev Heiden and Gunther Mai. Weimar: Böhlau, 1995, 463–86.

Lehmann, Bernhard. *Katholische Kirche und Besatzungsmacht in Bayern 1945–1949 im Spiegel der OMGUS-Akten.* Munich: Neue Schriftenreihe des Stadtarchivs München, 1994.

Leiber, Robert. "'Mit brennender Sorge': März 1937–März 1962." *Stimmen der Zeit* 87 (1961/62): 417–26.

Lenski, Reinhold. "Pfarrer Dr. Philipp Haeuser (1876–1960)—ein Kämpfer für den Nationalsozialismus." Lecture delivered at the 14th scholarly meeting of Local Historians in the Administrative District of Schwaben, Irsee, November 29–30, 2002.

Lenz, Hubert. *Der katholische Geistliche im weltlichen Recht.* Trier: Paulinus, 1932.

Lepper, Herbert, ed. *Volk, Kirche und Vaterland: Wahlaufrufe, Aufrufe, Satzungen und Statuten des Zentrums 1870–1933. Eine Quellensammlung zur Geschichte insbesondere der Rheinischen und Westfälischen Zentrumspartei.* Düsseldorf: Droste, 1998.

Letter of Barnabas, in *The Apostolic Fathers.* Trans. and ed. Kirsopp Lake. Cambridge, MA: Harvard University Press, 1952, 335–409.

Lettl, Josef. "Die Arbeitsgemeinschaft für den religiösen Frieden 1938." Diplomarbeit, Katholisch-Theologische Privatuniversität Linz, 1981.

Leugers, Antonia. *Gegen eine Mauer bischöflichen Schweigens: Der Ausschuss für Ordensangelegenheiten und seine Widerstandskonzeption 1941 bis 1945.* Frankfurt: Josef Knecht, 1996.

Lewy, Guenther. *The Catholic Church and Nazi Germany.* New York: McGraw-Hill, 1964.

Liebmann, Maximilian. "Rein zur Zeit des Nationalsozialismus und nach dem Zweiten Weltkrieg." In *Stift Rein 1129–1979: 50 Jahre Kultur und Glaube.* Festschrift zum Jubiläum. Ed. Paulus Rappold, Karl Amon, Helmut Mezler-Andelberg, Norbert Müller, and Ileane Schwarzkogler. Graz: Rein, 1979, 252–92.

———. *Kardinal Innitzer und der Anschluss: Kirche und Nationalsozialismus in Österreich 1938.* Graz: Institut für Kirchengeschichte der Theologischen Fakultät der Karl-Franzens Universität Graz, 1982.

———. *Theodor Innitzer und der Anschluss: Österreichs Kirche 1938.* Graz: Styria, 1988.

———. "Bischof Hudal und der Nationalsozialismus—Rom und die Steiermark." *Geschichte und Gegenwart* 7 (1988): 263–80.

———. "Ottokar Kernstock, der missbrauchte Dichter." *Zeitschrift des Historischen Vereins für Steiermark* 85 (1994): 381–93.

———. "Ottokar Kernstock: Gefeierter, geschmähter und missbrauchter österreichischer Dichter." In *Ottokar Kernstock Leben—Gedichte—Erzählungen.* Vorau: Zimmermann, 2003, 6–37.

Lintl, Martin. *Flucht aus dem Kloster: Bekenntnisse und Enthüllungen des Karmelitenpriors Martin Lintl.* Berlin: Deutscher Verlag für Politik und Wirtschaft, 1939.

Littell, Franklin H. *The Crucifixion of the Jews.* Reprint, Macon, GA: Mercer University Press, 1986.

Lob, Brigitte. *Albert Schmitt O.S.B., Abt in Grüssau und Wimpfen: Sein kirchenpolitisches Handeln in der Weimarer Republik und im Dritten Reich.* Cologne: Böhlau, 2000.

Lohalm, Uwe. *Völkischer Radikalismus: Die Geschichte des Deutschvölkischen Schutz- und Trutz-Bundes 1919–1923*. Hamburg: Leibniz, 1970.

Loidl, Franz. *Religionslehrer Johann Pircher: Sekretär und aktivster Mitarbeiter in der Arbeitsgemeinschaft für den religiösen Frieden 1938*. Vienna: Kirchenhistorisches Institut der katholisch-theologischen Fakultät, 1972.

———, ed. *Arbeitsgemeinschaft für den religiösen Frieden 1938/1939: Dokumentation*. Pts. 1 and 2. Vienna: Kirchenhistorisches Institut der katholisch-theologischen Fakultät, 1973.

Lortz, Joseph. *Katholischer Zugang zum Nationalsozialismus*. Münster: Aschendorff, 1933.

Luckens, Michael B. "Joseph Lortz and a Catholic Accommodation with National Socialism." In *Betrayal: German Churches and the Holocaust*. Ed. Robert P. Ericksen and Susannah Heschel. Minneapolis, MN: Fortress Press, 1999, 149–68.

Luža, Radomír. *Austro-German Relations in the Anschluss Era*. Princeton, NJ: Princeton University Press, 1975.

———. "Nazi Control of the Austrian Catholic Church, 1939–1941." *Catholic Historical Review* 62 (1977): 537–72.

Madl, Hartmut. *Pater Coelestin Maier (1871–1935): Gründerabt des Missionsklosters Schweiklberg und Apostolischer Administrator in temporalibus der Kongregation der Missionsbenediktiner von St. Ottilien*. Winzer: Josef Duschl, 1999.

Maier, Joachim. *Schulkampf in Baden 1933–1945: Die Reaktion der katholischen Kirche auf die nationalsozialistische Schulpolitik, dargestellt am Beispiel des Religionsunterrichts in den badischen Volksschulen*. Mainz: Matthias Grünewald, 1983.

Marschler, Thomas. *Kirchenrecht im Bannkreis Carl Schmitts: Hans Barion vor und nach 1945*. Bonn: Nova & Vetera, 2004.

Martin, Matthias. *Der katholische Weg ins Reich: Der Weg des deutschen Katholizismus vom Kulturkampf hin zur staatstragenden Kraft*. Frankfurt: Peter Lang, 1998.

May, Georg. *Kirchenkampf oder Katholikenverfolgung? Ein Beitrag zu dem gegenseitigen Verhältnis von Nationalsozialismus und christlichen Bekenntnissen*. Stein am Rhein: Christiana, 1991.

Mayer, Joseph. *Gesetzliche Unfruchtbarmachung Geisteskranker*. Freiburg: Herder, 1927.

———. "Die Lebensraumfrage der Völker im Lichte der christlichen Naturrechtsauffassung." *Schönere Zukunft*, November 12, 1939.

Meier, Kurt. *Die Deutschen Christen: Das Bild einer Bewegung im Kirchenkampf des Dritten Reiches*. Göttingen: Vandenhoeck & Ruprecht, 1964.

———. *Der Evangelische Kirchenkampf*. 3 vols. Göttingen: Vandenhoeck & Ruprecht, 1984.

Melis, Damian van. "Katholische Kirche und Politische Säuberungen: Gesellschaftliche Neuordnungspläne im Zeichen der Entnazifizierung und des Endes der DDR." *Neue Gesellschaft* 9 (1992): 816–22.

———. "Der katholische Episkopat und die Entnazifizierung." In *Siegerin in Trümmern: Die Rolle der katholischen Kirche in der deutschen Nachkriegsgesellschaft*. Ed. Joachim Köhler and Damian van Melis. Stuttgart: W. Kohlhammer, 1998, 42–69.

———. *Entnazifizierung in Mecklenburg-Vorpommern: Herrschaft und Verwaltung 1945–1948*. Munich: R. Oldenbourg, 1999.

Merkl, Peter H. *Political Violence under the Swastika: 581 Early Nazis*. Princeton, NJ: Princeton University Press, 1975.

Minuth, Karl-Heinz, ed. *Die Regierung Hitler*. Vol. 1: 1933/34, pt. 1: January 30–August 31, 1933. Boppard am Rhein: Harald Boldt, 1983.

Missalla, Heinrich. *Wie der Krieg zur Schule Gottes wurde: Hitlers Feldbischof Rarkowski. Eine notwendige Erinnerung*. Oberursel: Publik-Forum, 1997.

———. *Für Gott, Führer und Vaterland: Die Verstrickung der katholischen Seelsorge in Hitlers Krieg*. Munich: Kösel, 1999.

Moritz, Stefan. *Grüß Gott und Heil Hitler: Katholische Kirche und Nationalsozialismus in Österreich*. Vienna: Picus, 2002.

Morsey, Rudolf. *Die deutsche Zentrumspartei 1917–1923*. Düsseldorf: Droste, 1966.

Müller, Hans. *Katholische Kirche und Nationalsozialismus: Dokumente 1930–1935.* Munich: Nymphenburger, 1963.

Müller, Josef. *Die deutsche Ehe.* Bamberg: Otto, 1938.

Münch, Ingo von, ed. *Gesetze des NS-Staates.* 3d rev. ed. Paderborn: Ferdinand Schöningh, 1994.

Munro, Gregory. *Hitler's Bavarian Antagonist: George Moenius and the* Allgemeine Rundshau *of Munich, 1929–1933.* Lewiston, NY: The Edwin Mellen Press, 2006.

Murawski, Friedrich. *Die Juden bei den Kirchenvätern und Scholastikern: Eine kirchengeschichtliche Skizze als Beitrag zum Kampf gegen den Antisemitismus.* Berlin: C. A. Schwetschke, 1925.

———. *Die politische Kirche und ihre biblischen "Urkunden."* Berlin: Theodor Fritsch, 1938.

———. *Jesus der Nazaräer der König der Juden: Eine Darstellung nach den Quellen.* Berlin: Theodor Fritsch, 1940.

———. *Wehrgeist und Christentum.* Berlin: Theodor Fritsch, 1940.

———. *Das Gott: Umriss einer Weltanschauung aus germanischer Wurzel.* Berlin: Theodor Fritsch, 1941.

———. *Der Kaiser aus dem Jenseits: Bilder von Wesen und Wirken Jahwehs und seiner Kirche.* 2d ed. Berlin: Theodor Fritsch, 1942.

Nanko, Ulrich. *Die Deutsche Glaubensbewegung: Eine historische und soziologische Untersuchung.* Marburg: Diagonal, 1993.

Neuhäusler, Johann. *Kreuz und Hakenkreuz: Der Kampf des Nationalsozialismus gegen die katholische Kirche und der kirchliche Widerstand.* 2d ed. Munich: Katholische Kirche Bayerns, 1946.

Neuner, Josef, S.J., and Jacques Dupuis, S.J., eds. *The Christian Faith in the Doctrinal Documents of the Catholic Church.* Rev. ed. New York: Alba House, 1982.

Nicholls, William. *Christian Antisemitism: A History of Hate.* Northvale, NJ: Jason Aronson, 1993.

Nieborowski, Hubert. "Bekenntnis zum Führer: Ein deutsches katholisches Priesterwort." *Volksparole* (August 1934).

———. "Katholisch—kein Kampfruf! Ein zweites deutsches Priesterwort." *Volksparole* (September 16, 1934).

Noakes, Jeremy, and Geoffrey Pridham, eds. *Nazism: A History in Documents and Eyewitness Accounts, 1919–1945.* 2 vols. New York: Schocken Books, 1984.

Nowak, Josef. "Der Devisenprozeß Dr. Seelmeyer: Ein Generalvikar ging unschuldig ins Zuchthaus." In *Das Bistum Hildesheim 1933–1945: Eine Dokumentation.* Ed. Hermann Engfer. Hildesheim: August Lax, 1971, 507–29.

Opfermann, Bernhard. *Das Bistum Fulda im Dritten Reich: Priester, Ordensleute und Laien, die für Christus Zeugnis ablegten.* Fulda: Parzeller, 1987.

Padberg, Rudolf. "Reinhard Heydrich und das Beichtgeheimnis." In *Das Erzbistum Paderborn in der Zeit des Nationalsozialismus: Beiträge zur regionalen Kirchengeschichte 1933–1945.* Ed. Ulrich Wagener. Paderborn: Bonifatius, 1993, 289–96.

Patin, Wilhelm. *Beiträge zur Geschichte der deutsch-Vatikanischen Beziehungen in den letzten Jahrzehnten.* Berlin: Nordland, 1942.

Pauley, Bruce F. *Hitler and the Forgotten Nazis: A History of Austrian National Socialism.* Chapel Hill: University of North Carolina Press, 1981.

Persch, Martin. "Der Diözesanklerus und die neuen pastoralen Laienberufe." In *Geschichte des Bistums Trier.* Vol. 5, *Beharrung und Erneuerung 1881–1981.* Ed. Bernhard Schneider and Martin Pesch. Trier: Paulinus, 2004, 174–215.

Peters, Edward N. *The 1917 Pio-Benedictine Code of Canon Law.* San Francisco, Ignatius Press, 2001.

Peterson, Edward N. *The American Occupation of Germany: Retreat to Victory.* Detroit, MI: Wayne State University Press, 1977.

Phayer, Michael. *The Catholic Church and the Holocaust, 1930–1965*. Bloomington: Indiana University Press, 2000.

Phelps, Reginald H. "'Before Hitler Came': Thule Society and Germanen-Orden." *Journal of Modern History* 35 (1963): 245–61.

Pieper, Lorenz. "Christentum und jungdeutscher Gedanke." In *Jungdeutscher Orden, Katholizismus und Zentrum*. Kassel: Jungdeutscher Verlag, 1924, 13–19.

Pine, Lisa. *Nazi Family Policy 1933–1945*. Oxford: Berg, 1997.

Piper, Ernst. *Alfred Rosenberg: Hitlers Chefideologe*. Munich: Karl Blessing, 2005.

Pirchegger, Simon. *Hitler und die katholische Kirche*. Graz: Verlag der N.S.D.A.P., 1933.

Poewe, Karla. *New Religions and the Nazis*. NY: Routledge, 2006.

Prantl, Helmut, ed. *Die kirchliche Lage in Bayern nach den Regierungspräsidentenberichten 1933–1943*. Vol. 5, *Regierungsbezirk Pfalz, 1933–1940*. Mainz: Matthias Grünewald, 1978.

Preuschoff, Hans. *Pater Eduard Gehrmann SVD (1888–1960): Diener der Kirche in zwei Diktaturen*. Münster: Historischer Verein für Ermland, 1984.

———. "Zur Suspension der Braunsberger Professoren Eschweiler und Barion im Jahre 1934." *Zeitschrift für die Geschichte und Altertumskunde Ermlands* 15 (1989): 115–38.

Prunč, E. "Simon Pirchegger." In *Österreichisches Biographisches Lexikon, 1815–1950*. Vienna: Österreichische Akademie der Wissenschaften, 1983, 90–91.

Puschner, Uwe, ed. *Handbuch zur "völkischen Bewegung" 1871–1918*. Munich: K.G. Saur, 1999.

———. *Die völkische Bewegung im wilhelminischen Kaiserreich: Sprache, Rasse, Religion*. Darmstadt: Wissenschaftliche Buchgesellschaft, 2001.

Rainer, Johann. "Bischof Hudal und das Wiedererwachen Österreichs 1944 in Rom." In *Kirche in bewegter Zeit: Beiträge zur Geschichte der Kirche in der Zeit der Reformation und des 20. Jahrhunderts*. Festschrift für Maximilian Liebmann zum 60. Geburtstag. Ed. Rudolf Zinnhobler, Dieter A. Binder, Rudolf Höfer, and Michaela Kronthaler. Graz: Styria Medien Service, 1994, 305–16.

Recker, Klemens-August. *"Wem wollt ihr glauben?" Bischof Berning im Dritten Reich*. Paderborn: Ferdinand Schöningh, 1998.

Rehberger, Karl. "Die Stifte Oberösterreichs unter dem Hakenkreuz." In *Das Bistum Linz im Dritten Reich*. Ed. Rudolf Zinnhobler. Linz: OLV-Buchverlag, 1979, 244–94.

Reifferscheid, Gerhard. *Das Bistum Ermland und das Dritte Reich*. Köln: Bohlau, 1975.

Reimann, Viktor. *Innitzer, Kardinal zwischen Hitler und Rom*. Vienna: Fritz Molden, 1967.

Repgen, Konrad. "Christen im Widerstand: Am Beispiel des Kulturkampfes der Bismarckzeit und des Kirchenkampfes der Hitlerdiktatur." In *Ich will euch Zukunft und Hoffnung geben*. 85. Deutscher Katholikentag, Freiburg, September 13–17, 1978. Paderborn: Bonfacius, 1979, 256–73.

Reuther, Rosemary Radford. *Faith and Fratricide: The Theological Roots of anti-Semitism*. Reprint, Eugene, OR: Wipf and Stock, 1997.

Rhodes, Anthony. *The Vatican in the Age of the Dictators (1922–1945)*. New York: Holt, Rinehart & Winston, 1973.

Richter, Ingrid. *Katholizismus und Eugenik in der Weimarer Republik und im Dritten Reich: Zwischen Sittlichkeitsreform und Rassenhygiene*. Ferdinand Schöningh, 2001.

Riegler, Markus Johann. "Augustiner-Chorherren und Augustiner-Chorherrenstifte Österreichs im Ringen mit dem Nationalsozialismus." University of Graz, 1998.

Rinderle, Walter, and Bernard Norling. *The Nazi Impact on a German Village*. Lexington: University Press of Kentucky, 1993.

Rißmann, Michael. *Hitlers Gott: Vorsehungsglaube und Sendungsbewußtsein des deutschen*

Diktators. Zurich: Pendo, 2001.

Rösch, Mathias. *Die Münchner NSDAP 1925–1933: Eine Untersuchung zur inneren Struktur der NSDAP in der Weimarer Republik*. Munich: R. Oldenbourg, 2002.

Roschnik, Konrad. *Die nationale Gefühls- und Gedankenwelt in Kernstocks Gesamtwerk*. Vienna: University of Vienna, 1934.

Rosenberg, Alfred, ed. *Handbuch der Romfrage*. Munich: Hoheneich, 1940.

Roth, Claudia. *Parteikreis und Kreisleiter der NSDAP unter besonderer Berücksichtigung Bayerns*. Munich: C. H. Beck, 1997.

Roth, Josef. *Katholizismus und Judenfrage*. Munich: Franz Eher, 1923.

——. "Für Gott und Vaterland: Ein offenes Wort in ernster Sache." *Der Jungdeutsche*, March 4, 1925.

——. "Katholischer Pazifismus? Gedanken über Eigenpersönlichkeit und Eigenrechtlichkeit des Staates: Ein Wort an Vernunft und Gewissen." *Gelbe Hefte, Historische und politische Zeitschrift für das katholische Deutschland* (1926): 686–700.

——. "Der Weg der Frontsoldaten." *Gelbe Hefte* (1929): 317–23.

——. "Gedanken zum Münchener Stahlhelmtag." *Gelbe Hefte* (1930): 114–21.

——. "Um die allgemeine Wehrpflicht." *Gelbe Hefte* (1930): 321–59.

——. "Feminismus im öffentlichen Leben der Gegenwart." *Gelbe Hefte* (1932): 441–450.

—— [Walter Berg, pseud.]. "Die Kirche ist alt geworden." *Der Deutsche Glaube* 3 (March 27, 1935): 125–27.

——. "Die katholische Kirche und die Judenfrage." In *Forschungen zur Judenfrage*. Vol. 4. Hamburg: Hanseatische Verlaganstalt, 1940, 163–76.

Ruland, Ludwig. "Die Katholiken und der 12. November." *Maingau* (November 9, 1933).

Rummel, Peter. "Joseph Kumpfmüller (1869–1949)." In *Die Bischöfe der deutschsprachigen Länder 1785/1803 bis 1945: Ein biographisches Lexikon*. Ed. Erwin Gatz. Berlin: Duncker and Humblot, 1983, 420–21.

Rynne, Xavier. *The Third Session: The Debates and Decrees of Vatican Council II, September 14 to November 21, 1964*. New York: Farrar, Straus & Giroux, 1965.

Samerski, Stefan. "Der geistliche Konsultor der deutschen Botschaft beim Heiligen Stuhl während der Weimarer Republik." *Römische Quartalschrift für christliche Altertumskunde und Kirchengeschichte* 86 (1991): 261–78.

Sanfilippo, Matteo. "Archival Evidence on Postwar Italy as a Transit Point for Central and Eastern European Migrants." In *Revisiting the National Socialist Legacy: Coming to Terms with Forced Labor, Expropriation, Compensation, and Restitution*. Innsbruck: Studien Verlag, 2002, 241–58.

Schematismus der Diözese Würzburg.

Schematismus der Geistlichkeit des Bistums Augsburg.

Schematismus der Geistlichkeit des Bistums Eichstätt.

Schematismus der Geistlichkeit des Bistums Passau.

Schematismus der Geistlichkeit des Erzbistums Bamberg.

Schematismus der Geistlichkeit des Erzbistums Breslau.

Schematismus der Geistlichkeit des Erzbistums München und Freising.

Scherzberg, Lucia. *Kirchenreform mit Hilfe des Nationalsozialismus: Karl Adam als kontextueller Theologe*. Darmstadt: Wissenschaftliche Buchgesellschaft, 2001.

Schlund, Erhard, O.F.M. *Neugermanisches Heidentum im heutigen Deutschland*. 2d ed. Munich, 1924.

Schmaus, Michael. *Begegnungen zwischen katholischem Christentum und nationalsozialistischer Weltanschauung*. 2d ed. Münster: Aschendorff, 1934.

Schmid-Egger, Barbara. *Klerus und Politik in Böhmen um 1900*. Munich: Robert Lerche, 1974.

Schmidtke, Friedrich. *Die Einwanderung Israels in Kanaan*. Breslau: Borgmeyer, 1933.

Schmitz-Berning, Cornelia. *Vokabular des Nationalsozialismus*. Berlin: de Gruyter, 1998.

Schmitz, Walter, and Clemens Vollnhals, eds. *Völkische Bewegung, konservative Revolu-*

tion, *Nationalsozialismus: Aspekte einer politisierten Kultur*. Dresden: Thelem, 2006.

Scholder, Klaus. *The Churches and the Third Reich*. Vol. 1, *Preliminary History and the Time of Illusions, 1918–1934*. Trans. John Bowden. Philadelphia: Fortress Press, 1988.

Scholz, Nina, and Heiko Heinisch. *". . . alles werden sich die Christen nicht gefallen lassen": Wiener Pfarrer und die Juden in der Zwischenkriegszeit*. Vienna: Czernin, 2001.

Schröcker, Sebastian. "Theologische Fakultäten im Dritten Reich." *Der Staat* 20 (1981). (BA Koblenz, NL 1516 Schröcker)

———. "Der Fall Barion." In *Kirche und Kirchenrecht: Gesammelte Aufsätze*. Ed. Werner Böckenförde. Paderborn: Ferdinand Schöningh, 1984, 25–75.

Schumacher, Martin, ed. *Die Reichstagsabgeordneten der Weimarer Republik in der Zeit des Nationalsozialismus: Politische Verfolgung, Emigration und Ausbürgerung 1933–1945. Eine biographische Dokumentation*. 3d ed. Düsseldorf: Droste, 1994.

Schütz, Waldemar, and Rolf Kosiek, eds. *Deutsche Geschichte im 20. Jahrhundert*. Rosenheim: Deutsche Verlagsgesellschaft, 1990.

Schwalbach, Bruno. *Erzbischof Conrad Gröber und die nationalsozialistische Diktatur: Eine Studie zum Episkopat des Metropoliten der Oberrheinischen Kirchenprovinz während des Dritten Reiches*. Karlsruhe: Badenia, 1985.

Šebek, Jaroslav. "Die Äbte Alban Schachleiter OSB und Ernst Vykoukal OSB." In *Die Benediktiner und das Dritte Reich*. Ed. Ambrosius Leidinger, O.S.B. Maria Laach, 2002, 29–48.

Senn, Wilhelm Maria. "Das Komplott des Schweigens in der Judenfrage," *Katholische Wehr*, August 1930.

———. *Katholizismus und Nationalsozialismus: Eine Rede an den deutschen Katholizismus*. Münster: Abwehr, 1931.

———. *Halt! Katholizismus und Nationalsozialismus: Meine zweite Rede an den deutschen Katholizismus und—nach Rom*. Munich: Franz Eher, 1932.

Sereny, Gita. *Into that Darkness: An Examination of Conscience*. New York: Random House, 1983.

Shuster, George N. *The Ground I Walked On: Reflections of a College President*, 2nd enl. ed. Notre Dame, IN: University of Notre Dame Press, 1969.

Smith, Helmut Walser. *German Nationalism and Religious Conflict: Culture, Ideology, Politics, 1870–1914*. Princeton, NJ: Princeton University Press, 1995.

Soetens, Claude. "The Ecumenical Commitment of the Catholic Church." In *History of Vatican II*. Vol. 3, *The Mature Council Second Period and Intersession, September 1963–September 1964*. Ed. Giuseppe Alberigo and Joseph A. Komonchak. Maryknoll, NY: Orbis, 2000.

Spicer, Kevin P., C.S.C. "To Serve God or Hitler: Nazi Priests, a Preliminary Discussion." In *Remembering for the Future 2000: The Holocaust in an Age of Genocide*. Vol. 2, *Ethics and Religion*. Ed. John K. Roth and Elisabeth Maxwell. London: Palgrave, 2001, 493–508.

———. "Last Years of a Resister in the Diocese of Berlin: Bernhard Lichtenberg's Conflict with Karl Adam and his Fateful Imprisonment." *Church History* 70 (2001): 248–70.

———. "Gespaltene Loyalität: 'Braune Priester' im Dritten Reich am Beispiel der Diözese Berlin." Trans. Ilse Andrews. *Historisches Jahrbuch* 122 (2002): 287–300.

———. *Resisting the Third Reich: The Catholic Clergy in Hitler's Berlin*. DeKalb: Northern Illinois University Press, 2004.

———, ed. *Antisemitism, Christian Ambivalence, and the Holocaust*. Bloomington: Indiana University Press, in association with the United States Holocaust Memorial Museum, 2007.

Spotts, Frederic. *The Churches and Politics in Germany.* Middletown, CT: Wesleyan University Press, 1973.

Stachura, Peter D. *Political Leaders in Weimar Germany: A Biographical Study.* New York: Simon & Schuster, 1993.

Stasiewski, Bernhard, ed. *Akten deutscher Bischöfe über die Lage der Kirche 1933–1945.* Vol. 1, 1933–1934. Mainz: Matthias Grünewald, 1968.

——, ed. *Akten deutscher Bischöfe über die Lage der Kirche 1933–1945.* Vol. 2, 1934–1935. Mainz: Matthias Grünewald, 1976.

——, ed. *Akten deutscher Bischöfe über die Lage der Kirche 1933–1945.* Vol. 3, 1935–1936. Mainz: Matthias Grünewald, 1980.

Stehle, Hansjakob. *Eastern Politics of the Vatican 1917–1979.* Trans. Sandra Smith. Athens: Ohio University Press, 1981.

——. "Bischof Hudal und SS-Führer Meyer: Ein kirchenpolitischer Friedenversuch 1942/43." *Vierteljahrshefte für Zeitgeschichte* 37 (1989): 299–22.

——. *Graue Eminenzen—Dunkle Existenzen: Geheimgeschichten aus vatikanischen und anderen Hinterhöfen.* Düsseldorf: Patmos, 1998.

Steigmann-Gall, Richard. *The Holy Reich: Nazi Conceptions of Christianity, 1919–1945.* Cambridge: Cambridge University Press, 2003.

Stempfle, Bernhard. *De Scriptis Editis Doctoris Philosophiae Maximiliani Fastlinger Monacensis.* Munich: Sonntag, 1918.

——. *Staatsanwalt! Klage Sie an des Klassenkampfes!* Munich: Franz Eher, 1929.

Stockums, Wilhelm. *Das Priestertum: Gedanken und Erwägungen für Theologen und Priester.* Freiburg: Herder, 1934.

Stüken, Wolfgang. *Hirten unter Hitler: Die Rolle der Paderborner Erzbischöfe Caspar Klein und Lorenz Jaeger in der NS-Zeit.* Essen: Klartext, 1999.

The Tablet. "German Priests and the Nazi Party." Reprint. *Catholic Mind* 40 (January 8, 1942): 17–24.

Tal, Uriel. *Christians and Jews in Germany: Religion, Politics, and Ideology in the Second Reich, 1870–1914.* Trans. Jonathan Jacobs. Ithaca, NY: Cornell University Press, 1975.

Tischner, Wolfgang. *Katholische Kirche in der SBZ/DDR 1945–1951: Die Formierung einer Subgesellschaft im entstehenden sozialistischen Staat.* Paderborn: Ferdinand Schöningh, 2001.

Tröster, Werner. "'. . . die besondere Eigenart des Herrn Dr. Pieper!' Dr. Lorenz Pieper, Priester der Erzdiözese Paderborn, Mitglied der NSDAP Nr. 9740." In *Das Erzbistum Paderborn in der Zeit des Nationalsozialismus: Beiträge zur regionalen Kirchengeschichte 1933–1945.* Ed. Ulrich Wagener. Paderborn: Bonifatius, 1993, 45–91.

Vereb, Jerome-Michael, C.P. "*Because he was a German!*" *Cardinal Bea and the Origins of Roman Catholic Engagement in the Ecumenical Movement.* Grand Rapids, MI: William B. Eerdmans, 2006.

Vogel, Wieland. *Katholische Kirche und nationale Kampfverbände in der Weimarer Republik.* Mainz: Matthias Grünewald, 1989.

Vogt, Timothy R. *Denazification in Soviet-Occupied Germany: Brandenburg 1945–1948.* Cambridge, MA: Harvard University Press, 2000.

Volk, Ludwig, S.J. *Der Bayerische Episkopat und der Nationalsozialismus, 1930–1934.* 2d ed. Mainz: Matthias Grünewald, 1966.

——. *Das Reichskonkordat vom 20. Juli 1933: Von den Ansätzen in der Weimarer Republik bis zur Ratifizierung am 10. September 1933.* Mainz: Matthias Grünewald, 1972.

——, ed. *Akten Kardinal Michael von Faulhabers 1917–1945.* Vol. 1, 1917–1934. Mainz: Matthias Grünewald, 1975.

——, ed. *Akten Kardinal Michael von Faulhabers 1917–1945.* Vol. 2, 1935–1945. 2d. rev. ed. Mainz: Matthias Grünewald, 1987.

Vollnhals, Clemens, and Thomas Schlemmer, eds. *Entnazifizierung: Politische Säuberung und Rehabilitierung in den vier Besatzungszonen 1945–1949.* Munich: Deutscher

Taschenbuch-Verlag, 1991.

Wagener, Ulrich. "Unterdrückungs- und Verfolgungsmaßnahmen gegen Priester des Erzbistums Paderborn in der Zeit des Nationalsozialismus: Ergebnisse einer Untersuchung der Kommission für Zeitgeschichte." *Theologie und Glaube* 75 (1985): 51–62.

Wagner, Georg. *Simmerberg—Chronik einer kleinen Pfarrei im Westallgäu*. Weiler-Simmerberg: Pfarreiarchiv, 2000.

Waite, Robert G. L. *Vanguard of Nazism: The Free Corps Movement in Postwar Germany, 1918–1923*. 2d ed. Cambridge, MA: Harvard University Press, 1970.

Walterbach, Carl. *Katholiken und Revolution: Eine Verteidigung gegenüber den Angriffen auf die Führer der deutschen Katholiken*. Berlin: Germania, 1922.

Weis, Roland. *Würden und Bürden: Katholische Kirche im Nationalsozialismus*. Freiburg: Rombach, 1994.

Weiß, Otto. *Der Modernismus in Deutschland: Ein Beitrag zur Theologiegeschichte*. Regensburg: Friedrich Pustet, 1995.

Weissenberger, Paulus. *Das Benediktinische Mönchtum im 19./20. Jahrhundert (1800–1950)*. Beuron: Beuroner Kunstverlag, 1952.

Weitenhagen, Holger. *Evangelisch und deutsch: Heinz Dungs und die Pressepolitik der Deutschen Christen*. Cologne: Rhineland-Verlag, 2001.

Witetschek, Helmut, ed. *Die kirchliche Lage in Bayern, 1933–1943*. Vol. 2, *Regierungsbezirk Ober- und Mittelfranken*. Mainz: Matthias Grünewald, 1967.

———. *Die kirchliche Lage in Bayern, 1933–1943*. Vol. 3, *Regierungsbezirk Schwaben*. Mainz: Matthias Grünewald, 1971.

Wolf, Heinrich. *Die Entstehung des Jungdeutschen Ordens und seine frühen Jahre 1918–1922*. Munich: Wolfgang Lohnmüller, 1970.

———. *Der Jungdeutsche Orden in seinen mittleren Jahren 1922–1925*. Vol. 1. Munich: Wolfgang Lohnmüller, 1972.

———. *Der Jungdeutsche Orden in seinen mittleren Jahren 1922–1925*. Vol. 2. Munich: Wolfgang Lohnmüller, 1978.

Wolf, Hubert. "Pius XI. und die 'Zeitirrtümer': Die Initiativen der römischen Inquisition gegen Rassismus und Nationalismus." *Vierteljahrshefte für Zeitgeschichte* 53 (2005): 1–42.

———. *Clemens August Graf von Galen: Gehorsam und Gewissen*. Freiburg: Herder, 2006.

Wolf, Hubert, and Claus Arnold, eds. *Der Rheinische Reformkreis: Dokumente zu Modernismus und Reformkatholizismus 1942–1955*. 2 vols. Paderborn: Ferdinand Schöningh, 2001.

Wollasch, Hans-Josef. "War der katholische Priester und Eugeniker Joseph Mayer ein Wegbereiter der NS-Euthanasie?" *Caritas* 91 (1990): 411–29.

Wurster, Herbert W. "Zur Geschichte des Bistum Passau im Dritten Reich." *Passauer Jahrbuch für Geschichte, Kunst und Volkskunde* 28 (1986): 244–95.

Zahn, Gordon. *German Catholics and Hitler's Wars: A Study in Social Control*. New York: Sheed and Ward, 1962.

Zeender, John. "The Genesis of the German Concordat of 1933." In *Studies in Catholic History*. Ed. Nelson Minnich. Wilmington, DE: Michael Glazier, 1985, 617–65.

Zentralstelle des Volksvereins für das katholische Deutschland, ed. *Der Nationalsozialismus und die deutschen Katholiken*. Mönchen-Gladbach, 1931. (DAEI, NS-Zeit)

Ziegler, Walter. "Die deutschen katholischen Bischöfe unter der NS-Herrschaft: Religiöses Amt und politische Herausforderung." *Historisches Jahrbuch* 126 (2006): 395–437.

Ziemke, Earl F. *The U.S. Army in the Occupation of Germany, 1944–1946*. Washington, DC: Center of Military History, United States Army, 1990.

Index

igung des jüdischen Einflusses auf das deutsche kirchliche Leben), 182–83, 188, 191–94, 201–3, 215

Jaeger, Lorenz, 195–200, 211–13, 233
Jankowski, Berthold, 259
Jann, Johannes, 259–60
Jesus: ancestry of, 182, 189–91; and Aryan race, 107–8, 133, 189; as Führer, 100; Haeuser on, 107–8, 117, 128–29, 133, 226; R. Kleine on, 182–83, 189–91, 200
"Jewish Question", the: *Catholicism and the Jewish Question* (Roth), 42–44, 58–59, 98; and ecumenism, 181–94, 201; Haeuser on, 108–9, 117; Heuberger on, 137; Pircher on, 230; R. Kleine on, 158, 216–17, 230
Jews: B. Stempfle on, 38–39; baptism and conversion, 6, 7, 60, 108, 189–90; Bolshevism, 229; Catholic charities, 59; and crucifixion, 6, 11, 107, 134, 216, 230; as enemies, 128; exclusion of, 43, 48, 105, 109, 156; Haeuser on, 107–8, 112, 127–29, 133–34, 225–26; Heuberger on, 137; Huber on, 40; influence of, 35, 41, 60, 76, 82, 106–9, 216–17; R. Kleine on, 156, 188–91; Roth on, 42–43, 133. *See also* antisemitism; Judaism
John the Baptist, 119, 189
Johnson, Helmuth, 48
Judaism: banning of, 192; and Christianity, 98, 155, 182–83, 193–94, 230; Haeuser on, 103, 127–31, 133–34; Heuberger on, 153; Judeo-Christian heritage, 82; *The Letter of Barnabas*, 103; R. Kleine on, 188–92
Jungdeutscher "Jungdo" (Young German Order), 45, 48, 50–51, 57
Justin, German, 103

Kaeufl, Georg, 260
Kandler, Hermann, 260–61
Kania, Franz, 261
Kapferer, Friedrich, 180–81, 184, 261
Kappel, Michael, 261–62
Kast, Hermann, 24
Katholikentag (National Catholic Convention), 18–19
Keller, Hermann (Peter), O.S.B., 90–91, 262
Kellner, Walter, 262–63
Kempf, Richard, 220–21

Kernstock, Ottokar, 33–34
Kerrl, Hanns, 6, 95, 96, 162
Kertzer, David, 9
Kiefer, Karl, 140, 147–49, 151
Kiefl, Franz Xaver, 109
Kirchberger, Alois, 263
Klehr, Joseph, 263
Klein, Kaspar, 50, 79–80
Kleine, Josef, 263
Kleine, Richard, 154–202; antisemitic ideology, 155, 159, 178, 184–94, 201–2, 216–17, 230; biography, *66*, 153–54, 234, 264; and bishop Machens, 162, 213–15; and Brücker, 178–82, 185, 201; Catholic *Index* incident, 160–61; Catholic Study Group, 184–89, 193, 201; censorship, 233; church/state relations, 163–68, 195–201, 215, 228–29; "Decalogue Letter," 199–201; denazification, 212–17, 234; Duderstadt gymnasium, 154, 158–60, 202, 212–15; ecumenism and the "Jewish Question," 181–94, 201; German Catholicism, 163–68; German ecumenism, 178–81, 215; Group for Joint Reconstruction Work, 181–82, 191, 195, 201; and Hitler, 154–56, 158, 162, 175; Institute for the Study and Eradication of Jewish Influence on German Church Life, 182–83, 188, 191, 201–3, 215; and Jaeger, 195–200; and Karl Adam, 184–93, 202, 231; and National Socialism, 154–55, 157, 161–62, 212–15, 229; National Socialist priests' group, 173–78, 201; and Pircher, 168, 173–78, 201–2; Protestant/Catholic pastoral letter, 197–99, 201; redeeming the church and society, 155–58; SA song incident, 158–60; on *Volksgemeinschaft*, 11, 16, 164–67
———. *views on*: Bolshevism, 194–201; Jesus, 182–83, 189–91, 200; the "Jewish Question," 216–17, 230; Judaism, 188–91; Sermon on the Mount, 182, 193–94, 215
———. *writings*: *Der Deutsche Weg* contributor, 157; "Judaism and Christianity," 216; *An Open Letter of Catholic Germans to Their Volk and Fellow Christians*, 163–68; *Redemption!*, 155–57, 184; *The Volk Testament*, 182–83
Knobloch, Wilhelm, 264

7, 13, 15–16, 86, 126, 142, 157, 301n28; Vetter commemoration sermon, 19–20
Reichstag: burning of, 81; 1924 election, 111–12; 1930 election, 31, 32; 1933 Hitler speech, 7; Oberwittelsbach election rally (1936), 21–22; rise of NS-DAP, 6–7, 31, 124–25
religious antisemitism: banning of Judaism, 192; Catholic theology, 6, 11, 188–91, 229–31; Germanization of Catholicism, 184–86; Kleine on Judaism, 155, 188–94, 216; origins of Jesus, 107–8, 133, 189–91; Pieper speaking tour, 47–48; responsibility for crucifixion, 6, 11, 107, 134, 216, 230; tradition of, ix, 9, 107, 109, 226, 230. *See also* antisemitism/antisemitic ideology; racial antisemitism
Rempe, Karl, 283–84
Reventlow, Ernst zu, 179–81
Riegelsberger, Johann Gottfried, 25
Riemers (Duderstadt gymnasium director), 213–14
Riesterer, Albert, 25, 26
Rietberg monastery, 210
Rintelen, Friedrich, 206
Ritter, Emil, 157, 164–66, 167
Röder, Ernst, 284
Rohesche Home for the Poor and Aged, 77–78, 79
Rohm purge, 76
Rosenberg, Alfred, 7, 31, 37, 50, 78–81, 100, 117; *Handbook on the Roman Question*, 97; *Myth of the Twentieth Century*, 160–61
Rössger, Paul, 93
Roth, Josef, 93–100; antisemitic ideology, 42–43, 48–49, 59–60, 96; biography, 34, 42–44, 284–85; *Catholicism and the Jewish Question*, 42–44, 58–59, 98; on Christianity, 98; death and funeral, 99–100; *Deutscher Tag* (German Day) prayer service, 48–49, 59; German national church, 95; "God and Fatherland" lecture, 57–58; and Haeuser, 115; informant for SD, 97; and Käthe S., 98–99; military/paramilitary service, 42, 57, 58; Ministry of Church Affairs, 88, 95–97; on National Socialism, 93–94, 96, 231; "The Path of the Front-Line Soldiers," 58; photographs, 63, 67–69; Plan of Action, 96; publica-

tions, 57–60; rebuilding the party, 57–60; rise of in Third Reich, 95–99; SA membership, 68, 94; and Schachleiter, 56, 85, 93–94, 95; Stahlhelm Day rally, 54, 59; on *Völkisch* Movement, 57–58; as "Walter Berg," 98
Ruhr occupation, 46
Ruland, Ludwig, 285
Rust, Bernhard, 159, 162

SA (*Sturmabteilung*, storm troops), 22, 61, 68, 77–78, 83, 85, 94, 158–60
Sailer, Albert, 286
Sandkuhl, Franz, 29, 286
Sant 'Onofrio monastery, 37–38
Sauerbruch, Ferdinand, 142
Schachleiter, (Jakob) Albanus, O.S.B., 80–93; antisemitic ideology, 35; biography, 34, 35–37, 90, 287; death of, 91; and Engelhards, 55–56, 87; flag blessing, 47; German nationalism advocate, 36–37, 53, 62; Good Friday sermon, 53; and Haeuser, 126–27; and Heuberger, 150, 153; and Hitler, 35, 56, 80–81, 83, 85, 88, 93; on National Socialism and Catholicism, 80, 87, 89, 90–91; NSDAP membership ban, 56–57, 84; photographs, 61–63; and Pieper, 88, 94; and R. Kleine, 164; rebuilding the NSDAP, 52–57; removal of ecclesiastical faculties, 81, 83, 86–87; reprimands, 53–56, 80, 84, 87–88, 90; and Roth, 56, 85, 93–94, 95; Schlageter services, 46–48, 52–53, 85; St. Ursula (Munich) sermon, 53; state funeral, 91–92; under Hitler's rule, 80–93; Vogt correspondence, 232
"Schachleiter Linz affair," 80–87
Scharnagl, Anton, 222
Scheglmann, Alphons Maria, 109
Scheyern abbey, 86
Schick, Hans, O.S.Cam., 287–88
Schips, Anton, 288
Schirach, Baldur von, 92
Schlageter, Albert Leo, 46–48, 52–53, 85
Schlund, Erhard, O.F.M., 97
Schlund, Robert Alfons, 26
Schmaus, Michael, 14–15
Schmid, Joseph, 129–30
Schmidt, Hermann, 12–14
Schmidtke, Friedrich, 288
Schnitz, Joseph, 103

EAST BATON ROUGE PARISH LIBRARY

3 1659 03275 6765

DISCARDED
FROM

EAST BATON ROUGE PARISH
LIBRARY
BATON ROUGE, LOUISIANA

EAST BATON ROUGE
PARISH LIBRARY
MAIN